A Force to Be Reckoned With

(A History of Granbury's Texas Infantry Brigade, 1861-1865)

Volume I

Danny Sessums

Copyright © 2017 Danny Sessums

SECOND EDITION

All rights reserved.

Cover Image: Meg Murrey Designs.
Special Thanks to Living Historians Jim Branson, George Susat, Clive Siegle and Harold Hammett photographed.

ISBN-10:
0-9897838-8-X
ISBN-13:
978-0-9897838-8-0

Contents

Acknowledgment i

Preface 1

Chapter One 5

Chapter Two 109

Chapter Three 171

Chapter Four 223

   A Force to Be Reckoned With Volume II coming soon; 307

Bibliography 310

ACKNOWLEDGMENTS

As is often the case when a writer takes on a project of this magnitude, it's only through the generous support of friends and associates that its completion is assured. To those who so willingly gave so much, I owe you for all the handholding and coaxing me down an agonizing path. Though they admittedly will know who they are, I can't refrain from publicly thanking several for that long-term support! Foremost are Homer Kerr and Kathleen Underwood, who at the University of Texas at Arlington perused what surely must have been a "tortured" treatise. And to Anne Bailey, now retired but formerly at Georgia Southern University, who served as mentor and friend, for demanding this volume be pushed to completion. Likewise, to a mutual mentor, Norman Brown from the University of Texas at Austin, who believed as much as anyone that these Texans warranted all that might be penned of them. Thanks goes also to Art Bergeron, late of the U.S. Military History Institute, who also perused an early manuscript and gave of his knowledge. If a scholarly work's been the consequence, those five are entitled to a fair share of praise.

But thanks must also go to Barbara Huval, of Lamar College-Port Arthur, for reading an interim manuscript and laboring to address a myriad of stylistic errors so the volume might read better otherwise than it would have. And to Larry Hewitt, who offered various viewpoints, please accept this thanks. Another to whom much is owed is Scott McKay of Roswell, Georgia, who generously shared material with this writer relating to the 10th Texas Infantry. And to Lawrence Jones III, of Austin, thanks for permission to use images from that vast collection. Also, much thanks to Tawdra Kandle for editing this manuscript. And last, but not least, recognition is due those in the "living history" fraternity who helped broaden my awareness of the sociocultural values this volume relates. Finally, to my noble spouse, Candace, this work is especially dedicated to your challenging me to finally get this over with!

Danny Sessums

PREFACE

"I hate the idea of causes, and if I had to choose between betraying my country and betraying my friend, I hope I should have the guts to betray my country."

E. M. Forster

Some fifty-odd years ago, encouraged by a grandfather (with whom I was living at the time, he not being long out of the penitentiary), this writer began a long-tenured study of the "Civil War," as it is today identified. Although Northerners designated that conflict the "War of the Rebellion," the "War Between the States" is the term Southerners are still wont to declare it. No matter the term employed, this conflict proved most destructive to both parties in terms of loss of life and exhaustion of treasuries. In this writer's view, this fight directly led to the destruction of the Republican formula for government that the "Founding Fathers" had so ardently striven to achieve. What follows in the body of this work is a history of a large group of Texans who entered the war on behalf of families and friends, and in a vain attempt to reclaim a "confederate government" that had supposedly dissipated with the adoption of the Constitution of 1787.

Historians write in terms of relevance, in other words, hoping to articulate that which they discover through research in a quest to somehow assist their generation to better understand their collective past and relate it to how we got to where we are today. As most of my formal and informal education occurred many decades ago, the generations since may likely fail to understand the context of this unique treatise, for the current generation is quite far removed from the beliefs of my generation, just as were the soldiers and civilians who witnessed the tumultuous times herein were to my own. To better understand the texture of the "Texian" mind-set that set men into motion for the front, it's imperative to somewhat understand those salient facts that governed their eventual conduct.

That a perpetual union was not contemplated in the adoption of the Constitution of 1787 can be seen in the myriad examples of efforts at dissolving the national government by various states for one reason or another after its passage. Included are such acts as the Essex Junto and Hartford Conventions before 1820 and South Carolina's threat centered on the Abomination Tariff circa 1830. In fact, as historian Kenneth Stampp so well articulates in Chapter One of *The Imperiled Union: Essays on the Background of the Civil War* (Oxford University Press. Oxford. 1978, viii), "as far as I have been able to discover, a substantial case for a perpetual Union was not devised until several decades after the adoption of the Constitution." In point of fact, then, this writer is of a mind-set to believe that what the founding fathers meant by their hope to "form a more perfect Union" makes better sense when viewed in juxtaposition with their attitude about the vexations that had occurred during the Confederation government that had previously managed America's governmental affairs.

This writer also feels that in the Supreme Court case of *Texas vs. White* (1869), wherein the all-Northern judges declared that secession was not legal, it's imperative to understand that this was closing the door in the wake of the disastrous war that preceded that opinion and *was not* based on the arguments raised at the time of the Constitution. Merely stated, a "Right of Revolution" existed at that time and would perhaps have been the legitimate title for abandoning the national government. So many thousands of people then (and an even remarkably larger number today) believed the national government had become so corrupted by 1860 that it couldn't be salvaged in its extant form. Please bear in mind, it was the national government at the time that decried the secession movement to be only a rebellion. However, purely and simply, given that the purpose of a rebellion is supplanting by force one controlling authority with another, this was *not* the South's intent. As the southern states came to believe that the three branches of the national government had equally failed them, they ardently felt they had the right to peaceably withdraw from it, but as we see, they were prohibited from doing so through a lengthy, and costly, conflict.

As westward expansion came about in the early to mid-nineteenth century, in recognition that a rapidly expanding industrial society in the North was competing with an increasingly rural expanding agrarian South, continuous efforts were required in attempts to somehow maintain a semblance (and affect a continuing social and political harmony) between the competing sections. The Missouri Crisis of 1820 led to a wholesale aggravation of both parties, and the compromise barely averted war at that time. By 1836, with Arkansas entering the Union, a concerted effort led to the accelerated creation of Michigan, and thus when Texas applied for admission, she was denied. In point of fact, Texas came into the Union in 1845 in a most unusual manner, a "Joint Resolution of Both Houses of Congress," oddly enough, with authority to subdivide into some five states in total, retaining its public lands (as well as its $10 million debt), and a guarantee from the national government that it would resolve the hostile Indian problems which she had long suffered. (And in the main, this would be an argument as to why Texas could leave the Union, as the national government had failed to keep its promise.)

But the war with Mexico destroyed the ability of the nation to remain united, in that each side wanted to keep the other from taking over the lands acquired by the Mexican Cession. By 1850, then, the stage had been set, and for Southerners (and my Texians), each year seemingly brought about one crisis after another. Readers should review the Compromise of 1850; the presidential election of 1852; the Gadsden Purchase of 1853; the Kansas-Nebraska Act and Birth of a Regional Republican Party in 1854; "Bloody Kansas;" the Dred Scott decision of 1857; Lincoln-Douglas debates; and John Brown's raid on Harper's Ferry in 1859. In Texas, a storm of arson fires swept the state, and the tentative assignment of the cause was said to be Methodist ministers fomenting slave uprisings across the state to prevent the state's westward expansion. (As to the latter, see the remarkable article of William W. White, "The Texas Slave Insurrection of 1860," in The

Southwestern Historical Quarterly (Jan., 1949), vol. LII, # 3, pp. 261-85.)

So when secession came, Texas became the seventh state to declare it had the right to leave the Union, and subsequently, to join the Confederate States <u>after a popular vote of some 45,000 for and 15,000 against</u> its leaving. Having previous to this adopted, in 1858, a uniform militia act in case of need, all men between the ages of eighteen and thirty-five began to enroll in their counties' Texas State Troops organizations.

Chapter 1

"Texas: A Land of Opportunity"

Texas had grown appreciably in the years between war with Mexico in 1848 and the onset of the secession crisis a little more than a decade later. Within a scant twelve-year period, thousands of new settlers flooded into the Lone Star State, with eager immigrants from other states in the U.S. joining those from strife-torn lands to begin life anew in the frontier west. Those arriving via steamship, whether from the Atlantic Seaboard or Europe, habitually passed through the ports of Galveston and Indianola, predominantly settling the southwest portions of the state. Here, they vied with a largely Hispanic population, folks who had come earlier from other Southern states, or from the North and Midwest.

Many still came via clipper ships or, if better off, on the lively packet steamers, averting overland corridors that often proved more time-consuming and arduous, if perhaps less expensive. For the most part, robust people, who included both adventurers and the lower classes, once ashore, found the requisite means to adjust to a society in flux; and this while openly competing with hostile natives, including Hispanics, whose numbers continued to swell, and those earlier-arrived Southerners, many of whom called themselves "Texians," all seemingly hellbent on protecting their unique status vis-a-vis these new intruders. This heterogeneous complex produced unique subcultural identities, some alike, others atypical of other states, often more difficult to penetrate than even the hostile environment itself. Despite these marked dichotomies, nevertheless, the state seemed to be the land of milk and honey to those immigrants arriving during the decade of the 1850s.

So rapid had been this population boom that it can be safely stated it catapulted the spread of civilization westward by hundreds of miles. Earlier frontier communities, like Ft. Worth, Waco, Austin, and San Antonio, had grown so rapidly as to seem cosmopolitan by

Texas standards by 1860. While cognizant of the growing number of problems created by such a rapid influx of peoples coming from varied backgrounds, the state seemed to welcome strangers with open arms. From a pragmatic viewpoint, in reality, it had little choice but to make the best of the boom so long as it lasted.[1]

Despite such diverse backgrounds, well before this time, the state had become very much politically and socially linked to her deep-southern neighbors to the east, often referring to that region simply as the Deep South. Long-tenured Texans generally espoused similar views toward the states' rights attitudes of those sister states situated along the Gulf Coast. After all, it had been those states that had early on contributed the greatest number of immigrants, and even in more recent years, transplanted Southerners yet outnumbered those arriving from foreign or domestic areas. While these folks could scarcely expect foreign-born, or their counterpart, to adopt the same ideological views, nevertheless, they demanded support of their political ideology.[2]

Not surprisingly, these later-arriving immigrants could readily detect their decidedly pro-Southern bias despite the sheer vastness of the state, and the fact that there had developed so many distinct subcultures made it unique for those now settling here, each being recognizably different from one another. Undoubtedly, East Texans had forged (and maintained) stronger political, economic, and social ties than was apt to be the case for those living in either the northern, southern, or "frontier" sections of the Lone Star State. Only in Central Texas did the lines begin to blend together, but even there, the sections remained as much unalike as similar. Some of this came from the unique values of the peoples settling them, but also, to a certain extent, to the demands of the land itself. During the 1850s, this new frontier subculture also underwent new developments,

---

[1] A good account of 1850 Texas is that by Randolph Campbell in "Texas and the Nashville Convention of 1850," *Southwestern Historical Quarterly*, Vol. 76 #1 (1972), pp. 1-14. Hereafter, the quarterly will be cited as *S.W.H.Q.*

[2] *Ibid.*, pp. 2-3.

though this state was obviously in a great condition of flux as tensions arose.[3]

In some ways, Texas appeared to be at the forefront of the raucous political infighting that marked the growing turbulence of the nation in the late 1850s, and even within the state, the disparate regions often split into political factions as a result. As the swing of national events drove the more easterly Southern states toward secession in 1860, Texas likewise swung toward the extreme Southern states' rights stance being espoused by its easterly neighbors. By late 1860, the momentous issue of secession further exacerbated political turmoil within Texas, as the state considered its relationship to the Union; if anything, this made for even more intense circumstances.[4]

A Southerner from an upper-tier Southern state, Tennessee, the clearly anti-secessionist Governor Sam Houston wryly tried branding his secessionist opponents to be either tyrants or traitors. Led by prominent political figures, such as Senator Louis T. Wigfall and Judge O. M. Roberts, these anti-Houston men chastised the governor's seeming reluctance to align himself with the Deep South, and as a result, political debate waxed hot and heavy in the Lone Star State during the fall of 1860. Already, two years before the state had passed a uniform militia act in 1858, requiring a state militia organization in case it came to more than just angry words. In was in this vexing quandary that its citizens watched in December, 1860, as first South Carolina, then a month after, Mississippi, Alabama, Georgia, and Florida withdrew by a still-debatable process called secession. (Note: There's never been a U.S. Congressional act, a

---

[3] There are any number of works that provide an in-depth treatment of Antebellum Texas. For example, see David Meinig, *Imperial Texas: An Interpretive Essay in Cultural Geography*, (Austin, 1980), pp. 45-89; and, Walter Buenger, Jr., "Antebellum Texas and the Lower South," in *Essays in History: The E. C. Barksdale Student Lecture Series*, vol. 7, 99-131; or Terry Jordan, "The Imprint of the Upper and Lower South in Mid-Nineteenth Century Texas," *Annals of the American Association of American Geography*, vol. 57, pp. 667-90; and Llerena B. Friend, "The Texan in 1860," from *Texas Vistas: Selections from the Southwestern Historical Quarterly*, 1980, pp. 119-34. Lastly, see Ernest M. Winkler, ed., *Journal of the Secession Convention of Texas, 1861*, (Austin, 1912).

[4] *S.W.H.Q.*, 76, #1, pp. 3-4, 13-4.

presidential executive order, nor a Supreme Court case that declares secession unconstitutional.)

As had Texas' next-door neighbor, Louisiana, the Lone Star State increasingly displayed an extreme sentiment with respect to secession, creating a groundswell of support for a similar move in Texas to also act; only in response to this growing fervor had Governor Houston been provoked into calling for a special session of the state legislature in February to act as to the state's fate. Already, ardent extremist factions within the state had eclipsed his power by deciding to call for a state convention, and they hurriedly demanded for the meeting to be held in late January. Across the state, most people held their breath in anticipation as to what might be the decision rendered by the conflicting entities.[5]

Once assembled at Austin in late January, convention delegates rapidly debated and quickly adopted a secession ordinance, to the mortification of Governor Houston's supporters. The convention, however, wisely decided that the matter should be submitted to a general vote of on the issue, set for February 23, before going on to appoint commissioners to attend the convention of other Southern states already set for Montgomery, Alabama. Interestingly, voters soundly ratified the state secession measure by a three-to-one majority, thus prompting Houston to reject the offer by President-Elect Abraham Lincoln to send U.S. troops into the state in an effort to prevent them leaving the Union. During these crucial weeks, Houston witnessed a continuing erosion of supporters, and when required by the state convention to swear an oath of allegiance to the newly formed Confederacy, instead opted to permit himself to be removed from office and let his lieutenant governor supplant him.[6] The convention reconvened on March 2, confirming the

---

[5] *Confederate Military History: A Library of Confederate States History, written by distinguished men of the South*. Evans, Clement A & Roberts, Col. O. M., eds. NY: The Blue & Grey Press. (reprint). Unknown date; also see Fehrenbach, T. R. *Lone Star: A History of Texas and the Texans*, (NY, 1985), p. 347.

[6] A number of those who afterward fought in Granbury's Brigade served in the secession convention; among them were John Gregg from Freestone County; Allison Nelson of Bosque County; Roger Q. Mills of Navarro County; and T.S. Anderson of Colorado County, from Texas in the War, 1861-1865, (Hillsboro, 1965), pp. 175-180; especially see Roger Q. Mills letter of January 22, 1861,

popular vote in support of the secession ordinance, and then proceeded to adopt resolutions severing the state's ties to the U.S. by appointing members to tender Texas' incorporation into the Confederate States, already ongoing at Montgomery, Alabama. And lastly, the Committee of Public Safety had been created to attend to the immediate needs of the state, focusing on two major issues: 1. removal of U.S. troops from Texas and taking possession of forts and supplies, and 2. to provide for defense of the western frontier, where Mexican bandits and Indians had proven to be a problem. As one of his last public measures, on March 4 Houston issued a proclamation announcing the acceptance of the popular vote for secession. [7]

Houston's successor, Governor Edward Clark, was to oversee the actual dismantling of U.S. military posts and arrange for the orderly removal of regular army troops from Texas, then supplanting these garrisons with a rapidly increasing state militia. The convention had mandated the Committee of Public Safety to increase the state militia based on legislation passed back in 1858 in order to ensure orderly preparations for a war everyone was beginning to see over the horizon. By the end of February, the state had been incorporated into the Confederacy at Montgomery, and with their main agenda items completed, the convention came to a rather abrupt end.[8] State authorities worked quickly to establish an umbrella defense for the frontier and proceeded to ready the state militia to act should a Union invasion transpire, and further, to do all that could practically be done

---

Austin, Texas, in the Mills Papers, Box 2F42, University of Texas Special Collections, Austin. The latter hereafter cited as the Mills papers.

[7] Even previous to this, James H. Rogers had been sent by the Committee of Public Safety to Louisiana, and there secured a "loan" of a thousand muskets for the state's use. Half of these were shipped to Messrs. Murphy & Co. of Jefferson, Texas, and would be used to arm two companies of the 7th Texas later that year. *Confederate Military History*, p.23. On May 6, 1861, at least one of the companies later composing the 6th Texas Infantry had been ordered to Indianola, Texas to detain U.S. troops arriving there to be sent by ship to the north, that being Capt. E. A. Pearson's Co. from Matagorda, in *O.R.*, I, 4, p. 632.]

[8] On Feb. 2, the Public Safety Committee had been assigned the authority to seize all federal property within the state, *Texas in the War*, p. 199.

to solicit enlistment in the volunteer regiments that would be raised for Confederate service once war should erupt. Militia units needed to be sent to the frontier fully equipped to hold the U.S. Army posts as those detachments vacated them, as well as to conduct scouting missions well beyond the settlements. Also, troops would have to be stationed at convenient points along the coast so as to prevent a seaborne invasion. The value of a militia force that could be brought into service as needed, and as readily discharged when not needed, would have to do until regular army units could be raised.

And should fighting ensue, the state's militia could be further used as a resource for providing troops in the form of volunteer regiments to the new national government, and therefore all eligible men needed to be officially enrolled if that call came. While authorized under state laws, such volunteers would need to arm and equip themselves pending the national government's ability to meet those needs. Also, this organization would allow them to perfect their command structures, schedule periodic, if rudimentary drills, and be prepared to instantly turn out if and when an emergency came. As spring advanced, a groundswell of registering occurred across the state, with men swarming into their county courts to register. Few expected the conflict to be a protracted one, and even if fighting came, few would heed the advice of those cognizant of the potential demands arising from the state's secession.[9]

In the wake of the firing on Ft. Sumter, South Carolina, on April 12, 1861, a clamor arose upon Abraham Lincoln's call for 75,000 militiamen to quell what the U.S. termed as a "rebellion" of the South. This action actually caused an even greater groundswell of support than that of secession itself, as now both the able-bodied and not so militiamen hastened to recruiting locations. In many places throughout the Lone Star State, emotions ran so intense that it seemed they threatened to take off the entire adult male population.

---

[9] An illustration relative to the state militia can be seen in the creation of Capt. Samuel McAllister's Co. (later in Granbury's), their militia name being the "Alamo Rifles," sworn in March 27, 1862. When their muster-roll went to the adjutant general's office at Austin, it advised that the company had been mustered, and "offered as a whole company under the Act of 1858." See their muster-roll copy in the Texas State Archives, Austin.

Rural farmers enlisted alongside their stock-raising counterparts, joining factory hands, store clerks, lawyers, and physicians as they vied to enlist in hastily raised militia companies.[10] Even early on in the process, age scarcely played a role, with underage recruits enrolling alongside old codgers who could barely remember their own childhoods. Those of wealth enlisted as frequently as did the poor or middle classes, thus making the earliest militia companies representative of the communities from which they were formed. Many of both the older and younger groups would, not surprisingly, be granted discharges for not meeting the requisite physical, mental, or emotional elements needed to actively serve. Such awareness often didn't surface until the men began to depart their home communities.[11] An early example of the frenzied reaction in the aftermath of Ft. Sumter came at the tiny frontier village Buchanan, in Johnson County. Here, on June 3, 1861, some 300 men enlisted in a local militia organization that took on the air of outdoor gathering. And from the fairgrounds in Austin, another group of recruits were exhorted to enlist in a local militia company that denominated itself the "Travis Rifles." Even in those two areas of the state where secession proved to have lukewarm support, counties experienced few difficulties getting volunteers once the war came on. And these often hastily raised companies seemed to be a clear source for men of

---

[10] To better understand the militia/volunteer system evolved in 19th-century America, the reader should review U.S. Congressional legislation relating to organizing armed services. For both the role of militia and volunteer forces, see "The Uniform Militia Act of 1792," U.S. Congress, 2nd, 1st Session, Ch. 33: pp. 271-4; and further for volunteer units, "The Provisional Army Act of 1798," U.S. Congress, 5th, 2nd Session, Ch. 47: pp. 558-561. Each entity served on a different basis in governing the military in perilous times, at least until conscription laws came about during this time. A good analysis of U.S. and C.S. military command structures is provided in Kenneth J. Hagan & William R. Roberts. Eds., Against All Enemies: Interpretations of American Military History from Colonial Times to Present. NY: Greenwood Press. 1986; and, James M. Morris, America's Armed Forces: A History, (NJ, 1991).

[11] "Cause," as it was referred to then, as well as even today, can be a nebulous term, but seems to center on defending one's state against outright invasion, the "invader" in this case being U.S. troops. For a sound analysis of the "states'-rights" question, see Against All Enemies:, pp. 133-154.

stature wanting to raise entire regiments.[12] Those not interested in serving, or not pressed to join, often found it very convenient to help the local community's militia ready for active service. Often, such activities began with the local county court, though in larger municipalities, special committees often were formed to secure supplies, including weapons, uniforms, and field equipage. The well-to-do found themselves called on to furnish land on which the men could be rendezvoused, it needing to be suitable enough in size to provide both camping and training grounds. Meanwhile, merchants were persuaded to donate the requisite supplies, including furnishing logistical support to get both the men and supplies to camp. Available supplies of cotton and wool would be needed to convert into uniforms and tents, plus supplying the wants of the soldiers for camp equipage and wagons needed to transport stores. Local craftsmen, such as blacksmiths, coopers (barrel-makers), and tanners, likewise tendered their services, ranging from converting sporting guns into serviceable weapons, or supplying canteens and haversacks (to carry rations), while the last supplied leather goods that went for belts, cartridge and cap boxes, and bayonet scabbards.

Though perhaps not as professionally organized initially, almost every community sported a women's sewing circle that assisted tailors in sizing, cutting, and stitching fabric together to make jackets, pants, shirts, and drawers, along with sundry other items, including socks, gloves, and the requisite "housewife," a sewing kit to be used by the men in the field.[13]

The local press similarly got caught up in the patriotic groundswell, with firms printing appropriate training manuals, plugging local recruiting efforts, and chronicling the men's experiences. Occasionally, they even offered sage advice that could help the novice recruit when he left for camp. An interesting early

---

[12] Record of the Johnson County militia formation came from the Layland Museum Gallery Lecture Series #3, (Cleburne, 1980), p. 3. On the "Travis Rifles," see their muster-in roll at the Adj. Office, State Archives, Austin, Texas. Hereafter cited as State Archives.

[13] Dean Labenski, ed., "Jim Turner, Co. G, 6th Texas Infantry, C.S.A., from 1861 to 1865," Texana, vol. XII, p. 150; also, Charles D. Spurlin, ed., The Civil War Diary of Charles Leuschner, (Austin, 1992), p. 4. Labenski's article will hereafter be cited as Texana, with vol. & pg. #; Spurlin's as Charles Leuschner.

article that appeared in the *Dallas Herald* (and was reprinted by other papers) cautioned recruits on avoiding pitfalls. Recalling service from the late war with Mexico and written under the striking heading of "Advice from an Old Soldier," a writer admonished recruits to:

1. Remember that in a campaign more men die from sickness than by the bullet.
2. Line your blanket with one thickness of brown drilling. This adds but four ounces of weight, but doubles the warmth.
3. Buy a small India Rubber blanket (only $1.50) to lay on the ground, or to throw over your shoulders when on guard duty, or during a rain storm. Most of the eastern troops are provided these. Straw to lie on is not always to be had.
4. The best military hat in use is the light-colored soft felt, the crown being sufficiently high to allow space for air over the brain. You can fasten it up as a continental in fair weather or turn it down when it is very wet, or sunny.
5. Let the beard grow so as to protect your throat or lungs.
6. Keep your entire person clean. This prevents fever and bowel complaints. Wash your body every day [,] if at all possible. Avoid strong coffee or oily meat. Scott said that the too free use of these together with neglect to keep the skin clean cost too many a life in Mexico.
7. A sudden check of perspiration by chilly or night air often causes fever or death. When thus exposed do not forget your blanket.[14]

Militia companies, following their formation, then reported to their respective county courts as well as to the state Adjutant General's Office. That would bring about, hopefully in an orderly way, assignment to Confederate regiments once called upon to furnish regiments for service outside its boundaries, the state being obligated, however, to secure a local unit's permission to so do. As

---

[14] 7. [Dallas Herald, Dallas, Texas, May 22, 1861. Slight variations of this article appeared in other papers, including the Clarksville Standard. See John C. Grady and Bradford K. Flemly, Suffering to Silence: 29th Texas Cavalry, C.S.A., (Nortex Press, Quanah, Texas. 1975), pp. 11, 17.]

will be seen, problems quickly emerged as to exactly which entity, state or national government, had the authority to commission troops for Confederate service. As a consequence, often the levies sought by the national government met with little to no cooperation from the state. Thus, already such problems pointed to the thorny conundrum as to which held supreme sovereignty. (The Uniform Militia Act of 1792 had attempted to address the problem by nationalizing state militias in national emergencies, taking control from the state and placing it under the chief executive officer's authority. But such actions had not often sat well with some states and had met with outright resistance from others.)

While there was divergence of opinion and ignorance on what the grand scale of the conflict would assume, the frenzied recruiting from spring and early summer had brought forth a plethora of independent companies, battalions, regiments, and even legions, some made known to the state, others only to the national government, but oftentimes to neither. Many individual Texans as well, as bodies of troops, had reported to Richmond, Virginia, during the summer, the Confederate capital having been relocated after Virginia's secession in May. This state of confusion would lead to Texas units being formed in far-off locales, like Kentucky, Missouri, or even in the Indian Nations.[15]

Following a flurry of that summer at Manassas, Virginia, and near Wilson's Creek, Missouri, many Southerners assumed the war would soon be over. Consequently, continuing to raise new commands seemed superfluous if the North might soon stop fighting. To their chagrin, it seemed as if these two major disasters had actually stiffened the North's resolve to continue on, and with fall looming, recruiters again began to canvass the state seeking recruits with which to form further units. Again, confusion reigned arising from the often-helter-skelter approach by both state and national leaders as to who should regulate the new commands thus raised, each claiming it had primary authority over the other. This further threw recruiting efforts into disarray. Combined with the all-too-

---

[15] *Confederate Military History*, pp. 58-71; also, see the short article by this writer, "Co. D, 4th Texas Cavalry, Arizona Brigade," in *Military Images*, vol. 3, p. 4. Cited as *Military Images* hereafter.

frequent misrepresentations made by recruiters to bring in new recruits, coupled with a cantankerous attitude many Texans had for military service, it was actually pretty amazing that the system didn't collapse under its own weight.

COUNTIES FROM WHICH THE 6TH TEXAS INFANTRY REGIMENT ENLISTED

In South Texas, one effort to raise an infantry command came at summer's end, following efforts on both the state's and national government's parts. From Richmond, Samuel Cooper had, on June 12, sent an order to the new Texas dept. commander, Earl Van Dorn, to raise some twenty companies "for the war, unless sooner discharged." The Confederate president would appoint all field officers, but the companies were to elect their own commanders. On the 30th, Governor Ed Clark had received a request to establish "two camps of instruction at accessible points," where the men would be mustered into service, organized, and receive initial drill instruction. Both points were on railroads, with one being established near Victoria. A Maj. Alex. M. Haskell and Lt. J.H. Dinkins would oversee the initial effort by putting together a depot, muster in and supply their troops, and command them. In September, these officers selected Nuner's Mott (a beautiful copse of oak trees surrounded by the coastal plains) as the rendezvous site. One recruit described this point, at the end of the rail line, thus: "The position . . . is a central one, as you can start from it and go to any part of the world with a furlough."[16] The first company arriving came from Calhoun County, led by Capt. Alexander Phillips, Jr., marching into camp on Sept. 27. These men referred to themselves by their militia name, the "Lavaca Guards." It received as its designation Co. A, 6th Texas Infantry Battalion. Three days later, a second arrived, Capt. James Rupley's Lone Star Rifles, which hailed from Victoria County, becoming Co. B. Alonzo Bass brought in the third detachment on Oct. 3, hailing from Gonzales County, Bass being both the former district attorney and his county's sheriff. The next was Capt. E. A Pearson's "Matagorda Coast Guards," he having been a physician in Matagorda County until raising this company. It arrived Oct. 4 and became Co. D. A month later, a fifth contingent reached the camp, led by Capt. John White, the men coming from Guadalupe County. They arrived Oct. 30 and were assigned to be Co. E. Only days later, a Bell County company arrived, under Capt. William Bradford, and registered in as the Bell County Invincibles prior to being mustered in on Nov. 3 as Co. F. And finally, a company led by Capt. Rhoads Fisher arrived after a long march from Austin, the Travis Rifles, but soon after designated Co. G. Fisher was the son of a former Texas Navy officer, who had also signed the Texas Declaration of Independence.[17]

---

[16] [Charles Spurlin, ed. The Civil War Diary of Charles A, Leuscner. Austin: Eakin Press. 1992. See pp. 1-2. They also rented the nearby Victoria Male Academy as a hospital for $50.00 a month. At the time the San Antonio and Mexican Gulf railroad linked Victoria with Indianola on the coast. A good map of the region is that of Capt. Calvin D. Cowles, comp., The Official Military Atlas of the Civil War (NY reprint), Plate CLVII. Hereafter cited as Military Atlas.

[17] The muster rolls for some of these companies are housed in the state archives at Austin, Texas. For reference, see Co. D, # 457, pp. 1-11; Co. F, #1243, pp. 1-4; and for the two remaining companies that would enlist in the regiment, you

The field officers appointed to the regiment included Col. Robert R. Garland, a former captain from the 7th U.S. Infantry, the Virginian being confirmed Dec. 12 to rank from Sept. 3. He would be assisted by Thomas S. Anderson, an Austin attorney who had once served as the Texas secretary of state and more recently as a delegate to the secession convention, now serving as the Lt. Col. Maj. Haskell, who had been formally in charge of the battalion in its infancy, had been transferred from the regiment, with Capt. A. H. Phillips supplanting him in that role. Initially rejected by the men, he went on to well serve the regiment as its first permanent major.[18] [

Earlier that summer, Garland had traveled to Dallas to conduct the mustering in of two cavalry regiments, but by the fall had found a more permanent home with the 6th Texas. In the shaded oak grove, he established a headquarters to await the arrival of the ten companies needed to form a volunteer infantry regiment. By now, the War Department had stipulated that all such regiments be mustered in for three years or the duration of the war, whichever expired first. Additional companies were solicited to apply for incorporation to raise the strength from a battalion to those required for a regiment of volunteer.[19] The various muster rolls of the companies entering Garland's command reflect the general ethnic diversity that then existed in South Texas. For example, the "Matagorda Coast Guards," afterward Co. D, had more than thirty Germans enrolled, with five others claiming Irish descent and at least a smattering of Portuguese, Swedish, Danish, English, and French origins. Also surprising is the number of Northern-born recruits appearing on regimental rolls, representing states such as Maine, New York, Massachusetts, and Indiana. Numerous others listed their

---

will find Co. G, as # 1429, pp. 1-7; and Co. K as #.1333, pp. 1-3. A muster-roll for Co. E of the 6th was copied from *Seguin Enterprise* of Oct. 26, 1900, compiled by a company member, P.S. Sowell.

[18] O.R., I, 4, p. 108, regarding Garland's appointment, and see Charles A. Leuschner, p. 2-3.

[19] Concerning the three-year requirement, see O.R., Series I, vol. 4, p. 131, G. O. #11, November 6, 1861, Headquarters, Military Dept. of Texas; reprinted in vol. 9, p. 700.

former residences as Florida, Mississippi, or Louisiana, but Tennesseans predominated from the Southern states.[20]

Other companies reflected similar diversity in composition, depending on where they originated, gauging by their rolls. A De Witt County contingent, for example, bears Prussian names like Prutz, Obstein, Peter, Reidel, and Zowada on its rolls. In fact, it originally had to drill using only German commands, this making for a unique appearance in what must have appeared to be a polyglot military unit. The soon-to-arrive "Alamo Rifles," afterward designated as Co. K, seemed to be denominated by Hispanic surnames, and as it came from San Antonio, reflects names of Navarro, Bustillos, Garcia, Fremon, and Miguel on their rolls.[21] But variations came not only in cultural affiliation; even the ages of the recruits varied substantially from one company to another. Though the "Alamo Rifles" averaged only eighteen and a half years old, the Matagorda detachment averaged just over twenty-eight. But that latter company did have several men forty years or over, with one listing his age as fifty-two at the time of enlistment. Mere boys, ranging in age from twelve to fourteen, served as field musicians in several companies, and there appears to have been no upper age limit, so long as the individual seemed to be active enough to keep up with the demands of the service.[22] []

Visitors to Garland's camps thought the command to be a rather heterogeneous one, but this also drew the curious out to watch the regiment brought together. Because of the variance in age and ethnic composition, and recruits coming from such far-flung points, Garland quickly realized he would have his hands full, even as a regular army officer, in trying to whip these new charges into shape. However, under his strict regimen, the men would quickly learn what the French tactician Alfred Jomini was referring to in his well-read

---

[20] See muster-in rolls copied from the Adj. General's Office in the state archives at Austin, especially Co. D; also, see Charles A. Leuschner, p. 2.

[21] Original muster-roll of companies D and K, 6th Texas Infantry, State Adj. General's Office, Austin.; Charles A. Leuschner, p.4; and see Appendix # 4 at the end of the manuscript.

[22] Muster-rolls of Co. D & K, 6th Texas Infantry Regiment, Adj. Office, Austin.; *Charles A. Leuschner*, p. 2-4.

volume concerned with the *Art of War*.²³ The fall months would prove crucial for instilling Garland's harsh brand of military authority over the men, and like most Texans at the time, those efforts did not always go well with men who had hadn't been subjected to such demands. Most, though by means not all, would make the requisite adjustments to become worthy soldiers, of course, over a period. Gradually, the process began to be understood, and, realizing the importance of their evolution, many felt a desire to share their transition from civil to military life through diary entries or through letters addressed to loved ones back home. It is due to such accounts that we are afforded a good idea of this transformation process. [For a report of deserters who left the Matagorda Coast Guards even prior to its setting out for Victoria, see their rolls in the Adj. Office, Austin, Texas.]

A young recruit who had enlisted in the "Travis Rifles," which afterward became Co. G in Garland's command, dramatically captured his company's metamorphosis during this time, providing remarkable insight for this conversion. According to Jim Turner, even prior to departing Austin for Victoria, he realized the impact of their departure in the community being left behind.²⁴ His captain, twenty-eight-year-old Rhoads Fisher, came from a family with a long military background, and obviously knew well the requirements in getting his Austin compatriots ready for their service ahead. Knowing that neither his strapped state, nor the national authorities, could materially assist in arming and equipping his men, Fisher turned his eyes instead to his local community for assistance. An eager population responded, forming committees to address their most pressing needs for uniforms, weapons, accouterments, and the camp equipage. While much of this equipment would later be

---

²³ Considered the authoritative treatise of war and tactics in this era, Alfred Jomini's two-volume set, Precis de l' Art de la Guerre, or as translated, The Art of War, was considered to be about the best conceptual manual for schooling both officers and recruits in tactical deployments.

²⁴ Dayton Kelly ed., "Jim Turner, Co. G, 6th Texas Infantry, C.S.A., From 1861 to 1865," in Texana, vol. 12, (1974), pp. 149-178. Hereafter cited only as "Jim Turner".

reflected upon as being of dubious quality, nevertheless, all of it had to serve until such time as other resources could be brought to bear.[25]

Seeking gray uniforms, he convinced the ladies in the community to weave a material together that included black and white thread to render the desired color, referred to as "salt and pepper cloth," each then being trimmed with green tape. At a respectable distance, it gave the uniform a gray appearance. Local tailors had cut and sized the material, utilizing military patterns in order to fabricate the uniforms. Additionally, a sizeable store of cotton canvas had been found that was quickly converted into wall tents large enough to sleep six men, with each having a "fly" that provided further cover from the elements.[26]

Not all those moving to the rendezvous would sport such proper clothing; in point of fact, many preferred homespun garments made of material referred to as "jeans." But the Lavaca Guards must have challenged the Austin company in appearance, as they wore custom-fitted clothing made of "linen jeans with a narrow red stripe, [with] blue-flannel frock coats trimmed with red braid, and blue caps with patent leather visors and silver 'LG' letters sewed to the front." Unlike other companies raised for the regiment, the Lavaca Guards arrived at Victoria in style, having traveled partway via an ocean steamer, then transferring to private railway cars; meanwhile, the Matagorda Coast Guards rode the rails as well, but in ordinary coaches after their arrival at Indianola.[27]

In Austin, meanwhile, at the city armory, the men received antiquated flintlock muskets that had been stored for many years. These were brought out and cleaned thoroughly, making them ready for service. However, local gunsmiths then altered the weapons to fire percussion caps, also supplying bayonets that slipped over the barrel end to lock into place. Also, leather goods found at the armory proved to be durable as well, albeit worn. This included cartridge boxes, bayonet scabbards, and waist belts. Skillets, kettles, pots, and mess tins likewise came forth as donations by area merchants, who

---

[25] Texana, p. 151.]

[26] Ibid., p. 150.

[27] Charles A. Leuschner, p. 4.

also furnished a sufficient number of wagons to transport the bulky equipage to Victoria. This included excess clothing, hygiene, and other non-essential items, such as pens, pencils, and writing paper, enough items to fill the wagons supplied. At last, with everything prepared, on Nov. 2 the company rendezvoused at the armory and loaded their gear, ready to depart Austin and head for the coast.[28]

Private Turner wrote of the exhilaration all possessed now that they made ready to start: "[Now,] when [we]. . . stood in line with bayonets fixed we presented quite a war-like and formidable appearance." On that memorable Saturday, with everything ready, the Rifles got underway, Turner trying to characterize the stirring scene that greeted them:

"The company assembled at the armory and loaded our tents into the wagons. We . . . then marched up Congress Avenue to the corner of 9th St., where the company was presented a beautiful silk flag, the stars and bars of the Confederacy, in the presence of a large crowd of people.

Patriotic speeches of presentation and acceptance were made, and after giving three hearty cheers, the company marched down the street amidst cheering and waving of handkerchiefs by the people who thronged the sidewalks. At noon we crossed the Colorado . . . at the ferry . . . just above Glasscock's Mill, and proceeded on our way to . . . war."[29]

While commissioned to be 6th Texas Infantry Battalion, Garland had put off elections pending the arrival of the Travis Rifles. He knew, however, that three more companies would be required to raise the command to a regimental standing, so he continued to scour the region for three more companies.[30]

Even previous to the Austin company's arrival, Garland had instituted a very strict camp regimen, knowing the need to quickly convert the men quickly into a well-disciplined crowd. He had recently read the Confederate *Articles of War* to the men, it being virtually a verbatim copy of the U.S. edition from which it had been

---

[28] Texana, p. 150.

[29] Ibid., pp. 150-1.

[30] Ibid.]

copied. He knew that his new charges would not readily take to the demanded regimen required to make them like the regulars commanded before the war. Not surprisingly, early on, an atmosphere of suspicion and mistrust had developed that would occasionally lead to conflict between the new commanders and those they commanded. This attitude was especially noted by Turner, who wrote of their Colonel:

> Col. Garland was an old army officer, having spent twenty-five years in the regular army, was a perfect martinet, and everything had to be done in strict accordance with military rules. He kept us hard at work drilling, and [soon] converted the regiment into a machine which could move with clock-work precision.[31]

It took quite some time for the Travis Rifles to arrive at Nuner's Mott; in fact, he took the better part of two weeks to move to the coast, the company finally reaching there on the morning of November 14, as the men became used to the continuous marches. The first night had been spent on Onion Creek before continuing on to reach Lockhart, after which they moved via Gonzales, thence the final leg to Victoria. In the meantime, the Nuner's Mott site had been designated as Camp Henry McCulloch, in honor of the overall commander who commanded the troops within Texas at the time. The men from Austin found themselves assigned a company street that ran at right angles to the battalion color line, where they set up their tents. Being the last company to reach the locale before the New Year arrived, they discovered they had been designated as Co. G in the battalion.[32]

They, like the companies that preceded them to Victoria, with virtually no fanfare, found their militia names quickly fell into disuse, those flashy titles being supplanted by mere alphabetical

---

[31] Texana, p. 152; On Garland's attitude toward the Texans, see also Charles A. Leuschner, p. 3. The Articles of War proscribed the rules and regulations governing those in the military, for both officers and enlisted personnel.

[32] Ibid., p. 151.]

designations. And while many preferred to continue their militia titles for some time to come, the new designations would continue throughout the rest of their service. The first company to arrive had become Co. A, and the 7th from Austin became Co. G. It appears that the nominal arrangement from the old U.S. service had been retained, so that when they filed out onto their color line for drills, Co. A was assigned as the far-right flank company maneuvers, the second found itself posted on the left flank, and the remaining ones alternated between the two. And, indeed, this would be the case when the 7th Texas was mustered in just after Garland's. Immediately, the neophytes joined with their sister companies in learning the rudiments of drill utilizing *Hardee's Light Infantry Tactics*.[33]

As stipulated in the regulations, in addition to having a lieutenant colonel and major as wing commanders, it was required that other staff officers be appointed for the benefit of the battalion. Garland appointed the remaining staff, including the adjutant and sergeant major positions, as well as other subalterns; perhaps an indication of nepotism is suggested by Garland's appointment of a nephew to act as the sergeant major. The other staff positions included a commissary officer to secure provisions, a quartermaster for clothing, ordnance officer for arms and ammunition, a surgeon, chaplain, as well as a small number of men appointed to compose a regimental band.[34] Already, discipline problems had occurred, often resulting as soldiers attempted to establish either a reputation or to draw attention upon themselves. This mixture of raw, mostly inexperienced recruits encountering often-intransigent officers, who

---

[33] Originally published by brevet Lt. Col. William Hardee while in the prewar U.S. Army, this manual went south with him to serve as the "bible" for training soldiers in the most modern linear tactics. Titled as *Rifle and Light Infantry Tactics: For the Exercise and Maneuvers of Troops When Acting as Light Infantry or Riflemen*, (Memphis, 1861). Hereafter cites as *Hardee's Tactics*.

[34] For these appointments see muster-in rolls of Field, Staff and Band, 6th Texas Infantry, Old Army and Navy Records, in Record Group 109, National Archives, Washington. Hereafter cited as RG 109, Washington. According to Charles A. Leuschner, pp. 2-3, While Co. A through G had been mustered between Sept. 27 and Nov. 14, companies H, I, and K would not reach the command until March and April, 1862.

(like their colonel) attempted to impose strict control, resulted in petty misconduct, which often brought about arrests and time in the guardhouse. One writer, Jim Turner of Co. G, seemed to be genuinely bemused by these behaviors: "The boys were always ready for a frolic, but never committed any [significant] depredations nor . . . anything serious enough to be punished by more than imprisonment in the guardhouse a day or two . . .."[35] Though he already had his hands full with myriad other issues, Garland nevertheless deemed it essential for the good of the service to ensure conformity by the rank and file, and resorted to ordering different levels of punishment for those involved in obvious behavior; in the worst cases, this might feature the bucking and gagging of those who committed major infractions. This proved to be unreasonably harsh, even dangerous, to those being punished. This punishment required soldiers to squat, have their hands tied behind their backs, and either a bayonet or stick to be thrust between their teeth for a period.

A significant number of other matters confronted Garland, reflecting the chaos coming from intransigent bureaucrats, causing many headaches for him. Over and over, he attempted to resolve these, but often found that his pleas for assistance fell on the deaf ears of overworked officials. Perhaps through luck or providence, his most pressing demand, that of arming his men, finally was resolved. This came about as U.S. forces from the frontier posts arrived at Victoria for movement to Indianola, where they were to take steamers for their trek back to the north. They were required to surrender their weapons and accoutrements to local Confederate authorities before being reissued to the Texans.[36]

> Jim Turner of Co. G wrote of this gift, pointing out:
> Not long after our arrival in camp our reconstructed muskets and antiquated accouterments were taken from us, and the entire regiment was armed with new Springfield muskets with percussion locks; also, new belts, cartridge boxes, etc. The guns were smooth,

---

[35] Texana, 152.

[36] In O.R., I, 4. p. 632, G. O. # 4, in May, 1861, Capt. Pearson's company had been sent to Indianola to detain Union soldiers reaching that point for transshipment north.

and buck-and-ball cartridges were to be used with them.[37]

While these would be smooth-bore muskets, more than likely the U.S. model of 1842, they were far preferable to the sporting guns many of the men still carried, even if they had one unpleasant aspect: "They had," penned Turner, "[the] . . . characteristic of the mule; when fired they were as nearly dangerous to the man behind the gun as those we [had recently] discarded."[38] While still at Victoria, one muse from Co. B, Private R. R. Gilbert, wrote several not-so-praiseworthy articles to a Houston paper regarding his regiment. Among the more poignant was one written with respect to their muster-in: "You solemnly swear that you will stay in the army as long as this war lasts and fight to the best of your ability; that you will not growl at your rations, and be content with eleven dollars a month, whether you get them or not, so help you God." A second, suggestive of their being in a backwater area of the war, suggested one might leave the local community (where his company had been raised) and go to virtually any other spot in the world, to escape the boredom.[39]

That Garland was an old-line officer in the prewar regular army is testified to by Jim Turner of Co. G, who wrote of him as "being a perfect martinet, and everything had to be done in strict accordance with military rules. He kept us hard at work drilling and converted the regiment into a machine which could move with clockwork precision." Obviously, his twenty-five years in the old army had prepared him for the task of taking raw recruits and making them into an effective tactical unit, despite all the trouble he experienced in the process.[40]

---

[37] Ibid., p. 152.

[38] "Jim Turner," p. 152. Several companies had received military rifles, care of their county courts, when originally raised, but they varied in caliber and some were not in the best of shape.

[39] R. R. Gilbert, " High Privates Confederate Letters, 1861-2-3-4-5," Austin: Eugene Von Boeckmann. 1894. 2nd Ed., p. 6.

[40] "Jim Turner," p. 152.

On October 17, Garland received orders from Henry McCulloch to send five of his companies to Pass Cavallo, on Matagorda Bay, he having previously reconnoitered the area beforehand, upon hearing that Union naval vessels had been observed sounding the bay as if to land shore patrols on the mainland. The men were to carry along two days' rations and only a single blanket, along with forty rounds of ammunition. He deemed it prudent to station several detachments from several companies at convenient points in order to deter such activities. The command traveled via rail the railroad first to Indianola, before marching overland to Saluria in order to protect that point and stop depredations from enemy landing parties supposed to be operating in the area. After dining on sumptuous seafood there, and perusing the beach to gather seashells as they watched for the enemy, the companies ultimately returned to Victoria, from which on December 14 Garland reported to Brig. P. O. Hébert his handling of affairs along this section of the coast.[41]

Other than the Lavaca Guards and Travis Rifles, each of which had reached Camp McCulloch well uniformed and equipped, most of the remaining companies made little progress in clothing and equipping themselves. This prompted Garland's quartermaster to search for ways to adequately address the clothing issue, meeting with limited success. However, not long after returning to Victoria, the thorny issue of uniformly clothing the men would be addressed by his ordering a large quantity of cloth from the Lone Star Mill at Huntsville Penitentiary. The prison had been converted by the state in the prewar era to produce broadcloth woolen and cotton cloth, but only in recent months had it been converted to war production, with the intent to meet the growing needs of the military. Through persistent efforts, on December 26, 1861, the regiment received 4,951.3 yards of brown kersey, 1,200 yards of cotton jeans, and 4,968.1 yards of osnaburg muslin. A second shipment arrived just two days later, consisting of 2,031.3 yards of heavy osnaburg for use in making tents. And finally, on January 2, another 2,048 yards of

---

[41] O.R., I, 4, p. 108; 144; 156-7.

brown kersey and 2,031.1 yards of osnaburg reached the regiment's camp.[42]

As was commonly the case, regimental quartermasters had to make arrangements to convert the material into uniforms and tents by what was known as the piecing-out process, whereby the material was cut to size from patterns by tailors and then sent out to ladies to hand-finish the uniforms. The kerseys went to make coats and trousers, cotton osnaburg was used for interior linings and pockets, while the thicker, off-white cotton-duck material was used for tents to accommodate the entire command. The issue of these goods produced a decidedly military effect upon what had been motley-appearing assemblage of troops, and with winter fast approaching, they couldn't have come at a better time.[43]

By January 1862, the regiment had made remarkable progress, both in uniforming and equipping the men as it had in perfecting its drill regimen. That such progress had occurred since their enlistment in October was attested to by Maj. Macklin Stith, an inspector with the State Adjutant General's Office, who advised that, in the latter category, Garland's command had to be the best-drilled regiment he had observed within Texas.[44]

So much had this proved to be the case that the wag Gilbert, writing under his pseudonym of High Private, submitted another letter to the *Houston Telegraph* that appeared to mock Stith's assessment of Garland's command. The men had become, according to Gilbert, "as well drilled as drilling machines in the 'miseries' of *Hardee's Tactics*." And he further went on to make the following observation of a recent drill session:

> The other day an officer came here from headquarters to inspect me. I went out to the parade ground and the

---

[42] O.R., I, 4, p. 101; also, for the quantity of cloth shipped to Garland, see Copies of Correspondence, Box 4-8407, Huntsville Penitentiary Papers, Texas State Archives, Austin. Hereafter cited as Huntsville Penitentiary Papers.

[43] "Jim Turner," Texana, p. 152.

[44] Adj. Macklin A. Stith to Governor Francis R. Lubbock, State Archives, Austin. Lubbock had supplanted Edward Clark, whose term as Governor had expired the previous November.

whole regiment followed me in order to witness the inspection. They placed me in the rear [rank] of Co. B, which went ahead to crowd the others along . . . I was then drummed and fifed and witnessed around the parade ground three times. First on a walk, then on a trot, and then on a gallop. They did not put me through my facings, though pacing and running are my favorite gaits. I then turned three somersets [sic] and one deadset [sic] to prove my ability and soundness.

I next wheeled to the right and to the left, in sections and [by] platoons, and the whole regiment followed to see if I did it right. Eyes righted, lefted, and fronted; and at last came up standing as a guidepost. There I rested and gazed around for marks of approbation. A small boy asked me how I felt. **He did not ask me again that day!** [author's emphasis added] After granting a reasonable time, I was ordered to Prepare to Open Ranks, then To the Rear, Open Order, March. This I did with becoming dignity. At this stage I recollected a maneuver I had never performed . . . . When with tremendous sounds your ears asunder, with gun, trumpet, blunderbuss and thunder, said I, started off with my left foot and took two steps with that foot for every one I took with the right.[45]

From the men's perspective, Garland remained aloof and somewhat detached from the rank and file, firmly believing it necessary to maintain such deportment in order to better exercise control of the men. He did take a hands-on interest in administering the drills, however, by personally supervising the intricacies involved

---

[45] "High Private," Houston Telegraph, Feb. 12, 1862; and reprinted in R. R. Gilbert, High Private's Confederate Letters Written for the Houston Telegraph During the War of 1861-2-3-4-5-, with a Short Autobiographical Sketch of the Author, (Austin, 1890), p. 4. Hereafter cited as High Private.

in the complex evolutions the men were being required to learn. While they might not fully comprehend the import of the drill regimen, nor were they likely to ever appreciate the need to maintain the haughty behavior that Garland exuded toward them, the men, interestingly, seemed to gain an ever-increasing pride as they observed the progress made. And while High Private might continue to vent his spleen over what he took to be an over-demanding training regiment, this measure of self-awareness would prove most beneficial upon their reaching the front.

Gilbert's intent had been to inject some degree of humor into what had become a less-than-pleasing adjustment to military service. The more studious among them might well appreciate the need for mastering these repetitive drills and complex movements being learned, but even ordinary privates seemed pleased by their progress. And, no doubt, the time-consuming, and tedious, drills brought about better discipline as well, which seemed to instill a better sense of pride in what they were accomplishing.

By February, an ever-increasing supply of material flowed into Garland's camp, and not just in ordnance stores, but commissary and quartermaster goods as well. With respect to the former, the battalion had received some 2,000 pounds of powder, 7,000 musket balls, 250 pounds of buckshot, 6,000 cartridge wrappers, 20,000 percussion caps, and five tons of pig lead in that single month alone! The issuance of such huge amounts of munitions, mused High Private, would cause the soldiers to "shatter a few human natures, or it will not be the fault of our sharpshooters."[46] Similarly, a small train of five wagons had also arrived in camp, filled completely to the guards with quartermaster supplies, especially additional clothing and blankets, along with a thousand pairs of brogans to be distributed among those most in need. Once issued, they supplied the wants of virtually everyone in the ranks, and, in tandem with the recent arrival of tents, meant the remaining winter months would be spent in relative comfort. Though little activity had occurred outside camp, during February, several companies had once again been dispatched to Ft. Esperanza, near Saluria Bayou, on the 6th. Here the men drove piles and erected other defensive works before returning to Camp

---

[46] "High Private," in the Houston Telegraph, February 14 & 23, 1862.

McCulloch.[47] The rest of the winter months found them committed to an incessant regimen of drill, guard mounts, and the inevitable work details, only occasionally getting a few hours off. While they may have been somewhat miffed by the lack of action, in reality, the men truly profited from the opportunity to perfect their command and to get properly supplied. In what little off-duty time they got, the men perused the latest papers to read on events in far-distant theaters, sent and received letters from those back home, or simply lounged around camp looking for something interesting to do to wile away the time. Still, most eagerly looked forward to that time when they might see the elephant; in other words, experience their first taste of combat. And some must have wondered how they might react when that time came.[48]

A continuing dilemma had greeted Garland as the New Year came on, for he was still short the requisite number of companies required to increase his command from a battalion to a regimental strength, since he still had only seven companies mustered in. Across the state, recruiting had fallen off sharply over the fall months, prompting the new governor, Lubbock, to threaten the wholesale conscription of all males from which to fill existing units or form new ones, noting the 6th Texas Battalion to be one of those still needing companies to meet a regimental status. Apparently, his cajoling produced results, for three additional companies would arrive in the coming months to be incorporated into Garland's command before the end of April.[49]

---

[47] Ibid; also, Charles A. Leuschner, p. 6; "Jim Turner" in *Texana*, p. 152.; as well see the Compiled Service Records, 6th Texas Infantry, State Archives.

[48] Joseph Allan Frank and George A. Reaves, *Seeing the Elephant: Raw Recruits at the Battle of Shiloh*, (NY, 1989), pp. 2-3.

[49] Muster-in rolls reveal that Co. H came aboard on March 27, followed by Co. K on the 31st; then finally by Co. K which entered the regiment April 11th, State Archives; also, see *Charles A. Leuschner*, p. 4.

-Seventh Texas Infantry-

Meanwhile, over in East Texas, as fall began, even as Garland still struggled to raise a command of his own, yet another infantry regiment began to coalesce. The genesis for the 7th Texas Infantry came about through the efforts of a prominent Fairfield politician, John Gregg, who, originally hailing from Alabama, had arrived in Texas in 1851. Establishing a successful law practice early on in Freestone County, he went on to serve as a judge for the 13th Judicial District Court. As early as 1860, along with William L. Moody, he had raised a militia company designated as the Freestone Freemen. Gregg represented Freestone County at the Secession Convention in '61 and heartily supported the effort to withdraw from the Union, after which he had obtained an appointment to represent the state in the 1st Confederate Congress. Upon receiving that summer authority to raise a regiment of his own from the secretary of war, L. P. Walker, Gregg resigned his Congressional seat to return to the Lone Star State to accomplish his goal.[50]

As had previously been done with regard to Garland, the War Department appointed Gregg to the rank of colonel and, with a host of connections in that region, he began searching the eastern part of the state for companies that would consider joining his command. He advised interested parties to contact him if willing to report immediately, for he had assurances from Richmond that his regiment would be sent to an active area as soon as it rendezvoused and completed its initial organization. His original rendezvous site had been set for Tyler, as an article in the *Dallas Herald* of September 25, by Capt. Jack Davis, stipulated that: ". . . acting under instructions from Col. John Gregg, calls upon members of the 7th Texas to rendezvous at Tyler by the 22nd, preparatory to joining their comrades at Vicksburg." As winter would soon be upon them, "they are requested to bring with them as much winter cloth as they can . . ." But hectic matters forced changing both the place and time

---

[50] James Lynn Newsom's doctoral dissertation, "Intrepid Gray Warriors: The 7th Texas Infantry, 1861-1865". Ft. Worth: T.C.U. Press. 1995, p. 2-3 hereafter city as "Intrepid Gray Warriors"; see Texas in the War:,pp. 6, 80, 176.; also, Walter P. Webb, ed. The Handbook of Texas, 2 vols., (Austin, 1952), vol. 1 p. 733. Hereafter cited as The Handbook of Texas.]

of the rendezvous, the site selected soon being altered to Marshall, with a date of October 1 being at last agreed upon. Though obviously already designated the 7th Texas Infantry, more often than not, in its correspondence the command is simply listed as Gregg's regiment.[51] Correspondence reveals Gregg to have been at Nashville September 20, on his way back to Texas to start assembling his regiment. In the interim, however, he messaged Henry McCulloch with a call for that officer to supply arms for his command, but none were on hand at the time, according to McCulloch, and therefore not forthcoming. The men would, therefore, be forced to bring whatever weapons they could furnish from their resources, or else await War Department arrangements to furnish them. If they supplied their own, a promise was made to reimburse them for their value at the time of mustering in. Appeals for those already having interested companies were printed in area newspapers, stressing the requirement to be at Marshall no later than October 1, if at all possible.[52]

The selected rendezvous site would be at the old fairgrounds just outside Marshall, and here Gregg established a headquarters to await the arrival of companies indicating a desire to join his command. All but one of the companies would come from East Texas, that single exception being Capt. Hiram Granbury's Company from Waco, in McClennan County. The remaining companies would come from the East Texas counties of Kaufman, Henderson, Rusk, Upshur, Smith, Cherokee, and Harrison. In fact, this last county supplied two entire companies for Gregg's regiment, even as others inquired as to how they could become attached to Gregg's battalion.[53]

---

[51] For the term of service for Gregg's command, see Sandra L. Myres, ed., *Force Without Fanfare: The Autobiography of K. M. Van Zandt*, (Fort Worth, 1968), p. 79. Cited hereafter only as Force:; also, see O.R., I, 4, 131.

[52] O.R., I, 4, p. 108. The "Texas Republican", at Marshall, wrote that donated weapons could be left at either "G.G. Gregg's" or "Bradfield and Tilley's."

[53] Perhaps the best Hiram Granbury biography is that published by Tom Holder of Ft. Worth, Texas, found at http://www.battleofraymond.org./holder.html. The family came to America in 1655. Hiram's father, Seth, had been a Baptist preacher, and in reaction to a religious crisis in 1845, wherein the Baptist Board of Foreign Missions of Boston and the American Home Mission Society in New York both decided to exclude southern Baptist slave holders equal rights before

The first company that became associated with Gregg's command came from well beyond the East Texas area, this being the Waco Rifles led by Capt. Hiram B. Granbury, it having been formed earlier in the summer. Interestingly, this company had unsuccessfully tried to be included in several other commands before becoming part of Gregg's. Unlike many of the hastily raised companies formed that summer for Gregg's regiment, Granbury's would come into the organization as a well-equipped company; having acquired both tailor-made uniforms and full military equipage, these men presented a rather striking contrast to others reporting in at Marshall.[54]

At a special meeting of the McClennan County Commissioner's Court on July 31, a sum not to exceed $600 had been authorized to purchase clothing and camp equipment for Granbury's company, "provided that the tents, camp utensils, etc., not used by Capt. Ryan's company [also raised here] be used as a portion of the above and provided that if said company does not go into active service, then said equipage is to become the property of McLennan County." This didn't mean that everything else would flow as smoothly for these men as did the provision of suitable uniforms.[55]

---

the National Baptist Union, he realigned with the newly established Southern Baptist Association. He passed away in 1850 while Granbury was a student at Oakland College in Raymond, Mississippi. He willed Hiram a "saddle horse, eighty dollars, a bed, bed-stand, some clothing, and an eight-year-old slave named Oliver." Graduating from the Liberal Arts College in 1851 with a law degree, because of a split in the Democratic party over the Compromise of 1850, Granbury decided to emigrate to Texas. Eventually settling in central Texas, he chose Meridian, just west of Waco, practicing his craft in both communities. See also, Force:, p. 79.; W. W. Heartsill, Fourteen Hundred and 91 Days in the Confederate Army. Jackson, Ms. 1953 reprint, pp. 262-3, states that in addition to the two serving in Gregg's regiment, five others came from Harrison County, two who later would be part of the 17th Texas Cavalry that would serve in Granbury's Brigade. Hereafter cited as *Fourteen Hundred:*.

[54] Texas in the War, 5, 78.

[55] Tony E. Duty, "The Home Front: McLennan County in the Civil War," Texana, vol. 12, (1974), p. 203.

COUNTIES FROM WHICH THE 7TH TEXAS INFANTRY REGIMENT ENLISTED

Interestingly, long after Granbury's company had departed Waco, this same court was still wrangling with some contractors' bills over what services had been provided the Rifles. For, on February 17, 1862, officials struggled to reconcile their outstanding accounts relative to companies raised in the county, including Granbury's: "R. J. Talley[,] having presented his accounting for balance of an account for cutting coats for E. D. Talley's company, and which . . . was turned over to Granbury's company by altering and fitting same," was entitled to payment for his services. As will be later seen, Granbury's charges had many more serious issues than this trifling affair.[56] Of the remaining companies, other than those coming from Marshall itself, none had made nearly the progress that

---

[56] Ibid., vol. 12, p.204.]

Granbury's had, and as a consequence, more often than not, these had reached the rendezvous site sporting all manner of clothing, and in several cases, having virtually totally worthless equipage. The single element most common to these men came about as they made their appearance in gaudy "battle" shorts rather than the uniforms common to regular military units. Gregg continued to wrestle with how to address his most important needs, especially that of arms, with his repeated appeals making hardly any impact upon harried state officials. For example, in far-off Southeast Texas, on October 7, an article in the *Galveston News* indicated that they expected to be supplied with "arms from [the] San Antonio Arsenal before leaving for Corinth, Mississippi; the order for 1,000 muskets with accoutrements has [already] gone to [Brig. Earl] Van Dorn."[57]

Since BG Paul Hébert couldn't fill Gregg's order either, he referred that request to BG Henry E. McCulloch, who had only recently taken command of the northern subdistrict of Texas at Tyler. Already strapped beyond his ability to supply other units still undergoing organization, McCulloch could do little other than endorse Gregg's request, forwarding it to Richmond with the endorsement that: "as arms for this regiment are not on hand, I of course, could not comply . . . ." By this time, however, most of the companies were either on, or soon would be on, the march to Marshall.[58]

Another company that would join Gregg's command came from Kaufman County, just east of Dallas, and which had originally been known by its militia name, the Kaufman Light Infantry Company. It had changed its moniker, however, when a couple of local merchants agreed to contribute both money and supplies to help equip the company; henceforth, it was to be known as the Johnson Guards to recognize those store owners' contributions. The men had elected as captain Edward T. Broughton, Jr., better known to the men simply as "Tom." Fortunately, this officer immediately commenced a long series of correspondences with his wife that would continue

---

[57] Galveston News, Galveston, Texas, Oct. 7, 1861. Neither this Arsenal, nor any other source within the state, could ever expect to even partially supply Gregg's needs for very few military arms existed within the state.

[58] O.R., I, 4, p. 108, letter from Brig. H. McCulloch to Brig. P. O. Hébert.

almost throughout the entire war. His first missive, mailed from Van Zandt County, September 17, 1861, let his spouse know that he'd made good progress in reaching that point in their trip to Marshall and that he hoped to make a short stop in neighboring Smith County long enough to gain additional recruits for his company. He next encamped at some point between Starrville and Tyler, where he wrote her a second letter on Thursday, September 26.[59]

A third company joining Gregg's regiment came out of Smith County, where a volunteer company eventually gathered on the town square in Tyler to be formally sworn in. Drawn up in regular military order on a street that bordered the courthouse, the men enlisting in the Lone Star Rebels made the following oath to the new national government:

> We do solemnly swear that while we continue in the service we will bear true faith and yield obedience to the Confederate States of America, and that we will serve <u>them</u> faithfully and honestly against <u>their</u> enemies and that we will observe and obey the officers appointed over us all according to the rules and articles of war. [underscore added by this writer to show their belief that this was a confederation of independent, sovereign states.][60]

Following the presentation of a company guidon, this company likewise headed for Marshall, where, with others, it would await orders for going to the front. On October 6, the *Texas Republican* noted the Smith county contingent's arrival, "a splendid company from Smith [County,] c[o]mm[an]ded by Capt. [William]

---

[59] Edward T. Broughton to his wife, found in The Broughton Collection, Coll. # 1993.24.02 & .03 (a&b), Smith County Historical Society archives, Tyler, Texas. See also Danny M. Sessums, "Capt. Edward T. Broughton, Jr., 7th Texas Infantry, C.S.A.," in Chronicles of Smith County, Smith County, Texas, Vol. 45, pp. 23-47. Cited hereafter as the Tom Broughton letters.

[60] Dean W. Turner, ed., "Major John Dean," Chronicles of Smith County, vol. 3 (1964), p. 25. Hereafter cited as Chronicles.

Smith[,] formerly editor of the *Tyler Sentinel* . . ." having just reached Marshall. . . .[61]

Two Harrison County companies also decided to join Gregg's regiment, these being Capt. Kleber M. Van Zandt's Bass Grays and Capt. W. B. Hill's Texas Invincibles. Van Zandt, who had earlier served in the Grays company, had left to form another company, and afterward recalled the excitement that then existed in his county on the eve of this conflict, feeling the need, perhaps, to justify why the war had come about:

> The people [hereabout] saw the shadows of war as early as 1859. Agitators from the North came to our part of the state and began doing all they could to excite the slaves to rebellion. Conditions became so serious that in 1860 the white men . . . organized an association to provide protection by placing look-outs on duty each night. We began to plan to aid the South if the call should come.[62]

A close relative of Van Zandt's had initially raised the former company that bore his last name as its the Bass' Greys, but prior to the company departing for active service, so many recruits joined that this second company had been formed at Marshall, that one denominating itself the Texas Invincibles, under the leadership of Capt. William Hill.[63]

Unlike their predecessors who composed the 6th Texas Infantry, the 7th shared a much more homogenous relationship in that almost 90% of these men traced their origin to Southern states. In fact, just ten recruits reported themselves as being of Northern birth, that same number noting their birth as being in foreign countries. Of more than considerable interest, in light of how many recent writers focus on Southern history, is the matter of slavery.

---

[61] Texas Republican, Marshall, Texas, microfilm rolls, Tyler Public Library, Tyler, Texas. After this, cited as Texas Republican.

[62] *Force:*, 77.

[63] See muster-in rolls of Companies D & G, 7th Texas, State Archives, Austin; Force: p. 264.

Several companies had as few as 4% of their men as slave-owners, while the highest, a Harrison County company, listed some 16% of their recruits as owning slaves. These records support this writer's belief that chattel slavery proved not to be a compelling reason that even these Eastern Texans had a great interest in this issue as their basis for joining the army.[64]

What was it, then, that had prompted most of these men to volunteer for such arduous circumstances? "It was the invasion by the North that fired the South," wrote Kleber Van Zandt as the reason most of his comrades expressed as their basis for enlisting. Another soon to become elevated in this regiment to the rank of field officer, William Moody, decried: "You know with what spirit I joined. That it was for neither fame nor gain, but an uncontrollable sense of duty to my country." In fact, it's interesting to note that most of the soldiers expressed favorable sentiments toward their slaves, often asking their spouses in letters to tell the "negros (sic) howdy."[65]

At last, orders arrived directing that Gregg move posthaste toward the Mississippi River; ostensibly, his destination would be to report upon his arrival at Corinth, Mississippi. On October 10, a very ill-equipped and under-strength battalion composed of just seven companies began its first march, hoofing it overland from their first camp at Sulphur Springs, some sixteen miles east of Marshall, to reach first Shreveport, Louisiana, then on to Monroe, where they boarded the cars of the Vicksburg, Shreveport, and El Paso Railroad for the brief trip to Vicksburg. Upon reaching the last point, according to Capt. Broughton of Company C, Gregg received orders to again take rail cars from Vicksburg, this time north to Memphis, Tennessee, from whence he would report his regiment's expected arrival at their duty station, somewhere beyond Bowling Green, Kentucky.[66]

A second contingent of two more companies of the 7th Texas that had been too late in reporting to Marshall to travel with the main

---

[64] See *Intrepid Gray Warriors:*, p. 8.

[65] *Intrepid Gray Warriors*: p. 10.

[66] "Capt. Edward T. Broughton, Jr." in Chronicles 46, pp. 26-7; *Intrepid Gray Warriors*, p. 16; *Force*, p. 80.

body had followed after the other seven by several days, at last overtaking the battalion at Memphis, then falling behind again on the rail line that took the battalion on to Hopkinsville, Kentucky. This last place would actually serve as their new duty station once the regiment was reunited, the two-company complement arriving there just a day after the others arrived. The two latter companies were those of Capt. J. W Brown and E. T. "Tom" Broughton (the latter appears to have been joined by a Henderson County contingent that had fallen in temporarily with the Kaufman men, since they were neighbors, and understrength also). These men had had to remain a day longer in Memphis, awaiting transport, though reaching their new duty station in time for the regiment's formal mustering in.[67]

    During their last leg, the men found themselves ensconced in dilapidated boxcars that encountered inclement weather as the train moved northward, the horrid conditions causing the men to suffer tremendously. A combination of freezing rain (which at one point turned to hail) and howling winds made for a very grueling trip. Upon arriving in Memphis, they boarded an eastbound train that took them to Nashville, where, if anything, the weather grew even worse each passing mile. Arrived at Nashville, the battalion booked passage aboard a steamer that took them via the Cumberland River to Clarksville, some fourteen miles south of the Tennessee-Kentucky border. In so doing, the men passed near a small village called Dover, where they witnessed an unassuming fort then undergoing construction back of the town. Little could they have realized that this point, later designated Ft. Donelson, would witness the culmination of their first military campaign. After debouching at Clarksville, the companies then marched north to Hopkinsville, reaching there on or about November 3. After a night near the

---

[67] See Capt. "Tom" Broughton's letter of Nov. 6, 1861, sent from Clarksville, Tenn., detailing his arrival there pending his continuing on to Kentucky; also *Intrepid Gray Warriors*, pp. 20-1; for the amalgamation of the Henderson and Kaufman county companies, see *Force:*, p. 82; as well, see the letter of "R.R.H." in the *Texas Republican* of Marshall, Texas, Nov. 30, 1862, of the seven companies arrival and the tragic drowning of a new recruit while at Clarksville, he having just enlisted while at Memphis.

landing, the once-again reunited nine companies of the 7th Texas fell in on the 6th and marched out east of town to reach their camp.[68]

As the men settled into their new camp, Col. Gregg brusquely wired Gen. Albert S. Johnston, department commander, of the regiment's arrival and of the lamentable conditions amongst the men due to their exposure on the trip up from Texas. He advised he had just 749 men present in camp, advising further that five men had perished from sickness along the way. As a consequence of this arduous trip, Gregg complained that ". . . we have more coughs and colds [now] than I ever saw among the same number of men."[69]

Gregg likewise announced that his regiment would be officially mustered in shortly, but that that he had only nine men (rather than the ten customarily found in a full regiment), indifferently armed, none of whom were capable of immediate service. By this time, the consolidation of the Kaufman and Henderson County contingents had already been completed, with the eventual appointment thereafter of Capt. S. T. Bridges of the Henderson County group to serve as the commissary officer of the regiment after elections held just after Gregg's report. Gregg advised that Company A, Capt. C. W. Alexander's company from Waco (Alexander replaced Granbury as company officer due to the election of Granbury as major), had reached Hopkinsville with no weapons, and only due to the generosity of the state of Louisiana had the Kaufman and Smith County companies acquired a loan of muskets, which the Pelican State government desired be returned as soon as weapons could be issued these men. A fourth company, Capt. R. S. Camp's Texas Patriots of Upton County, had left its arms at the Clarksville armory, being told they would be issued better ones at Hopkinsville. Of the remaining companies, most had brought either sporting rifles or shotguns with them, and many of these were already out of working order. In a December 21, 1861 edition of the *Texas Republican* at Marshall, however, readers were advised that

---

[68] *O.R.*, I, 4, 524-5 & 495-6, W. W. MacKall, Asst. Adj., Bowling Green; also, see *Force*: p. 80.

[69] *O.R.*, I, 4, p. 525, report of Col. John Gregg to W. W. MacCall.

the 7th Texas had just been issued Enfield rifles dated 1861 and stamped "London Tower."[70]

As a consequence of having only nine companies, this obviously understrength command would remain composed as such in the forthcoming campaign, even after sending recruiting parties back to Texas in search of additional recruits for the 7th. As expected, Gregg of course retained his appointment as colonel, with Massachusetts native J. M. Clouth of Marshall easily capturing the post of lieutenant colonel and an increasingly popular Hiram B. Granbury getting the nod as major. And as had been the case with the 6th Texas Infantry previously, these selections forced the elevation of several lieutenants to assume command of both Clough's and Granbury's former companies.[71]

It had apparently been intended that Gregg's regiment would be attached to Brig. Lloyd Tilghman's Brigade, as a note sent that officer on November 1 indicated that Gregg's regiment should reach Clarksville that day. On the 13th, however, Gen. Tilghman advised his commander, Gen. Albert S. Johnson, that "Gregg has a fine body of men, but no one to drill them;" then proclaimed that he had been asked "to nominate . . . several [instructors]. . . in my old regiment" to oversee their instruction. Unfortunately for all involved, the noncommissioned officer sent over to the Texans' camp proved to be a former Prussian by the name of David Hirsch, who drew the unenviable role of breaking these Texans "to the bit," by serving as their initial drill master.[72] As might have been anticipated, the Texans took an immediate dislike for what they took to be a "foreigner's" arrogance, and thus they quickly set about deflating his ego. And, unfortunately, Hirsch proved to be his own worst enemy, and in one of the earliest drill sessions, he literally and figuratively

---

[70] *Ibid.*, I, 4, 525; also *Texas Republican*, Marshall, Texas, Dec. 21, 1861. The Henderson County men had officially denominated themselves the "Kickapoo Rangers," after a tributary creek that flowed through the eastern half of that county.

[71] *Force:*, pp. 80-1.

[72] *Ibid.:*, p. 81, where Van Zandt advises that only he and one other Texas officer had any military training previous to reaching Kentucky. Hirsch had previously served in the 3rd Kentucky Infantry. Also, see *Intrepid Gray Warriors:*, p. 23.

took a nose-dive while instructing them. Van Zandt offered up a vivid account of that first episode:

> [One day] as Mr. Hirsch was galloping back and forth across the field on which we were drilling, everything [suddenly] stopped. I looked around but could not see anything of horse or rider. The boys, with a look of astonishment, were [all] pointing in one direction. In a moment, a horse came scrambling out of a sinkhole. Close behind the horse came a rider, unhurt, but much crestfallen. When the boys realized Mr. Hirsch was not hurt, they all started laughing [at him].[73]

At another point, Hirsch invited a large group of locals out to watch him as he put the Texans through their paces; he was obviously bent upon impressing the observers with his adroit skill as an instructor, which, unfortunately, also backfired. Having put the men through a very rigorous physical drill regimen, one obviously meant to draw attention to him, he had at last drawn the regiment up into line of battle, cautioning the men to be ready for a simulated bayonet assault. After ordering bayonets to be fixed, he followed this by an extraordinary command he'd recently inculcated to them. Announcing loudly, "three times three and a tiger," the men were expected to count to three, repeat this twice more, and, while shifting their rifles to the "charge bayonet!" position, emit an ear-splitting scream that, unfortunately, drowned out all further commands by their instructor. Hirsch, who had previous to this ridden his charger to the center of the regiment, apparently expected to lead his charges. The shouting, however, coupled with the simultaneous shifting of arms, caused the horse to bolt.[74]

The spectators watched intently as Hirsch's horse bolted down the slope in front of the regiment, then ran as fast as they could in a vain attempt to keep close behind Hirsch on his panic-stricken horse. Down the hill went both rider and mount, the animal continuing its frantic flight up the far side of the neighboring ridge to

---

[73] *Ibid.:*, 81.

[74] *Ibid.:*, p. 81.

disappear over the top. Few of those witnessing the event could fathom what this meant, though the soldiers following after Hirsch quickly grasped the meaning. Most of them continued to whoop it up as they followed after horse and rider, until they too disappeared over the crest of the hill. Finally, a much-embarrassed Hirsch regained control of his mount and bellowed out to the rapidly following Texan line: "Hell-fire! Halt!" Obviously much crestfallen, Hirsch meekly dismissed the men and rode away, leaving both they and the public to ponder the meaning of his final maneuver.[75]

Having suffered severely from the weather on the way to Kentucky, and being further sapped by seemingly endless drills they labored under, not surprisingly, men increasingly began to take ill, being susceptible to the dreaded diseases endemic in camps where rural dwellers found themselves thrown together. Though measles and mumps predominated amongst the men, these diseases quickly led to an increasing number of men appearing on sick rolls as not "present for duty." To further exacerbate matters, not long after reaching Hopkinsville, a substantial part of the regiment found itself having to endure a forced march of over thirty-five miles to reach the town of Princeton, just northwest of Hopkinsville. Leaving Camp Alcorn, as their camp had been labeled by this time, about 250 of them had to rapidly march through increasingly cold weather to reach that community. They remained there but a few days before returning to their former camp. If anything, the weather on the return trek proved to be even worse, as freezing rains and gale-force winds struck the column not long after it got on the road. Lt. Col. Clough afterward advised that this forced march became the basis for a litany of diseases that struck the men, the elements being driven right through their lightweight clothes. Moreover, having to sleep upon frozen ground, wrapped only in soaked blankets and not allowed campfires, produced intense suffering.[76]

One of those grossly affected by the weather was Capt. "Tom" Broughton of Company C. He outlined in a letter to his wife that they had lived well enough while in Princeton, quartered in buildings of Cumberland College, and that "several loads of

---

[75] *Ibid.:*, p. 82.

[76] *Ibid:*, pp. 83-4. *Intrepid Gray Warriors*, p. 24.

provisions," including full rations, complete with "with coffee, sugar, etc.," had come his way. He further advised that his company now counted just seventy-seven men on their roll, but that he felt they were in a fix and "we will have to fight or retreat before long."[77]

As previously noted, upon their return from Princeton, those requiring medical attention more often than not found the ". . . hospitals [were] . . . without beds, blankets or furniture of any kind . . . , [and] the Post [being] without medicine," and that "the Brigade [hospital was] without competent directors and physicians . . ." In tandem with a recent outbreak of measles, many a man who might otherwise have been saved by competent treatment soon began to fall by the wayside. Then, sans forewarning, Gregg got orders just after Christmas to immediately send his sick back to Clarksville, as the enemy could be expected to move on Hopkinsville at any moment. This resulted in additional deaths that might have been averted had the sick remained in camp, surgeons now finding themselves issuing medical discharges for many men now totally disabled, burial details finding themselves called upon to hack holes into the frozen ground in which to inter the remains of the dead. In an early January letter, Lt. Col. Clough wrote that at least 130 of his Texans alone had perished since reaching Kentucky two months before.[78]

The number of deaths within the 7th Texas was variously reported. On January 22, Capt. Moody noted that Adj. William Douglas reported no deaths as occurring that day, the first time in two months in which no one had died. According to another source, the figure had risen to 166 deaths while still at Hopkinsville, another twenty-five men being discharged on disability certificates as being permanently impaired. This represented close to 26% of the regiment's strength, with the men not even having come close to making contact with the enemy. Of note also is the fact that the

---

[77] "Tom" Broughton letter, November 16, 1861, "Capt. Tom Broughton", in *Chronicles*, vol. 46. pp. 28-9.

[78] *Force:*, pp.84-5. And, in a January 4, 1862, letter, Capt. "Tom" Broughton had advised his wife he had come down with "intermittent fever," already having been sick for three weeks, and his weight dropping to only 110 pounds; moreover, he noted that fifteen of his company had recently died.

unimpaired had to not only wait constantly on sick comrades, but take over the other camp duties still required.[79]

The never-ending drills continued to be conducted, despite the arduous circumstances faced, with Capt. William Moody noting in a letter home he "would become sick if he had the time." However, as he had to rotate with the other officers still able to do duty, every ninth day he had to set out pickets and conduct outpost duty, the latter forcing him to cover well over fifteen miles on that day. On a normal day, however, camp guards had to be posted no later than 7:30 a.m. The companies, after sick call was over, were drilled until 10:30, after which officer's call for studying the evolutions of the line followed until noon. This preceded battalion drill at 2:00 p.m., with dress parade coming at 4:30. What little free time the men had afterward they put to use in visiting one another to gossip, in letter writing, or by trading any surplus goods they had with the locals or others in the army.[80]

Even while these Texans struggled to survive the harsh winter weather and the demanding marches they had to often make, not long after New Year's Day, signs of increasing enemy activities seemed to command notice. Northern newspapers made it clear that BG Ulysses S. Grant had just occupied Paducah, Kentucky, and rumors abounded he would soon follow that up with a simultaneous thrust up both the Tennessee and Cumberland Rivers in order to threaten the capture of Nashville, Tennessee. If successful, this would place his army in Johnston's rear, and Johnston realized that he must plan to concentrate his widely dispersed forces in order to prevent the Volunteer State from being overrun. He could only do that by abandoning Kentucky to the enemy and withdrawing southward immediately. Situated on the two vital waterways stood a duo of earthen forts in the northwestern corner of the state that could be potentially relied on to stave off Grant and hold his army in check until Johnston could bring all his troops together. Were he to not succeed, Johnston would likely be flanked from Kentucky altogether, and perhaps lose Tennessee in the process. Dispatching requests to the War Department for immediate reinforcements, he began also

---

[79] *Intrepid Gray Warriors*, p. 29 also, *Force:* p. 84.

[80] *Intrepid Gray Warriors*, pp. 27-8.

retreating toward Dover, just below the Kentucky-Tennessee line. Johnston wrestled with how best to respond should Grant actually attempt to cut him off by getting into his rear. In a letter dated January 22, 1862, Capt. "Tom" Broughton specifically mentioned the Federals seem to be "fitting out an expedition from Cairo- to come up the Tenn. & Cumberland River," noting both Fts. Henry and Donelson and that "if they do we, the brigade . . . will [likely] be sent to one of those places."[81]

For his part, Grant indeed had plans in the works for penetrating deep into Tennessee, employing naval warships and using troop transports to haul his army, using gunboats to reduce the two rebel strongpoints as part of this riverine excursion. Should he gain possession of both, this would enable him to advance either upon the state capital of Nashville, or else move on down the Tennessee into Alabama, cutting off Tennessee completely. Johnston's far-flung army didn't have the resources to concentrate either by boat or rail; he therefore would have to resort to arduous, time-consuming marches in order to concentrate his forces. In anticipating Grant's course of action, Johnston surveyed his troop dispositions to determine which force to send to either fort, if that had to be done. Incidentally, due to the closeness of the rivers west of Dover, the forts lay only a scant fifteen miles apart. Ft. Henry dominated the winding course of the Tennessee at that point, with Ft. Donelson guarding the river approach via the Cumberland, this latter point being the place Gregg's men had passed in moving to Kentucky some months before.[82]

Having ample support from the Navy, and occupying an inside track via the two rivers, through a rapid deployment of his forces, Grant might seize either one or the other, of perhaps even both, before Johnston could even withdraw from Kentucky. If successful, Grant would likely maneuver his opponent's army out of

---

[81] See Broughton's letter of Jan. 22, 1862, in *Chronicles*, vol. 45 (2014), pp. 31-2; for the campaign itself, see also Robert U. Johnson and Clarence C. Buel, eds., *Battles and Leaders of the Civil War*, 4 vols., (NY, 1884-89), p.379; and Shelby Foote, *The Civil War, A Narrative*, 3 vols. (NY, 1986):, 1, p. 88. Hereafter cited as *Battles and Leaders*, and *The Civil War*.

[82] *The Civil War:*, I, pp. 170-5.

Tennessee completely. His immediate targets, therefore, were to be these twin bastions on the two rivers, barely a day's march separating the two. The weaker work, Ft. Henry, had been laid out at flood-plain level on the river, Ft. Donelson being in better shape, as it sat on rising ground just back of the city of Dover. While hopefully mutually supportive, should either fall, it would lead to the loss of the other. Each must remain intact, therefore, in order to prevent the enemy's utilizing the two streams as a means to penetrate deep into Confederate Tennessee.[83]

Grant's army began to concentrate before Ft. Henry on February 4, 1862, and after a severe drubbing by Union gunboats the next day, the rebel commander BG Lloyd Tilghman (the same who had earlier commanded a brigade to which the 7th Texas had initially been assigned) had caused the fort's big guns to be spiked before surrendering to the enemy. Flushed by his initial success, Grant took possession there and put his men in motion via several parallel roads that led east toward Ft. Donelson. In the interim, he sent the naval gunboats back down the Tennessee, up the Ohio River, and entered the Cumberland to move back in the direction of Dover. The flotilla expected to arrive at Ft. Donelson in time to assist with its reduction through coordination with Grant's land forces. Grant hoped to reduce Donelson before Johnston could get reinforcements there, or at the least have its garrison abandon that site before being surrounded. Should Donelson fall, this would spell disaster for Confederate arms in the west. With the potential for disaster looming, Johnston knew he needed to act quickly, and forcibly.[84]

Upon learning that Grant had succeeded in capturing Ft. Henry, Johnston quickly ordered every command within supporting

---

[83] For a thorough account of Kentucky and Tennessee events in late '61 and early '62, see Jim Stanbery, ed., "A Confederate Surgeon's View of Ft. Donelson: The Diary of John Kennerly Farris," in *Civil War Regiments*, Vol. 1, #3, pp. 7-19. His regiment, the 41st Tennessee, would later serve as part of Gregg's Brigade at Port Hudson, La., which would contain the 7th Texas Infantry as well.

[84] See maps of the area shown as Plate XI, #s 1 thru 7, in the *Military Atlas*. For the composition of BG Charles Clark's Brigade, he having supplanted Tilghman in command of the brigade to which the 7th Texas belonged, as of January 31st, see *O.R.*, I, 7, pp. 852-3

distance to move immediately southward in the direction of Dover. Among those receiving such orders, BG Charles Clark's brigade (to which the 7th Texas Infantry had recently been assigned) made ready to march in that direction. The Texans had remained idle near Hopkinsville throughout January, but just three days after Ft. Henry's loss, word came to break camp and take up a forced march to Dover. Near daybreak on February 9, the 7th Texas Infantry began a first critical leg of that trek, the men enduring a tortuous twenty-five-mile forced march that took them to Clarksville, Tennessee. The same afternoon, by virtue of General Order #1, published at Ft. Donelson, an announcement came to camp that Gregg's regiment had been assigned to a brigade to be headed by Col. T. J. Davidson (Col. Clark at the time being absent) and that brigade had been attached to BG Bushrod Johnson's division. It seemed at the time that the opportunity for the 7th Texas Infantry to "see the elephant" was close at hand.[85]

On the following day, the 7th Texas boarded steamers during the early morning hours, the ships casting off immediately for a hurried trip downstream to Dover. Disembarking there, the men and their equipage quickly offloaded, the men were marched out west to a line that had previously been staked out atop a ridge just to the rear of Dover, the lines clearly indicating the position where they were expected to throw up earthworks. Rumors abounded that, flushed with success, Grant's army would very soon reach their front. A decided urgency prevailed, and the soldiers instinctively sensed that which was expected of them.[86]

Orders required that a defensive line be built large enough not only to accommodate those troops already there, but also others who would reportedly be on the way to Dover. Engineers had laid out a semicircular defense, known as a *crémaillère* line, running from just north of the village of Dover, curving back southward to the west of the original fort, then curving back eastward below the town to intersect the river below. Frustrated by a paucity of entrenching tools, nevertheless the Texans went to work with a will

---

[85] *O.R.*, I, 7, p. 353; *Ibid*.:, p. 338, 359, 407-9, 852-3.

[86] For an overview of the Ft. Henry-Donelson campaign, see *Battles & Leaders*, I, pp. 368-429.

to fortify that portion of the line assigned the regiment. Work details went at it with shovels to throw up a parapet, as one recalled, of "small saplings . . . thrown lengthwise along the outside margin of the ditches, dug some five feet wide and two . . . deep, the dirt [being] thrown upon the saplings." Upon completion, the works would afford a "protection of about five feet in height;" the walls would scarcely provide protection against continuous artillery bombardment, however.[87]

The outwardly curving line snaked along across numerous ridges and valleys and, as shown on the maps in the *Military Atlas*, extended just over three miles in length. The overall commander on scene, BG John Floyd, split his force into two wings, with his right under command of BG Gideon Pillow, and the left included all forces there under the control of BG Simon B. Buckner. This latter division included Clark's brigade (including the 7th Texas), with Gregg's Texans holding a portion of the line that overlooked the fork of Indian Creek. The regiment had arrived at Donelson on Tuesday, February 11, and after finishing their rifle pits, work parties expended additional effort in felling trees out in front and making abatis with them. These consisted of sharpening the branches of felled trees pointing in the direction from which the enemy could be expected to attack, the men interlacing the limbs in order to slow the enemy's approach. Meanwhile, nearby staff officers superintended the placement of field guns, hauling in ordnance supplies, and selecting sites for temporary hospitals.[88]

---

[87] O.R., I, 4, p. 552; also see Ibid., I, vol. 7, p. 407, Report of Capt Jack Davis, Co. E, 7th Texas; as well as Force: pp. 85-90, wherein Capt. Van Zandt advises he sprained a foot during the march out and had to take off his brogans and go barefoot due to swelling!

[88] *Battles & Leaders*, I, p. 409. Unfortunately, Gregg's after-action report, found in *O.R.*, I, 7, p.376 (# 68), was not drafted until six months after the battle and is far too brief to adequately record the regiment's involvement.

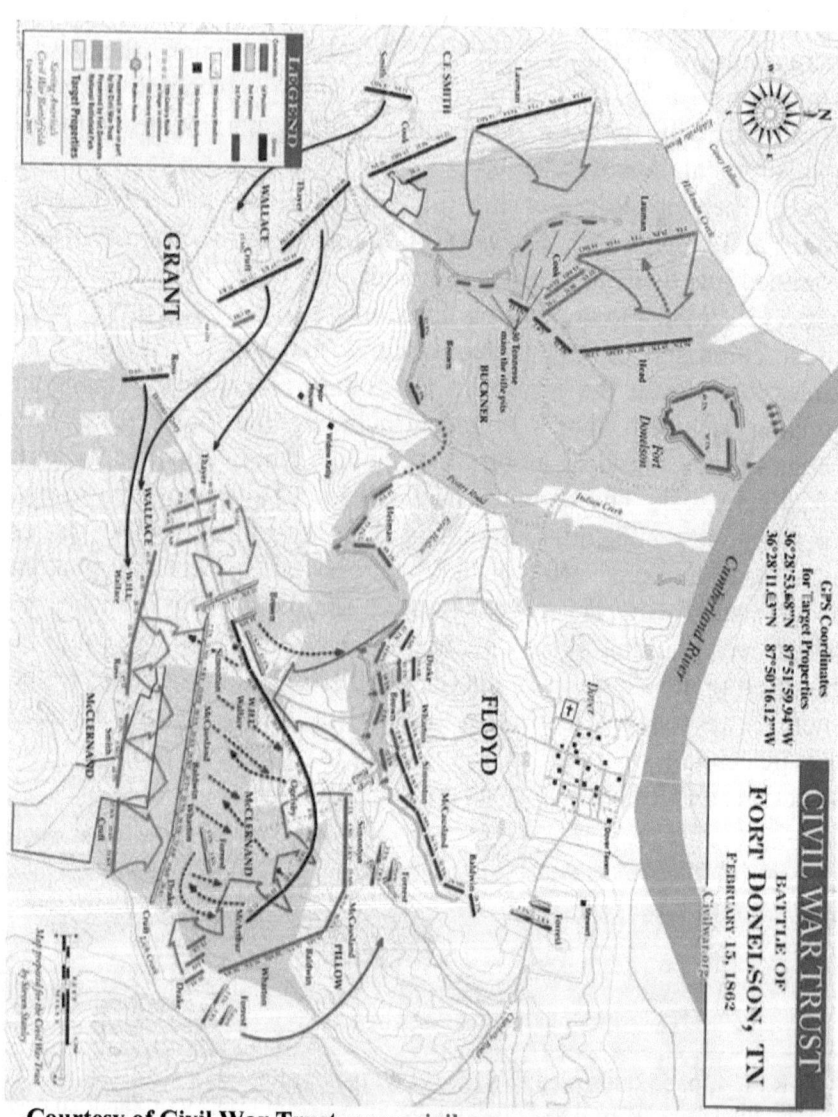

Courtesy of Civil War Trust, www.civilwar.org

On the following day, February 12, Grant's army began to arrive in force before Ft. Donelson, as he intended to implement rapidly his overall plan to surround and invest the works to cut off any escape the rebels might attempt. He dispatched BG John A. McClernand's 1st Division to continue southward to a point where the road connecting Donelson to Ft. Henry passed into Dover, instructing that officer to move further to the south until occupying the Wynn's Ferry road, thereby cutting off escape in that direction also. He next ordered BG C. F. Smith's 2nd Division to deploy his regiments north of the main road, his left flank stretching over to Hickman Creek, which would close off Floyd's right.[89]

Soon after McClernand's arrival, his skirmishers drove in their rebel counterparts deployed along Barn Hollow late in the day, and a desultory fire continued for some time afterward. The next morning, Thursday the 13th, a brisk artillery fire began to search out the main in this southern area. In the meantime, the 7th Texas Infantry had been moved from near the center of the works toward the left of the rebel line, this ultimately placing it as the fifth regiment from the far left flank. The first true attacks in the area came close to noon of the 13th, but these were easily beaten back. Artillery fired concurrent with this reconnaissance by the enemy killed Lt. E. B. Rosson of Co. A and slightly wounded Thomas Jordan of Co. G. The balmy weather that both parties had experienced prior to the Federal arrival began to turn that day, with skies clouding over and the wind swinging around to the north and the thermometer plunging to near zero by dark. Snowflakes had begun to spot a dreary landscape, and by dawn of the following day, the bitterly cold winds swirled the flakes directly into the men's faces, stinging them as they arose early that morning. As fires had been prohibited on either side, most everyone began to feel adverse effects from the cold. Those not

---

[89] *The Civil War:*, 1, pp. 198-9. For an overview of the Federal movements during the Ft. Donelson campaign, see Lew Wallace's, "The Capture of Fort Donelson," in *Battles & Leaders*, 4 vols, (reprint), vol. 1, pp. 398-429. Also, Col. William Baldwin's report (# 53) of his 2nd Brigade's action, along with that of Lt. R. B. Ryan's report (# 65) of Davidson's Brigade (to which the 7th belonged) and to Col. John Simonton's report (# 66), who commanded Davidson's Brigade during the breakout effort on Feb. 15th, found respectively in *O.R.*, I, 7, pp. 338-9; 371-4; 376; & 407.

detailed directly for sharpshooting duty tried huddling in nearby ravines in a mostly wasted effort to stave off the biting wind. For those about to enter this, their first engagement, time would reveal the wretched circumstances that would, ever after, cause them to reflect upon war's total cruelty.[90]

The two armies spent a miserable night that Thursday, the rapidly falling snow and howling winds making it all the more so as everyone considered his fate ere the passage of another day, each anticipating that war's full fury was apt to be unleashed at first light. Surprisingly, however, that day passed rather peacefully, as both armies still needed time to prepare for the fight all knew to be coming. As the predawn darkness fell away once again, Union gunners strained to sight their field pieces before opening a savage barrage that, in the vicinity of Barn Hollow, featured a converging fire on the rebel works. Solid shot, spherical case, and shells smashed into parapet walls, whilst others bounded along harmlessly overhead, the exploding rounds producing a gut-wrenching noise among those inside the Confederate works. Around noon, enemy gunboats steamed up to a point above the fort to add their even greater explosions to the cacophony of sounds as their swishing bombs came at the Texans from the opposite direction.[91]

Gradually, as the enemy gunners gained the range of the rebel works east of the hollow, numerous rounds began to explode over them, hurling their lead and iron fragments into those trying to shelter themselves within the flimsy works. This barrage continued all day, with the resulting thunderclaps turning silent as the sun began to set, the night giving the men their only respite. Within the works, after nightfall, the Texans set about repairing the damage inflicted by direct hits, and to further bolster their parapet. Work details were rotated so that no single soldier would be unduly

---

[90] *The Civil War:*, 1, p. 200; see also Gregg's report # 68 in O.R., I, 7, p. 376, and Capt. Jack Davis' report, p. 407-9.

[91] Ibid; also, see report # 62, by BG Bushrod Johnson in *O.R.*, I, 7, 361; O.R, I, 7, p. 408. wherein Capt. Davis states four gunboats bombarded the fort. In the map supplied by the Civil War Trust for the Battle on Feb. 15, note that shells passing above the fort would have enfiladed Floyd's position from the rear. This map is a very close approximation as to the position of the 7th Texas stood during that day before attacking the Federal left.

strained over their continued efforts. When men did speak, they did so in muted voices, and only as they went about performing their sundry duties. Many pondered what their fate might be on the morrow, though rumors suggesting that already discussions had been held at headquarters for a surrender by higher officers. A cursory check on the Texans by their officers found their morale remarkably high, however; the men were seemingly confident, though awaiting the expected arrival of reinforcements to occur at any moment.

On the morning of the 15th, according to Col. William Baldwin, commanding the 2nd Brigade in Bushrod Johnson's division, his regiments had been ordered to form outside and to the left-rear of their fieldworks, ostensibly to launch an attack in a column of platoons expecting to strike the enemy's right. Having advanced only a quarter of a mile, Pillow had these men recalled, and they countermarched back to their former positions in line.[92]

Unbeknownst to the men in this sector, sometime after midnight and 1:00 a.m. on the 15th, following a council of war by his principal officers, BG Gideon Pillow (who had arrived on the 9th to take overall command) instructed BG Bushrod Johnson to once again prepare his division for a flank movement to his left that would, hopefully, break the Federal right wing apart in the neighborhood of the Wynne's Ferry road, allowing the escape of the entire garrison. Preparations had begun immediately by alerting those units expecting involvement to get ready to move out. The men were to carry their knapsacks, blanket rolls, and all the rations that they could carry in their haversacks. Scheduled to be launched long before sunup, the lead brigades were to initiate a wheeling assault that would slowly pivot to their right, this enabling the rebels to seize and hold the roads in that area open. These troops would hold there until the remainder of the garrison could make its way out via the Charlotte and Forge roads.[93]

On the opposite end of the line, Floyd's troops were to generate sufficient noise by feigning an attack in order to hold the enemy in place opposite their front, thereby preventing the sending

---

[92] Report # 53, by Col. William Baldwin, *O.R.*, I, 7, p. 338.

[93] *Ibid.*:,1, 7, pp. 338-9; 361, p. 409; p. 433. See the Civil War Trust map relating to this breakout attempt.

of any reinforcements from Union left to their right; in other words, over to Bushrod Johnson's position. Should Johnson succeed in this assault, these troops would utilize the seized roadways for escaping from Ft. Donelson, after which they move toward Nashville. All of the troops in this initial attach had to be in position no later than 4:00 a.m., with the understanding that these troops on the Confederate left would form in the same place, and at the same time as had been dictated the previous evening.[94]

Though the plan for the troops at the far-left attack was to be in place no later than 4:00 a.m., soon it was discovered that Col. Davidson's brigade had failed to arrive, owing supposedly to the illness of that officer. For those in the 7th Texas, forming part of Davidson's detachment and thus leading the attack, the previous night had seen them cooking three days' rations in preparation, but now Col. Baldwin's brigade nervously awaited the arrival of the other, as it was to act as the pivot point for the preliminary assault. According to Gen. Johnson's orders, the two brigades would advance by a column of regiments, right in front, to spearhead the breakout attempt, this leaving Gen. Pillow's remaining force to follow the left wing, making their escape while Johnson's brigades held the roads open. If conducted according to plan, the Confederate brigades in this first assault would gradually wheel to the right in order to hit the enemy perpendicularly from their right; in other words, delivering a head-on attack upon the very end of the Union line. The troops at the inner portion of the wheel, Davison's brigade, would bear the greater responsibility of rolling up the enemy's right, while those of Baldwin's, to their left, were charged with extending the opening a successful attack would make.[95]

Though rather simple in concept, in actuality an attack of this magnitude, made in predawn circumstances, required a great deal of harmony between the mostly inexperienced regiments, plus a close coordination between them that, at this point in the war, simply didn't exist. Another perplexing problem had to be what Grant's response

---

[94] *The Civil War:*, vol. 1, p. 206; Report # 53, in *O.R.*, I, 7, p. 338; also, # 62, p. 361.

[95] Report # 62, *O.R.*, I, 7, p. 206; also # 53, *O.R.*. I, 7, pp. 338-9; and *Battles & Leaders*, I, p. 415.

might actually be, provided the Confederates succeeded in their mission. Unfortunately, after dawdling for several hours while awaiting the arrival and deployment of Davidson's regiments, it was about 6:00 a.m. before Baldwin began his advance, his columns having a greater amount of terrain to circumvent in order to strike the enemy from the rear. Davidson's brigade trailed in echelon and as the right-rear of Baldwin's command, Col. John Simonton having supplanted as the temporary commander of Davison's brigade.[96]

Whatever the outcome might be on the Union right in the early morning hours of February 15, it would likely determine the fate of an army seemingly ensnared by Grant's corps. Should the attack succeed, the rebel army would then march eastward to join those other units of Johnston's army rumored to be concentrating near Nashville; if not, they would become the first major rebel army taken prisoner in the war. While not possessing much information as to the enemy's actual position, nevertheless, Johnson's subordinates would lead their commands forward with alacrity to cover the almost mile and a half of broken ground to reach McClernand's right. They would afterward learn, much to their chagrin, that Grant's right was in the process of being reinforced by the just-arrived division of BG Lew Wallace. This would allow McClernand to shift his entire division further right than on the previous afternoon before settling in for the night.[97]

Before the advancing began, the Texans had been ordered to load their Enfields. In the process, the men instinctively, if nervously, swung their cartridge and cap boxes to the front, "feeling" as they executed the maneuver to ensure their cartridges were available for use. Anxious moments passed as each man methodically checked their caps, with some toying with bayonet shanks still seated in their scabbards. Now ready for the contest, once they had received the command "In Place! Rest!" they awaited the issuance of further orders. At last, just as the sun began to rise at their backs, whispered commands floated the length of the companies to "Fix Bayonets,"

---

[96] *Ibid*, I, 7, pp. 339, 362, and Report # 68, Col. John Gregg, 7th Texas, p. 376. Submitted Aug. 8, 1862, after his exchange, Gregg's report is, unfortunately, decidedly brief and therefore not as useful as would be desired.

[97] *Battles & Leaders*, I, pp. 408-9.

and they executed this almost as quietly as the commands had been issued. Men who had on many another occasions so nonchalantly practiced such routine motions now sensed their muscles become taut, and their eyes straining through the predawn darkness to fix the location of the enemy lines of battle.[98]

Simonton, in command of Davidson's brigade, had formed it in a copse of woods directly opposite the slumbering forms of the men in Col. Richard Oglesby's 1st Brigade of McClernand's division, the Texans having already arrived within a quarter mile of the enemy's advanced picket posts, nervously awaiting the command that would send the men forward. Some among them probably offered up simple prayers, while others spoke occasionally in low, muted tones. Company officers labored to rectify any alignment defects, vainly trying to maintain that peculiar type of detachment that made men in the ranks understand that a fight was certainly in the offing.[99]

Across the west bank of Barn Hollow, Oglesby's men had just begun to stir from what had been an uncomfortable night for them as well, when just after sunrise, the rebels were brought to attention. So far, not a round had been discharged to disclose their imminent attack, and for now, the stirring Yankees remained oblivious to the densely packed columns that stood poised not far out beyond their advanced pickets. For what appeared to those awaiting the word to advance, these minutes passed interminably as they awaited the order to move forcibly forward. And when that order came, the solid wall of regiments plunged downward into the flat woods to their front, the noise so low as to catch some of the enemy soldiers yet asleep.

In a formal report filed not long after the battle occurred, left-wing commander BG Bushrod Johnson advised he initially had placed Davidson's brigade, 7th Texas included, earlier that morning of the 15th some four regiments from his left flank. In case of failure, a rallying point had been established there in case the assault was

---

[98] *O.R.*, I, vol. 7, p. 408, report # not shown but submitted by Capt. Jack Davis of Co. E, indicating that "we did not know the force of the enemy or the number and locality of his batteries." It's interesting to note that McClernand's division had Lick Creek to its rear; a very dangerous position to be in.

[99] *Civil War Trust*: map reveals the actions of Feb. 15, 1862.

turned back. Irritated that this brigade had not "appear[ed] punctually," he eventually had gotten the regiments therein formed out in front of their works, but further south of their original positions. Later, when Baldwin's brigade first came under fire, Johnson ordered Col. Simonton to move forward with the whole of Davidson's brigade. The brigade began its advance in a column of companies, moving with files right, before deploying into a column of companies, with that same configuration. The 7th Texas trailed at the rear both the 3rd (23rd) Mississippi and 8th Kentucky Infantry regiments as the brigade continued to advance.[100]

According to Col. Simonton of the 1st Mississippi Infantry, temporary brigade commander, when performing these changes of front while passing forward, they could clearly make out the enemy's troops stirring on several small hills back to the west, these Union regiments appearing to be "encircling our entire left wing." Because of the irregularities of terrain and the heavy vegetation encountered, all four regiments in the brigade remained in column for another quarter mile until encountering a direct fire, at which time he directed the regiments be thrown "forward into line." Due to a disarrangement within the 3rd (23rd) Mississippi line, the 8th Kentucky was immediately moved by its right flank at the double-quick to become the new anchor for their right flank, receiving heavy fire while doing so. Shortly afterward, Simonton ordered Gregg to move his Texans by that same flank, likewise at the double-quick, which took this regiment out beyond the furthest regiment to the right, a companion regiment of the brigade, the 1st Mississippi Infantry. This made Gregg's regiment the extreme right of the flanking force, which Gregg's regiment "executed with as much coolness . . . and in as good order as if they had been on review."[101]

Having arrived at the bottom of a ridge that lay directly opposite their original deployment position, the brigade began an ascent of the steep hill; if anything, the enemy fire seemingly increased with each step, with most of those balls, remarkably, passing harmlessly overhead, said Col. Simonton. The regiments continued up the hill, "loading and firing as they moved." Just before

---

[100] *O.R.*, I, vol. 7, pp. 360-2, report # 62, dated March 4, 1862.

[101] *O.R.*, I, 7, p. 373.

reaching the crest, the Texans came under heavy fire from the enemy at virtually point-blank range. This resulted in the instant death of Lt. Col. J. M. Clough of the 7th Texas. Because of his short stature, he had remained mounted and was struck by a ball that went clear through his head. Here also fell Capt. William B. Hill and Lt. J. W. Nowlin, both killed not far from Clough. Capt. K. M. Van Zandt of Marshall, Clough's closest friend in the regiment, later testified that Clough "was shot through the brain and never breathed after falling . . ." By this time, the 7th Texas crested the ridge, having virtually exhausted its ammunition; a detail was sent back for more rounds.[102]

William Baldwin's 2nd Brigade of Johnson's division had led off the advance, being immediately followed by Col. Simonton's Brigade (including the 7th Texas), further to the rear of Baldwin's line. Lt. R. B. Ryan, A-D-C. to Simonton's (formerly Davidson's) brigade advised that the regiments of the brigade didn't deploy into a regular battle line until about halfway up the slope on the ridge where the Union right rested. The 3rd Mississippi constituted the right regiment, the 8th Kentucky forming to that regiment's left, followed by Gregg's 7th Texas, and, lastly, by the 1st Mississippi. Coming under heavy fire, the 3rd deployed into line first, the 8th Kentucky being hit so hard that the regiment moved into a hollow to the right of the 3rd Mississippi. Soon, however, both the 7th Texas and 1st Mississippi moved via their right flank, coming onto line to the right of the 3rd Mississippi and 8th Kentucky by undoubling and moving by the left flank back toward the front, the 7th Texas ending up as the far right regiment of Davidson's brigade. According to Ryan, near the brow of the hill "Colonel Gregg's regiment met with severe losses while near the top of the hill; in some places it seemed as if a whole rank fell at a time." Summarizing his report, Ryan again mentions the 7th Texas by stating that: "The Seventh Texas seemed to have lost half their members."[103]

Col. Simonton's report of their action, unfortunately, was not filed until September 24, 1862, as he had been a POW in the north until that time. He assessed the situation thus, giving the composition of the brigade: "The brigade was formed in column under the crest of

---

[102] *Force*: p 89; also *O.R.* I, 7, p. 373; see also, Gregg's report on p. 376.

[103] *O.R.*, I, vol. 7, pp. 371-2, report # 65, dated March 6, 1862.

a hill in rear of and to the left of the rifle pits . . ." The enemy appeared to be posted "behind the crests of a number of small hills in front and to the right of our rifle pits, and encircling our entire left wing." While still in a column, the brigade had not advanced 400 yards before being fired into. He had ordered both Gregg's 7th Texas and the 1st Mississippi to move at the double-quick to form a line of battle to the right of the remaining regiments of his brigade, noting that both regiments moved "with as much coolness and their commands in as good order as if they had been on review." Afterward, they advanced upslope against an enemy "four times their number." For an hour, the fighting continued intensely. Gregg's Texans were moved further to their right to prevent the enemy from flanking the brigade in that direction, but the enemy broke while they were apparently in motion. They withdrew some "few hundred yards in rear of their first position."[104]

Additional regiments had been sent forward to support this first line, the taxed soldiers of Simonton's command taking a brief respite before moving on again: "I ordered the subordinate officers to rectify their alignments, which was quickly done; [and] I again ordered an advance, which was promptly obeyed by all, . . . [and] the enemy was again driven from his position" and four pieces of Schwartz's (Illinois) came into his hands. These two attacks drove the enemy back over a mile and half, he said, and the "enemy had disappeared behind the crests of a range of hills about a half a mile in our front . . ." He identified them as belonging to both McClernand's and W. H. L. Wallace's divisions. It was during a pause at the latter place that an order arrived calling for Simonton to halt his attack.[105]

---

[104] *O.R.*, I, 7, pp.373-4, report # 66, Sept. 24, 1862

[105] Ibid., p. 374. Of remarkable interest (considering where it surfaced was found at, The Library: The University of Texas At Austin, which incorporates a report by Adj. W. D. Douglas, who presented a tabulation of numbers involved casualties suffered by the 7th Texas at Ft. Donelson. He records 305 actually in the ranks going into the fight on the 15th, suffering a loss of "sixty-one killed, wounded and missing; 7 escaped, and 324 surrendered as prisoners of war." This extremely odd compilation of those who suffered what at the hands of the enemy at Ft. Donelson, and are listed by company. See OFFICIAL REPORTS OF BATTLES EMBRACING THE DEFENCE OF VICKSBURG, a subtitle report noting the "Casualties of the Brigade of Col. Simonton at Fort Donelson." MG Earl Van Dorn. Richmond, VA. Smith, Bailey & Co. Dec. 1862.

According to Col. Gregg's brief report, not submitted until August 8, 1862, during the second of three assaults he reports having captured a "6-pounder, with ammunition and horses." He continued to "press them until a third force was seen drawn up in a ravine near a clearing; and upon this we pressed and continued to fire until it also broke and fled . . . ." Continuing his report, he states that "although the slaughter of the enemy had before been very great, their difficulty in getting through the felled timber [there] caused our fire to be much more destructive upon them at this place." For well over a mile, all one could see was that "the earth was strewn with the killed and wounded of the enemy." Early on in the fighting, a private of Co. G named George Blain had brought to him a major post of the Eighth Illinois Infantry; his regiment was Oglesby's Brigade in McClernand's Division. He further reported that "of the 350 to 360 officers and men he led into the fight, that 20 were killed on the field and 34 were disabled by wounds."[106]

In his synopsis of his report on the end of the fight on the 15th, Col. Simonton advises that during the final assaults, the brigade "was furnished with ammunition [chiefly gathered from the slain of the enemy] and the command brought to a rest." The men remained in this last position for some hours awaiting instructions, and were at last ordered "for us to march inside the rifle pits," without a shot being fired or the enemy appearing out front. On returning to his original lines, "I had not fully occupied my position in the rifle pits when an order came to me to move at double-quick to the right of our line." The men were immediately re-formed in their ranks and moved off toward their right, but were halted and ordered back to their former position.[107]

As to the final location of Simonton's brigade at the end of the attack, BG Bushrod Johnson, division commander, noted they were "driving the enemy slowly from hill to hill until about 1:00 p.m., when we reached a position nearly opposite the center of the left wing of our trenches." After describing other incidents from this series of attacks, he observed that the "Eighth Kentucky, Seventh

---

[106] Ibid, p. 376.

[107] Ibid, # 66, p. 374, Sept. 24, 1862, obviously done after Simonton's parole from a Northern camp.

Texas, and First Mississippi, . . . suffered, perhaps, the greatest losses" of the whole division. And, according to Bushrod Johnson, after returning to their works, they "remained in the trenches until between 1 and 2 a.m. on the 16th, . . . I drew out my whole command with a view to cut our way through the enemy's right and retreat . . . ." Upon doing so, he formed his command in a column of regiments about 3:00 a.m., only to learn from his then-commander, BG Simon Buckner (he had replaced both Pillow and Floyd, who had previously fled) to prepare their surrender. By daybreak, all of the garrison remaining at Ft. Donelson had suffered the embarrassment of surrender.[108]

A sidebar report by Col. William Baldwin, the 2nd Brigade commander, alludes to his having been observed as Simonton's regiments moved forward into action, he advising that Col. McCausland's Virginia Brigade had been sent from their rear in order to extend his own threatened right flank, as the "First Mississippi, Colonel Gregg's [Seventh] Texas, and Lieutenant-Colonel Lyon's Eighth Kentucky Regiments [of Simonton's Brigade] had been moved still farther to the right, the latter [8th Kentucky Infantry] being thrown back perpendicularly to our line to prevent the enemy's taking advantage of the cover afforded by the slope of the ground to our right." This documents that Simonton's brigade had actually become the fulcrum of the general wheeling movement, with the 7th Texas serving as the lynchpin upon which the entire division took its direction.[109]

Shocked by the Texans' spirited advance, Oglesby's 8th Illinois had recoiled from Gregg's attack, though they unleashed an especially destructive volley fire at point-blank range into the Texans' ranks before stampeding to the rear as the 7th steamrolled right over those attempting to stand their ground. Following their initial collision, the men of the 7th Texas pressed forward, until halted for replenishing their cartridge boxes, before advancing to a second ridge about a half-mile in the rear of the first. This brought the 7th Texas to a position that enabled the regiment to hit the right flank regiment of Col. W. H. L. Wallace's 2nd Brigade, the Texans

---

[108] O.R., I, 7, p. 361-2; see as well, Gregg's report (# 68), p. 376.

[109] O.R, I, 7, p. 339.

this time striking the 11th Illinois, commanded by Lt. Col. T. E. G. Ransom, on end. In a spirited, sanguine contest, the Texans drove Ransom's regiment away from this second line, during which the Texans took the single gun captured from Capt. Adolph Schwartz's Battery B, 2nd Illinois Light Artillery. Their infantry supports driven back, the gunners had tried to limber up and get off also, though they lost four more guns in the process.[110]

Col. Gregg's narrative continued:

> In . . . half an hour their line broke, and we pursued them to the next ridge [beyond]. . . . I caused the regiment to continue . . . and to keep up a continuous fire, and in a short time the second line broke and fled, leaving in our hands one six-pounder [gun]. . . . We continued to press them until a third force was seen drawn up in a ravine, . . . and upon this pressed . . . [also], and continued to fire, until it also broke and fled.[111]

A company officer within the 7th Texas thought all along that the primary object of their attack had been to carry the enemy battery, knowing that to be essential to either seizing it or driving it away. Having previously wrecked the first infantry regiment struck, the 8th Illinois, the Texans had next pressed on to strike the right flank of Lt. Col. Ransom's 11th Illinois Infantry. In another deadly encounter at point-blank range, Ransom was numbered among those

---

[110] *Battles & Leaders*, vol. I, pp. 417; 429. Losses for both brigades struck by Simonton's Brigade proved to be heavy, with Oglesby's 1st Brigade tabulating losses of 184 killed, 603 wounded and 66 captured; that of Wallace's 2nd Brigade numbered 99 killed, 350 wounded and 98 missing; for the role played by the 7th Texas in seizing a gun from Schwartz's Btty., see Capt. T. J. Beale's biographical entry in Mamie Yeary, ed., *Reminiscences of the Boys in Gray*. Austin. 1912., p. 8.

[111] *O.R.*, I, 7, 376. To see where the 7th Texas operated, see the map of Ft. Donelson, TN, copied courtesy of the *Civil War Trust*; as well as *Military Atlas*, plate XI, #s 6 & 7. These maps locate both the positions of Oglesby's brigade and Schwartz's battery at the onset of the fighting, as well as W. H. L. Wallace's brigade.

felled there, suffering a severe wound even as his regiment broke and fled to the rear. In a rather extraordinary quirk of fate, Sgt. Stanley M. Warner of the 7th Texas was a former classmate of Ransom's at Norwich University and passed within steps of Ransom, though did not learn that until later.[112]

The most significant loss for the Texans, other than the sheer number of casualties suffered, came in the tragic death of a regimental favorite, Lt. Col. Jeremiah Clough. A Massachusetts native, he had married a Southern woman, and when the war came, he cast his lot with his adopted state. A sharpshooter's bullet through his temple toppled him from his horse, killing him instantly. Capt. Van Zandt revealed how Lt. Arch Adams "went to the body while the bullets were flying around him like hail and secured his watch, memorandum book, purse, etc." Later that night, after returning to their original trenches, a detail recovered Clough's remains from a debris-strewn field and, after fabricating a makeshift coffin out of an Enfield rifle crate, temporarily interred him within their own lines.[113].

After their surrender, Capt. Van Zandt had Clough's body exhumed, and, along with Maj. Hiram Granbury, sought Grant's permission to take his body to Clarksville, where it was re-interred. While there, Granbury made arrangements for his wife's safety, as she had taken a residence there when Granbury's regiment had moved to Ft. Donelson. Afterward, both returned to Ft. Donelson to join their comrades for trans-shipment to a northern prisoner of war camp. But reports by various individuals engaged on that fateful day help form a more in-depth record of events relating to the Texans.[114]

While a sizeable escape route had been opened beyond McClernand's right flank as a consequence of the attack, Gideon Pillow, the on-scene rebel commander, had chosen not to exploit it by extricating the left-wing troops; ostensibly, this came about as a consequence of Grant launching a counterattack on the Confederate

---

[112] Beale biography, in *Reminiscences*, p. 8. Also, see Gregg's report of the capture of Maj. John Post of the 8th Illinois by Private George Blain of Co. G, *O.R.*, I, 7, p. 376.

[113] *Force:*, p. 89.

[114] *Force:*, p. 91.

right, during which time Pillow ordered his attacking force engaged in the breakout effort to return to their works. That a breakout attempt was to be executed is confirmed by Col. Simonton's report; he noted that the men had been formed to move toward their right during the night, only to find themselves being countermanded and ordered back into their former positions. This remarkable failure to extricate even part of the army when such an opportunity had presented itself sealed his men's (and his own) fate, for the rebel army faced no other choice but surrender. While Col. Nathan B. Forrest would lead his cavalry regiment and several hundred other soldiers out via a backflow swamp to make good an escape, unbelievably BG John Floyd took his entire Virginia Brigade to the landing, commandeering sufficient transport to ferry his men across the river during the night.[115]

Here at Ft. Donelson, the Union's overall commander would earn his remarkable sobriquet as "Unconditional Surrender" Grant, stemming from his demand communicated to the rebels that they would be accorded "no other terms." The decisions made by Gen. John B. Floyd and Gideon Pillow in averting surrender in resigning their posts and taking their own men out let the final surrender fall on the shoulders of BG Simon B. Buckner. As the senior officer remaining within the environs of Ft. Donelson, Buckner only agreed reluctantly to march the remainder of the garrison out the following morning to complete their capitulation.[116]

The exact number of casualties for the 7th Texas is apt to never be known with a certainty, due to the separation of the participants immediately after the battle. Gregg advised in his report that the regiment entered the fight with 350 to 360 officers and enlisted men present and lists a loss of "20 killed and 34 disabled by wounds." An even odder place for a report to turn up relative to regiment's casualties is that furnished by Adj. W. D. Douglas in the

---

[115] *The Civil War:*, I, p. 212; *Battles & Leaders*, I, p. 426; also, see Capt. Jack Davis' report, *O.R.*, I, 7, p. 407, wherein he records evacuating most of his men in a boat as well during the night. Both Floyd and Pillow would be relieved from command in the wake of their egregious decisions to flee for their own personal safety.

[116] *Battles & Leaders,* I, p. 426; *Force:* pp.89-90; and *O.R.* I, 7, pp. 362-3.

Official Reports of Battles Embracing the Defence (sic) of Vicksburg, by MG Earl Van Dorn, and the Attack Upon Baton Rouge by MG (John C.) Breckenridge, In it, Douglas lists the known casualties by name and rank, along with his summation that the 7th lost sixty-one killed, wounded, or missing of some 391 present at the start of the fight. Further, he notes the escape of seven men and that 324 soldiers were afterward surrendered.[117]

Once it became apparent the army would be surrendered, many a man slipped away from camp, ultimately making their way to freedom by various means. Some made their way back to Texas and found themselves subsequently assigned to the 22nd Texas Infantry, though a considerable number of others traveled due south to link up with Johnston's army, then in North Mississippi. A published account advises that twenty-seven men from the 7th Texas, led by their regimental chaplain, found themselves temporarily assigned there to the 9th Texas Infantry, pending the regiment's formal exchange. Eventually, this number rose to some fifty men, all finding themselves attached to the 9th Texas at Iuka, Mississippi.[118]

The morning of the 16th, a Sunday, found the Texans still at Donelson disconsolate. They realized that though they had performed their duty, most expressed openly their frustration and embarrassment as prisoners of war. But they soon found themselves even more disheartened upon learning they were to be marched out and forced to stack arms. After this, the prisoners were escorted under armed guards (in lots) to the wharf at Dover, where they boarded steamers for what would turn out to be an arduous trip north. Moving upriver, they made a short stop at Cairo, Illinois, where the men were again split into groups, based upon their rank, before being issued two day's rations and departing by rail cars to distant camps that had been hastily converted to house them. What appears to be a

---

[117] Maj. Earl Van Dorn. *Official Reports of the Battles Embracing the Defence of Vicksburg and the Attack Upon Baton Rouge*, (Richmond, 1863), pp. 115-7.

[118] For a report of those assigned to the 9th Texas, see the John King Papers, Jenkins Garrett Special Collection, the University of Texas at Arlington, Arlington, Texas. Serving as the Adj. of the 9th Texas, King reported the men's arrival and temporary assignment. Hereafter cited as the King papers. As relates to the 22nd Texas assignment, see the Thomas O. Moore biography from *Reminiscences*, p. 536.

September report made out later by Northern authorities, and identified only as "W.D. #521," was a list of all officers and enlisted personnel who had been incarcerated in various camps throughout the north.[119]

The guards had briefly herded them into a temporary holding pen at Cairo like so much livestock, before "culling" their officers and senior noncommissioned officers to forward them on to camps in Ohio. Immediately afterward, the enlisted men and lower-grade non-coms boarded rail cars bound for Chicago, guarded by three companies of the 52nd Illinois Infantry. Here they found a stockade fort containing numerous barracks that had formerly served as a training camp for newly recruited U.S. soldiers. This infamous POW facility would house thousands of captives, initially Mississippi and Tennessee regiments that had accompanied the Texans on their trip up from Tennessee.[120]

Not much could be favorably spoken of the converted Chicago camp that was to serve as a temporary home for the thousands of Southerners captured at Donelson. While much has been made over the years of Northerners who suffered horribly while in Southern camps, the treatment accorded those at Camp Douglas verifies that most Northern camps ranged from despicable to just tolerable. Perhaps some of this could be attributed to the sheer number of prisoners taken during the early months of 1862, but these were certainly aggravated by insufficient amounts of even the basic necessities of life, whether that be stoves, medicines, soap, etc., all of which resulted in an unnecessarily high mortality rate among these Confederate soldiers. With hardly an extant medical facility, and as often as not guarded by third-rate soldiers who seemed to revel in

---

[119] Discovered in a memorandum records file, RG 109, at the National Archives, Washington, and dated September, 1862, it lists the POW camps that the officers and sergeants were then held, noting that the remaining con-coms and privates had been incarcerated at Camp Douglas, in Chicago, Illinois. By that time, both Col. Gregg and Maj. Granbury had been forwarded to Ft. Warren, Boston harbor, the bulk of the officers being held at Johnson's Island, near Sandusky, Ohio. [Styled "War Dept. Memorandum 521, S. 1862-Surrendered at Ft. Donelson, Gregg's 7th Regt. Texas Vols."; also, see *Intrepid Gray Warriors*, p. 45.]

[120] *Force:*, p. 91; *Intrepid Gray Warriors*, p. 46.

subjecting the captives to abject cruelty, these places often assumed the reputation of living hellholes. In conjunction with the abysmal conditions faced by men not enamored with the inclement winter weather they faced soon after arriving at Chicago, the result was severe physical and emotional trauma experienced by the prisoners.[121]

Most believed that the aggravated conditions experienced at Camp Douglas confirmed a genuine lack of concern on behalf of U.S. officials with those prisoners in their charge. One of the Texas officers sent to Camp Chase, outside Columbus, Ohio, observed how his fellow officers encountered brutal treatment there as well. Thirty-two of them found themselves billeted in a room that measured just fourteen by twenty-eight feet, which, interestingly enough, initially included eight personal servants also. They slept on rudely constructed tiers of bunks nailed to exterior walls, the rows commencing at virtually ground level and running up to just under the rafters. This meant that each bunk had to accommodate three prisoners each in order to just get everyone off the floor. And it was as readily apparent that sanitary conditions were not a major concern, at least judging from the poor drainage, along with the location of the camp's sinks. The clear lack of sanitation and cleanliness, coupled with a paucity of blankets, straw, etc. to use as bedding, quickly caused even healthy men to begin suffering. That this was the case is evidenced by the mortality table for the rank and file of the regiment who died between March and September while incarcerated at Camp Douglas, a whopping sixty-five men.[122]

The prisoners had initially hoped not to be long held in such primitive circumstances, but each passing month resulted in a general

---

[121] For a list of the sixty-five Texas soldiers of the 7th Texas that died while at Camp Douglas before being repatriated, see *Confederate States Soldiers and Sailors who died at Camp Douglas, Illinois,* Kalamazoo: Privately Published. 1980. In Appendix 3 of this volume is an extrapolated list this writer compiled for this regiment. That this was not a unique situation can be seen by reviewing rolls of the dead from the other seven regiments that would ultimately compose Granbury's Brigade, who died at Camp's Douglas and Butler, in Illinois. Cited hereafter as *Confederate Soldiers and Sailors*.

[122] *Ibid.*; also see Capt. Van Zandt's matter-of-fact report of incarceration at Camp Chase, Ohio, in *Force:* pp. 91-3.

lessening of hope for survival, with many suspecting they might not live long enough to be exchanged. What they would not discover until much later was that the long stay came about because of disagreements on the exchange process by those serving as POW commissioners. While the cold would begin to abate by late April, it was replaced by a stifling summer sun that quickly set in. But at least the proportion of soldiers dying in camp began to diminish somewhat with the arrival of warmer weather. Not forced to perform hard labor (which might at least have helped maintain their physical stamina), instead the men lay idly about camps, cautiously awaiting word of an exchange being arranged.[123]

While their physical strength might not be sapped by the absence of exercise, boredom caused the weeks, then months, to pass by interminably. The more industrious among them learned to fabricate trinkets from discarded bones and the horns of slaughtered livestock; they cut and then polished them to offer for sale or trade to the guards, or to the numerous spectators who flocked out to gawk at them, giving them some semblance of income. Other major diversions included playing townball, and other games, along with group discussions delving into the fields of politics and religion, including those relating to issues that had spawned the existing conflict. Reading, singing, or writing letters to friends and loved ones at home kept the men occupied otherwise; they especially enjoyed the times when men gathered together around their campfires at night to harmonize before lights out.[124]

Mail came through the lines only infrequently, and when it did, it was usually some months old and heavily censored by their captors. Col. John Gregg advised from Ft. Warren, Boston Harbor, that Maj. Granbury had been prevented from seeing his sick wife, who had recently arrived at that point to be near him. From hawking their bone and horn wares, the prisoners could receive tokens that

---

[123] *Force:*, pp. 93-5; also, Appendix 3 by this writer for the death list of the 7th Texas Infantry.

[124] *Force:*, p. 95. Also, see letters from Col. John Gregg to Capt. W. L. Moody, March 8, & April 22, 1862, and that sent by Maj. Hiram Granbury to Capt. Moody on June 23, 1862, Xerox copies acquired courtesy of the Mary Moody Northern family collection, Galveston Library, Galveston, Texas.

could be deposited with camp sutlers to purchase what few amenities were found there. Often, they received the latest published Northerner papers that, while innately biased, furnished some sense of what was transpiring in the world beyond their prison walls. However, by late June and on into July, word gradually filtered down that the long-postponed Dix-Hill cartel had been reinstituted, and they might therefore expect an early release from captivity.[125]

It the interim, officers in Gregg's regiment kept in as close contact as censors would allow. Col. Gregg's letter of July 1 advised Capt. W. L. Moody that "your censor is so much more liberal than ours, as to what is to be written by a prisoner." But "plague on these restrictions any how (sic), don't you just hate them?" While it would take another month before that exchange came about, he seemed genuinely surprised when advised of the rumors that he'd supposedly been killed at Donelson. In Boston, he had met several Irish Catholics from the city, remarking: "They are clannish," but that "I rather like these Catholics."[126]

But it was not until mid-August that the actual agreement that would result in the exchange of the prisoners on a wholesale basis came into effect. Already at Boston, both Col. Gregg and Maj. Granbury had been alerted to their parole that month, with Gregg being swapped for three first lieutenants and one second lieutenant, while Granbury went for one first lieutenant and one second lieutenant. Both of these officers were then forwarded to Aiken's

---

[125] *Force:*, p. 96; Maj. Granbury's letter of June 23rd, in addition to discussing their "playing football and pitching quoits," discussed a new rumor "that we hope this time there will no abortion, but that a good healthy personal exchange" will take place. Known thereafter as the Dix-Hill cartel, this exchange program provided pro-rata formulas providing for swapping man for man, officers for officers, and a pro-rata of so many enlisted men for an officer, etc. See Coll. # 1988.2.1688, p. 1.

[126] *Ibid,;* also, see Col. Gregg's letter to Capt. William Moody, July 1, 1862, Mary Moody Northern collection, # 1988.2.1690; wherein he mentions that eight Texans were then held at Ft. Warren. Also, see Capt. "Tom" Broughton's letter envelope of May 23, 1862, carried by a released P. O. W. from Johnson's Island, Sandusky, Ohio, but postmarked at Richmond, Va., some months later, and at last delivered to his wife.

Landing, Maryland, before being transshipped to Richmond, Virginia.[127]

-Tenth Texas Infantry-

Even as the 6th and 7th Texas Infantry Regiments underwent organization in the fall of 1861, another infantry regiment later destined to serve within Granbury's brigade came into existence. And unlike the 6th Texas Infantry before it, while this regiment couldn't trace its origins to the Texas Gulf Coast, it did undergo its formation near Galveston. One of the most important seaports in the state, Galveston became the terminus of a major rail line that intersected with the state's interior via Houston. Most of the companies of the 10th, however, sprang from what can only be best described at the time as frontier counties: Anderson, Limestone, Johnson, Freestone, Bosque, and Coryell counties contributed sizeable contingents to that regiment. Only two came from anywhere near where the regiment actually completed its organization. One originated at Millican, in Grimes County, while the other enrolled in Washington County. Initially named after its original commanders, as Allison Nelson's Regiment, it eventually received the designation as the 10th Texas Infantry.[128]

Essentially the brainchild of Waco attorney Allison Nelson, the regiment quickly seemed to take on his persona. Born in Fulton

---

[127] *Intrepid Gray Warriors*: p. 59; *Force*: p. 96; and Gregg's letter to W. L. Moody, July 1, 1862, Coll. # 1988.2.1690.

[128] Compiled service records of the 10th Texas Infantry, RG 109, National Archives, Washington, D. C.; for Allison Nelson's biography, see Mike Polston, "Allison Nelson: Atlanta Mayor, Texas Hero, Confederate General," in *Atlanta Historical Society Quarterly Bulletin*, (fall, 1985), pp.19-25, hereafter "Allison Nelson"; also, *Texas in the War:*, pp. 14, 89. Scott MvKay of Georgia graciously furnished much print material relative to the 10th Texas from his research of the regiment, including many ordnance returns, for which I'm very grateful.

County, Georgia in 1822, during the Mexican War, Nelson served in that state's militia forces before sojourning as a filibusterer in Cuba during the early 1850s as an officer in Francisco Lopez's army. Once he returned stateside, he moved on to become involved in the Bloody Kansas episode of 1854, returning to Atlanta the next year to enter the political arena there.[129]

Having served a short stint as mayor of Atlanta, he resigned under duress and moved his family west, settling eventually at Meridian in Bosque County. After serving for a brief time as the state's Indian agent, in 1858 he enlisted in the Texas Rangers under Lawrence "Sul" Ross as a lieutenant, serving against hostile Comanches out beyond the frontier. He afterward studied law before serving in the state legislature. Even as war began to loom on the horizon, Nelson had relocated his law practice to the larger community of Waco. A staunch states' rights Democrat, and an ardent secessionist, he participated in the state secession convention in January 1861 as one of the more vocal advocates supporting Texas' withdrawal from the Union. While avidly supporting the state's becoming part of the Confederacy, he seemed to drift more toward military matters, and as a consequence, he strove to gain authority to raise his own regiment. In an October 17, 1861, edition of the *Galveston News*, the paper advised its readership that "Col. A. Nelson, of Bosque County, . . . was commissioned by Hébert to raise a regiment of infantry for coast defense, [asking us] to report that he had succeeded in raising ten companies. . . ." The Confederate secretary of war appointed Nelson a colonel on October 15, 1861; he was expected "to [both] muster and command" the regiment."[130]

The Galveston paper hyped Nelson's efforts in raising the regiment:

---

[129] "Allison Nelson", p. 20; and *Texas in the Civil War:* p.14. See also Scott McKay's *A Timeline History of the 10th Texas Infantry*, chap. 2, p. 2. Hereafter cited as *A Timeline History*.

[130] Comp. Serv. Rec., RG 109, NA; *Galveston News*, Oct. 17, 1861; *A Timeline History*.

Col. A. Nelson, of Bosque County, who but a fortnight ago, was commissioned by [Paul O.] Hébert to raise a regiment of infantry for coast defense, returned here Saturday last, from the upper country, to report that he had succeeded not only in raising ten companies, but half a dozen more had been offered; and he came down to know what disposition would be made of them. He left again on Sunday; and his companies will be down this week. **They are for the war** [author's emphasis]. Col. Nelson is an old soldier, both in regular and frontier service; he is active, cool and brave, and only asks to get his men near enough the enemy to use the bayonet."[131]

Nelson requested the companies to rendezvous at Galveston, where the regiment would be formally organized and mustered into service. The selection of this city satisfied any number of objectives for the state: it would provide an effective force to defend the city against an invasion by sea, whilst the men could be easily supplied via a rail line linking Galveston with the state's interior. Interestingly, only eight of Nelson's ten companies would initially be mustered in between October 13 and November 1, but like Garland's 6th Texas, the two remaining companies required to bring it to regimental strength wouldn't arrive until after New Year's Day.[132]

To assist Nelson in organizing the command, Roger Q. Mills of Corsicana joined him soon after and became an avid supporter. He eventually was appointed lieutenant colonel. Previous to this, Mills had served in Col. Elkanah Greer's South-Kansas-Texas Regiment (later known as the 3rd Texas Cavalry) and had fought at the Battle of Wilson's Creek, Missouri, the previous August. The *Texas Republican* of Marshall, Texas had printed a verbatim letter by him, dated August 22, 1861, on his experience in Missouri. In addition to these officers, a stock-raiser (a.k.a. rancher) named Robert B. Young

---

[131] *Galveston News,* October 17, 1861.

[132] See muster-in rolls of Nelson's Regiment, Texas Infantry, Adj. Reports, State Archives, Austin; also, RG 109, National Archives, Washington; and *A Timeline History*, chapter 2, p. 1.

of Waco likewise received the nod as major. The companies reporting only spent ten days at Galveston before being relocated to Virginia Point, opposite the island itself, where they were put to work on an earthwork designated as Ft. Hébert, named to honor their district commander, BG Paul O. Hébert. And like its companion regiment, the 6th Texas, the men on the point would spend the coming winter months learning the rudiments of drill and trying hard to enliven lives faced by what many saw as an overall monotonous existence.[133]

In an October 22 letter, Mills had signified to Maj. Samuel R. Davis his acceptance of the position of lieutenant colonel, as authorized by President Jefferson Davis, advising he would report himself to Nelson for duty (note that he thought then that Nelson's regiment was the 6th and not the 10th Texas Infantry). Almost at the same time, the earliest reporting companies had been designated as Companies A, F, and H and mustered in with two others, B and E, having been enrolled on the following day. And about this same time, up in Johnson County, Texas, another company had begun to come together, due to the efforts of Capt. William Shannon of Buchanan, the county seat (and southwest of Ft. Worth). The previous May, Shannon had enlisted fifty-six recruits in what the men denominated as the Rock Creek Guards, though they eventually became Co. C. in Nelson's command. And another Johnson County company that had been mustered into the state militia the previous June would join the regiment, though not actually arrive in camp until the following January. They had to change their initial name as the Stockton Cavalry when they became Co. I. And lastly, a conglomerate company consisting of recruits joined from neighboring Coryell and Bosque counties would be the last to reach

---

[133] A good biography of Mills is Alwynn Barr's, "The Making of a Secessionist: The Antebellum Career of Roger Q. Mills," in the *Southwestern Historical Quarterly.*, 79 (1975): pp. 9-44; on Mills' Wilson's Creek letter, see "A Texan at Wilson's Creek," published in *Civil War Times Illustrated,* Vol. 17, (Jan. 1979) pp. 46-7. Cited afterward as *C.W.T.I.* For a most interesting letter pertaining to Mills' participation in the secession convention that previous January, see his of January 22, 1861 letter, the "Roger Q. Milles ["Mills Papers," Call Box 2F42, University of Texas at Austin; for Young's biography, see *A History Timeline,* p. 2; and Compiled Service Records, Record Group 109, NA, Washington.

Virginia Point, becoming Co. K. This last rounded out the requisite ten companies needed to justify its regimental status.[134]

COUNTIES FROM WHICH THE 10TH TEXAS INFANTRY REGIMENT ENLISTED

By early November, the earliest recruits to arrive had begun to record their initial experiences of being in the army. Isaiah Harlan, a private in Co. G, had just enlisted with three other comrades in Capt. J. S. Lauderdale's Co. G from Washington County. Of great import to him seemed to be their perilous circumstances. If the enemy did come: "I am of the impression that if the Lincolnites were to make a vigorous attack upon the place, that it might be very easily taken, and the whole rest of us." Already ill, he had not fared well, and as for performing active service, he hadn't drawn either arms or

---

[134] C.S.R. of companies A through K, from RG 109, N.A.; *A Timeline History*, chapter, 2, pp. 1-32. A copy of the militia rolls of the "Rock Creek Guards," dated May, 25, 1861, and of the "Stockton Cavalry," dated June 3, 1861, marked # # 192, were copied from the State Archives, Austin.

clothes and had lost his carpetbag on the stage on the way down to Galveston. Consequently, he had only a single pair of pants to make do with and not much else. Only four days later, November 5, Pvt. Benjamin Seaton had enlisted in Harlan's company, noting in his diary that day that "everything in camp is quited [sic] and but little excitement. We receive news almost every day from the eastern states of their fighting...."[135]

Seaton's off-hand remarks confirm the universal impression at the time that the war might already be nearing an end, and frankly, he seemed to have fast become bored with military life. Nevertheless, the regiment would continue to prep for war as the tedious winter months passed by.

Seaton might have recanted his opinion about their boring circumstances, for only a few days afterward, an incident transpired that signaled that war had suddenly come close to hand. On the 10th, he observed that:

> ... the [U.S.S.] Santee, as she was getting short of provisions, [decided] she would throw a few shells into Galveston to see how she would stand them, thinking they would vacate, [but] they were mistaken.[136]

The other chronicler in Co. G., Isaiah Harlan, who had earlier presumed that "if the Lincolnites were to make [a] vigorous attack [on] the place [they] might be very easily taken," now penned a short note to his "ma," on the 10th also. In it, he acknowledged that while their tents seemed to be good, "we are on the ground and I can't tell how long we will stay." However, he and his tent-mates shared "a mattress and six or seven blankets, [at least] on this score nothing is lacking." He still lamented the loss of his carpetbag, along with his

---

[135] This typescript letter of Isaiah Harlan to a brother Eliphalet, Nov. 1, 1861, comes from the Confederate Research Center, Hill College, Hillsboro (hereafter noted only as C.R.C., Hill College); Col. Harold B. Simpson, ed., *The Bugle Softly Blows: The Confederate Diary of Benjamin M. Seaton*. Waco: Texian Press. 1965, p. 1. Hereafter Simpson's work will be cited simply as *The Bugle*.

[136] *The Bugle:*, p. 1.

wallet and extra clothing, thinking it to have been pilfered on the way down. He also wrote about the rations received, of "beef, bread and coffee[,] with bacon enough to grease with." He grumbled over having to drill three to four hours daily, concluding his letter by stating that "I am going to have my likeness taken and sent up to you."[137]

Around Galveston, the men found that for the most part, they had to take things pretty much as they came, with apparently quite a number of them not thinking the strict military regimen imposed as necessary. Though complaints of a lack of military equipment continued, the men being issued squad-size tents had at least gotten them out the weather, though not protected from myriad critters living in the sand. Virtually everyone spent some hours daily on guard duty, alternating with four hours on and off. They were subject to be called out a moment's notice. Having few other demands, this left them plenty of off-duty time to spend on personal business. Some speculated as to whether they would ever get into a fight, though Harlan voiced that if they did, he hoped to "turn out to be a coward." He requested those back home to write as often as possible to help fill his free hours and to keep him abreast of matters there, lest he succumb to the "melancholy business" that other comrades suffered from.[138]

On the same day Harlan sent his November 10 missive, Benjamin Seaton made a diary entry advising of the recent excitement in Galveston occurring when the blockade vessel, the *U.S.S. Santee*, "as she was getting short of provisions, [decided] she wo[u]ld throw a few shells into Galveston to see how they wo[u]ld stand them . . . The enemy must have been surprised to see the ladies of the town atop the roof of the tallest building looking out at the ship " . . . as if to say if you come here we will whip you . . . ." But on November 24, Isaiah Harlan complained to his brother about a very touchy subject the men appeared frustrated over: "We have not yet received our arms and the Lord only knows when we will." Irritated

---

[137] Isaiah Harlan letter, November 10, 1861, C.R.C., Hill College. Hereafter cited as Harlan letters. A Bosque County resident since 1857, another letter dated August 30, 1858, shows him to be running livestock for a living.

[138] *Ibid*, letter of Nov. 10, 1861.

by this, he complained: "We committed a great error in sending those back we had; but we were told that we would draw them." In fact, the only good news he noted was that "very little sickness [existed] in the Regiment."[139]

November had brought with it the first inclement weather they had experienced, and prompted by this, the men began to write home about acquiring more substantial clothing, the likes of which only those back home could supply. On November 24, Isaiah Harlan wrote his brother, Alpheus, that he needed several overshirts and a pair of trousers, "of good strong coarse stuff. Have breast pockets put [in]to them," he advised, referring to the shirts. And if nothing else, he'd soon have need of a hat, "but I'll [likely] send to Houston for it." Though still very rudimentary, "We drill a little every day. That is we form, right and left flank[,] and file[,] mark time, counter-march, and right about a few times and then dismiss." Obviously, the men still had a long way to go to learn the sophisticated evolutions they needed.[140]

During this same month, 4th Cpl. Aaron Estes of Co. B had written his wife from Virginia Point about their circumstances as the month came to an end. Cautioning her to not be alarmed should they come under attack, he alluded to an increasing number of enemy contacts around the point. The fortifications had been all but completed near Galveston's east end and were now approaching that point near the bridge at the western end. Importantly, due to increasing enemy pressure from out beyond the bar, "wee (sic) have been drilling very hard fore (sic) several days and making every priperation (sic) that wee (sic) can be fore a fight. Wee intend to do the best we can fore (sic) ower (sic) self and Country."[141]

As December advanced, the potential for hostilities showed no sign of abating, in part resulting in a recent increase in drills, which perhaps kept minds off the dearth of supplies and bland diet they experienced. And now soldiers began complaining about their

---

[139] *The Bugle;* p. 1; Isaiah Harlan letter, Nov. 10th and 24, 1861, CRC, Hill College.

[140] Isaiah Harlan to Alpheus, Nov. 24, 1861, CRC, Hill College.

[141] Aaron Estes letter of Nob. 29, 1861, Estes letters in Special Collections, Baylor University, Waco, Texas.

personal discomfort. Harlan alludes to just that in a letter written on December 5, wherein he pronounced that "Galveston will be abandoned, it is considered impossible to defend it with the forces here." In a letter drafted December 15, he further advised his brother, Eliphalet, that he's become "very tired of 'blue' beef and tough biscuits - a little grease would help greatly." He asks that his brother to send him a supply, along with potatoes and "six or eight pounds of coffee." He also advised that all non-combatants had been ordered off the island and all ammunition had been removed to the Virginia Point. At the end, he complained that: "We need more men and arms and better arms and a great deal more cannon[,] and that of a large[r] size."[142]

Two days later, he sent a follow-up letter to his brother, Alpheus, in which Harlan recommended that Alpheus put in all the food crops he could raise. Advising he'd been sick again, Harlan went on that "we drill a great deal more than we did. Some of the boys complain at it, but I should think they ought to." And he disclosed that a rumor in camp had spread that they might, at last, be paid for their service, in which case his brother could use that money to pay their taxes. As will be seen down the road, not much would come of this for many months to come. That the disaffection Harlan expressed seemed to be growing; Benjamin Seaton's diary entry of December 23 stated: " . . . we are now drilling from 6 to 8 hours every day and we think it is vary (sic) hard to do to be commanded by a set of white men to have command of another one . . . ."[143]

During these months, the regiment began to fill many of the necessary staff position officers to meet its needs, Dr. William Gantt being appointed surgeon by BG P. O. Hébert, with the elevated rank of major. About this time also, Capt. George Hearne had been selected as the regimental adjutant on November 4, and 2nd Lt. George B. Jewell of Co. C. found himself detailed as the regimental ordnance officer on the 8th, these supernumerary posts being necessary to bring the regiment into compliance with regulations.

---

[142] Isaiah Harlan letters, December 5, and 15, 1861. The term "blue" beef would be best described today as what is referred to today as "extra-heavy aged beef," or worst, that marked "reduced for quick sale!"

[143] Isaiah Harlan letter of Nov. 17, 1861 C.R.C, Hill College; *The Bugle*, p. 2.

Interestingly, in a letter written on December 10, despite illness, Maj. Roger Q. Mills advised his spouse that there was "some apprehension that the enemy will land one division of their army at Sabine Pass and take charge of the R. R. to N. O. and come to take Houston" (from behind, which would obviously make Galveston untenable). Irrespective of this rumor, he forced an optimistic response toward this view: "I believe the Lord of hosts will deliver the enemy into our hands."[144]

Previously, on December 1, Pvt. I.P. Jones of Co. H had written his aunt and uncle that his enlisting in the 10th Texas seemed to him to be "like [joining] the 'old' regulars[;] [as] its go it from six o'clock in the morning till eight of a night." He noted that seventy-two enlisted men had been entered upon their rolls at this time, bringing the company close to full strength. With rumors rampant that Galveston would be evacuated, and with orders having arrived mandating that all remaining government stores and non-combatants be removed from the island, it seemed readily apparent to most everyone that the troops there must also be removed from Galveston if they were to be saved. While extra duty men had been assigned by this time to commence their winter quarters, they ceased this pursuit once abandonment seemed probable. However, the men continued to improve their fortifications, even throwing up additional works nearby in order to successfully defend against enemy forces that might be landed to their rear. It was during these hectic weeks, moreover, that typhoid fever began to make its appearance within the ranks, causing many deaths and the disablement of many others from continuing to serve in the regiment.[145]

Writing in early January 1862, Cpl. Aaron Estes advised that he too had not been well, "but able to [k]nock about. There is a rite [sic] amount of sickness in camps." He writes that the recent bad weather had ameliorated and that "some of those large cannon have arived [sic] here, wee [sic] have three rifle cannon here. They say they will shoot 7 miles." Rumors continued to abound of their

---

[144] R. Q. Milles letter to his spouse, Dec 10, 1861.

[145] James, John and Martin Jones letters from Anderson County, Special Collections, Baylor University; Isaiah Harlan letter, Dec. 15, 1861, to Eliphalet, C.R.C. Hill College; *The Bugle:*, p. 3.

receiving an enlistment bonus, along with wages, but "wee [sic] haven't been paid yet, but (the captain) thinks that wee [sic] will be paid off in a short time, so if I live I will bee [sic] at home bee [sic] twixt [sic] this and spring." Teasing his wife over his long absence, he suggested that she "would like to see my wooly head." Bringing this letter to a close, he promised to bring her "some pretty sea shells," perhaps even "a little con[c]k shell."[146]

That circumstances weren't all that could be asked for at the point is obvious in the violent death of 4th Sgt. Robert L. Franklin, of Co. C, who had been killed in an artillery accident on December 19. And just afterward, a company commander had submitted a special request for a supply of discharge forms on December 21, in order to discharge a dozen men out of Co. D. The dramatic increase in premature death through incipient diseases, coupled with the sheer inability of some enlisted personnel to perform the requisite duties of a soldier, led to further reductions in force. So much so was this the case that before the final month of the year had ended, a decision had been reached to send out recruiting parties to visit respective counties in search of additional recruits to bring companies back to their necessary strengths. Included among these were 43-year-old 2nd Lt. Daniel Boatright of Co. K, along with 1st Lt. James J. Ligon, age 37, of Co. C, each of whom had been sent home on recruiting duty.[147]

Perhaps not atypical among the recruiting parties was Lt. Ligon of Johnson County, who obtained several recruits there, including fifteen-year old William O. Wynn, who enlisted as a musician and noted his home as near Comanche Peak in the western part of the county. He advised that he had been a cowboy before the war, having often pursuing "the wild savages" frequently found in the Brazos River bottoms. That winter, he had ventured to the county seat of Buchanan with his boss, the latter opting to enlist in the Rock Creek Guard. Unable to sleep that night, Wynn decided to go back into town the following day and enlist. He recorded this momentous

---

[146] Aaron Estes letter of Jan. 5, 1862, Estes special collection, Baylor University.

[147] *A History Timeline*, chapter 2, pp. 20-1; also, chapter 2, p. 23; also, the compiled service records of the 10th Texas reveals that at this time only 431 officers and men appeared on the rolls, where close to a thousand were required to possess full regimental strength.

occasion in an off-handed manner: "After he [Lt. James Ligon] had gotten his hundred men all strung in line, he said, 'Now, gentlemen, raise your right hand, pull off your hats, and I will . . . administer the oath to you[,] or muster you into service." Wynn had recanted the first time an effort had been made to recruit him, as he was underage and had returned to his home. It wasn't until early 1862 that Ligon again came up from Galveston to gather up more recruits. Again, Wynn had gone to town, and as he termed it, "afraid the war would end before I got to see a Yankee," he and some twenty other men enlisted on February 2, 1862. Drawn up in line again, each was requested to raise his right hand, after removing their hats, "and he [Ligon] cussed us in[to] the army . . . ."[148]

Also reaching their camp in January, in addition to new recruits, were special requisitions that included undershirts, shoes, tents, spades, axes, hatchets, mess pans, camp kettles, and even canteen straps. As an example, Capt. Pendergast's company received twelve undershirts and twenty-six pair of shoes (ranging from size six to ten), along with wool socks and underwear. And Capt. John Formwalt of Johnson County, recently promoted from a private in Co. C to raise another company from the same area (afterward Co. I), had submitted a special requisition and received the following items: two officer's tents, two company tents, four spades, four axes, four hatchets, eight mess pans, eight camp kettles, and sixty-two canteen straps (one and a half yards to the strap). And, lastly, on the 28th, a special requisition submitted by Capt. Byron Bassel of Co. K brought his men many of the same items that Formwalt's company had received, but additionally saw him obtain twenty-four quires of paper, several dozen envelopes, thirteen pens, a gill of ink, and one pen holder. A day later, Dr. Gantt received for his field hospital twenty cots and mattresses, along with twenty pair of sheets and

---

[148] See muster-roll of Wynn in C.S.R. N.A., Washington; copy in possession of writer that details his enlistment as a musician, this transpiring on January 3, 1862; however, also see his accounts of his service in a later-in-life autobiography privately published in 1912, pp. 34, 40-2. Wynn's statements in his somewhat dubious volume, printed in Paris, Texas, should be correlated by other accounts, as some of his assertions are clearly refuted by others and caution ought to be used in citing his work. See also, *A History Timeline*, chapter 2, p. 24.

pillowcases, six chamber pots, fourteen shirts, and a yard and a half of oilcloth, these items being required for the large number of men who had recently begun to contract the measles.[149]

Cpl. Aaron Estes of Co. B wrote to try and console a brother, Ed. B. Estes, then serving in the 7th Texas Infantry at Hopkinsville, Kentucky, saying just how lucky his own regiment had been when compared to the sickness that his brother professed to have witnessed way up in in the Bluegrass State. Though the measles had broken out, the men otherwise had plenty of beef and bread, some molasses, and were expecting vegetables to be sent over to them soon. As "fore (sic) clothing and blankets we have plenty." He advised that the men still hadn't been paid as of the date of his letter, January 29, 1862. That he and his comrades in the 10th were doing well in the way of firearms at this point is attested to by his report that "wee [sic] are all gitting [sic] very well drilled and I have got the best musket that ever burnt powder. I can hit a yanky [sic] 2 hundred yeards away . . . ."[150]

And one of Cpl. Estes' messmates, a private named Silar Barber of Co. B, had likewise written Aaron Estes' brother, Ed, that same day (and likely mailed in the same envelope) advising how concerned they were in learning of the great number of men in the 7th Texas Infantry who had already died of disease, reporting that recently two men had been run over and killed on Virginia Point by railroad cars. He and his comrades did sometimes cause minor problems in their regiment through miscreant behavior, though their officers "tries to keep them all out of [the] cused [sic] place."[151]

Of growing concern to most everyone seemed to be a rift that had grown between those at the regimental staff level and those serving in the ranks, due in large part to the perception of the enlisted men that many of their officers seemed to have recently begun to distance themselves from their charges. This growing animosity might flare up at any moment, in large part because those in the

---

[149] *A Timeline History*, chapter 2, p. 24 & pp. 32-3.

[150] Aaron Estes letter, Estes special collections, Baylor University. As to the extent of the measles outbreak, see J. P. Jones letter of Jan. 14, 1862, also in Jones special collections, Baylor University.

[151] Silas H. Barber, Co. B, 10th Texas, addressed to Ed Estes of the 7th Texas, found in the Estes family special collections, Baylor University.

lower ranks thought that their leaders possessed little interest in their men's welfare, one private noting this even by the seeming unwillingness to adequately superintend their drills: "Most . . . of our officers are such gofers [sic]," lamented Isaiah Harlan of Co. G, "that they can't learn anything." And even 4th Cpl. Aaron Estes of Co. B, in a letter shared with his family, stated flatly to them on this point: "If I am a solger [sic] [,] I intend to act on honorable [sic] prineables [sic] and I shall expect to bee [sic] treeted [sic] in the same way, but it don't look much like it . . . ." That degree of confidence so necessary to good relations between officers and enlisted men, perhaps more important even in volunteer regiments, appears at this time to be nearing the breaking point. And as will be seen later, this would, in large measure, become the precursor to an open revolt.[152]

With the arrival of the final two companies at the point to fill out the regiment, its status was raised from a battalion to a regimental organization. These two new contingents, companies I and K, had also been raised out on the Texas frontier, and warranted special attention in order to integrate them into the new organization and allow them to catch up with their eight other companies, both in equipping themselves and in perfecting their drill. Respectively mustered in January 16 and 28, both had a lot of catching up to do. Several other regiments having been mustered in with a full complement of companies meant that Nelson's command would be belatedly numbered the 10th Texas Infantry Regiment.[153]

One of those late-arriving companies that had enrolled in January 1862 hadn't actually reached the coast until late that next month, as they encountered many difficulties in getting all the men together and then locating suitable transportation. Capt. Formwalt's Stockton Cavalry, as that company from Johnson County had formerly been known, had reached out to recruits in the neighboring counties of Coryell, Erath, Bell, Bosque, and McLennan in order to fill its ranks. Due to the considerable delays they experienced, once arrived near Galveston, Capt. Formwalt had felt duty-bound to

---

[152] Isaiah Harlan letters, Feb. 19, 1862, CRC, Hill College; and Aaron Estes letter of Feb. 14, 1862, Estes special collections, Baylor University.

[153] Compiled Service Records, RG 109, NA, Washington; *The Bugle*: p. 3; *The Timeline* pp. 29-30.

publicly thank those folks who had rendered aid in helping to get this company to the coast. A public memorial of thanks had been printed by a Houston paper, wherein Formwalt lauded the citizens of both Acton and Buchanan in Johnson County for having hosted ". . . elegant parties, dinners, and suppers given the company" prior to its departure from the county.[154]

The last company to arrive to complete the 10th Texas organization had come about through the effort of Overton F. Davenport, who had gained permission from Capt. Brice Hartgraves of Co. H on December 10 to return to Coryell County, and there raise another company, of which he had been elected a lieutenant. John Bassel was elected to serve as this company's new captain. Co. K likewise had to make a long trek to Virginia Point, arriving there not long after Capt. Formwalt's company had arrived. Like others, it included men from surrounding counties in order to fill its quota.[155]

Though service on the coast might had seemed idyllic to those back home, such had not proven to be the case at all. What with camp diseases, an inadequate number of supplies, and increasingly inclement weather on the coast during the winter months, along with the rising dissension within the ranks, many a man was in a foul mood. Momentous events had begun to transpire in the Mississippi River valley not long after the New Year began, and they quickly threatened to bring their tranquil service on the coast to an end. This had actually begun in mid-February following the twin losses of forts Henry and Donelson in central Tennessee that had led to Albert S. Johnston's army falling back all the way to northern Mississippi, virtually giving up Kentucky and Tennessee as a consequence. In a bold stroke soon after, Union forces had moved via the Cumberland River to seize Nashville on February 23, making it the first Southern capital to fall to the enemy. Then, in early March, Confederate forces in Northwest Arkansas had been soundly defeated at the Battle of Pea Ridge (Elkhorn Tavern), and had fallen back to the Arkansas River valley before being moved off to the

---

[154] *Houston Tri-Weekly Telegraph*, Feb. 5, 1862.

[155] See Joe R. Davenport's *Incidents of the Life of W. G. Davenport Which Occurred During the Civil War*, an unpublished manuscript, (San Antonio, 1994), pp. 2-5. Hereafter cited as *Incidents of the Life of W. G. Davenport*.

northeastern part of that state. Unless drastic action was quickly taken to rectify the sudden turn of events, the war along the Mississippi River and Trans-Mississippi west stood a good chance of being over before spring arrived.[156]

The race to save those states both east and west of the mighty Mississippi seemed to be of paramount importance, for the loss of that river meant the destruction of communications for either side and perhaps the end of entire war. In the wake of the Ft. Donelson disaster, on February 24, BG Paul Hébert in Texas received an urgent telegraphic message to "send forward to Little Rock [immediately] . . . all the troops in your command, for the defense of the coast, except such as are necessary to man your batteries." Hébert immediately alerted all units already under arms and capable of moving to begin preparations for a move forthwith toward the valley of the Mississippi, further alerting those units still undergoing organization that they too would be sent off as well once completed. Obviously, among those immediately ordered to Arkansas from the Texas coast would be Garland's 6th Texas at Victoria and Nelson's 10th Texas near Galveston.[157]

While by this time both had the requisite number of companies needed, each had also been much reduced in strength as the weather turned bad over the winter. Each had dispatched many sick men to hospitals, or out into the country to be attended in private homes, while still others were away on recruiting duty or on furlough, and therefore much time would pass in getting them back into camp, delaying the move considerably. Mid-January had shown the 6th Texas having only 643 effectives, whilst a February 28 report of the 10th Texas had seen just 636 men present.[158]

---

[156] See *Battles & Leaders of the Civil War*, vol. 1, pp.398-429, & 314-337; also, *The Civil War:*, vol. 1, pp. 208-214, and pp. 282-291.

[157] *O.R.* I, 9, p. 700; also, *Charles A. Leuschner*, p. 7. Interestingly, typhoid fever had erupted among the men of the 10th, and "the weather has been so bad," said Isaiah Harlan of Co. G "that we have been drilling but little," letter of Feb. 19, 1862 C.R.C, Hill College.

[158] The 6th Texas figures are those reported by "High Private" in *Houston Tri-Weekly Telegraph*, Jan. 31, 1862; those for the 10th are reflected in *O.R.*, I, 9: p. 701.

As signs of approaching spring came on down along the Gulf Coast, the blustering trade winds signaled that milder temperatures that would come by early March. Within Galveston, this first week marked Texas' Independence Day, as well as marking the first anniversary of the state's secession, and it was deemed appropriate to mark the occasion. Indeed, the 10th Texas had joined several other provisional army troops and local militia organizations in a massive parade through the city, after which a Grand Review had been held of the close to 5,000 participants who were present. One 10th Texas private took the occasion as being akin to the "revolution of 1836," comparing the current conflict with that which saw the republic win independence from Mexico.[159]

Pvt. Isaiah Harlan's response, however, perhaps seemed a little more flowery, when, after participating in the patriotic parade, he remarked that provided "the Lincolnites don't get me . . . ," the struggle would be continued "so long as there is a prospect of achieving independence." And should that not be the ultimate outcome of this war, he added: "I don't care a copper whether I live or die." Harlan probably echoed the sentiments of many men that each had a duty to defend "southern rights" and that if "every man in the Confederacy should do his duty . . ," the South would stop the North from perverting the Constitution." As the conflict seemed to be inexorably moving into a second year, Harlan felt compelled to record the feelings at this critical time: "Some of our boys are considerably discouraged on account of our reverses in Tennessee," he observed, but "others are still cheerful and hopeful" about the outcome.[160]

Another writing of the disasters in the center, the Jones brothers in Co. D, 10th Texas, wrote on March 9 from Ft. Hébert that rumor had it they might soon be moving via boat to some point,

---

[159] Isaiah Harlan letter, March 7, 1862, to brother Eliphalet, CRC, Hill College; also see *The Bugle:*, p. 3. Harlan perhaps paraphrased one of his superiors, Lt. Col. Roger Q. Mills, who had during the secession crisis expressed his opinion that all Texans had an obligation to turn out in what he called an "imperative sense of duty I owed to my country in [this, its] . . . most trying hour," Roger Q. Mills letter, Jan. 22, 1861, Mills papers, Box 2F42, Special Collections, University of Texas archives, Austin, Texas.

[160] Isaiah Harlan letter, March 7, 1862, CRC, Hill College.

though if not, then perhaps they'd be sent to the Red River, or on into the Indian Nations. They believed their comrades in the company would whip the enemy, because they "are well drilled and spunky," though one man had recently offered a "thousand dollars to take his place" as a substitute soldier, and he had seen in the local paper that the enemy had Nashville by that point.[161]

And like the Jones brothers, many others on the coast carefully perused the newspapers for more details on those far-off events being experienced in distant theaters. Not long after Independence Day, the *Houston Tri-Weekly Telegraph* advised readers of the aftermath of the Ft. Donelson surrender, copied from a Northern paper: "Late prisoners [we learn, are incarcerated] in Chicago. [U.S. troops] had in charge 899 prisoners, including some of the Texas Rgt., [of] Col. Gregg, most of them are sharpshooters from eastern and central Texas. Among the prisoners we found Orderly Sgt. Stanley M. Warner of the 7th [Texas Infantry, who] . . . by a remarkable circumstance between the 7th Texas . . . and 11th Illinois [Warner and Lt. Col. T. E. G. Ransom] were pitted against each other outside the trenches . . . . These two [regiments] almost decimated each other, suffering far more [casualties] than any other [commands] on either side."[162]

Though most rank-and-file soldiers yet remained in the dark over many of the nagging problems that had surfaced between national and state leaders, in Austin, Governor Francis R. Lubbock, who had succeeded Edward Clark, likely exacerbated recruiting problems with a recent declaration that state, and not national authorities, had the ultimate responsibility for commissioning officers in regiments from the state, as well as authorizing the raising of new troops there. In fact, he'd recently sent a menacing letter to the War Department, in which he lectured Richmond authorities as to their issuing blanket commissions without first consulting the governor. Lubbock asserted that this would result in continued confusion in his efforts to orderly raise new units, and, after all, wasn't that what both the state and national government wanted? In

---

[161] Signed as J. P. Jones, in Jones family letters, Jones special collections, Baylor University]

[162] *Houston Tri-Weekly Telegraph*, March 14, 1862, State Archives, Austin.

Richmond, ongoing attempts to commission Texans of stature to independently raise new commands breached the very cornerstone of the state's sovereignty and must therefore be stopped.[163]

The arguments almost reached the boiling point when, not long after, the War Department wired Governor Lubbock a levy for fifteen additional regiments, which the governor again took to be an unconstitutional action by the national government, sparking another outburst by him. The continuing conflict over who held the preemptive right to award commissions personally galled Lubbock and would lead to further frustration, as he hinted that such actions might just irreparably damage the relationship between the state and its national counterpart. Lubbock ended a scathing letter by demanding Richmond stop meddling in the state's affairs, especially in light of the recent requests for the state to supply additional regiments. Lubbock sternly lectured that some action must be immediately taken to lessen the conflict in order to avoid a complete breakdown of the troop-raising system, and unless his counterpart acquiesced to those demands, this dispute would likely continue to grow worse.[164]

Few, if any, of the men in the army ever learned of the imbroglio, and most couldn't have cared less had they known, for their attention had now turned to how best get their commands ready and underway. The self-proclaimed "High Private," R. R. Gilbert of the 6th Texas Infantry, had recently (if facetiously) chronicled some of the momentous changes his regiment experienced as they made ready to move to the seat of war:

> This month of March has brought me marching orders, as I anticipated. If it had not, [then] I should have [really] been 'April fooled.' I am to be an 'Arkansas traveler,' via Houston . . . to overtake Van Dorn up the White River. I fear there will be some

---

[163] See Lubbock's letter in *O.R.*, IV, 1, pp. 977-9. Though afterward an avid Jefferson Davis supporter, Lubbock nevertheless felt that Richmond's efforts interceded with the state's internal affairs and such appointments ought to reside only in his office.

[164] *Ibid.*

faltering [however, among the men] . . . for the want of shoes. The scarcity of this article has been produced by our Sutler. He purchased . . . shoes from the Mexicans. They were snugly packed in boxes marked: 'This side up with care.' Not understanding Spanish, [he] turned the boxes over and all the soles dropped off. Fact is, they were picked before they were ripe.[165]

Such a huge undertaking would prove to be more difficult than most would have thought necessary, and may well have been the reason why High Private somehow managed to depart the regiment upon its reaching Houston.

Meanwhile, on March 23, orders had arrived at the 10th Texas headquarters to likewise commence a movement as soon as possible, this prompting Col. Nelson to immediately dispatch a detail to Houston to arrange for suitable field transportation to serve his regiment's needs. Two days later, on the 25th, Benjamin Seaton of Co. G left for Houston to help arrange for wagons and teams sufficient to meet the regiment's needs. He noted in his diary that the regiment had been ordered to Little Rock and that he had to be ready to move between April 10 and 15. To facilitate their movement, Nelson divided the regiment into its two wings, each to move somewhat independently of the other, at least until arriving at the railhead at Millican, fifty miles northwest of Houston. The first five companies boarded the cars of the Galveston to Houston rail line on the 29th, transferring there to the Houston and Texas Central to commence the second leg that would take them all the way to Millican. The second wing followed on the 30th, passing through Houston as well to reach Millican. From there, the rest of the trek to Arkansas would have to be made by overland marches.[166]

The second wing overtook the first at Millican and then began the serious business of organizing the overland marches. Here the men were joined by a train of twenty-two wagons awaiting loading, drawn by 130 mules. All of this would be essential for

---

[165] *Houston Telegraph*, March 19, 1862, State Archives, Austin, Texas.

[166] *The Bugle:*, p. 3.

hauling all their camp equipage, surplus baggage, ammunition, and so on. There was a dearth of working teamsters available, and some soldiers found themselves drafted temporarily to serve as "mule skinners." After loading the regimental wagons, the men cleaned and oiled their weapons and accoutrements, washed and packed surplus clothes, and otherwise made ready to get underway.[167]

With everything at last stowed away and all seemingly anxious to get on the road, on April 16, in the afternoon, Nelson had the order of march read at dress parade before dismissing the men, who were in "high Spirits fer [sic] the march." Reveille sounded at 3:00 a.m. the next morning, the men quickly stumbling out of their tents to hurriedly answer nature's call, after which they had a formal roll call. Dismissed afterward to hurriedly gulp down their meager fare, the men quickly fell in, eager to march away from "Camp Brazos." The entire command, inclusive of the long train, was ready to move at 5:30; when placing himself at the head of the column, Nelson rose in his stirrups to issue the command of attention, followed by the order: "Shoulder Arms! In Two Ranks! Right Face! Route Step! March! Arms at Will!"[168]

Stirred up by patriotic tunes that seemed to float the whole distance of the column, the soldiers stepped lively to the band's cadenced music, with the cumbersome train following at the end of the column; the whole, however, moved at a lively pace. From a distance, the regiment took on the appearance of a giant millipede as it snaked its way northward, the column filling up some two miles of roadway. While bound initially for Dallas, their first trek took the column in the direction of Springfield, Nelson sensing that the men would need some time to become acclimated to the rigors of long-distance marching; therefore, he kept them on the road only long enough to cover an initial eight-mile march before halting the column at Johnson's Pond.[169]

---

[167] *Ibid.*:, p. 3. Seaton would continue for some time to serve as wagon master, seemingly enjoying this job.

[168] *Ibid.*: p. 5.

[169] *Ibid.* To see the actual roads they followed see plates CLVII & CLVIII in Military Atlas.

The next day saw the regiment streaming down what is today's Texas Highway 6, the men covering some fifteen miles and passing through Booneville to arrive within seven miles of Wheelock, on "a vary [sic] warm and butiful [sic] day." The 19th found the regiment making a grueling eighteen-mile march amidst a heavy rainstorm, and the men "camped five miles on the other side" of Wheelock: "Rained all day - a cold rain, a hard day's march," wrote waggoneer Benjamin Seaton. The wagons had fallen somewhat behind that day, but overtook the regiment late that night. By now, virtually everyone had begun to suffer blistered feet, chafed thighs, or a combination of both. Though needing to rest weary bodies, the men found it almost impossible to sleep because of their rashes and their near state of exhaustion. The following day (the 20th), a Sunday, the road began to pass through rising terrain, the regiment moving through Owensville and going into camp on a creek flowing into the Little Brazos River. Monday, the 21st, saw the column proceeding thirteen miles and encamping two miles north of Alta Springs. As they neared the village of Springfield, where some of these men formerly resided, many of them seemed to be close to exhaustion as they snaked "through a pararie [sic] country and hot." On Wednesday, the 23rd, the regiment took a left fork off the main road that led to Tehuacana Springs Post Office. It was near here that Nelson got orders to turn back east and head for Alexandria, Louisiana, rather than continuing on into Dallas. After a short respite, allowing both men and animals to recover somewhat, the men found themselves visited in their camps by "a great many ladies," who spent the day visiting with the men as they recuperated and purchased some much-needed supplies.[170]

While in camp near the famous springs, word reached the regiment that the Confederate Congress had at long last passed a conscription act that included compulsory military service for able-bodied males between the ages of eighteen and thirty-five. What remained unclear, however, was how this might affect those either over- or under-age, as quite a number of both served in the regiment. Some likely pondered on just what the war was coming to when this

---

[170] *Ibid.*:, p.5-6; also, James H. Hurst diary entries of the dates recorded, transcript from the CRC, Hill College.

new government had thought it necessary to force men into the military. And some probably reflected on what a sad state of affairs it was that such drastic act had to be put in place.[171]

Questions immediately arose as to which way the regiment would now head and what their ultimate destination was to be. A private from this area, who had been on a short leave in order to visit friends nearby, passed on the rumor that the regiment would first go to Alexandria, thence to Memphis, and then on to Corinth, Mississippi, rather than to Arkansas, as had originally been expected. He advised the regiment had laid over a short while at "the Comanche crossing on Navasoto (Creek), below Tehuacana," needing to make arrangements to "secure . . . some [badly needed] flour."[172]

After passing the word along to the men of the change in orders, Nelson swung the head of the column toward the northeast, following rural roads to reach Fairfield on April 28. Beyond there, the men encountered Trinity River well out of its banks, causing a significant delay in ferrying the men across the swollen channel at Bonner (Barnard's) Ferry, which was not accomplished until May 1. An "easy" march of only twelve miles took the column into Palestine on May 2, the men marching through "a butiful paprarie [sic] country-tho [sic] very warm." On the 4th they crossed the Neches River, and marched into Rusk the following day. Here, James Hirsch of Co. A recorded in his diary: "Oh! God, that I could see my lovely home again." Having briefly stopped over at Fairfield to conduct regimental business, Col. Nelson returned to his command at Rusk, and "no regiment was [ever] prouder to see their commander."[173]

Though having been gone only since April 17, the men greeted their commander's return with lusty cheers, while some among them bandied good-natured barbs about his supposedly

---

[171] Isaiah Harlan letter, April 25, 1862, to Alpheus, CRC, Hill College. This act allowed some adult males, notably those owning or overseeing twenty or more slaves, to opt out of military service; this measure soon took on the unflattering term of the "twenty nigger law." For the provisions of the Conscript Act, see A. B. Moore, Conscription and Conflict in the Confederacy. NY: 1924, pp. 12-26.

[172] Isaiah Harlan letter, April 25, 1862, to Alpheus, CRC, Hill College.

[173] James H. Hurst diary, May 5, 1862, CRC, Hill College.

"malingering" in the rear. A day after he returned, another messenger arrived, bearing the quite sobering news that New Orleans had just fallen into enemy hands: "That is a sad thing for a gang of soldiers to hear when they are struggling for liberty", wrote one private. And just afterward, rumors began to circulate of another supposed calamity, that the enemy had continued up the Mississippi from the Crescent City to seize Memphis as well. If such a rumor proved true, it might mean that these men would be permanently cut off from the eastern Confederate states. Apparently not distressed by the news, Pvt. J. P. Jones of Co. D wrote from Rusk that "some of the cleverist [sic] girls in the world is in Palesteen [sic], . . . they are more friendly to us privates than to the officers." He also recorded the return of Col. Nelson, noting, "I never heard such hollowing (sic) in my life."[174]

That discipline problems had become a thorny issue by this point is evidenced by the fact that on May 8, Capt. John Kennard of Co. A arrested both his subordinate officers (lieutenants J. J. Brooks and A. J. Edmonson) for supposedly refusing to obey a direct order. After imposing a minor punishment upon them, and admonishing both, each was returned to duty. Having received word at Camp Regan on the 7th that they would now be headed toward Little Rock, soon another order reached their camp "to change hour (sic) route again to Schreveport [sic]." On the 9th, the regiment entered Panola County, now passing through great pine forests and having to march over very sandy roads. The regiment moved on the main road from Rusk to reach Mt. Enterprise before continuing on to reach Grand Bluff on May 10. Here the men halted another time as they made ready to get across the Sabine River.[175]

Maj. Robert Young, who previously had to stop on business like Nelson, here rejoined the regiment about the time it marched

---

[174] James Hurst diary entries of May 5-6; see also the letter of J. P. Jones, penned in Cherokee County, on May 5th; Jones special collections, Baylor University; and Isaiah Harlan letter, May 11, 1862, to his mother, wherein he thought they were expecting to now be re-routed to Little Rock., CRC, Hill College.

[175] *The Bugle:*, p. 7; Hurst diary entry, May 8-10, 1862; Isaiah Harlan letter, May 11, 1862, CRC, Hill College; also, W, O. Wynn, Co. C, 10th Texas infantry, from *The Biographical Sketch of an Old Confederate Soldier*, p. 46.

into Carthage. The 9th found the regiment crossing the Sabine, where it went into camp on the road heading toward Elysian Fields; here the men would spend their last night in the Lone Star State, many for the last time. Isaiah Harlan of Co. G wrote his "ma" from there that orders had arrived that the regiment "would not take the boats at Shreveport on account of the [Mississippi] river being blockaded" by the enemy; instead they would now head "to Little Rock, where [the regiment had] first [been] ordered."[176]

After a half-day's march, the regiment crossed the boundary line separating Texas from Louisiana, halting briefly at Greenwood in the latter state about noon of the 14th, then continuing on into Shreveport in the early evening hours. By this time, the marches seemed to have become less arduous, even though the weather had gotten hotter, so that marches of twenty or greater miles a day presented few obstacles, even though rainy weather made travel more difficult. At Shreveport, the commissary officer purchased ten days' rations, disbursing enough to meet the immediate needs of the men before arranging to have the regiment ferried across the Red River into Bossier Parish. Once across that stream, the regiment went on to go into camp on the edge of Bossier City.[177]

Now, after getting over the Red and having made arrangements for the next leg of marching, the regiment struck out north, obviously now bound for Arkansas rather than the Mississippi River. Some those who had given out before now, or had become too sick to continue the march, were put aboard a steamer that would carry them up the Red to land them at Fulton, Arkansas; here, the overland column was expected to catch up with the sick. After being offloaded at Fulton, the officer in charge contracted with local teamsters to convey the sick into the nearby Washington community, where the ambulatory cases would profit from a well-earned rest.

---

[176] See Hurst diary entries of May 11-12, 1862, CRC, Hill College; and *Ibid.*, Isaiah Harlan letter of May 11, 1862.

[177] Pvt. Hurst of Co. A noted in his diary May 13 that he had been taken ill, suffering from both chills and fever, CRC, Hill College; and Isaiah Harlan had earlier advised that "my bowels have been slightly deranged," and that fifteen to twenty men of his regiment had been left along the way due to sicknesses, and recording that four or five men had died prior to May 11, 1862, *Ibid.*

Here they would be able to seek hospital treatment even while they awaited the arrival of the marching column, which wouldn't overtake them for many days. One of the sick aboard the boat, Isaiah Harlan of Co. G, wrote that the vessel carried forty or fifty sick soldiers, including him; nevertheless, he announced that "we have fared as well as any Rgt. [regiment] that has gone from Texas thus far."[178]

The rest of the men continued moving northward again, via easy marches that normally took them no more than fifteen or twenty miles a day. A private in the overland column noted they passed through the communities of Rocky Mount, Plainville, and Red Land, all in North Louisiana. And James Hurst of Co. A noted that the marching column actually crossed into the state of Arkansas on May 18, having crossed both Bossier and Caddo parishes in the process. Another private, however, Benjamin Seaton of Co. G, advised that the regiment actually crossed the state line on Saturday, May 17, with the men camping that night at the Walnut Hills. The next day's march, on the 19th, had them making only twelve miles, as "we had a hard rain on us and after the rain we had an abundance of mud to contend with." Their march on the 20th took them through Conway in the direction of Lewisville, which they reached on the 22nd. However, this last trek proved to be anything but enjoyable, for as James Hurst indicated in his diary on the 20th, "we have lost three men . . . [in] the last two days, the cause of their death was hot marching." Sporadic rain along the way caused many of the creeks to go out of their banks, flooding the country and turning the roads into quagmires, making the marches quite grueling, and the final day's march into Washington, if anything, even less enjoyable than the preceding ones; it was reported that they floundered through a veritable sea of mud.[179]

Having had to inter several of their dead along the roadsides due to sunstroke, the men straggled into Washington after a nine-mile march, again wet through and through from another heavy storm during the night. The men made a camp a mile and a half

---

[178] Isaiah Harlan, May 21, 1862, CRC, Hill College; also, *The Bugle:*, p. 8., May 14th.

[179] Hurst diary, May 20, 1862, CRC, Hill College; also, *The Bugle:*, pp. 8-9, wherein Seaton notes the "roads to be very mud[d]y and sloppy."

below town. Here they reunited with those who had previously traveled upriver by boat to Fulton and then carried aboard wagons to the same point. Persistent rumors had it that Memphis had been captured, and great anxiety seemed to prevail amongst soldiers and civilians alike in Washington. Everyone understood the ramifications should this rumor prove true, but for the men of the 10th Texas, this meant they were apt to remain for the present west of the Mississippi River. Whether factual or not, events along the Mississippi would continue to make an impact on the troops already in or on their way to Arkansas from the Lone Star State. Such hearsay would play a pivotal role in decisions being made in the recently created District of Arkansas, now under the command of BG Thomas C. Hindman, as it would actually work out to help bolster his forces at an especially critical time.[180]

Now reunited, Nelson's regiment subsequently moved its camp a mile or so west of Washington, where it awaited the arrival of the regimental train. The townsfolk appeared pleased to see the Texans arrive in their neighborhood, at least gauging from a newspaper article that appeared in a local paper about the time they left there:

> The splendid Infantry Regiment from Texas under the command of Col. A. Nelson struck their camps and marched through our town early Monday morning, on their way to Little Rock. Every one of our good citizens express the highest admiration of this regiment. Its good condition and orderly conduct speaks highly of its officers; whilst the appearance of the men, their excellent drill, and well-appointed arms, give us assurance of most efficient service in the protection of the state. This regiment has an

---

[180] Isaiah Harlan letter of May 21, 1862 C.R.C, Hill College; J. P. Jones letter of May 25, 1862, Jones special collections, Baylor University. This new Trans-Mississippi Dept. would incorporate the recently established District of Arkansas, but wouldn't be officially announced till May 26, the day the 10th departed for Little Rock.

excellent brass band. Our citizens tender . . . thanks for the delightful serenade last Saturday night.[181]

For some, the layover at Washington provided them their first opportunity to attend regular church services since departing from Millican a month before. Still, others used the free time ibyn doing their laundry or sundry other chores, though some chose this time to catch up on their sleep or to engage in camp gossip with comrades. Quite a few used this chance to forward letters to those at home, describing what had happened to them of late or speculating on where they might be headed once they left Washington. Some even used their off-duty time in companionship with the citizens who ventured out to their camp to enjoy a friendly visit.[182]

Not everything was so copasetic, however, as John P. Jones noted in a letter of May 25. Announcing to friends back home that eight men had died since he had returned to the regiment from his own confinement, he advised that "the country here would kill the devil. Even the frogs has got the chills, they are laying about the edge of the water just shaking the warts off them[selves]," plus he'd never seen so many ticks, they "all are along the road waiting for the cows to come . . , I will put on next Sunday for five hundred curricomes [mercurochrome] and the same for hands to use them."[183]

As to their departure from Washington, the local newspaper, the *Washington Telegraph,* dedicated an entire paragraph on the regiment's leaving the city:

> Military. The splendid Infantry Regiment from Texas under the command of Col. A. Nelson, struck their

---

[181] *Washington Telegraph,* May 28, 1862, Southwest Regional Archives, Washington, Ark.

[182] Hurst diary entry, May 25, 1862, CRC, Hill College; wherein he expresses a genuine pleasure in attending local church services. Cpl. Aaron Estes of Co. B related to his parents about men who'd been felled in the recent marches with "inflammation of the brain" from overheating. See the letter to his wife, May 29, 1862, from "Arkansas, Hempste[a]d County," in Estes special collections, Baylor University.

[183] John P. Jones letter, Jones special collection, Baylor University.

camps and marched through our town early Monday morning on their way to Little Rock. Every one of our citizens express the highest admiration of this regiment. Its good condition and orderly conduct speaks highly of its officers, whilst the appearance of the men, their excellent drill, and well-appointed arms, give us assurance of most efficient service in the protection of the State. This regiment has an excellent brass band. Our citizens tender their thanks for the delightful serenade last Saturday night, in the course of which they were addressed by the honorable L. S. Green.[184]

On the 26th, the regiment began a more northeasterly march, reaching Cotton Creek after a short thirteen-mile jaunt. The following day, the regiment reached, and crossed, the Little Missouri River, before making camp three miles further on. The physical conditions encountered had not improved materially as they moved in the direction of Little Rock, the regiment encountering heavy rains that caused even smaller streams to leave their banks, between which the men often had to struggle through primordial swamps. In crossing an overflowed stream on the 28th, they experienced great difficulties in getting across the swollen streambed, having to rebuild a washed-out bridge there in order to get their train over that point. While awaiting the arrival of several boats with which to erect a pontoon bridge, several of Capt. Kennard's men swam across rather than awaiting the completion of the bridge. In an effort to instill discipline in men who seemed determined to do as they pleased, Kennard had the miscreants lug their heavy knapsacks the next day as punishment. Beyond Arkadelphia, Bayou De Fouche proved to be no easier a stream to get over, but the men ultimately ended up safe and sound on the opposite shore, ready for the final leg that would carry them into Little Rock.[185]

---

[184] *Washington Telegraph*, May 28, 1862, SWRA, Washington, Arkansas.

[185] Hurst diary, May 28, 1862, CRC, Hill College; and see Benjamin Seaton in *The Bugle:* p.9.

"We had a hot, unpleasant march today," James Hurst recorded in his diary, as "the soldiers suffered from the heat very much." After crossing the Washita River at Rockport on June 1, the 10th Texas spent the night near that village (present-day Malvern) before continuing up and over lofty hills and stony ridges that led into Benton, which they reached on June 3. Here they encountered one additional large stream, the Saline River, the men discovering it to be in a flood stage as well. Once safely over that stream, the regiment paraded through that city, before moving rapidly on a last leg of the march that took them to within a few miles of Little Rock, which they reached on June 4. Here they cleared a large campsite just off the Benton road, southwest of the capital, this place designated Camp Texas. Nelson and his entourage rode on into town to confer with Maj. Thomas C. Hindman, who had assumed overall command there May 31, while the men set up their tents, then gathered firewood and water for cooking and cleaning themselves up. Hindman advised that Nelson keep the men well in hand and to be ready to move the regiment at a moment's notice, as rumor had it that the enemy appeared to be, even then, moving on the city from the northeast.[186]

Of greatest importance, according to James Hirsch of Co. A, was the need to acquire shoulder arms for those with none, or bearing ones of an antiquated type. And apparently Nelson received an assurance from Hindman that he would supply their wants in that area as soon as possible. Isaiah Harlan of Co. G advised his mother on the 8th that "the troops in this department are not yet drilled, being mostly dismounted cavalry and new recruits." As "the army is yet unorganized," little could be expected in this quarter other than "skirmishing for some time yet and that will be confined to the cavalry."[187]

---

[186] James Hurst diary, June 4, 1862, CRC, Hill College; *The Bugle:*, p. 10; Isaiah Harlan letter, June 8, 1862, CRC, Hill College; and see also Lt. Col. Roger Q. Mills' letter of June 5, 1862, to his spouse in the Roger Q. Mills family papers, Dallas County Fair Park Collection, Dallas, Texas. Hereafter cited as the Mills papers, Dallas, to differentiate them from other letters by the writer found at the State Archives, Austin.

[187] James Hurst diary entry of June 4, 1862, C.R.C.; Isaiah Harlan to his mother, June 8, 1862, CRC,.Hill College.

Nelson's second-in-command, Lt. Col. Roger Mills, had likewise written his wife soon after reaching Little Rock that Gen. Hindman seemed extraordinarily relieved by the arrival of their regiment, with the department commander paying him a compliment by acknowledging their regiment's discipline and physical appearance. Mills felt that the "Arkansas people are not turning as they ought to," and "to tell the truth they are a long way behind in Civilization anyhow," and "if they have a preference at all it is with the Yankees." In closing his letter written June 5, he asked that his wife convey a personal message to his servant's wife: "Ben sends a warriors love to his tender bride, he is still breathing vengeance against the Yankees."[188]

On June 8, Benjamin Seaton of Co. G made note that here had been conducted "a general inspection of the guns and knapsacks to sea [sic] how we keep our clothes in a soldier-like manner." And Isaiah Harlan of the same company, in a letter home of the same date, advised his mother that the enemy were believed to be within forty-five to fifty miles of the capital. By this time, Lt. Col. Mills had talked with several Missouri refugees in the city, and took them to be more supportive of the war and ready to join the Confederate side in order to return to their home state, contrasting with how the Arkansas natives seemed to express little more than lukewarm support for "the cause."[189]

It was apparent that Arkansas had been stripped of the better part of its military forces prior to the Texans' arrival, with the majority having only recently been sent across the Mississippi to reinforce Gen. Albert S. Johnston's army; the latter was supposed to be concentrating in North Mississippi. In the wake of the Shiloh disaster in April, coupled with the recent investment of the Confederate army that had just retired to Corinth, most of those regiments would likely never return west of the river. As a consequence, only through a strict enforcement of the recently passed draft law, Lt. Col. Mills, and the arrival of more Texans to bolster the Arkansas army already undergoing organization would a

---

[188] R. Q. Mills to his spouse, June 5, 1862 State Archives, Austin, Texas.

[189] Seaton, in T*he Bugle:* p. 10; and Roger Q. Mills letter of June 5, 1862, Dallas Fair Park.

total disaster be averted. The few who had come forward, and in Mills' mind those were admittedly few in number, had made a rather poor showing. Even the untrained eye within the ranks could sense the obvious: "Th[os]e troops in the department [already formed] are not drilled yet, being mostly dismounted cavalry and new recruits."[190] In Mills' mind, his regiment needed only guns and rations to be ready for the field, and they quickly began to receive the staples that could be brought in from rural Arkansas. For the most part, their rations would consist of slab bacon, mealy bread, and "blue" beef, the last being "Arkansas beef, worse than the meanest beef we [ever] got at Virginia Point last winter." If they were in the need of anything else, it would be a quick return to their drill regimen, and this they were apt to get in abundance. As both Isaiah Harland and Benjamin Seaton of Co. G recorded, drill in the manual of arms had begun in earnest on June 9, with word coming down from the top that the men needed to be ready "to march in two minutes after warning," though "for what purpose I know not," penned James Hurst of Co. A.[191]

Several days after that, a major change came about, though it may have met with more enthusiasm on the men's part, for on the 11th, a requisition was made out at Col. Nelson's headquarters to the department commander for several types of arms. The regiment received for its officers ten swords, and the enlisted men were issued 413 muskets, along with 354 each of cartridge boxes, belts, belt plates, bayonet scabbards, and gun slings. That these weapons were inferior in their minds might have been due to the fact that 300 flints accompanied the order. Nelson had supplied a return to his strength at that time, noting 40 officers and 767 men present.[192] Though not likely ecstatic to receive such an issue, the rank and file seemed to at least pride themselves on their military proficiency, especially comparing themselves to those other units recently coming in from Texas, and there existed a great esprit de corps amongst the

---

[190] Isaiah Harlan letter, June 8, 1862., C.R.C., Hill College

[191] Isaiah Harlan letter, June 8, 1862 C.R.C., Hill College; and James Hurst diary entries, June 9-11, 1862, CRC, Hill College; and *The Bugle:* p. 9.

[192] Compiled service records, 10th Texas Infantry, RG 109, copy supplied by Scott McKay of Atlanta, Georgia.

individual men. At this point, most, in essence, thought themselves to be the embodiment of the well-disciplined volunteer.[193]

The 6th Texas Infantry's overland move to Arkansas would follow a similar combination of transport, with short rail transport followed by long overland marches to reach its new duty station, which would turn out to be Pine Bluff. For unknown reasons, the 6th Texas required a greater amount of preparation prior to making the move. This may have been due to the regiment being further from Arkansas, thus needing a much greater amount of stockpiling of supplies initially because of having the greater distance to go. Or it may be that with the later arrival of its final complement of companies, it simply needed more time to complete its organization. Bor whatever reason, Garland's regiment did not get underway from their Victoria camp until the morning of May 22, by which time Nelson's regiment had already reached Washington, Arkansas.[194]

Initially, the 6th Texas marched due north, crossing the Lavaca River and marching on northward to reach Halletsville. From there, a shorter trek carried the regiment into Columbus, where they then crossed the Colorado River and marched on to Alleytown (often spelled Alleyton), where they took the cars of the Buffalo Bayou, Brazos, and Colorado road (a.k.a. the B.B. & B. & C. line), which had arrived not long before. Rather than taking the cars here, however, the regiment turned back southeastward toward Eagle Lake, where they arrived on May 30. After a short stint spent recuperating from tender feet, the men next moved eastward to Richmond, in Ft. Bend County, where they at last boarded the cars of the B.B. & B. & C. line for the short trip to Houston. Here the men changed lines, boarding the cars of the Houston and Texas Central

---

[193] Mills letter, June 5, 1862, to his wife, Dallas Fair Park Archives, Dallas, Texas.

[194] *Charles A. Leuschner*, p. 7.

line the following day, following the same route as had the 10th Texas, and bypassing Hempstead to reach the railhead at Millican.[195]

And like the 10th Texas before it, at the last point they found a train of wagons had arrived, and after sorting through and loading all their equipment, some three days later, the regiment made ready to embark on the cross-country march needed to take it to Arkansas. Near Navasota, an embarrassing event transpired, apparently the first major breach of etiquette by a member of the regiment worthy of note. While in camp there, Capt. C. P. Naunheim of Co. I. discovered his pistol missing from his tent, but the culprit was quickly discovered when he tried to sell the weapon to another soldier, and it was ultimately retrieved. The accused was court-martialed on the spot, and it was agreed to shave the convicted soldier's head, after which he was summarily drummed out of camp. Forced to ride straddle a fence rail, he was borne on the shoulders of several men to the edge of camp, and he further received instructions not to return to camp again.[196]

After crossing the Trinity River at Cincinnati, the regiment proceeded to Crockett, thence to Rusk to Palestine, marching afterward via the Seven Leagues Post Office to just south of Tyler. Arriving at this last town, the 6th Texas went into camp northeast of Tyler, named appropriately for the Northern Texas subdistrict commander, Henry McCulloch. The men were allowed to rest there for five days, enjoying this respite while staff officers went in search of badly needed supplies. While there, BG Henry McCulloch came out to camp to inspect and review the men. He could see that, just as had been the case with the 10th Texas, the men of Garland's regiment suffered from blistered feet or galled thighs, no doubt brought on by the rigorous marches made to get to this point. Franz Coller of Co. H advised his wife on June 28, 1862, that "there are several cavalry

---

[195] Gilbert Cuthbertson, ed. "Coller of the 6th Texas," in *Military History of Texas and the Southwest*, 9 (1972): p. 131; "Jim Turner," in *Texana*, vol. XII (1974), p.153; also, see *Charles A Leuschner*, p. 7. Hereafter, Cuthbertson's work is cited simply as "Coller."

[196] *Charles A. Leuschner*, p. 7; James M. McCaffrey. *This Band of Heroes: Granbury's Texas brigade, CSA*, Austin, Eakin Press. 1985, p. 6. Hereafter cited as *This Band of Heroes:* p. 6. The writer tried to determine who the culprit was but only determined that he had been in Co. G, and from Austin.

regiments here which, it is said, will be converted into infantry." He was likewise pleased to notify her that "a lot of praise as being the best-equipped regiment that has passed through here[;] although our weapons almost disqualified us."[197]

Pvt. Coller wrote again the following day to tell his wife that among the reasons for their layover at Tyler is that "we need to obtain boots and shoes, for it is much longer before we get better shoes, we won't have any to put on." Despite such efforts, however, "there are already some wo are barefoot." And speaking of rations, he advised that "we still receive enough . . . which consists of flour, cornmeal, rice, bacon, beef, salt and sugar." The only major item missing from their meals was "coffee, however, is very rarely . . . , but we buy barley and wheat" as a substitute for the "real java." And on the 30th, he added a postscript to his last letter that he'd received a knife she'd sent him, along with some tobacco. He expected that "tomorrow we go on the march again, however, I hope that it will not be far."[198]

Indeed, that was absolutely the case, as after laying over for almost a week, the regiment moved only to Starrville, five miles north of Tyler but in the same county. Next they headed for Gilmer, and lastly into the Dangerfield community. From this last point the regiment marched via Boston, where it would march through the expanse of the Red River bottoms, where long stretches of flatwoods stretched out before them. It took several days to reach the river itself, where they quickly passed over to enter Fulton, Arkansas.[199]

These Texans had found the going through this area quite different from the hills and valleys they had hitherto marched through. Capt. William Phillips of Co. A wrote: "In the last 200

---

[197] "Franz Coller," in "*Chronicles of Smith County*," vol. 12, # 1 (summer 1973), pp. 29-30. He wrote his wife three times in as many days from just north of Tyler.

[198] "*Ibid.*", pp. 30-1.

[199] *Charles A. Leuschner*, p. 8; *Military History of Texas*, vol. 9 (1971), p. 129. Also, relative to Franz Coller's letter to "Ottilie," his wife, on June 28, 1862, in *Chronicles*, vol. 12, # 1 (Summer, 1973), pp. 29-30 discusses observing a large spring near Tyler going to waste because it was not being used to brew lager beer!

miles we have had about ten miles of prairie . . . . I like the people much better than I do the country, the latter is too broken and sandy . . . ." And Pvt. Coller of Co. H recalled that "day after day we march in the woods and God knows if we will come out again." He reflected that the countryside through which they had just passed proved to be quite different from South Texas: "I have never seen such a poor region as we see here in east Texas and Arkansas." And private Benjamin C. Robertson of Co. C thought the region to be "the most degraded country I ever saw."[200]

The regimental band had previous to this ceased playing, except when they passed through the villages and small towns along the way, though they took up their instruments on July 1, when crossing the state line between Texas and Arkansas. And just like the 10th Texas Infantry before, the 6th Texas continued their march from Fulton to Washington, tracing the same route afterward as Nelson's regiment until reaching Rockport. Here the regiment lay in camp some ten days, according to Jim Turner of Co. G, as the measles had begun to break out amongst the men. Leaving many men sick in their wake, the regiment moved to Benton, where a courier found Garland, ordering him to halt his command at the crossroads pending a decision on where next the regiment might be sent. Several days passed before new orders arrived, directing that the regiment must move southeast to Pine Bluff, where Garland was to place his men in camp to await the convalescents left at Rockport to rejoin his command.[201]

Other than the raucous events surrounding the theft of Naunheim's revolver at the first of the march, little of note had otherwise occurred during the trip to Arkansas. Some fifteen recruits for Capt. William Harvey's Co. H overtook the regiment at Tyler, after being enlisted to serve in that command and having trailed the regiment the entire way from the Texas coast. Other than the paperwork required to formally bring them aboard, along with sundry other issues needing attention from the officers, nothing out

---

[200] For Coller's comments, see *Military History of Texas*, vol. 9 (1971), p. 132; also, *Charles A. Leuschner*, p. 8, as relates to both Phillips' and Robertson's comments.

[201] *Charles Leuschner*, p. 8; "Jim Turner, in *Texana*, vol .XII, p. 153.

of the ordinary disturbed the regiment's progress. And other than the abrupt change in terrain that went from the gently rolling prairies of Central Texas to the flatwoods and swamps of the eastern part of the state, then lastly the mountains they had to passed through in southern Arkansas, their major discomforts came from the incessant rains that fell, along with the measles outbreak that felled many a man. In fact, the march had proven to be a rather banal event overall, and mostly uneventful.[202]

Thus, by early summer, two rather well-disciplined, and reasonably well-equipped, Texas infantry regiments had reached Central Arkansas, one at Little Rock, the other encamped near Pine Bluff. Each had the capacity to be of efficient service, especially in case of a dire emergency, and it certainly seemed that might soon be the case, given that the enemy had by now come within fifty miles of the capital, and more recently, suggesting that a major advance might come via the Arkansas River toward either or both places. And though the rumors of Memphis having fallen turned out to be in error, at least for the moment, the prospects might certainly see the enemy coming from the northeast and taking the Arkansas capital, likely knocking the entire state out of the war.[203]

Matters in the western theater beyond the Mississippi seemed to have gone from bad to worse as summer approached, and Hindman's small army (if it could be called that at this time) remained concentrated in the central portion of the state or out on the far western frontier, with Hindman not even willing to consider going over to the offensive. In fact, it remained dubious whether any part of the state could be held, given the dire circumstances there, unless major reinforcement should arrive in time to bolster Hindman's mostly paper-strength army. Unionist sentiment had grown appreciably in the wake of recent military disasters, with

---

[202] See the supplemental muster roll of Capt. William Harvey's Co., Garland's Texas Infantry Regiment, dated June 1, 1862, copied from the State Archives, Austin; also, *Charles A. Leuschner:*, pp. 7-8; and see *Texana*, vol. 12, p. 153.

[203] *The Civil War:*, vol. 1, pp. 556-7.

many of its adherents looking for ways to take the state out of the Confederacy.[204]

Isaiah Harlan, of Co. G, 10th Texas, perhaps put it as succinctly as could be, stating in a letter of June 8 from Little Rock: "It is impossible to tell when we will begin active operations, at least with us small- . . . we might possibly get in a fight soon, but I do not think we are [ready]." Besides which, the army still had to be organized and put into better fighting condition before being exposed to more veteran enemy forces. Time alone would tell whether they'd reach that point before the Federal army arrived before the gates of the capital itself. Harlan's remarks echoed the thoughts of Lt. Col. R. Q. Mills, 10th Texas, who had on the same day written home that affairs in Arkansas appeared desperate.[205]

Those men just coming into military service under the conscription act would require several months at least to become organized and proficient and made into viable commands. Even then, it would require herculean efforts to equip, drill, and move these hastily raised troops to get them within range of the enemy. Hindman's heavy-handed enforcement of the draft within the state, coupled with his recent declaration of martial law, had made him so unpopular as to require a shake-up of command in the entire Trans-Mississippi. Richmond would assign MG Theophilus Holmes, or "Old Grannie," as the affable officer was known, to the command of the Trans-Mississippi Department. He would take the reins at a time when much doubt existed as to whether the Confederates could even retain Arkansas. As did his predecessor, Hindman, Holmes would have to adroitly employ his very limited resources in an effort to forestall further advances on the enemy's part until such time as a substantial force could be brought together in Arkansas. Only due to his skills of subterfuge over the the next few months would disaster be averted.[206]

---

[204] On the Arkansas situation in mid-1862, see *The Civil War*, II, pp. 45-6; also, Thomas L. Snead's, "The Conquest of Arkansas," in *Battles & Leaders*, III, pp. 441-461.

[205] Isaiah Harlan letter, June 8, 1862 CRC, Hill College; and R. Q. Mills letter, June 8, 1862, Fair Park Archives, Dallas, Texas

[206] Snead's, "The Conquest of Arkansas," *Battles & Leaders*, vol. III, p. 443.

In Texas that spring, Gen. Paul O. Hébert had ordered all available units in the state, including both the 6th and 10th Texas, to move toward Arkansas and the Mississippi River. At the same time, he advised Governor Lubbock to hurry up the enlistment of additional units the state could contribute to the Confederate cause. As summer came on, much of Louisiana and Arkansas had already been partially occupied, and the civilized tribes in the Indian Nations proved resistant to again serve outside their boundaries, making all minds in the Trans-Mississippi west understand that they must look to the Lone Star State for that assistance. The debatable point appeared to be whether that state could supply enough troops, and that quickly, before the Trans-Mississippi (including the Indian Nations) was overrun, a point debatable to both civilians and the military alike. For the present, all concerned seemed to look to Texas and how best to get whatever raw forces, and scant military resources there, could be brought to bear.

Chapter 2

Stopgap Measures

The early months of 1862 had dawned with great expectation, based on the most part on the previous year's military successes, but those hopes had quickly been dashed early on by a surprising number of military defeats. East of the Mississippi, the loss of all of Kentucky and most of Tennessee east of the river, coupled with multiple disasters in Missouri, Arkansas, and Louisiana, caused Confederate fortunes to plunge dramatically. Now, with spring coming on, it appeared as if the entire Mississippi valley was in peril of being conquered. After Gen. A. S. Johnston's death at Shiloh in early April, his army had withdrawn into northern Mississippi, and it appeared as if his second-in-command, Gen. P. G. T. Beauregard, might follow a Fabian policy with respect to defending Corinth, and he let it be known he might eventually have to abandon that rail hub also. It seemed that disaster loomed on an extraordinary scale.

The arrival of spring in Central Arkansas had brought with it a victorious Federal army that, in the wake of the debacle at Pea Ridge the previous March, had led to MG Samuel Curtis sidling eastward across the northern part of Arkansas toward the Mississippi, perhaps expecting to move on Little Rock from the northeast. With Memphis hanging by a thread, and Union forces occupying substantial portions of Southern territory on either side of the mighty river, the Trans-Mississippi had reached a chaotic pinnacle that could see it completely wrenched from the eastern Confederate states. Kentucky and Missouri might have to be permanently written off the ledger, and large portions of Tennessee and Arkansas had gone into enemy hands; where the next disaster might strike seemed to be on everyone's mind. After New Orleans' fall in April, Union naval forces could either move upriver to threaten either Mississippi and

West Tennessee or else penetrate into Arkansas by way of the state's major river systems that drained into the father of waters.[207]

In fact, April and May had seen an enemy flotilla descend the river from the north and seize Island #10 before continuing down to Memphis in early June. The South could scarcely afford to lose any more territory east or west of the river. At most, the Trans-Mississippi area had only small troop detachments with which to slow Curtis' southward advance, which must surely come in May, as he ostensibly had the Black and White rivers to use in supplying his army. In fact, his advance forces had already penetrated to less than sixty miles of the capital, as MG Hindman first, and afterward Gen. Theophilus Holmes, strove to raise an army to oppose him. To further compound matters for Holmes, the heavy-handed tactics Hindman had employed previous to his arrival had greatly hindered the cause, as it left the people in a state of great consternation.[208]

By mid-month, Curtis' army had begun to concentrate around Batesville; he hoped to utilize the major streams in the area as a source to help the army subsist until he could strike out southwest for the capital. Soon, the vanguard of his army had moved as far south as Searcy, a mere fifty miles northeast of Little Rock. If the capital fell, the Confederacy would inevitably lose the entire state. Extraordinary action had to therefore be taken, and quickly, if for no other reason than to bolster the citizen's sagging morale, if not Confederate fortunes within the state.

There was another potential that sprang from Curtis' position on the rivers there: he could conceivably link up with an enemy naval force bringing reinforcements coming from either North Louisiana, or, should Memphis fall, much-needed supplies could come south, then upward via the White or Arkansas rivers, and these forces might then cooperate with Curtis to take Little Rock through a pincer movement from north- and southeast. At the least, in so doing, Curtis could move his army overland to Helena, in Union hands already, gaining naval support at that point. It was such possibilities that harried military officials at Little Rock concerned themselves with.

---

[207] *The Civil War*, vol. I, pp. 353-71.

[208] *Ibid.*, vol. I, p. 292.]

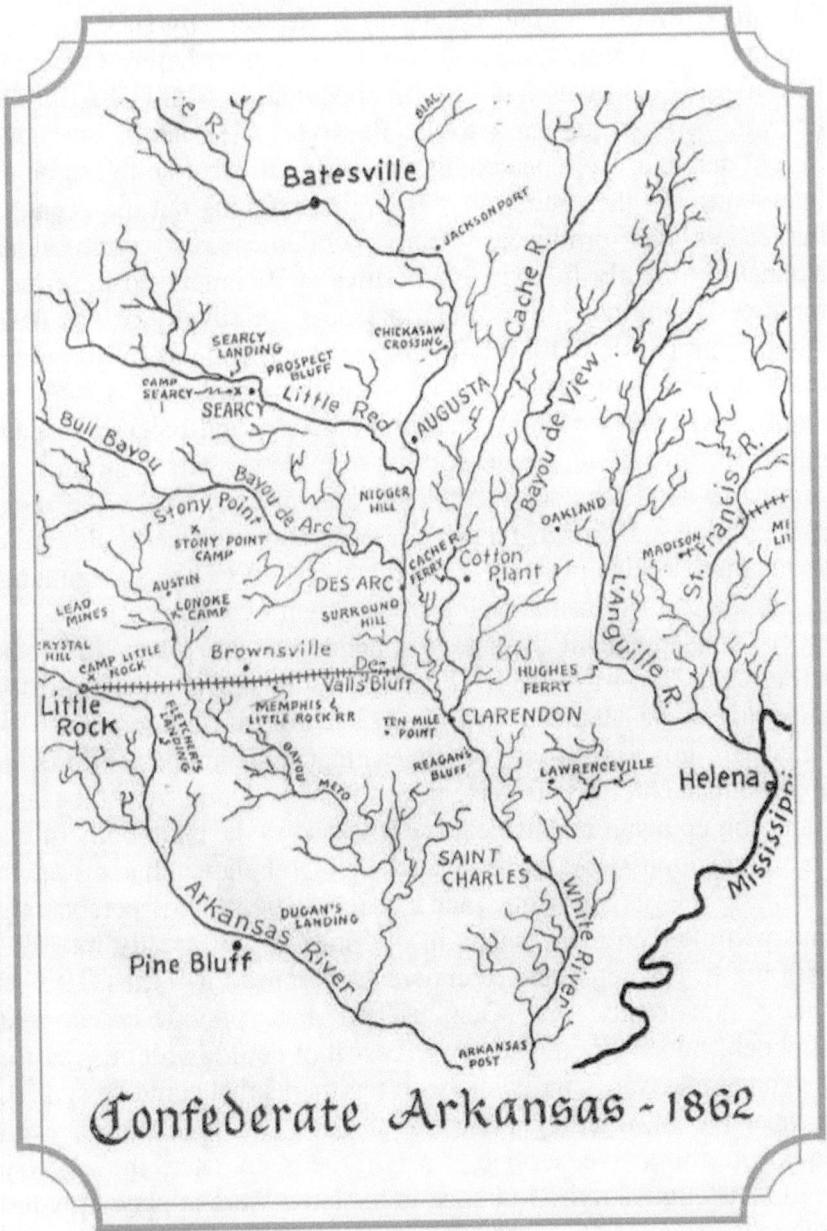

Confederate Arkansas - 1862

At Houston, Gen. Paul Hébert had responded to Secretary of War Judah P. Benjamin's order of February 24, 1862, of sending virtually every disposable force in the state toward the Mississippi itself. And Benjamin had mandated that "the men are to be pushed forward with all possible rapidity to Little Rock by such route as you may deem best." Scarcely two weeks lapsed before Governor Francis Lubbock, who had been in consultation with Hébert in the interim, penned quite a vitriolic missive to Benjamin over this formal demand. He repeated his opposition to what he felt to be an intervention in the state's internal affairs, pointing out the negative the orders had produced: "Many gentlemen had commissions emanating directly from the authorities at Richmond to raise men for twelve months, and in most instances for cavalry, it has been wholly impossible to fill infantry or cavalry regiments for the war." He vehemently protested further Benjamin's order to Hébert "to disband all twelve-months men immediately, and receive no men into the Confederate service for less than three years or during the war." Advising that some mounted commands had for the most part only recently been raised, the only comment he could make about these regiments was: "I believe that the cavalry regiments that are in the service have all provided their own arms . . ."[209]

In a poignant statement appended to his letter, Lubbock wrote that "a Mr. William Fitzhugh is raising another cavalry regiment to be attached to Col. M. T. Johnson's command." A rancorous governor went on to castigate Richmond's efforts in approving such efforts to raise troops independently from the state, summing up again his displeasure reflected in the main body of his communications: "As I have said . . . I believe this mode of obtaining men is all wrong, and I feel satisfied that if persons are thus permitted to raise troops in our state it will greatly interfere with the fifteen regiments proposed to be raised in Texas." It was readily apparently that Gen. Hébert had previously advised Lubbock, but for the present, the best that could be done was for the state to forward immediately all regiments that could be spared, irrespective of whether drilled or not, or, for that matter, even equipped for active service. As will be seen later, the cavalry regiments alluded to by Lubbock in his letter were to play a pivotal role in the state of Arkansas.[210]

---

[209] Sec. of War Judah P. Benjamin to BG P. O. Hébert, in *O.R.*, IV, 5, p.700; also, F. R. Lubbock to Sec. of War, J. P. Benjamin, *O.R.*, IV, 5, pp. 977-979.

[210] F. R. Lubbock to Sec. of War J. P. Benjamin, *Ibid.*, IV, vol. 5, p. 979.

Three cavalry regiments forwarded to Little Rock as a consequence of Hébert's orders were among a plethora of Texas units undergoing organization during the winter of '61 and the early months of 1862. These and others just beginning the process were later assigned to the organization that ultimately became Granbury's brigade, though all of them initially began their service as mounted units. In Northern Texas, several of those that had begun to come together during the previous fall did so under the auspices of on Middleton T. Johnson, who lived in the Dallas-Ft. Worth area and who had attempted to field an entire cavalry brigade. In a letter sent to the adjutant and inspector general's Office at Richmond, Virginia, on March 7, 1862, Johnson had gone to great length to demonstrate how this organization had come about. Having received a letter from the secretary of war's office in Richmond, dated October 18, 1862, he had been granted authority to raise a regiment, after which he would receive a commission as its colonel. Between then and the March, 1862, report to the adjutant and inspector general, Gen. Samuel Cooper, the command had by that time already grown from a single regiment until it encompassed a full brigade that would include five separate cavalry regiments.[211]

Johnson's communication noted the regiments to be incorporated into his provisional brigade, and that all five of them had been mustered into service by the time of this report. They included Col. William Fitzhugh's 14th (which Governor Lubbock had already alluded to previously), Col. George H. Sweet's 15th, Col. George F. Moore's 17th, and another unnamed at the time, but may have been Col. Nicholas P. Darnell's 18th Texas Cavalry. All of them had agreed to furnish their own mounts and their own arms, which, he bragged, included "good double-barreled shotguns," or if "not so armed [to] have good common hunting rifles." In addition to which, he advised that every recruit needed to be "provided with good pistols and nearly all have large knives." They had been instructed, upon mustering, to head for Clarksville, Texas, where a camp of instruction had already been established,

---

[211] M. T. Johnson, Senior Col. Commanding, to S. Cooper, *Ibid.*, IV, 5, pp. 982-3

in expectation of their eventually moving via Little Rock to Corinth, Mississippi.[212]

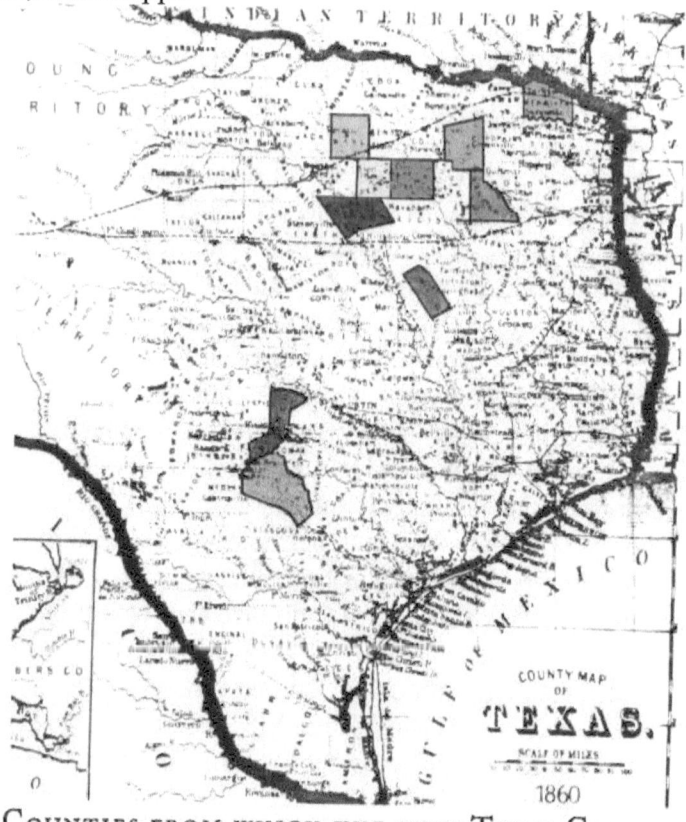

COUNTIES FROM WHICH THE 15TH TEXAS CAVALRY REGIMENT ENLISTED

The first of the regiments to come into existence had primarily been raised under the auspices of a prewar politician hailing from San Antonio, George Sweet, who had gained authority the previous fall to raise his own cavalry regiment. He did this with the belief that his command would either be destined for service in the Indian territory or out on the western frontier against hostile Plains Indians. Armed with little more than a colonel's commission, Sweet had proceeded to Dallas later that fall, bent upon locating a

---

[212] *Ibid.*

rendezvous point at which to bring together the requisite ten companies needed to complete his regiment.[213]

Some of his companies began to reach Dallas by mid-December, though some would not reach there prior to the early months of 1862, some only dispatching Sweet of their intent to join his regiment. In an open letter distributed to prominent men in the state that had requested information on his organization, Sweet requested all companies be ready to move to the rendezvous site as quickly as organized, emphasizing again the need for every man to furnish his own arms and mounts for service as ranging companies. The site he selected for the rendezvous lay just southeast of Dallas, known locally as Fair Park, and here Sweet established his headquarters to await the arrival of those companies wanting to be part of this regiment.[214]

Among the later-arriving contingents to reach Dallas had been one raised at Decatur, Wise County, out on the Texas frontier. One of the newer recruits wrote that it had just 200 registered voters in the county, the men ranging from teachers to store clerks, though many were cowboys. He advised that after their formal swearing-in that "lots of Dexter's best had been put under their jackets, [and] the remainder of the day was put in cavalry movements round and round the square." He emphasized later that their enlistment be taken as patriotic in nature: "We did not then and do not to this good day, believe in the peaceable secession of any of the states, but **we**

---

[213] *Texas in the War*, pp. 26, 116. Initially referred to as the 2nd Regiment, M. T. Johnson's cavalry brigade, Sweet's command is sometimes erroneously referred to as the 15th Texas Infantry, perhaps springing from its later having been dismounted and converted to infantry. Oddly enough, a second Texas regiment had received the same designation as Sweet's, but that regiment had later been renumbered as the 32nd Texas Cavalry. Sweet had formerly served in Hood's Texas brigade in Virginia but had returned home when authorized (and armed with his commission) to raise his command; see "Fifteenth Texas Cavalry," in *The Handbook of Texas Online*, Texas State Historical Society, Austin.

[214] Original muster-in rolls of several companies are found in the adjutant general office records at Austin, as well as in RG 109, National Archives, Washington. Interestingly, the Washington rolls notes the regiment to have been mustered into service on April 1, 1862, for twelve months, though the state's rolls bear dates ranging from March 1 through 31.

believed in the right to rebel," [author's emphasis added] and that was why they called themselves rebels."[215]

Earlier, a contingent of men had ridden in from Central Texas, including brothers Daniel and Woodson Park, both in Co. A, who recorded their earliest service with the command. Of the trip up, Daniel's letter of February 20 to his wife stressed that they "faced a keen north wind every day as we came up," and, as a consequence, their horses had just about been played out. Now ensconced at the fairgrounds, he disclosed that "we have no tents [at this time] yet but will in a few days." He advised that they expected to "leave this place in the co[u]rse of too [sic] weeks and go to Clarksville on red river." In a follow-up letter written on the 28th, he wrote that "we are still encamped at the same grown [sic], talk about moving to about 30 miles east of here to McKinney and stay there for a while." He ends his letter with the plea to "tell all the boys to come on that can come, that the South is needing men."[216]

On March 5, Daniel Park advised that the men's equipment had been appraised that day by the government; he was allowed $140 for his mount, $35 for a saddle, and $45 for his arms. On the day following, he expected the regiment to leave for McKinney "about 30 miles farther on toward the enemy." He believed she had written him, for he hoped that "I may get a letter from you to night as the eastern mail comes in to night." Woodson, his brother, added a postscript about paper being most difficult to purchase, so he wouldn't be sending along a separate letter.[217]

---

[215] Robert M. Collins, *Chapters from an Unwritten History of the War Between the States: The Incidents in the Life of a Confederate Soldier in Camp, on the March, and in Prison.* St. Louis: Nixon-Jones Printing Co. 1893. (Reprint by Southern Heritage Press, Widener, Ark.) Cited as *Chapters* hereafter. While published long after the war, it is remarkable in many ways and may have sprung from a diary, or letters written during the war, though none have surfaced.

[216] Daniel and Woodson Park letters of February 20 and 28, 1862. Courtesy of Betty Troutman of San Antonio; a Park family descendant who tendered them to this writer after hearing a lecture given on the brigade in 1992. Cited hereafter as the Parks letters, with dates.

[217] Daniel and Woodson Park, March 5, 1862, Park letters.

About the time that this letter had been sent, a recruit from northwest of Ft. Worth decided the time had come for him to enlist. Robert M. Collins had either kept an account or made meticulous notes of his wartime service, as his postwar publications remain one of the best in-depth sources for an intimate knowledge of the 15th Texas Cavalry. Originally published in 1893, it is a 332-page narrative of his adventures and fills a void that might have otherwise existed in chronicling the day-to-day history of the regiment. To that end, it's been a most valuable document in chronicling the events and the drama of war as viewed by a Northern-born frontier Texan at the time.[218]

As Collins recalled, the new recruits raised in Wise County needed all the help they could get from the locals in preparing to go to war. A prominent Decatur citizen, George B. Pickett, had received authority to raise a cavalry company in his community, Collins writing that local "merchants piled out . . . clothing, hats, boots and shoes, and men owning herds of horses were willing to give them up. As to arms to fight with, the variety in kind, caliber and quality, is beyond our powers of description." In one way alone did the men appear to be equipped the same, with everyone a wielding a huge side knife made by area blacksmiths from worn-out files, "old scythe blades, plowshares, cross cut saws, or anything else that could be had."[219]

For his part, it seemed obvious that "Captain" Sweet had no desire to include state officials in the formation of his regiment; he was seemingly dedicated to get the companies together and fully organized. In an election subsequently held February 26, in addition to promoting Sweet to colonel, William K. Masten of Dallas got the nod as Lt. Col., and on the 28th the men had selected George Pickett of Decatur to serve as major. The small complement of men who had come all the way up from San Antonio area to join Sweet's command had been formally designated as Co. A; oddly, it was to be the only one from that region, all the others originating in the North Texas area. Hardly had the men begun to reach Dallas than word began to

---

[218] Robert N. Collins. *Chapters from an Unwritten History of the Civil War*. St. Louis: Nixon-Jones Publishing Co. 1893. Hereafter cited simply as *Chapters*.

[219] *Chapters*., pp. 12-3.

be passed around that they would quickly be moved to another location, this coming about because of the huge number of measles cases that had broken out in camp. This prompted Sweet to change the rendezvous point from Dallas to nearby McKinney. Daniel Park advised his wife March 5 that they would move to Clarksville shortly, where they would begin to learn the proper drill required for a regiment. So the men remained just briefly at McKinney before making their way to Clarksville, where a camp of instruction had been established just outside the city limits.[220]

With the exception, perhaps, of those from South Texas, most of the men would be mustered in at a time when the conscription act was coming into operation, and this writer deems it important to understand that the men in the cavalry regiments composing Johnson's cavalry brigade all entered the service as volunteers. While some may have enlisted to escape the onus of being considered as conscripts, on the original rolls, all are shown as volunteers.[221]

Though originally orders from the War Department the previous fall had stipulated regiments would be accepted for only three years of service, for some odd reason this seemed not to be the case with many of the regiments raised at this time. All seemed to be accepted for a period of just one year, and since neither state nor national authorities could by this time supply arms or equipage, much less mounts, communities or the men themselves had to supply what they needed for mounted service. It had been promised at the time of enlistment that an evaluation board would establish the value of all such contributions, set the prices, plus pay a stipend based upon the distance men had had to travel reach their rendezvous point. Presumably, the men would ultimately be reimbursed, and

---

[220] See the "Fifteenth Texas Cavalry," *Handbook of Texas Online*, Texas State Historical Assn., Austin (http://tshaonline.org/handbook/online/articles/qkf08; Daniel Park letter of March 5, 1862, Park letters.

[221] See Rupert N. Richardson, Ernest Wallace, & Adrian Anderson, *Texas: The Lone Star State*, Princeton, 1988, 5th ed., pp. 211-3. Passed in April, the act took some time to circulate to the several states, allowing regiments in transition to be enlisted as volunteers.

additionally, each many would be paid wages based on the rank held.[222]

While still in Dallas, Pvt. Daniel Park of Co. A had written about anticipated movements, and that "if they [the Feds] are advancing on through Arkansas to[ward] Texas as we heard they are, we will soon march to meet them and put them to flight." Having not heard a word from home to that time, he had become anxious to hear "from you and my little babes." As will be seen, unfortunately, long delays and lost mail would become a major issue in communications between those on active service and the folks, or relations, back home.[223]

In a letter of March 22, he advised his spouse that he'd received her letter dated the 15th and that it had given him great comfort to at last hear from her. Unfortunately, his return letter related that he and his comrades were in dire straits, with many of them seeming to have come down with "typhoid pneumonia." A brother, Woodson, seemed to have suffered worst from the malady, which he attributed to the cold, rainy weather, and their still not having tents as of the date of this letter: "We are in the hospital in the town of McKin[n]ey . . . ten men of our company [are still] here, some sick and others awaiting on the sick, the company is gone [on] to Clarksville." Fortunately, a group of women had been waiting on them hand and foot and just recently "presented us with a fine melon pie and a bottle of wine." The women had only been gone a few hours when "a negro man with a fine wool mattress for Woodson to lie on" came over. He knew from whence this came: "The ladies of this town deserve great credit for their kindness to us," emphasizing that there had not let a day pass without one or more stopping by to be of service.[224]

On that same day, Pvt. William Young of Park's company wrote of being at the hospital serving as a "nurse" to those still

---

[222] [See *O.R.*, IV, 5, p. 131, dated September 10, 1861; also, Secretary of War Benjamin's order of February 13, 1862, in *O.R.*, I, 4, IX, p. 700.; but note also Gen. S. Cooper's April 9, 1862, endorsement to accept Johnson's brigade, "the regiments [to be] engaged for twelve months."

[223] Daniel Park, Park letter, March 5, 1862.

[224] Daniel Park, March 22, 1862, Park letters.

requiring medical attention. He mentions specifically of Woodson Park as being very sick; he believed they all had pneumonia. "Our captain has been very sick" also but had gotten somewhat better by this time. He had received a cursory assignment, for "they have made a water boy of me." His horse had contracted distemper, and this had prompted him to be detailed to the hospital, but his mount also seemed to be on the mend as well. He asked that she direct all future correspondence to him at Clarksville, "care of Captain V. P. Sanders, Second Regiment, Johnson's Brigade," as he expected to go there shortly.[225]

A last letter sent from McKinney, dated March 31, advises Daniel Park's wife that he was still at the hospital waiting on his sick brother, though the recovered men remaining expected to leave for Clarksville that evening: "I hate very much to be left behind," lamented Park, as "there are a great many soldiers here going on to war, nearly every man that can get on a horse is going . . ." The town, he advised, "is on the main northern rout[e] leading to Arkansas, Missouri, Tennessee, and Kentucky[,] so that soldiers from all parts of the state pass through here." He, sadly, had recently witnessed the remains of BG Ben McCulloch (killed at Pea Ridge, Arkansas, earlier in the month) pass by in the opposite direction; they bestowed military honors as the wagon bearing his body passed through. It had become common knowledge by now that the regiment would soon take up the march for Arkansas, and "there is some talk of dismounting some of the cavalry when we get to the main army. I hope that our regiment will not be dismounted for I neither want to go in infantry, nor loose [sic] my horse." And even as he wrote this, he observed that through the open window he watched as Col. W. H. Parsons' 12th Texas Cavalry passed down the road, obviously bound for Arkansas also.[226]

Upon arriving at Clarksville, for some unknown reason the regiment had to be completely reorganized, at which time staff officers had evaluated each man's equipage and dutifully noted the

---

[225] William Young to his sister, March 22, 1862, typescript copy from C.R.C., Hill College. The letters will be referenced hereafter simply as William Young letters, C.R.C, Hill College.

[226] Daniel Park, March 31, 1862, Park letters.

salient information on rolls that, presumably, were forwarded to Richmond so they could be reimbursed at some future point. Also listed again were commutation allowances to reimburse for travel and subsistence in the men's getting to the rendezvous point. This may have come from their reorganization at Clarksville. Months would pass, however, with no mention being made of reimbursement, and many a man began grumbling as to whether they'd ever be paid.[227]

Robert M. Collins, who had only recently enlisted in Co. B of Sweet's regiment and quickly found himself elected to serve as a lieutenant, dutifully recorded his first experiences in the regiment. Collins related what had prompted him to enlist, noting it was not so much a belief in the noble cause that provoked the move but rather an innate fear that "the ladies would present us with a hoop skirt" should he not go into the service. Embarrassed by the mere suggestion he might be a coward, he and several other men enlisted together about March 15, 1862.[228]

As with many other recruits coming from his county, they presented anything but the proper soldier's appearance, at least judging from the almost complete lack of military equipage available to them as they left for war. They had to scrape together anything resembling military equipment in a small frontier community with little to offer. Though merchants proffered hats, shoes, and clothing, area ranchers "owning herds of horses were willing to give them up" to supply their wants for horseflesh, but a dearth of military weapons led to the substitution of every conceivable type of civilian arm. These ranged from "double-barrel shotguns, some squirrel rifles, and . . . [a few] old-fashioned buck-and-ball muskets" donated to them, noted Collins. In a crude effort to supply himself with a long gun, he'd ferreted out a four-and-a-half-foot-long rifle barrel, somehow acquired out a working lock, before having it stocked and barrel sights mounted. Once complete, he speculated that he'd be able to

---

[227] See muster-in rolls of companies A-K, 15th Texas Cavalry, Adj. Records, state archives, Austin; also, RG 109, NA, Washington.

[228] *Chapters:* p. 14. This postwar account is a very good read for those wanting more in-depth information relating to his service during the war.

shoot "with the wind, against the wind, and at right angles to the wind."[229]

In one way alone would they all appear uniform, in that everyone seemed to have been able to acquire a long side knife to somewhat augment the limitations imposed by inferior arms. With the government unable to provide cavalry sabers, their long knives would have to suffice as a replacement. But in reality, the men actually preferred these long "bowies" over swords in most cases, for as Collins would later share in his musings, the men found it exhilarating to gallop through the forests lopping the tops off pine trees, this in some measure suggesting what might be the actual case if and when they at last came into contact with the enemy.[230]

Even as the neophytes engaged in such outlandish antics, Sweet remained in close contact with Col. Johnson, who kept Sweet posted as to the regiments that were being included within the still-forming brigade. For his part, Johnson also wrote Richmond that the brigade included his own 14th Texas Cavalry, along with Sweet's 15th, Col. William Fitzhugh's 16th Texas Cavalry, and Col. George Moore's 17th Texas Cavalry. It's possible that a final detachment might have included Col. Nicholas Darnell's 18th Texas Cavalry (which would also later become a part of Granbury's Brigade), though all but the last's regiment had received orders to head for Clarksville, where a training site called Camp McKnight had been established, which would be used to train those regiments being assembled there.[231]

Upon reaching Clarksville, Pvt. William Young, of Co. A of Sweet's own regiment, reported that just six companies of that regiment had reported in; these were put into a regular military order in the midst of a copse of shade trees bounded all around by gently

---

[229] *Chapters.*, pp. 12-3.

[230] *Ibid.*, p. 13.

[231] *O.R.*, I, 4, pp. 982-3, wherein Col. M. T. Johnson advises that Sweet's regiment had mustered in on March 10, followed by Moore's 17th on the 15th of the month, and that Darnell's 18th would shortly be likewise doing so. In *O.R.*, I, 4, pp. 977-9, Governor Lubbock especially names Johnson as one of those acting outside the scope of state authority, he expressing great umbrage at Johnson's behavior in the matter.

rolling plains. He drafted another letter on April 13, again to his sister, in which he advised that "we had a beautiful battalion drill yesterday." As to their trip up to this point, however, "I have seen more rainfall here since I have been here than I ever saw all together down there;" meaning his home near San Antonio. As a diversion, for sport, the men in camp were already engaging in "fighting some poor chickens . . ." He further reported that he had met several local belles, one of whom he "almost fell in love with . . ." the only peculiarities being, though while she was quite good-looking, "her hands were uncommonly large, her face . . . rather out of shape, and her foot was a little too large." On a more serious note, he observed that several sermons had already been preached in camp, and he and a fellow comrade had gone to the trouble to get their heads shaved as a measure to prevent the enemy grabbing their hair in a close-up fight. Moreover, they seemed to be continuously interrupted by military activities; he stated toward the end of the letter that: "There's the bugle. I must go to roll call."[232]

Despite seemingly interminable rainfall, their lives at Camp McKnight looked to be idyllic, for even though subjected to the vagaries of being in a camp of instruction, what with coming and going of civilians, the men hadn't been forced to make especially demanding adjustments to the new demands placed on them. A compatriot of Young's, Lt. Robert Collins of Co. B, wrote that they constantly had company, and more recently, increasing battalion drills; often the men left tried to figure out just what the impact of these deployments would be when they actually met up with the enemy. Nevertheless, that they were most impressive to both soldiers and spectators alike came from Collins' expression on their first evolutions of the line: "Strung out in line of battle on the prairie, it appeared . . . that we had enough men to whip the United States, with Mexico and Canada [both] thrown in."[233]

An interesting series of letters was written the same day, April 17, one from Dan Park and the other scrawled by J. McCann, both of Co. B, and likely sent in the same envelope, as both were found in the Park family letters. Daniel had written to his wife, while

---

[232] William Young letter, April 13, 1862, CRC, Hill College.

[233] *Chapters*, p. 22.

McCann addressed his to a family friend named Burrel Lann. The heavy rains had caused Park to address his letter as drafted while at "Camp Mud," rather than Camp McKnight. He and Woodson had just reached Clarksville from McKinney and "had some rain on us." In fact, the encampment, some three miles from town, had been subjected to "three heavy rains since we have been in this camp." For men who had been deathly sick only days before, the incessant rain must have been cause for concern. Rumor had it that they would soon leave for Corinth, Mississippi, and "we will start either saterday [sic] or monday [sic]" and that the regiments at Clarksville would all move via Washington, Arkansas. From there it was anticipated they would go to Pine Bluff, thence to Memphis, and finally on to Corinth. "There has been some talk in camp of our being dismounted[,] **the thing is now settled we are received as cavalry**." (Author's emphasis.) However, "being just twelve miles below Red River[,]" he thought they would probably cut across the "Indian Nation[,] then in[to] Arkansas." Recently his five-man mess had received sufficient fabric enough, and therefore, "we have been very busy for some days past in makin[g] a tent." With rain falling for almost two straight weeks, it's no wonder he had signed off as being at "camp Mud."[234]

In J. McCann's portion of the double letter to the Park family, addressed to Burrel Lann, he advised that A. S. Johnston had personally ordered their regiment to Corinth, but after Johnston's death in Shiloh in the weeks thereafter, the question now was where they might expect to be ordered as a consequence of that. A total of 76 men had been taken into their company, though many in their regiment had the full complement of a hundred soldiers or more. He joked that a mess-mate, Bill Stevens, "got wounded the other night in a battle during a stormy night in battle [when] the tent fell . . . and skin[n]ed his forehead." He suggested that Lann not consider joining the army just now, but wait till McCann had served out his twelve-month term and returned home, and if after that he still wanted to join up, that'd be all right with him.[235]

---

[234] Daniel Park letter to his wife, April 17, 1862, Park letters.

[235] J. McMann to Mr. B. Lann, April 17, 1862, Park family letters.

In the Wise County company that Robert Collins had joined, now listed as just Co. B, (whose militia name had been the Wise County Yankee-Catchers) he had recently seen himself elected to serve as a second lieutenant, placing more responsibility on his shoulders. Collins thought that what his stalwarts most needed at this point, perhaps, was a good circuit-riding preacher who would likely work wonders amongst his young charges, as, separated from polite society, they had lately taken up both card playing and swearing. In his new post, moreover, he found a considerable amount of necessary paperwork, along with the unwelcome responsibility of posting the guard details nightly.[236]

That the Clarksville community took a decided interest in the men of Sweet's regiment camping in their midst was evidenced by a column published in the *Clarksville Standard* on April 18. A flag had just been presented to Capt. Alsdorf Faulkner's Co. G, by a Miss Ida DeMorse of that city "in the presence of eight or ten hundred spectators," her father both owning and serving as editor of the *Standard* (he would afterward raise the 29th Texas Cavalry Regiment in that area). As some men in Faulkner's company hailed from the community, the young ladies had worked diligently to fashion an embroidered banner that sported the regimental name and number in fancy letters, with a bevy of young belles attending the impressive flag ceremony. This included a rather large assemblage of soldiers, citizens, and other guests who watched as Miss DeMorse gave the handsome silk banner to Sgt. D. L. McGary; who dutifully accepted it on behalf of the company.[237]

A second cavalry regiment destined to initially serve with Col. M. T. Johnson's brigade had earlier begun to gather over in deep

---

[236] *Chapters*, p. 16.

[237] *Ibid.*, pp. 16-22. This was most probably a company ensign rather than a regimental color, though the "attendance of thousands" that Collins conveys suggests otherwise.

East Texas. The progenitor of this regiment was an attorney, George Moore of Crockett; it would soon after be designated the 17th Texas Cavalry. A Georgia native, Moore had hailed from Alabama before relocating to East Texas in 1846, where he maintained his legal practice. A man of means by 1861, and well known throughout the East Texas area, he'd been authorized on February 1, 1862, to raise a cavalry regiment for Johnson's brigade in the state's eastern counties. Almost all of the recruits would come from that area, with three companies enlisting from Harrison County, a couple coming from Cherokee County, and one each from Nacogdoches, Smith, Rusk, Upshur, and Red River counties. With the exception of the last county, where just half the voters had supported secession, the remainder came from staunchly secessionist counties.[238]

After being commissioned, Moore set the rendezvous point for his companies at Jamestown, a tiny crossroads community east of Tyler, in Smith County. This had transpired between mid- and late January, but as there was a dearth of both mounts and arms, Moore had had to work tirelessly just to get all the companies together. Some weeks had been spent at Jamestown perfecting an organizational structure, and there the men had begun to at least learn the rudiments of drill. Orders arrived in early March from Johnson to Moore to quickly get his men on the road toward Arkansas, where they would link up with the other three regiments that were to move in that direction from Camp McKnight at Clarksville. As had been the case with the 14th, 15th, and 16th Texas Cavalry regiments, Moore had acquired authority to become part of Col. M. T. Johnson's provisional brigade. It was hoped the regimental structure would be completed prior to their actually joining the rest of the brigade, with this regiment hopefully profiting from its association with those earlier-raised regiments, believed to be further along in the process than Moore's command.[239]

---

[238] *Texas in the War*, pp. 26, 117. For a capsule history of the 17th Texas Cavalry, see *The Handbook of Texas* online, though it lacks a lot in providing a concise history of this command.

[239] See muster-in rolls, 17th Texas Cavalry, RG 109, National Archives, Washington; and Adj. General Reports, State Archives, Austin. Also, see *Texas in the War*, pp. 26, 117.

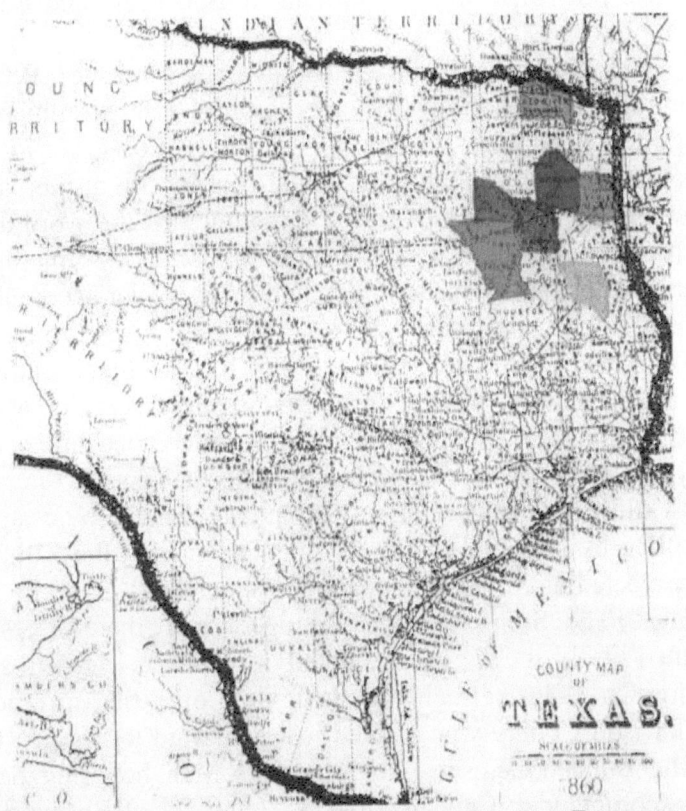

COUNTIES FROM WHICH THE 17TH TEXAS CAVALRY REGIMENT ENLISTED

As with many another regiments recruited during these critical early months of 1862, Moore's recruits varied considerably, ranging from men who had served in the war with Mexico in the 1840s to many underage youngsters who had never been together in a setting such as this. At least one company in particular benefited from the fact that one of their number had already seen service in the present conflict. Though only a teenager himself, Edward Perry of Harrison County had been attending a North Carolina military academy when the war began and had left before graduation to enlist in Co. A, 1st North Carolina Infantry, in 1861, where he initially served as that company's drill instructor. As a consequence of this experience, not surprisingly, he found himself appointed a second lieutenant in Co. K.[240]

Having displayed a better-than-average demeanor, Perry had gone on to serve with the 29th North Carolina, that recommendation coming from none other than his senior officer, Col. (later Lt. Gen.) Daniel Harvey Hill, following an initial trial by fire at the battle of Big Bethel, Virginia, June 10, 1861. Upon getting the word that his father passed away, he resigned his commission in Virginia in order to return home and help settle his father's estate. That accomplished, the talented youngster then enlisted in a company being raised in Harrison County. Armed with his previous military skills and leadership capability, he set about training new recruits when he reached "Jimtown." His skills learned as both cadet and non-com quickly caused his elevation as a leader in this company.[241]

Unlike the flashy militia title that had been the rage earlier in the conflict, by now most of the companies entering the 17th Texas Cavalry elected not to adopt the fancy militia names for their current companies. The Smith County contingent had, therefore, simply designated itself the Texas Mounted Volunteers, though simply becoming Co. C in the regiment at the time of muster-in. The men from Harrison County who arrived just afterward to become Co. E had earlier dubbed themselves as Hendricks' Men, honoring their 40-year-old commander, Capt. Sterling B. Hendricks of Elysian Fields. And Capt. Gil McKay's company (in which Lt. Perry initially served) chose to honor the death of a fellow Marshall officer, Lt. Col. Clough of the 7th Texas Infantry, who'd been killed at Ft. Donelson the previous February, designating themselves the Clough Rangers. And, as will be seen with many other companies raised during these hectic months of early 1862, the self-aggrandizing names were rapidly falling off in favor of simple company letters.[242]

---

[240] Edward C. Perry biography in *Reminiscences*, pp. 603-4. He'd returned to Texas upon the death of his father to attend to family matters and, afterward, enlisted in Capt. Gil McKay's company.

[241] *Ibid.*

[242] See muster-in rolls of companies C, E, and K, 17th Texas Cavalry Regiment, RG 109, N. A., Washington.

A recent volunteer for Co. H, Joseph H. Bruton, of Nacogdoches, Texas, appeared to be a typical Southern volunteer coming from deep East Texas. Though a married man with four offspring to care for, early on he had played a prominent role in his home county. His county court, on May 22, 1861, had appointed him as a precinct patrol leader in his neighborhood, placing twelve neighbors in his charge to assist patrolling their vicinity in anticipation of trouble occurring following the state's secession. Living at the time in the Linn Flat community as a moderately successful farmer, he had owned several and was a recognized leader in his community. Because of his being a family man, he had forgone entering regular military service until after several military disasters had transpired in the first months of 1862. Now feeling compelled to volunteer, on March 10 he joined Capt. I. J. Walkin's company at Douglas, Texas. This company reported to the command while it was encamped at Jamestown, seemingly eager to move on to the front.[243]

Also enlisting about the same time were Bryan Marsh and Z. H. Crow, both of whom joined Capt. John C. Robertson's company, having been recruited in Smith County. Serving in Co. C, both provided good glimpses of their military service, and they helped flesh out the regiment's earliest experiences. And both sent letters home to family concerning their service as new recruits. Bryan, who would quickly supplant Robertson as captain, had settled north of Tyler in 1854, and, while himself a family man, had felt the need to enlist. Two brothers, Darius and Edmund of Bryan's company, would perish in the Atlanta campaign in 1864.[244]

To assist Col. Moore, the men had elected Sterling Hendricks, captain of Co. C, to serve as second-in-command as lieutenant colonel, with John McClarty of Co. F getting the nod as

---

[243] "One Man's War: Capt. Joseph H. Bruton, 1861-1865," by Douglas Hale, *East Texas Historical Journal*, vol. XX, number 2 (1982), pp. 28-45. Hereafter cited as "One Man's War:." On page 30 of the article is a period military image as an officer.

[244] See "The Confederate Letters of Bryan Marsh," in *Chronicles of Smith County, Texas*, vol. 14, # 2, (Winter, 1975), p. 9. Hereafter, cited as simply *Chronicles*; also, "A Smith County Confederate Writes Home: Letters of Z. H. Crow," in *Chronicles*, vol. 4, # 2 (Fall, 1965), p. 11. Each cited hereafter as "Bryan Marsh" and "Z. H. Crow."

the regimental major. It's readily apparent from the muster rolls that great effort was made to divide equally the subordinate spots under the field officers so that most, if not all, the companies gained some representation at headquarters. On March 15, with their organization complete, Col. Moore reported that he would put his troops on the road from Jamestown to any place ordered before the end of the month.[245]

According to W. P. Fears of Nacogdoches, his company, being the first to arrive at Jamestown, received the designation of Co. A; it appears that the assignment of company letters came from the order in which each company came into camp. After establishing a headquarters and their own camp, the men drilled for some weeks awaiting the arrival of the other companies. That the companies arriving at Jamestown spent an appreciable amount of time learning the rudiments of service was attested to by Samuel Cooke of Co. E, who observed that "our first move was to Jimstown [sic], near Tyler . . . [where] we drilled a short time. . . ." He remembered that they drilled several hours in the morning, followed by a similar regimen in the afternoon. This writer advised that he personally conducted the drills, "as he knew a little having had some, which the officers had not." He was at Princeton University in 1858; after the John Brown raid on Harper's Ferry, Virginia, in late 1859, he transferred to a Southern school, attending Emory and Henry College. In this setting, he had already begun to notice the dichotomy between enlisted personnel and the officers. While obviously still in need of additional drill in order to perfect the necessary military discipline, many a man worried they would be sent off before becoming fully prepared. These underlying tensions had made their appearance even prior to their leaving Jamestown, and, if anything, seemed to grow appreciably as they made ready to head for Arkansas. As with many in their earliest training, men often complained bitterly about the officers' obvious arrogance in light of promises made, but not kept by

---

[245] Muster-in rolls of the 17th Texas Cavalry, RG 109, National Archives, Washington. Moore hailed from Nacogdoches, with Hendricks joining from Elysian Fields, and McClarty coming aboard from Henderson. Interestingly, the quartermaster and commissary officers, along with the regimental chaplain, all came from Gilmer, with the surgeon and assistant surgeon coming out of Dallas.

those who had so openly politicked for office. For the present, however, they would have to make do with circumstances, biding their time until they could deal with the pompous officers placed over them.[246]

A final mounted regiment destined to reach Clarksville later in the spring, like others before it, had likewise been consigned to M. T. Johnson's provisional cavalry brigade. The 15th Texas Cavalry had also begun to coalesce at Dallas, Texas, not long after Sweet's regiment departed from there. Its progenitor, Nicholas H. Darnell, had been in Texas since the mid-1830s and had helped found the republic. Not a well-known political figure, nevertheless, he'd served several terms in the state legislature before assuming the role as house speaker in 1842, but failing some years later in his quest to become lieutenant governor. Though still in the legislature, Darnell had in 1858 relocated to Dallas and, once settled in, helped steer his new constituents in the direction of secession by engaging in firebreathing orations directly aimed at the national government's inability to adequate defend the state's vast Indian frontier. He stressed the need for military action there should Texas leave the Union, and, not surprisingly, when conflict came, he decided to raise a cavalry regiment, which was early on to bear his name. Most of the companies in the regiment originated in the North Texas area, and most had enlisted ostensibly for frontier service.[247]

Despite being 54 years old by this time, he quickly resigned his congressional seat and announced his intent to raise a cavalry regiment. As early as June 21, 1861, the *Dallas Herald* had informed its readers that "Darnell to raise a Rgt. of Cavalry." As with the 15th Texas Cavalry before it, it was decided to rendezvous the various companies at Fair Park, at the southeastern edge of Dallas (in fact, at the same location Sweet had previously utilized). Persistent rumors

---

[246] Letter of Lt. Flavius Perry to his pa, May 13, 1862, in Joe R. Wise, ed., "The Letters of Lt. Flavius W. Perry, 17th Texas Cavalry, 1862-3," in *Military History of Texas and the Southwest*, vol. 13, #2, p. 12. Born at Douglas, Texas, in 1835, a Smith County town that no longer exists, near far from Jamestown. Cited hereafter as Flavius letters, *Military History of Texas*. Also, see "The War Years," in the *Southwestern Historical Quarterly*, vol. 74, #4, pp. 536-7. Hereafter cited as "The War Years," *S.H.Q.*

[247] *The Handbook of Texas*, vol. I, p. 465.

circulated that this command would either move to the Indian Nations initially, or else out on the state's northwest frontier. It was initially composed of eleven companies, rather than the ten companies common to volunteer regiments, with eight of them originating in North Texas, while three others (like the 15th Texas before it) came up from the vicinity of San Antonio to enter the regiment.[248]

Remarkably, four companies sprang from counties where secession had been uniformly repudiated, while five more came from counties where the ordinance had passed by less seventy percent; indeed, just two companies originated in counties that had voted for the measure by over eighty percent. Close to half of the men volunteered from locales that could only be described as frontier areas, which explodes the premise they were more energized over Indian incursions that invasion from the North. And like the other cavalry regiments that came into service at the time, Darnell experienced a litany of problems in acquiring suitable weapons and worthwhile mounts. He seemed not overly concerned about the welfare of those civilians left behind once his command departed Dallas, which prompted many living there to wonder why their communities were being left virtually defenseless.[249]

Fortunately, both for readers at the time, as well as the public today, the *Dallas Herald* chronicled Darnell's effort to bring this regiment into being, providing a rather unique image of their hectic origins. In the January 8, 1862 edition, the writer announced that "Darnell's Regiment [plans] to rendezvous [on] January 15." This was followed up in the paper on the 22nd, that "a Johnson County Co. joining Darnell's Rgt. had [just] marched [out] to [their] quarters at Reunion;" it provided a list of officers and even identified the bugler by name. In the same issue, a paragraph briefly noted that

---

[248] *Dallas Herald*, June 26, 1861; see as well, *Texas in the War:*, pp. 26, 117-7; and the author had copies of the muster-in rolls of Companies A, B,C,E,F, I, and K, 18th Texas Cavalry from the State Adj. General Office; and RG 109, N. A., Washington.

[249] See "Voting Record of Texas Counties For and Against Secession," in *Texas in the War*, pp. 185-6; also, see the muster-in rolls of companies A, B, E, F & K, found in the State Archives, Austin, while Professor Anne Bailey supplied the roles of Capt. Hiram Childress' company (A) from Johnson County.

Capt. John T. Coit's ninety-odd "brave and robust men of Dallas County [as having also been] mustered in." A third paragraph in the same edition announced that "another company for Darnell's has reached the river yesterday, etc. We hear they are from Belton." Three others are also written about: the Denton County Rebels was three miles southeast of town, "and [we] found [it and] the 'Montague Pioneers' on line drilling;" the same paragraph mentioned that each had their "camps organized, tents pitched in order, and [having a] rail fence around [their whole area] . . . ;" whilst "the 'Morgan Rangers' arrived here Friday . . . [having been] raised in Bastrop and Travis County's."[250]

This last-named company caused quite a stir upon their arrival, their recruits sporting uniforms that consisted of "yellow-grey tunic[s] and pantaloons made of penitentiary 'jeans,' [each] with two rows of brass buttons down the front of the coat and a stripe down . . . [the outer seam of] the pantaloons." Made from cloth loomed at the Lone Star Mill, Huntsville Penitentiary, two of its members, privates John Pickle and Malcolm Hornsby, display the natty appearance of those uniforms in images taken at the time, contrasting significantly with the homespun attire most of Darnell's other companies had upon arrival at Dallas.[251]

---

[250] *Dallas Herald*, January 8, 1862, p. 2; and January 22, 1862 editions, Dallas Library. In December, 1861, Capt. Hiram Morgan's militia company had received, via Huntsville penitentiary on orders from Governor Frank Lubbock, the following cloth: "716.2 yards of kerseys, 635.1 yards of osnaburgs, and 555.1 yards of cotton jeans; from which they obviously had uniforms and tents made. Huntsville Penitentiary Papers, State Archives Box 452.

[251] Huntsville Penitentiary papers, State Archives, Austin, Box 452.

COUNTIES FROM WHICH THE 18TH TEXAS CAVALRY REGIMENT ENLISTED

Next, a January 29 edition of the *Herald* reveals that Capt. Ed. C. Browder's company (from Dallas) had been "mustered into Darnell's Rgt. last Saturday." This edition went on to note that Darnell's regiment now included some eight companies, all "ready and mustered." A further paragraph in the same paper discussed the mustering in of "John T. Coit's Co. of Dallas Cty.," complete with the names of their officers and noncoms, noting that ninety-two men had already been enrolled.[252]

Soon after, another edition noted on page 2 that the "Hays and Williamson County 'Blues'" had arrived, once again providing the names of the principal officers in that company. And on page 3, the editor advised his readers that "Capt. [Hiram] Morgan accidentally knocks pistol off hook, wounding [him]self." The pistol had

---

[252] *Ibid.*, p. 3.

obviously discharged upon striking the ground, inflicting a serious groin injury. After another week had passed, the same paper advised readers that Darnell's regiment had just gotten orders to proceed to Kentucky, the columnist reporting that another company had been enlisted in Dallas for Darnell's, Capt. Middleton Perry's, who had eighty-three men already on the rolls. Not surprisingly, the paper failed to include articles of a more mundane nature, such as what the regimental organization was going to be or the insurmountable difficulties encountered in acquiring sufficient arms, mounts, and forage for its livestock.[253]

Though Darnell had hoped to remain in Dallas long enough to perfect his regimental structure, rumors began to fly in the wake of the Ft. Donelson and Pea Ridge fiascos that his regiment would sent off sooner rather than later, some still inferring their assignment would be Kentucky, though others peddled rumors the regiment would be apt to go to the Indian Nations. With Capt. Perry's eleventh company having joined the regiment, Darnell's command now sported more than enough to be classified as a full regiment, nominally receiving its designation as the 18th Texas Cavalry.[254]

Some rather interesting information concerning the 18th Texas' formation came early through letters penned to and from John T. Coit, of Plano, Collin County, where he and family members wrote of the circumstances that led to his company deciding to finally join Darnell's command. The same month, Darnell had announced his decision to raise a regiment that had made headlines in the *Dallas Herald*; in July, 1861, Coit had been solicited by none other than Col. John Gregg of the 7th Texas to agree to attach his militia company to Gregg's regiment, and a couple of weeks later, Coit had written Ed. C. Browder of Dallas, asking that his name be removed from Browder's company roll. And later, in August, he had been pitched by Col. Warren Stone, who held authority to raise a regiment of his own. Coit expressed great displeasure upon learning that Stone knew next to nothing about either drill instruction or

---

[253] *Ibid..*, Feb. 12, 1862.

[254] Though Capt. A. Farrar's Waxahachie company actually constituted the final (or eleventh) company, as it would be detached in the nations, ultimately the last company would be the one from Dallas proper.

organizing that regiment. A letter of September 23, sent by Col. M. T. Johnson, did attract Coit's attention, Johnson announcing he wanted to raise an infantry command, authorizing Coit to enroll his company with that command and to march his company to Dallas. Johnson also advised that Coit's men ought to adopt a uniform jacket, preferably of gray material.[255]

The most interesting correspondence came on January, 1, 1862, wherein a man named D. Malley of Dallas advises that Coit is not apt to raise a company due to his fears that Darnell's recent efforts would likely interfere with Coit's own efforts in that arena. A postscript strongly recommends that Coit ought to report with his men and himself as soon as possible to Darnell, as the latter's regiment might already have been filled. And a letter by Coit's wife, Cattie, in writing to her sister, Sallie, penned on January 27, advises that Coit's company had been mustered into Darnell's command "on Monday or Tuesday last week," and was even now encamped on White Rock Creek, "about 1/4 mile below Mrs. Scott's Crossing." Cattie advised that she could watch the company drill from her front porch as they march out onto the prairie. The following day, the 28th, she noted that the "rgt. is to go into camp at or near Reunion (Frenchtown) on top of Cedar Mt.[;] [though] John has only stayed in camp one night."[256]

A very illuminating letter in this series was authored by W. Thomas, C. B. Garwood & others from Dallas, dated February 13, 1862, in which Thomas opined in his note to Coit that: "Several members of Capt. [Hiram] Morgan's Co. want to see you concerning the election of field officers of the Rgt. (Darnell's). Will you notify us at what time you may come to our camp in Dallas to see us.[?]" It

---

[255] Letter from A. L. Aberchain to Col. Coit, July 15, 1861; letter from J. T. Coit to E. C. Browder, July 27, 1861; from John Coit to his brother, George, on Aug. 30, 1861; Col. M. T. Johnson letter, Johnson Station (present-day Arlington), Texas; E. T. Nicholson letter to Coit, from Dallas, Nov. 10, 1861; and letter by (Col.) Thomas C. Bass, Sherman, to Coit, dated Dec. 2, 1861, These are from a Master's Thesis by Jesse Guy Smith, entitled "A Calendar of the Coit and Moore papers." Commerce, Texas. 1936. Hereafter cited as "Coit and Moore papers." Fair Park archives, Dallas.

[256] Cattie to Sallie letter, Jan. 27, 1862, in Coit family papers titled: "Coit and Moore papers" my copies came from the Fair Park archives, Dallas, Texas.

appears from this letter that elections were about to be held in Darnell's regiment to select the field officers to run the regiment, and the men of this company were hoping to help elect Coit to the post of lieutenant colonel, the spot just under Col. Darnell.[257]

Another, but equally important, series of letters relating to the early formation of Darnell's regiment came from the Scurlock family, who lived near Alvarado, in Johnson County. In an early letter written to a brother, James Scurlock, on January 7, 1862 (he had previously enlisted in another Texas regiment), Mollie Scurlock writes from near Grandview that a younger brother, Malcolm, had "not gone off to try and get into the war yet but that if a school was held locally that Pa wanted Malcolm to go to school, but he does not seem to want to go, says he would rather join the volunteers and go and fight." In her letter, she alludes to the fact that another company has been raised locally by Hiram Childress, who was elected captain, and that this company "is going to Dallas to take up winter quarters until spring." While she thought that this company might become part of M. T. Johnson's provisional brigade, a letter of February 27, 1862, advised that Childress' company (with Malcolm now a part) had already become a part of Darnell's 18th Texas. Childress' Company, as the first accepted, became Co. A.[258]

Once in Dallas, the new recruits spent their off-duty hours either lounging around camp or frequenting the larger town's many taverns. Some, however, apparently aware of the seriousness of this new business, sought out churches in the area to commune whenever time allowed them that pleasure. Many recruits engaged in all manner of sporting contests, whether horse races, town ball games played in fields adjacent their camp, weather permitting, or friendly games of marbles. What with the arriving mail now bringing in almost endless accounts of military disasters in the lower Mississippi River valley, soldiering seemed to take on a more sober side. When word at last came, in the form of a directive from General Hébert, to

---

[257] "Coit and Moore's papers", Fair Park, Dallas Archives.

[258] Mollie A. Scurlock to brother James, Jan. 7th, 1862, as published in the *Grandview Tribune*, Grandview, Texas, Nov. 25, 1977, p. 4; *Ibid.*, Mollie to James, February 27, 1862.

be ready to take up the march at once, men saw this as the opportunity to at last "see the elephant" close at hand.[259]

The regiments encamped near Clarksville had also found themselves put on notice, with orders quickly spreading to rid the men of all unnecessary equipment. On April Fool's Day, the 15th Texas Cavalry received word to head for Corinth, Mississippi, though it would not actually get underway until ten days later. And Moore's 17th Texas Cavalry wouldn't depart until the 22nd; that regiment lingered some two weeks after Sweet's departure. In Dallas, Darnell had similarly received orders to move, but rather than toward the Mississippi, this regiment was to instead head north, bound for the Indian territory. It had been determined that Darnell's command must rush there to augment BG Albert Pike's Indian Brigade which had just withdrawn from Arkansas in the wake of the disaster known as Pea Ridge (or Elkhorn Tavern), Pike's force retiring toward the southern border of the Choctaw Nation with North Texas.[260] A much-maligned Pike, even while retreating into the Choctaw Nation, took time to flail at any and everything to do with the army in the aftermath of Pea Ridge. He lambasted both Richmond and Little Rock authorities for having "abandoned" the civilized tribes to an overwhelming enemy force, flushed with victory. If something were not done quickly to reinforce his Indian regiments, Pike complained, the Confederacy might just see the five civilized tribes renounce their treaties with the South and join up with the North. Halting at last within almost a stone's throw of the Red River, Pike put his Indians to work on constructing an earthwork designated Ft. McCulloch, where he would await further developments, unaware that the enemy had long since given up on pursuing his command. At a distance, it

---

[259] The slang term had been derived from the prewar circuses that toured about the country; these exotic stock normally accompanied pre-event parades through local villages, hence, "seeing the elephant" implied you were about to experience an extraordinary event.

[260] Lary C. and Donald L. Rampp, *The Civil War in the Indian Territory*, Austin, 1975, p. 9-10. Hereafter, cited as *Indian Territory*. While the Rampps don't portray Pike's withdrawal as panic-stricken, most other authorities do. See Jay Monaghan, *Civil War on the Western Border, 1854-1865*, NY, 1955, pp. 250, 257.

seemed as if Pike wondered just who the enemy really was, the dreaded Yankees or their "former Confederate friends!"

A few accounts shed light on what was transpiring with Darnell's regiment as it made its way north toward the nations. In a letter to his brother on April 14, 1862, Pvt. Malcolm Scurlock of Co. A announced they had arrived "at Nail's Mill on [the] Big Blue in the [Choctaw] Nation, twenty-t[w]o miles from Red River." He further advised that the 18th Texas Cavalry had been temporarily assigned to BG Pike's Indian Brigade for the moment. He further reported himself as being afoot, having recently lost his horse, but "I am armed with my old rifle [and a] five shooter." The men had been put to work digging wells and erecting cabins, and were supposed "to throw up breastworks."[261]

For some unknown reason, Lt. Col. John Coit had returned home for a short respite during this time, during which he informed his spouse what had been transpiring with the regiment. In a follow-up letter of May 12, and another on the 21st, his wife Cattie had written relatives that Coit's regiment had left Dallas about March 17 and got "into Choctaw Nation near Boggy Depot," before being confronted by Gen. Pike, who presumably bore orders retaining Darnell's regiment there. The men had been expecting to move eastward toward the Mississippi, but John (who had been at home eight days when she wrote on the 21st) had just left to return to the regiment, noting it at this time as being near Bonham, just inside Texas. They had apparently returned to North Texas to seek out provisions and were expected to head next toward Clarksville; she proudly announced her husband's selection as lieutenant colonel of his regiment: "The men like their new Lt. Col., a lot. That Col. Darnell is too much addicted to the use of ardent spirits" as to be an undependable officer, she reasoned, was the reason for Coit's promotion.[262]

---

[261] Malcolm Scurlock to his brother, James, April 14, 1862, printed in the *Grandview Tribune*, Nov. 25, 1977. The letter suggests the writer may have been equipped with either a Colt Revolving rifle, or a "five-shooter" pistol.

[262] Letters of Cattie Coit, to sister Sallie on May 12, and to her aunt Henryetta, in Cheraw, South Carolina, on the 21st of May, 1862, "Coit and Moore," Fair Park Archives, Dallas, Texas.

Though these Texans appeared destined to remain for some period in North Texas, in a series of rapid marches beginning April 10, the 18th Texas Cavalry had moved from their camp east of Clarksville to Fulton, Arkansas, splashing across the Red River there to ride on into Washington. The town newspaper, *The Washington Telegraph*, advised readers that Sweet's 15th Texas Cavalry had already cleared that town and was rumored to be somewhere between Pine Bluff and Little Rock, obviously having made a forced march to get that far. And it reported also that all of "M.T. Johnson's [Provisional] Brigade [had been] ordered by General Roane to Little Rock." And that also that "Col. N. H. Darnell's Rgt. (not yet attached to any brigade) . . . is just behind Fitzhugh's (16th Texas Cavalry) and would soon be coming." The 15th Texas Cavalry had indeed advanced to a point about midway between Pine Bluff and Little Rock, but it had then been ordered on to Little Rock, where it was to link up with BG Oscar Roane's command, rumored to be somewhere northeast of the capital. Each successive regiment paused only long enough to briefly rest their stock at Washington, and after re-outfitting, each continued its northeasterly path.[263]

With respect to the 17th Texas Cavalry, a rather insightful letter from then-Pvt. Bryan Marsh of Co. C, sent from Bossier Parish in Louisiana, spoke of an immense train of 43 wagons that accompanied their column as it moved through Louisiana. Louisianan women had greeted them along their route of march "singin[g] 'Dixie,' presenting[g] flowers & [always supplying] something[g] good to eat." He related, however, that they'd barely escaped with their lives while in the Shreveport area: "There was a Hurricane last[t] night that killed five horses & crippled fifteen or twenty others," though no soldiers were killed.[264]

---

[263] *Washington Telegraph*, May 14, 1863, SWRA, Washington, Arkansas..

[264] Bryan Marsh letters in F. Lee Lawrence and Robert Glover, eds., "The Confederate Letters of Bryan Marsh," in *The Chronicles of Smith County*, vol. 14, (winter/1975) # 2, p. 10. Afterward cited only as "Bryan Marsh," in *Chronicles*. On the regiments heading toward Napoleon, Arkansas, also see F. Lee Lawrence and Robert Glover, eds., "A Smith County Confederate Writes Home," also in T*he Chronicles of Smith County*, vol. 4, # 2, p. 11-2. The letters published therein were written by Z. H. Crow, he also being a member of Co. C.

Bryan Marsh related in a May 29 letter about his recent bout with sickness that prevented his keeping up with the regiment, but that he saw alarming times ahead for them: "the principle [sic] excitement [in the regiment] was re-organization, the soldiers in favor of it & the officers opposing it generally." Apparently, this had caused a rift within his own company; he advised that "I gave Louis Goodman a thrashing in Camden about his brother Robert; I made his face as black as a negroes [sic]." While separated now from his regiment, he had learned that it had made it into Little Rock, but that "General Ro[a]ne had ordered them toward Batesville on White River, [along] with six other regiments."[265]

The *Washington Telegraph* advised its citizens in a May 28 edition of the arrival of Darnell's 18th Texas Cavalry; the paper emphasized that "the cavalry regiment from Texas under command of N. H. Darnell is now here, [that] six companies are now in camp and the others daily expected to arrive with the trains, in order to proceed to Little Rock." The editor found the soldiers to be quite cordial and their physical appearance as favorable as any of the commands that had recently passed through. In a June 4 edition, it conveyed that the "splendid cavalry regiment under command of Colonel Darnell left here last Friday morning . . . they marched through our streets before leaving, and with various banners and fine-looking horses presented quite an imposing appearance." The 18th continued on to reach their next layover point, Benton, on May 3, where the men enjoyed a short rest period prior to heading toward Little Rock.[266]

Darnell's regiment found the march between Washington and Little Rock arduous; the men were often forced to swim their mounts over innumerable flooded rivers and streams, each seemingly flooded out of its banks from the incessant rains that spring. In

---

[265] "Bryan Marsh," in *Chronicles*, vol. 14, # 2, pp. 10-1. The six regiments mentioned were all from Texas.

[266] *Ibid.*, May 14, 1862; also, *Chapters:* pp. 24-5. This article confirms that the regiments traveled in two squadrons (each of two companies), to supply guards for both the front and rear of their immense train, the remaining six companies traveling as a separate body moving somewhat ahead of the slower moving train.

between those spots, their column normally moved unimpeded, often leaving their train far behind. Though it would appear that somewhere along the way, the regiments had all gotten orders to proceed toward Pine Bluff, with the expectation of continuing on to the Mississippi, as several of the regiments mention halts made in or near Camden, though the 18th Texas, following a short respite after crossing the Ouachita River, turned directly toward Little Rock, rather than continuing eastward.

And just as had Sweet's 15th and Darnell's 18th Texas Cavalry regiments, Col. Moore's 17th Texas Cavalry had taken to saddle in mid-April, but rather than heading toward Fulton to cross the Red River, the column swung due east, headed straight for Shreveport. Also, thinking themselves bound for the Mississippi, many of the men had a final opportunity to swing by their homes for a final visit prior to rejoining their command in Louisiana. And, unlike the forced marches that seemed to mark Sweet's and Darnell's progress, Moore's 17th continued to proceed at a more leisurely pace, their daily marches averaging between twelve and fifteen miles, with the regiment not reaching Shreveport until May 5. Here they were allowed a short rest, while learning that they would alter their course to move toward Napoleon, Arkansas, where they'd be ferried across the Mississippi. Almost as if presaging the future difficulties all would face, the regiment seemed to be scarcely in a hurry.[267]

After the near-miss by the tornado opposite Shreveport, two soldiers belonging to Co. A had sent letters home detailing their movements to and arrival at Camden. One came from of the pen of Lt. Flavius Perry, who advised his "Pa" that they had only reached the city just hours before; in it, he also decried the pervasive sicknesses that had arisen as they moved north from Shreveport. Of special interest to Perry was "a great confusion in the regiment yet," with the men seemingly very unhappy over their organizational structure. Almost nightly, some party or another in the ranks would present a petition demanding that all the officers resign, and only two nights prior to his letter, some six companies had petitioned Col. Moore to "order a reorganization of the whole business," a proposal that Perry appeared to endorse. While at Camden, the regiment's

---

[267] "Bryan Marsh," Chronicles, vol. 14, # 2, p. 12.

destination had been officially changed to Little Rock, though they'd now turn north in the direction of Pine Bluff.[268]

An unidentified soldier in Perry's Co. A noted the regiment departed Shreveport on May 8; with the roads north choked by heavy traffic, coming and going, his regiment had had to leave "a great many of those sick left twenty miles behind." In an attempt to overhaul his regiment, he seemed to be one unhappy soldier, even decrying the land passed through. He described it as "the poorest country we ever saw." He also went off about the people he encountered along the way, as they "look like ugliness was their only inheritance." Everything in South Arkansas left him in a state of despair: "There are no cows here. I haven't seen a dozen cows nor got a particle of milk since I have been in the state."[269]

By now, the military commander at Little Rock had established what was denominated as "The Army of the West," and appeared to be organizing the Texas units on their way there into a viable organization. As early as April 29, 1862, MG Earl Van Dorn had advised in a report to Richmond that the "Army of the West" included a third infantry brigade to be assigned to MG J. P. McCown's division in Mississippi, and it would consist of Johnson's own 14th Texas, Sweet's 15th Texas, Fitzhugh's 16th Texas, and Moore's 17th Texas (he had already denoted them all as dismounted troops on his return), though all were obviously still west of the river. And a separate report filed almost a month later still claimed that the same complement of troops belonged to his army; he went further by announcing it as the "Third Brigade" of McCown's division. Of special import is that Darnell's 18th Texas Cavalry is not reflected in either of these reports, lending credence to the suggestion that it still served as an independent organization.[270] Toward the middle of

---

[268] Lt. Flavius Perry, Co. B, 17th Texas Cavalry, May 13, 1862, in *Military History of Texas and the Southwest*, vol. 13, # 2, pp. 12-3.

[269] This unidentified soldier's letter of May 13, 1862, from "Camden, (on the Ouachita), CRC, Hill College. It's likely this may have been James P. Ford, as he mentions his serving in two separate capacities, one as acting quartermaster, the other as the acting commissary of subsistence. He may not have posted the bond required to hold either positions. Several of his letters surfaced while I was employed at Port Hudson, Louisiana, in the 1980s.

[270] *O.R.*, I, vol. X, Pt. 1, pp. 464, and 551.

May, and reflecting the growing strains thrust upon both the soldiers and their mounts, all of these cavalry regiments began arriving at Little Rock. A mud-spattered column, the 15th Texas Cavalry, reined up in the capital on May 15; the men were hurriedly sent over to occupy the well-manicured lawns adjacent St. John's College, where they set up camp for the time being. Carefully attending to the needs of their stock first, they awaited the arrival of their train while taking up quarters in the recently vacated campus buildings.[271] Everyone thought this to be their roughest test since enlisting, what with both the great distance involved and the rapid movements made, especially in light of the constant rains they had encountered along the way. For much of that time, they had sloshed through flooded bottoms, finding them replete with "mud and water . . . of equal depth," and their nightly beds consisted of "pine tops laid [up]on stumps" in fruitless efforts to keep them and their equipages dry. Lt. Collins of Co. B, 15th Texas, wrote of the physical impossibility of trying to determine where roadbeds ended and swamps took over. The only relief on the arduous marches came as young ladies in local communities gathered by the roadsides and tossed flowers at the feet of the soldiers' steeds while they passed.[272]

Perhaps the most troubling issues, other than the trek just completed, were the persistent rumors they had first heard when nearing Benton: that all of the Texas Cavalry regiments were to be dismounted and converted to infantry commands as quick as they reached Little Rock. Lt. Flavius Perry of the 17th Texas Cavalry advised that the column had reached Little Rock "sorter [sic] in a forced march," arriving May 20. He scoffed at the conditions he discovered in the capital:

> There is a great many sick soldiers left here . . . about six hundred of them and there is also a great many wounded here. I was up to see them yesterday and my eyes never beheld such a sight before. Some were dying and some looked like they would not live two

---

[271] William Young letter to a friend, May 18, 1862, C.R.C., Hill College.

[272] Richard Walker biography, in *Reminiscences*, p. 772; *Chapters:* p. 25; and see William Young letter of May 18, 1862., CRC, Hill College.

hours. Some wounded in both legs and some with both hands shot off and everything else you could mention all kinds of diseases. The Lord deliver us from such a place.[273]

Perhaps the most serious circumstance confronting them came through a rumor that all the cavalry regiments now arriving would have to be reorganized due to the recent implementation of the conscription act. Disconcerting to all was a provision that extended their terms of enlistment from just one year to three years. And with that came an equally distasteful element: the law provided that anyone under eighteen years of age or over thirty-five years was to be discharged, for this would further reduce an already-diminishing numerical strength, not even considering the separation of relatives, friends, and neighbors that had enlisted together. To compound matters, in the 17th Texas, Col. Moore resigned to return to Texas. He was quickly supplanted by Capt. William Taylor, who took over as the regiment's colonel. Even within individual companies, the act often made significant impact, as Pvt. Bryan Marsh of Co. C (who'd blackened the eyes of a chief competitor in his old company) found himself elected to serve as its captain. Fortunately for Lt. Flavius Perry of Co. B, he retained his post as a lieutenant there, and even though he acknowledged "we are fighting for a just cause," the changes occurring caused quite a row within the 17th. And Perry offered privately that ongoing changes in the regiment had created great dissension in the ranks: "We could have been bought then for a low price."[274]

If the distasteful reorganizations, coupled with continuing rumors of their being permanently dismounted, were not enough, the lackadaisical attitude shown by local residents contributed further to their disorientation. The few merchants encountered in the city demanded exorbitant prices for common wares, plus cash on the barrelhead from men who'd not received a cent in payment of their services to date. Few townsfolk appeared greatly concerned that their

---

[273] Flavius Perry letter, May 24, 1862, in *Military History of Texas and the Southwest*, vol. 13, # 2, p. 13.

[274] *Ibid*, p. 14.

common enemy by now had approached to within 45 miles, and eligible males openly spurned recruiting efforts. In fact, many a man vowed openly he would resist the implementation of the draft. The Texans quickly seized upon a negative term for the locals, referring to them derisively as "rackensackers." If not openly resistant, many remained skeptical of serving, or only lukewarm supporters of the Texans.

And for the most part, the same folks either remained aloof to those who had seemingly just come to their rescue, or else poked fun at their often-shoddy appearance or lack of military discipline. Attempting to explain the situation at the time, one Texan rudely proclaimed that: "We divide the country into three parts, to wit: Arkansas, Arkansaw, and Rackensack. We are of the opinion that we are now, and for several days have been, in Rackensack."[275]

The morale among the locals was not the only area warranting attention, however. Another was what to do with the myriad sick and injured soldiers who seemed to arrive hourly from the front. As a consequence, the capital had taken on the appearance of a gigantic hospital, with most public buildings overflowing their capacity to handle those requiring assistance. To further add to their overall misery, the measles epidemic left many regiments with almost as many men unavailable for duty as those helping out with the sick. Due to the generally unhealthy condition among both the men and their stock, drills had been temporarily suspended. This did give an opportunity to dash off a few hasty lines to those back home, detailing their travails to this point as well as their experiences since reaching the capital.[276]

One of funnier discoveries made by the men of Sweet's 15th Texas Cavalry, as it was not a life-threatening one, came as they approached Little Rock. Due to the heavy rains encountered along

---

[275] As employed here, this last term seems to have traced back to the Mexican War when a regular army officer derisively referred to Arkansan soldiers as not being worth much in the field, but were able to "rack-and-sack" a Mexican town faster than other troops in the army. See the commentary of George W. Guess in the *Arkansas Historical Quarterly*, vol. 48, # 4 (12/89), p. 328; also, see "Civil War Letters of George Allen," in the *S.W.H. Q.*, vol. 83, (July, 1979), p. 49.

[276] William Young letter of May 18, 1862, CRC, Hill College.

the way, the men found discovered that the huge side knives they brought along had rusted, and their rawhide scabbards had shrunk so much that the knives couldn't be drawn out of their sheaths. This rendered them useless, and the men began tossing their bowies into the river, fully expecting that at some point they would be issued genuine sabers. Some of these Texans saw a prison camp that had been built to hold enemy soldiers, and some got their first glimpse at the dreaded Yankees. Chronicled as a passel of Dutchmen who had been captured at Pea Ridge the previous March, among them was a foul-mouthed foreigner who projected quite uncivil remarks at the Texans gawking at him. He, in fact, challenged anyone outside the pen to fisticuffs, going on to boast that he could easily whip the entire bunch. For those observing from outside the enclosure, their chance to have just such a face-off would soon enough occur.[277]

Lt. Flavius Perry of Co. A, 17th Texas Cavalry, wrote about smaller skirmishes that had taken place northeast of Little Rock. He proudly noted the Texas units involved and the outcome of these contests, down to the number of casualties sustained by both sides. Admittedly minor in nature, such events still had profound effects upon both Perry and his compatriots. But the revulsion caused by seeing the badly wounded, some suffering from multiple gunshot wounds, or those that had lost limbs to a surgeon's scalpel, brought on war's true horrors. The city had a smell of death about it, he thought; he cautioned that for those who had just arrived, the impact of such sights could scarcely be understated. Those who had joined with a desire to observe the sublimity of war appeared taken aback by the sobering scenes of what war actually turned out to be.[278]

The 18th Texas Cavalry had seemingly trailed in the wake of the other regiments of Johnson's brigade all the way across North Louisiana and Southern Arkansas in relation to orders that directed the column toward the Mississippi River. And like the others before it, including the veteran 10th Texas Infantry, Darnell had split the command into its two wings: the first commanded by Lt. Col. John T. Coit, moved via the Camden road, reaching that city May 13. This wing rested, awaiting the arrival of the other wing, after which the

---

[277] *Chapters:*, p. 25.

[278] Lt. Flavius Perry letter, May 20, 1862, CRC, Hill College.

entire regiment moved on to Pine Bluff, veering to the left at the Little Rock intersection to proceed to the capital.[279] Darnell reported afterward that he had anticipated their crossing the Mississippi, but that Union gunboats had supposedly gained control of the river beforehand, this forcing the regiment to be instead hurriedly moved on to Little Rock; the regiment reached there on June 8. There, the on-scene commander, MG Thomas C. Hindman, realized that the new regiments arriving from Texas warranted a short rest after their taxing movements. As to their circumstances, for their part these men found a city in great turmoil, with many disorganized present and hastily raised conscript forces being billeted on every empty lot while their officers occupied hotel suites or commandeered private residences. Lt. Col. Coit of the 18th thought that little progress had been made in organizing the previously arrived troops, though some of them had apparently been in the city for quite some time.[280]

Even while the provisional brigade, as the 15th, 16th, 17th, and 18th Texas Cavalry regiments were known, worked to reorganize after reaching the capital, back in Texas, another trio of cavalry regiments was undergoing their initial organization. In the fall of the previous year, as the trees began to drop their leaves, George Washington Carter of Soule University, who had also been commissioned by Richmond, broadcast a call for volunteers, with which he expected to form a unique organization. The men enlisting would supposedly be a part of the only regiment of "Texas Lancers" to be raised in the state. Content not to only accept completed companies, Carter advertised that individuals and partially raised companies would be welcomed in the Lancers. Raised beyond the governor's authority, this would soon put Carter at odds with state

---

[279] John T. Coit to wife, Cattie, May 13, 1862, "Moore and Coit" family papers, Dallas County Archives, Dallas. Modern-day Coit Road in north Dallas appears to be named for this family.

[280] *Ibid.*

officials, and, as will be later seen, even at odds with the state's own citizenry.[281] By profession a Methodist clergyman, he had heretofore served as the president of Soule University and had received the endorsement of the church and the active support of two fellow pastors, Franklin C. Wilkes and Clayton C. Gillespie. While none of them possessed much awareness of military matters, each of the three had assiduously worked to generate interest in a special mounted unit. Wilkes, who had previous service as president of the Waco Female Academy, had been transferred to Galveston in 1861 to serve as an elder in the church's district there. And as a consequence, all three were to reap "great rewards from raising their flock of sheep."[282]

One illustration of the efforts to acquire recruits can be seen in a circular prepared and distributed to Texas newspapers beginning in November, 1861. Addressed to those worthy persons who considered themselves as representing the "Chivalry of Texas," its stirring appeal announced that interested parties ought to report themselves to Capt. F. J. Boggs at Chappell Hill. According to the broadside, the "1st Texas Lancers" would be a unique command in that the rank and file would be principally armed with lances, in lieu of the swords cavalrymen normally wielded. And, as the government couldn't supply the men's physical needs to any great extent, each recruit was requested to bring with him to the rendezvous site "two suits of clothing, a heavy blanket, a 'bowie' knife, and either a good double-barrel shotgun or hunting rifle; along with equipping himself with a serviceable pistol."[283]

---

[281] *The Handbook of Texas, supplement*, p. 148. Carter had come to Texas only in 1860, but had been an outspoken proponent of secession at the January convention, and had somehow managed not long afterward to wrangle a Colonel's commission directly from the War Department.

[282] A short biography on Wilkes is that in T*he Handbook of Texas, supplement*, p. 1113; for a background on C. C. Gillespie, see Norman D. Brown, ed., *One of Cleburne's Command: The Civil War Experiences of Capt. Samuel T. Foster, Granbury's Texas Brigade, CSA*, (Austin, 1981), p. xxxviii. This latter work is cited afterward as *One of Cleburne's Command:*.

[283] *Ibid.*

Such heady rhetoric appealed to many a recruit's masculinity when declaring:

> This will be the only Regiment of Lancers in the service, and Lancers are the most formidable cavalry in the world. The Lance simply takes the place of the sword in the charge, and is much the better weapon. Brave Men of Texas, the south is invaded; everything dear to us is at stake; there will be nothing to live for if we are conquered; this is the grandest contest in the world; Who will not be emulous of the privilege of taking part in the glorious strife?[284]

That such dramatic appeals met with success is evidenced by the fact that Carter soon had more than enough men to compose the single regiment; in fact, he had such numbers as to sufficiently form thirty-odd companies. Richmond quickly approved a request to organize this command into a brigade of three complete regiments. For its part, the War Department stipulated only that each regiment be mustered in for a period of three years, thus eliminating the calamity that had recently surfaced with other cavalry units undergoing organization that year.

The muster rolls of several companies in the 2nd Texas Lancers show that the men came from all over the state. Co. A alone consisted of recruits joining from Austin, Brazos, Montgomery, and Washington counties, enrolled between February 10 and March 1, 1862. Next came the Danville Mounted Riflemen as the second mustered; it was comprised mostly of recruits from Montgomery County and raised by a prominent physician in that community. From the Waco vicinity, Capt. William Taylor recruited men for Co. C in Lampasas, Comanche, Gainesville, Hamilton, Booneville, and a smattering of other communities adjacent to McLennan County. Included were Bosque and Coryell counties. Companies D, E, and H all came from three adjacent Southeast Texas counties, Jasper, Angelina, and Tyler, while Co. F came from Ft. Bend County, southwest of Houston. Others came from Jefferson and Tyler

---

[284] *Ibid.*, p. xxxviii-ix.

counties (Co. G), with Co. I originating in Karnes and Fayette counties and Co. K enrolled at Yorktown, Clinton, and Lavaca on the Gulf Coast.[285]

Of special interest to today's reader is a partial roll of Co. G, raised in and around Woodville, Texas, by Capt. C. W. Bullock. That roll, dated July 7, 1862, lists the following recruits' names as belonging to that company as of that date: "Indian Jack, Indian John, Indian Tom Poncho, Indian Johnson, Indian Jim Henderson, Indian John Scott, Indian Thompson and Indian Alexander." It's believed that most of these men were not long after separated from the company, either in Louisiana or Arkansas, returning to their home communities. They may well have been from the Alabama-Coushatta tribe that still resides in that vicinity.[286]

The final regiment of the brigade, initially assigned as the 3rd Texas Lancers, had likewise been organized by a Methodist minister, Col. Clayton C. Gillespie, and like the two previous regiments, it came into existence outside Hempstead, Texas in the late spring of '62. Composed at the start of eleven companies, most of these men came from Southeast Texas also. Liberty County contributed the greatest number of both individual recruits and whole companies, companies G, H, and I being raised mostly in that vicinity. But it also had held men from Galveston, Hardin, Tyler, Houston, and Huntsville counties; except for Co. E, which had been raised at the railroad town of Millican, Texas. Two of the companies recruited in Liberty County are reflected on rolls found on a blog site from a

---

[285] For the muster-in roll of Co. A, see 2nd Lt. W. H. Hensley, RG 109, NA, Washington; Co. B, courtesy of Karen McCann Hitt of Montgomery County, which reveals this company had originally been assigned to Beat 2, 17th Brigade, Texas State Troops, State Archives; Austin; Co. C, State Archives & RG 109, NA, Washington; Companies D & G, taken from *Sketches of Tyler County History*. Bevil Oaks, Texas. Whitmeyer Printing. 1986. pp. 182-191.; Co. F is reflected in the *History of Ft. Bend County*. Houston. W. H. Coyles & Co., 1904. pp. 273-274; and for Co. H (from San Saba County), see supplemental muster roll # 293, State Archives, Austin, dated April 8, 1862. In this latter company, the recollections of 1st Lt., afterward Capt. Samuel T. Foster in *One of Cleburne's Command:*, is perhaps the most authoritative work on the 2nd Texas Lancers, or 24th Texas Cavalry as it afterward became better known.

[286] *Sketches of Tyler County History*, p. 185.

resident there, and interestingly, quite a few of these men left one or more letters relating to their involvement with the regiment and the war itself.[287]

All three regiments, therefore, were mustered in for twelve months. The men's mounts and their arms were appraised and set out on the rolls, and interestingly, the thirty-plus companies then drew lots to determine which regiment they would be assigned to. Though a cash bounty had been promised as an incentive to gain recruits, that as well as the cash due the men for use of their horses and weapons would be long coming. In fact, it would be months before the men received any payment from the government, which would cause the men to begin to grumble from the time they left Camp Hébert, east of Hempstead, all the way up to Arkansas.[288]

The rendezvous point selected by Col. Carter at Hempstead was situated forty-five or so miles northwest of Houston, straddling the Houston and Texas Central Railroad. The officers had named the site Camp Hébert in honor of the district commander, BG Paul O. Hébert, and once arriving there, the tremendous effort needed to perfect their organizations got underway. In the meantime, Carter had gained authority to include the three regiments in a single brigade structure, as he served in overall command. Much had to be accomplished, and the New Year came and went, with the winter months seeing all three regiments struggling to complete their organization and acquire all equipage available.[289]

When Governor Lubbock became aware of yet another intentional circumvention of his authority by both Carter and Richmond, he decided to impede Carter's efforts in every way possible. He responded icily to a War Department query about Carter's command by writing that that officer's efforts would obviously "defeat every effort I can make to raise infantry

---

[287] See *http://libertycountyhistory.blogspot.com/2006/07/25th-texas-cavalry-regiment-company-b*, and *Ibid.*, company-h. See as well, Miriam Partlow. *Liberty, Liberty County, and the Atascosito District.* Austin. Pemberton Press. 1974. Pp. 212 for the roll of Co. G & I, dated June 30, 1862 and May 3, 1862.

[288] Bimonthly muster rolls of many of the men are on file in RG 109, Na, Washington, and reflect the values varied substantially from one man to another.

[289] *One of Cleburne's Command:*, p. xxxviii-xxxix.

[regiments]." He continued venting his spleen, moreover, by complaining that the War Department had in recent months been so focused on raising infantry commands at the request of Richmond, only to see the state undercut by national authorities in endorsing Carter's application without any hesitation.[290]

Though Lubbock might not have been able to totally derail Carter, he nevertheless seemed determined to do all in his power to interfere with that officer's efforts. In doing so, he would pointedly demonstrate to those in Richmond the price to be paid by those attempting to circumvent the state's authority. In the process, he believed he could demonstrate just what could be expected by those within the state who disregarded his authority in such matters. However, having by this time gained War Department approval to increase his command to a complete brigade of lancers, Carter's staff worked diligently to get all three regiments ready to move to the front.[291]

Their work nearing completion by mid-April, Carter began mustering in the three regiments. They were designated now the 1st, 2nd, and 3rd Texas Lancers. Ultimately, after an extraordinary march across Eastern Texas and North Louisiana, during which the uproar on behalf of disenchanted citizens would force Richmond to renumber them the 21st, 24th, and 25th Texas Cavalry regiments. Because of great personal efforts on behalf of facilitating Carter's attempt to maintain this as an autonomous brigade, Franklin Wilkes and Clayton Gillespie were awarded colonel's commissions, Wilkes taking over the 24th Texas and Gillespie assuming command of the 25th Texas. As the senior colonel, Carter would initially lead the brigade thus formed.[292]

---

[290] *Ibid.*, p. xxxix.

[291] *Ibid.*

[292] Carter's regiment would become the 21st Texas Cavalry, rather than the 1st Texas Lancers, with Wilkes' 2nd renumbered as the 24th, and Gillespie's designated the 25th Texas.

COUNTIES FROM WHICH THE 24TH TEXAS CAVALRY REGIMENT ENLISTED

Any number of lesser-known men would play important roles in the mad scramble that began after the New Year to secure recruits for the three regiments. Tyler County resident Robert R. Neyland, a Woodville attorney, had much earlier formed a company that adopted the title of the Woodville Sharpshooters. The company included at least two other local attorneys, W. P. Nicks and W. B. Cline. But before his company became attached to Wilkes' 2nd Texas Lancers, one of its members, 1st Lt. C. W. Bulloch, returned to Woodville and raised a second company that was afterward mustered in as Co. G in this same regiment. And it was this latter officer's company that bore the names of some twenty or more Native Americans that lived in the vicinity. In fact, Bullock's company didn't reach the regiment until July 7, 1862, when it was already on the road near Shreveport.[293]

COUNTIES FROM WHICH THE 25TH TEXAS CAVALRY REGIMENT ENLISTED

Among the men enlisting in Co. F of the 2nd Texas Lancers in March 1862 was a Galveston native, Robert Hodges, Jr. He had already seen service in the recent conflict, in mid-1861 joining John Ford's Mounted Regiment in South Texas, after which he enlisted in the 8th Texas Cavalry that September. Discharged from that unit in December as "unfit for further military service," in Kentucky, Hodges had returned to Ft. Bend County, and from there had enlisted in Co. F of Wilkes' regiment. Several letters covered this later

---

[293] James L. & Josiah Wheat, *Sketches of Tyler County*, (reprint) Bevil Oaks, 1986, pp. 183-5.

enlistment, commencing on April 4, 1862, and running all the way to March 25, 1865. He ultimately was promoted to lieutenant.[294]

Another set of early letters concerning Wilkes' regiment was penned by Pvt. Newton Allen of Co. D, commencing soon after his enlistment and the regiment's taking up the march for Arkansas. The first is dated May 18, 1862, and they ran intermittently until February 1864, when his spouse learned of his death in combat. This first series of letters reflects a lot of detail as to the 2nd Lancers' earliest activities in Texas and Louisiana, as will be seen shortly.[295]

In regard to Gillespie's 3rd Texas Lancers (25th Texas Cavalry), some four companies would trace their origins to Liberty County; one was formed on Tarkington Prairie, in a village bearing the same name, situated midway between the Trinity and San Jacinto rivers. There, a local schoolteacher named John R. Hardison had enlisted right after the premature demise of his wife during childbirth, and only a matter of weeks prior to his enlistment in March 1862. He had declared previous to this to a brother that: "I am giving every dollar I possess, and what else I can do in the way of procuring horses, guns and other equipment for those who are going" off to fight from his immediate vicinity. And it's probable that, thanks to his hard work afterward in helping recruit what afterward became Co. G, Hardison quickly found himself elected to the post of first sergeant in Capt. W. D. Davis' company from Liberty.[296]

---

[294] Maury Darst, "Robert Hodges, Jr. Confederate Soldier," *East Texas Historical Journal*, vol. IX, No. 1 (March, 1971), pp. 20-49. Hereafter, cited as "Robert Hodges, Jr., *E.T.H.J.*

[295] Xerox copies of Newton Allen's letters came from Joe Browder of Cleburne, Texas, and were transcribed by this writer.

[296] John R. Hardison letter to brother Edwin, March 16, 1862, Cain family genealogical collection; copies came from Elizabeth Ryan of Houston, Texas. Hereafter cited as John R. Hardison letters. See also the muster-in roll of Gillespie's 3rd Lancers in RG 109, NA. Washington, revealing that the regiment had eleven companies. Also, according to the Compiled Service Records, in RG-109, "Capt. Proudfoot's Company was merged into Co. H sometime after the[ir] muster of June 30, 1862." The records show that many men in Gillespie's regiment had formerly been in Nichol's 9th Texas Infantry Battalion, at Galveston, a six-month unit discharged in early 1862, RG 109, NA, Washington, D. C.

And on May 8, 1862, Jesse D. Lum of Liberty County had enlisted in Capt. J. N. Dark's Co. B of Gillespie's 3rd Lancers. What's important about his muster-in roll is that on the day after he enlisted, he was appointed first sergeant, with "drillmaster" entered below his name. On the June 30 roll, he's still shown as drillmaster, though in following months he's shown as having been promoted to the rank of second lieutenant, approved by none other than the department commander, Maj. Theophilus Holmes. Several of Lum's letters have survived and are instrumental, along with others, in helping to flesh out the earliest service of both the 2nd and 3rd Texas Lancers.[297]

When these Texans began to arrive at Camp Hébert, three miles east of Hempstead, they found several other organizations also bivouacked at nearby Camp Groce. Here several infantry regiments had likewise been brought together, and were getting their initial exposure to military life. Among them was a private named J. P. Blessington, a recently arrived recruit in the 16th Texas Infantry. From a distance, he watched Carter's men and noted that cavalrymen's circumstances contrasted decidedly from the Spartan circumstances the infantrymen faced. He wrote of Carter's men at the time:

> They do not fare badly in camp. Neat beds are contrived. Some are cots, others [are made of] saplings, or frames covered with cotton. On one side [of their tents] is a table, [upon which there are] books and novels, and most likely a bottle of "commissary" [whiskey]. Four flies form a mess-tent; and as the Col. and staff are going to dine, we will see what kind of fare they have. It consists of stewed beef, boiled ham, mashed potatoes, and a couple of chickens which some . . . Austin county housekeepers **were kind enough to raise for them**! (author's emphasis)[298]

---

[297] Compiled Service Record, RG 109, NA; also, see letters supplied by the Texas Confederate Museum, Nita Stewart Memorial Library & History Center, Midland, Texas, as Coll. # TCM 94.5; 7, 30-9.

[298] *One of Cleburne's Command:*, pp. xl-xli.

Having to subsist on a meager fare that included not much other than "blue beef" and cornbread, he and his comrades felt that some action ought to be taken to stop the cavalrymen's depredations upon local citizens.[299]

Both branches shared one thing in common, however, during their Hempstead stay. This came in the guise of sham battles staged between infantry and cavalry commands in the river bottoms adjacent to the camps. Most everyone openly engaged in these actions, obviously without the ramifications associated with real combat, and charges and countercharges became the norm between the "warring" parties. While such simulated combat provided some sense of what real fighting might be, and gave them an enjoyable break from their repetitive drill regimen, some serious injuries were inflicted upon some combatants, occurring mostly from blank rounds fired too close to one another, and gave an indication of the dangers involved even when trying to defeat one another. The fact that such simulations bore little reality to actual fighting conditions didn't seem to disturb anyone in the least.[300]

After the formal swearing-in ceremonies in April, Col. Carter furloughed all three regiments, maintaining only a skeleton crew required to complete paperwork and make all arrangements needed for the upcoming trek over land that had been ordered. This time off gave many of them a last sojourn to their homes, though they had instructions prior to leaving Hempstead to report to Crockett no later than May 15, where a cumbersome train of wagons would join them so they could be off for the front. Most of those on temporary furloughs reported back at the appointed time, or else sent word of when their return could be expected.[301]

After returning, the regiments departed Crockett on successive days, each given instructions to stop at a convenient point

---

[299] J. P. Blessington, *The Campaigns of Walkers Texas Division*. Austin: State House Press. 1994 (reprint), p. 29.

[300] Records on Carter's stay at Hempstead are rare, and often rather sketchy. One senses the men thought themselves out on a lark, rather than really practicing for war.

[301] *One of Cleburne's Command:* p. xl.

each evening, staggering their march so as to remain in contact with the other two regiments. This would make it easier to secure sustenance for both the men and their horses, and hopefully not adversely affect any one community through which the brigade would pass. With that understood, Col. Wilkes' 2nd Lancers (a.k.a. 24th Texas Cavalry) swung into their saddles on the morning of the 17th to lead the column away from Crockett, the regiment heading northeast to make camp near Alto that evening. The next day, Col. Gillespie's 3rd Lancers (a.k.a. 25th Texas Cavalry) trailed Wilkes' column, but bypassed the latter's regiment to encamp several miles northeast of Wilkes' camp. And, finally, Carter's 1st Texas Lancers, (a.k.a. 21st Texas Cavalry) followed after another day, moving via the same route, before halting midway between the other two so as to keep his headquarters in the center of the column.[302]

At Alto, Pvt. Newton Allen of Co. D, 2nd Lancers (24th Texas Cavalry) sent a letter to his wife, Helen, advising that the regiment had come 150 miles since leaving Hempstead and would next to the town of Douglas, in Nacogdoches County. Here a dispatch rider had overtaken the brigade, advising that "no more troops are wanted across the Mississippi River" and delivering new orders to go next to Shreveport. Especially disturbing to Allen and his comrades was the fact that the bounty money owed them had not yet come in and, he speculated, wasn't likely to arrive at all. The men placed the blame squarely on Col. Carter, with Allen pronouncing that Carter "will [not] be safe in a battle," because of the obvious lack of concern shown to the men's welfare. As a consequence, men had already begun to desert the regiments, with six to eight going missing in his own company. Further, they had already been forced to "press bacon and corn once," for the regiments had no funds on hand to pay locals for their stores. They indeed had only one pleasure still at this point, that being that "we have Coffee[,] the real jinuine [sic] Java[,] and make no mistake every time I drink it I think of home."[303]

---

[302] Newton Allen letter to his wife, May 18, 1862, from Camp Alto, in the Newton Allen letters, courtesy Joe Browder, Cleburne, Texas.

[303] *Ibid.*. The letter advises his wife to address return letters to Co. D, 2nd Texas Lancers, Carter's Brigade.

An earlier letter written by Pvt. Robert Hodges, Jr., of Co. F, 2nd Texas Lancers (24th Texas Cavalry), drafted April 4, had dealt with Carter's attempts to entice the soldiers to wait patiently for their pay: "I am certain that the bounty money is all a humbug." The soldiers felt cheated by the preachers-turned-politicians that had used the bounty as a means to get them to enlist, before failing miserably to supply the promised funds. Hodges, who had earlier seen service in the 8th Texas Cavalry, seemed ready to incite a riot amongst his comrades.[304]

Realizing by now that the state would certainly not be providing bounty monies, nor even purchase supplies for their march, Carter's men would be forced to seize, or "press," if they expected to survive as they made their way across the state. This had provoked the recently promoted Lt. Robert Hodges, Jr. to advise his brother on June 1 that "we will rove around over the country until we eat up all that we can get;" followed by his criticism that "this brigade has been a mixed-up affair from the beginning." He further suggested his brother could write him in care of "Laurissa [Larissa] Cherokee County, Texas," addressing his letters in care of "Capt. T. W. Mitchell, Co. F, 2nd Texas Lancers."[305]

And, not surprisingly, as should have been anticipated, there was little enthusiasm from those landowners along the way who received a visit from Carter's foraging parties; these citizens were forced to accept virtually worthless script or promissory notes for their commandeered stores, for which they knew there was very little likelihood of being reimbursed. Long and continuous were the outcries from those who found themselves imposed upon in this manner, and increasingly bitter became the demands from those pressed for supplies that the men engaged in such conduct be prosecuted to the fullest extent of the law. One Mt. Alto resident, W. W. Frizzell, wrote a fellow Texan, who just happened to be Confederate postmaster, John H. Reagan, vehemently protesting what was transpiring:

---

[304] See Maury Darst, ed., "Robert Hodges, Jr., Confederate Soldier," *East Texas Historical Journal*, vol. 9, #1, vol 1, # 9 (March, 1971), p. 30.

[305] "Robert Hodges, Jr.," E.T.H.J., p. 31.

> Notorious outrages are at this time being practiced in the way of plunder . . . by an armed party **professing to be Confederate soldiers and under the command of one Col. Carter** [author's emphasis added] . . . but all those professing to be officers acknowledge themselves void of any commissions to draw on the government for supplies. They are moving eastward . . . with a force of from 1,500 to 3,000 men, and remaining in each neighborhood just long enough to ravage corn-cribs and smoke-houses . . . ; **and even the defenseless widow meets with no mercy at their hands.**[306]

However, by the time state authorities could actually be brought up to speed, Carter's regiments had moved his command far beyond the governor's reach.

Instead of going to Larissa as had been rumored, the brigade turned northeast to reach Mt. Enterprise in southern Rusk County, where the column lay over for several days. While their mounts and they themselves needed rest, the men became increasingly sick as they moved along. They had already begun to leave men here and there along the route of march, suffering from a variety of illnesses. Robert Hodges, Jr. had written his brother on June 8 that "there is a great deal of sickness in our regiment." As they had moved along, first the mumps, then the measles began to appear amongst the men, and they were generally left at the homes of locals to be cared for. Pvt. Newton Allen of Co. D, 2nd Texas Lancers, reported at Mt. Enterprise that this factor had so reduced his regiment's strength that "our Rgt. is cut down to about 400 men[,] the rest of them a scattered from Crockett to this place sick." Indeed, he had also been taken sick on the 1st, at first believing himself to simply have a cold, but had also turned out to be measles. Having hoped for a quick recovery, "they went very hard with me. I was the worse sight you ever saw[,]

---

[306] *One of Cleburne's Command:*, p. xliii.

the skin on my face was in great red welts and felt if it was an inch thick."[307]

Lt. Robert Hodges of Co. F, 2nd Texas Lancers had likewise written from Mt. Enterprise on June 8; he had to stay with a sick comrade friend who "has a very interesting case of measles [sic]." He advised that the first battalion of his regiment had departed for Shreveport on the previous day, and his own wing expected to move shortly. That dissension had become increasingly prevalent amongst the men was pointed out by Hodge's follow-up letter of June 11. For some strange reason, "our Regt. is ahead [and] Col. Wilkes says he is going to keep it ahead [of the others]." Rumors abounded that "Col. Wilkes has command of the whole Brigade, four companies have taken a stand and they say they will not move from Shreveport until they get their bounty." It seemed to be that tougher times had fallen amongst the troops as they forged ahead on the march to Shreveport.[308]

Upon entering Louisiana, these men began to learn that their reputation for liberal foraging in East Texas had actually preceded them, with the residents in the Pelican State looking upon Carter's brigade with jaundiced eyes. Their infamous foraging expeditions had provoked a considerable disdain amongst the wary citizens they encountered daily along their route of march. So much had this been the case that on June 10, the *Caddo Gazette* published a village proclamation ordering all drinking establishments closed, and the mayor suggesting strongly that Carter's command might well want to encamp at McNutt Springs, well outside the city limits. The editor strongly endorsed a proposal that the brigade be sent quickly to "meet the enemy as soon as practicable," couching his words so as to actually appear to be in support of Carter's Texans.[309]

---

[307] Newton Allen to his wife, June 10, 1862, sent from "Hospital, Mt. Enterprise." Signed at the bottom: "Direct as Follows [:] Newton Allen[,] Co. D[,] 2nd Rgt., Carter's Brigade, Texas Lancers ", Newton Allen letters, Joe Browder, Cleburne, Texas Also, see *E.T.H.J.*, vol. 9, #1, p. 32, wherein Lt. Hodges reports of the numerous sick being left at that point as well.

[308] Robert Hodges letter, June 11, 1862, *E.T.H.J.* vol. IX, No. 1 (March, 1971, pp. 32-3.

[309] The *Houston Tri-Weekly Telegraph*, of June 20, 1862, reprinted from the *Caddo Gazette* of June 10, 1862.

With various kinds of sickness decimating their ranks, all three regiments had little choice but to lie over for some time in the Shreveport vicinity to let the diseases run their course and the displaced men return to their camps. Soon after reaching Shreveport, Carter dispatched Col. Wilkes to Richmond, charging him with looking into the promised bounty owed and when it might be forwarded; further, he was to lobby the War Department to continue to maintain their independent brigade status as well as make suggestions on their future service. In the interim, Carter was unfortunately either unable or unwilling to halt the men's depredations upon the locals, as by now they had become expert at pressing any and everything of value desired and a lot that wasn't. It seemed, according to Pvt. Newton Allen of Co. D, 2nd Texas Lancers, that their attitude may have arisen from the lack of adequate medical attention. He advised his wife Helen that "we were sadly neglected by the doctors," and "there was several died there and from neglect . . . ." To compound matters, he had styes in both eyes at this time and still suffered somewhat from his bout with the measles.[310]

Allen went on to report that just 308 of the 960 men enrolled in the 2nd Texas Lancers could report for duty. By this time, it had become common knowledge that the brigade would next head for Little Rock. A remarkable episode came when Allen commented on an unusual event that had transpired just before his June 21 letter to his wife:

> Last night a boat arrived at this place to get bacon and flour for New Orleans[.] It was found out later she was a spy[.] She was taken about midnight by our company and aboard of her was sixteen hundred cotton cards that had been sent to trade to the Union men. They will be confiscated.[311]

---

[310] Newton Allen letter, June 21, 182, courtesy Joe Browder, Cleburne, Texas. He did acknowledge that as of late: "We have plenty to eat and that is good meal, flour, bacon, been, peas, sugar and vegetables."

[311] *Ibid.* June 21, 1862.

But he indicated best the prevailing attitude amongst the men in what he appended to the bottom of his letter: "I am not well satisfied with my Rgt.[,] but I will make the best of a bad bargain." But storm clouds could clearly be seen on the horizon.[312]

And it may well have been such attitudes that prompted the launching just afterward of a junior officer and a small detachment from Wilkes' 2nd Texas Lancers. They slipped down the Red River, ostensibly to break up an illegal trade thought to have sprung up between those in enemy-occupied New Orleans and some upriver merchants who were supposedly profiting from trade with those on the Federal side that had hard money. This party soon returned, bringing with them some 5,000 pounds of powder, five tons of lead, 6,000 yards of jeans cloth, and lesser amounts of quicksilver, quinine, a sorely needed bullet-pressing machine, and a quantity of real coffee, taken from the enemy.[313]

That Capt. William Taylor's sortie made quite a "splash" can be seen by the reaction of Governor Thomas Moore after he learned of the mission. In a very emotional letter hurriedly dashed off to Richmond, Moore specifically names Taylor, going on to advise that the officer ought to be an embarrassment to the army for what Moore labeled as "bullying and threatening language and manner" employed during a "brutally practiced extortion and outrage" against the Louisianans living downstream. Demanding a court of inquiry to examine the matter, he covertly threatened overt actions on his part: "[If not done], My marksmen may save [you] the trouble" should such wanton acts continue to occur.[314]

About July 1, Col. Wilkes returned with the bounty money, but rather than turning those funds over to Carter, he promulgated orders that formally detached his 2nd Texas Lancers, along with Gillespie's 3rd Texas Lancers, from Carter's command. Then, without another word concerning the bounty money, Wilkes promptly led his regiment northward, taking all the funds with him.

---

[312] *Ibid.*

[313] *Houston Tri-Weekly Telegraph*, July 8, 1862; this may be related to an event Allen refers to in a June 21 letter.

[314] *One of Cleburne's Command:*, p. xliv.

Gillespie's regiment followed Wilkes' trek toward Arkansas, probably leaving Carter to wonder just what Wilkes' private mission in Richmond might have been. Shortly afterward, a crestfallen Carter got his men likewise saddled up; they headed for Pine Bluff, where all three regiments had been ordered.[315]

The 3rd Texas Lancers had obviously followed much the same path as had the 1st and 2nd Texas Lancers in getting to Shreveport, though it appears that their paths diverged somewhat upon reaching there. On July 17, 1862, Lt. Silvier P. Baillio of Co. G had written from Camp Fullerlove at Keatchie, Louisiana that the "1st and 2nd regiments [Texas Lancers] left for Little Rock two or three days ago." He went on: "We do not know when our regiment will be able to leave, for about half are sick; it is almost all cases of measles. About 15 have died, all after measles." About the same time, back in Texas, BG Paul Hébert had issued a quite animated General Order #11, dated July 11, deploring the seizure of property from private citizens by "independent corps [of troops], raised by . . . direct authority from Richmond and with orders to report to some command or general outside the department of Texas." It all probability, this order sprang primarily from the abuses attributed to Carter's men in moving to the front.[316]

That a combination of higher-ups had entered into the fray is pointed out in Lt. Baillio's next letter, written July 27: "The regiment is in a great uproar. We received orders from the General in Little Rock [MG Theophilus Holmes] to dismount us. All the soldiers swear they will not go afoot." That this had reached disturbing proportions is seen in his next statement that " . . . there are forty or fifty who have deserted, and they are deserting every night." The basis for this, he deduced, was "to put us in the infantry is that there is no grain in Arkansas to feed the horses."[317]

---

[315] *Ibid.*:, pp. xlv-xlvi.

[316] Letter from Silvier Baillio, July 17, 1862, obtained from www.civilwarbull.org/forum/messages/4339.html; *One of Cleburne's Command:* p. xlv; *O.R.*, I, XV, pp. 822, 824-5.

[317] Silvier Baillio, July 27th, 1862 in www.civilwarbull.org/forum/messages/4340.html

That this action brought about a considerable ruckus amongst the cavalrymen is readily demonstrated through letters sent from the Shreveport area in August. Among those, one penned by W. S. Boothe of Co. G, 25th Texas, on the 15th, proclaims flatly that "We have had a general revolution of things in this Command Since I last wrote you. In the first place we, or at least the most of us[,] were dismounted, in the next the notorious Carter Brigade has been disowned by the authorities of the war department[,] and we are now known as the 25th Reg[.]Tex[.] Cavalry." And if that weren't enough, within his own company, "last and worst of all most of the men have been Sick and five had died in our camps." He expressed the desire that "if the horses now here are Sent home[,] I will be detailed to go with them[;] [and] probably return then . . ." to the regiment.[318]

That this action had brought about much dishevelment within that regiment is reflected by a letter penned some afterward by a "new" private assigned to Co. I, 25th Texas Cavalry. The soldier, Pvt. C. B. M. Horton of Liberty County, had been hired as a substitute for another soldier; he was paid $800 to take that man's place. This letter, written October 16, 1862, advises his wife not to pay that amount back to that soldier, who in the meantime had gone home, only to be compelled to go back into the service by the conscription law:

> If Ab McMurtry wants that money back[,] you keep it by all means[,] doe [sic] not listen to anything any one sais [sic]. I speak of this because of the Conscript law has come out for he was warned of it before I was taken in his place by the proper authority at the time when he was puthing [sic] me in his place[.] Show this to him if he should make any effort to git [sic] it[.] he said he would run the cosequences [sic] any how.

---

[318] W. S. Boothe letter, August 15, 1862, Pearce Civil War Collection, Navarro College, Corsicana, Texas. This letter points out their new regimental designation and was sent to: Mrs. Mary A. Boothe, Tarkington Prairie, Cole Springs P. O., Polk County Texas; also marked via Hun[t]svill[e]. Hereafter cited as W. S. Boothe letters, with date.

Horton went on to advise that he'd been sick ever since entering the military, and sadly, he died not long afterward while in an enemy POW camp at St. Louis, Missouri.[319]

During these trying times, Lt. J. D. Lum of Co. B, officially now called the 25th Texas, on August 22 had, though sick with a cold and sore throat, been back in his roles of acting drillmaster, and "am drilling the men from morning until Knight (sic)." Though many of his comrades yet remained sick with the measles, many were getting well, though "some are quite weak yet." The regiment, moreover, was expected to ". . . leave these camps next Wednesday and go on toward Little Rock . . . ." He finished his missive by admonishing his wife to remain vigilant toward their offspring: "Tell Emmitt and Pat to be good boys and obey you, and Lizzy and Mat to be sweet girls for me; they must Kiss the baby for me, and you must Kiss them all." At this point, all future correspondence should be addressed including their new 25th Texas Cavalry designation.[320]

As the three regiments began to arrive near Pine Bluff, they discovered signs posted upon trees along the route being traveled, as well as handbills everywhere advising that Carter's regiments would be dismounted upon reaching that city. In a remarkable response to this seeming lack of justice, Carter would pocket those orders and continue on until reaching the camps of Col. William Parsons' Texas Cavalry brigade, where he arranged to keep his regiment mounted and attached to that command. In the final analysis, this perhaps left both Wilkes' and Gillespie's men pondering as to who had gotten the final laugh on whom. For soon after reaching Pine Bluff, the 24th and 25th Texas Cavalry (Dismounted) found themselves afoot and assigned to a brigade in the command of Col. Robert Garland at Camp Holmes. He was to personally see to the conversion of these cavalrymen to infantrymen, utilizing his own regiment, the 6th Texas

---

[319] www.civilwarbull.org/forum/messages/4340 & 4342.

[320] J. D. Lum, August 22, 1862, Texas Confederate Museum Collection # TCM 94.30.7, Haley Memorial Library & History Center, Midland, Texas. Hereafter cites as Lum letters, date, and collection # 94.30.]\

Infantry, as the nucleus around which to integrate the dismounted cavalrymen.[321]

Thus, by midsummer, seven of the eight organizations that would afterward compose Granbury's Texas Infantry Brigade (the 7th Texas Infantry being the 8th, still languishing in Northern prison camps), had begun to coalesce in Central Arkansas. All of them would spend the next few months either engaged in peripheral activities or assigned to camps of instruction, each receiving the rigorous training necessary to instill discipline and perfect their tactics. For the moment, Garland's brigade would remain outside Pine Bluff, though they too would have their moments as fall came on.[322]

But even as Garland's command underwent its formal organization at Camp Holmes, closer to Little Rock, Col. Allison Nelson's 10th Texas Infantry, Col. George Sweet's 15th, Col. William Fitzhugh's 16th, Col. William Taylor's 17th, and Col. Darnell's 18th Texas Cavalry found themselves, almost immediately after arriving there in May, sent to stem MG Samuel Curtis' advance upon the capital. Ultimately, Nelson would receive orders to organize a second infantry brigade centered upon his own 10th Texas Infantry, which was to incorporate Sweet's 15th Texas Cavalry, Taylor's 17th Texas Cavalry, and Darnell's 18th Texas Cavalry.

At Little Rock, MG Thomas C. Hindman had hurriedly made the decision by mid-May to send the recently arriving Texas Cavalry regiments northeast of the capital and to report to BG Albert Rust, who had standing orders to somehow harass and cut off any and every detachment sent out by MG Samuel Curtis in his quest to obtain forage and foodstuffs in order to supply his famished army because of an overextended supply line. This would act to bring these Texans into their first actual combat with an enemy, and it was hoped they would make the best of it. On Rust's front, several skirmishes had already occurred in an area near Searcy and beyond on the Little Red River road that led to Batesville. On the 19th and 21st, skirmishes had been engaged in an effort to slow, if not halt,

---

[321] *O.R.*, vol. 4, pt. 1, p. 209, issued as G. O. # 26, July 9, 1862.

[322] *Texas in the War*, pp. 117-19.

Curtis' thrust southward. These actions would be but the prelude to more extensive operations that were to follow in coming months.[323]

In essence, then, Arkansas would see the transformation of two sizeable Texas forces in the eastern part of the state: one centered around Little Rock attempting to protect the city against Curtis' forays coming via the northeast, and the other occurring due to the posting of a Texas Brigade near Pine Bluff for the purpose of defending the Arkansas River below Little Rock from any enemy force approaching the southeast. Each command would employ the opportunity to profit from two seasoned infantry regiments around which it was expected that two new brigades would come into existence. A very illuminating element is that all three regiments of Garland's regiments had originated for the most part in South Texas, while all of Nelson's regiments came from the northwestern part of the state. Therefore, though almost all Texans for most of their service, each regiment had its own subculture based upon where it originated, as will be seen. The two infantry regiments, having been longer in service and obviously more systematically trained and better drilled at this time, would serve as valuable anchors around which the remaining dismounted cavalry regiments must coalesce.

Up in Chicago, meanwhile, and all across many of the Northern states by now, stalwart veterans of the 7th Texas Infantry yet languished in stifling prison "pens" that spring and summer, following their embarrassing surrender at Ft. Donelson the previous February. With the rank and file held at Camp Douglas in Chicago, and a majority of their officers housed first at Camp Chase, Columbus, Ohio, or afterward on Johnson's Island on Lake Ontario (where they had been forwarded after a time), mere survival seemed

---

[323] Ronald A. Mosocco. *The Chronological Tracking of the American Civil War per the Official Records of the War of the Rebellion.* Williamsburg, Va. James River Publications. 1994. Hereafter cited as Chronological Tracking, with page #.

to be uppermost in virtually every soldier's mind. Only through surviving would there be the prospect for one day returning to the Southland, where they could only await an opportunity to expunge their reputation and dispense justice to those who had accorded them the barbaric treatment that had needlessly, in their opinion, been inflicted on them. By now, they had withstood their test by fire on those cold, barren hills outside Ft. Donelson, and seen many a comrade succumb to an even more horrid death than they had experienced in the form of a slow, excruciating demise in Northern hands. Many had perished, and many more would not last until their exchange, thus leaving many a surviving comrade dedicated to somehow wreak revenge. For the present, driven by their passion to exact retribution against a foe they deemed detestable, most could hardly await exchange.[324]

---

[324] For a record of the deaths in the 7th Texas Infantry while at Camp Douglas, see *Confederate States Soldiers and Sailors*, appended at the end of this volume. Also, see the letters of Col. John Gregg and Maj. Hiram Granbury sent out from Ft. Warren, Boston Harbor, where these two officers were separately held.

Thomas F. Bates
Private Co. D 6th Texas Infantry

Jonah Pickle
Private 18th Texas Cavalry
Courtesy Austin History Center

James Alexander Westmoreland
Private Co. E 17th Texas Cavalry
Dismounted

William Michael (Billy) Westmoreland
Private 17th Texas Cavalry
Dismounted

James A. Hughes (post war image)
Co. K, 10th Texas Infantry
Courtesy of Cheryl Abbott

Captain John Johnson, Co. A,
15th Texas Cavalry
Courtesy of Gary Ritchie

Brigadier General John Gregg
Courtesy Southern Methodist University,
DeGolyer Library, Central University
Libraries

Brigadier General Hiram B. Granbury

To see more images please visit http://tiny.cc/SessumsPinterest

A Confusing State of Affairs

One extraordinary scene greeted the novice Texas regiments reaching Arkansas during the late spring and early summer months of 1862. Just prior to their arrival, MG Earl Van Dorn had withdrawn virtually all disposable troops in Arkansas to cross the Mississippi in order to bolster Gen. Albert S. Johnston's army already withdrawing from Kentucky and Tennessee into northern Mississippi. This left Arkansas wide open to Curtis' Yankee army, which had moved across the northern parts of the state and now threatened to move south via the White and Black rivers to attack Little Rock from the northeast. A token Confederate force existed in the Little Rock area, while a diminutive force lay at Ft. Smith in the wake of the Pea Ridge disaster, suffered from both embarrassment and disorganization, and it would be months before it once again became a viable military force.[325]

Even if brutally reinforced, the recently initiated conscription law would take quite some time to bring in additional forces, and in Arkansas, these would prove to be both indifferently armed and inadequately trained, most being devoid of even the simplest military skills. Van Dorn's departure had no doubt prompted Curtis to advance toward Central Arkansas and thus threaten the capital itself. On May 5, his army had advanced to Batesville, only ninety miles from the city; he reported a seasoned army of 12,422 men prepared to take the capital. Prior to leaving Arkansas, Van Dorn had placed BG Oscar Roane in charge of gathering a mixed bag of troops with which to hold Central Arkansas until anticipated reinforcements could arrive from Texas and the conscripted Arkansans could be brought to bear. It appeared that little short of a miracle must transpire in order to avert disaster in the state, and the residents

---

[325] *The Civil War*, I, p. 556-8.

looked to Texas as the most expedient resource to come to their aid.[326]

Meanwhile, hamstrung by a tortuous supply line that stretched all the way back to Rolla in central Missouri, Curtis had painstakingly continued to advance until by mid-month; his forward elements had come to within fifty miles of the capital. At this latter place, harried state officials accused the national authorities of having abandoned the state, and if something were not done, and quickly, the state might just abandon the cause and drop out of the conflict. Amidst a flurry of angry letters and telegrams, going one way for the most part, earnest appeals came from the few officials who still remained within the capital. The War Department in Richmond had belatedly responded by assigning a native son, MG Thomas C. Hindman, to take over command of the entire state.[327]

Hindman had reached Little Rock on May 31 to hurriedly assess the potential for holding the capital, correctly guessing that the traditional means for going on the offensive were, simply put, not at hand. Van Dorn had not only taken away the army but had stripped the state of every available resource with which to make war, leaving a logistical nightmare for Hindman, even if he were able to field an army. He knew that until more help arrived, he could only adopt an aggressive defensive-offensive strategy, based as much upon ruse as substance, confusing Curtis so that he could hang on to the state until resources from beyond its borders could be brought to bear.[328]

As his first order of business, Hindman declared martial law, despite understanding that this might raise the ire of a populace not openly supportive of war in the first place. He next urgently requested support, in the form of men and material, from surrounding states, as well as from the other side of the Mississippi. Finally, in what appeared to be an act of desperation, he ordered the forcible enrollment by conscription of every able-bodied male within the state, ordering the establishment of camps of instruction and

---

[326] *Ibid.*, vol. I, pp. 556-8.

[327] *Ibid.*, p. 556. Also, see *O.R.*, I, vol. X, pt. 1, pp. 373 & 405 for Union operations at this time, and p. 830 for Enclosure #2, wherein Hindman assumed command.

[328] *O.R.*, I, vol. 10, pt. 1, pp. 29-36, Report of MG T. C. Hindman.

converting every scrap of materiel that could be adapted to equip those troops being raised. And it was during these critical first weeks of his tenure that so many Texas commands, including the 6th and 10th Texas Infantry, 15th, 17th, and 18th Texas Cavalry, and the 24th and 25th Texas Cavalry (Dismounted) came within his control.[329]

With Little Rock serving as the physical hub of the state due to its central location, this meant it might be attacked from virtually every direction, except the southwest. Curtis might well continue to sweep down from the northeast, as just as easily, an enemy force could do the same from the northwest part of the state. And, in the wake of the loss of Memphis soon after Hindman's arrival, enemy gunboats could at any time steam up the Arkansas River and attack the capital from either the east or southeast. In fact, it had already been reported that a Union navy flotilla had sounded the mouth of the White River, ostensibly determining whether they might steam up that stream to link up with Curtis' army marching south from Batesville.[330]

With Pine Bluff situated on the Arkansas some fifty miles southeast of Little Rock, that area could serve as a staging area from which to guard against movements advancing from the southeast. And it's highly likely that just such a prospect had led to the posting of Garland's 6th Texas Infantry, soon after augmented by Wiles' 24th and Gillespie's 25th Texas Cavalry (Dismounted), to serve as a blocking force against an enemy advance from that direction. And while serving in that capacity, it would allow the two dismounted regiments to profit from an association with the more-seasoned infantrymen in Garland's regiment, but admittedly, all three still needed more time to become adept at soldiering.

The more immediate threat, however, remained northeast of the capital, where Curtis' snail-like approach required the greater amount of attention, and thus Gen. Hindman next turned his attention

---

[329] *Ibid.*, p. 34. One indication of the dire straits Hindman had to resort to was the uprooting of several condemned artillery tubes at the Little Rock Arsenal, having them wrenched from the ground and mounted on home-made gun-carriages.

[330] Thomas Snead, "Conquest of Arkansas," *Battles & Leaders*, 3, pp. 441-61.

in that direction. Unfortunately, the only immediate means he had at hand was a mixed bag of Arkansas and Texas, along with just-arrived Texas units and others supposed to be on the way. He must somehow slow Curtis' advance until such time as his new levies and the out-of-state units could be brought into the field. To accomplish this object, Hindman began in late May to dispatch a patchwork force of "rackensackers" and the recently arrived cavalry units at and east of Little Rock to go pounding up the dusty country lanes in the direction of Searcy and Batesville, bearing orders as well to scout well beyond both points. All had orders to verify the enemy's positions, to probe for all possible weak points, and try to fix the enemy columns, thereby stalling Curtis' movements through a disruption of his overextended supply lines. So dire were the consequences that Hindman called for the "killing [of] cattle, ripping the carcasses open and throwing them in" rivers, creeks, and bayous to prevent the enemy's access to potable water.[331]

On the Federal side, Curtis had only recently wired Washington of his success in winning over many locals in this part of the state; he reported that "the people [hereabouts] . . . are [now] disposed to yield" for re-establishing national authority. Curtis proclaimed that "a provisional government is desired, and as soon as we can occupy and hold Little Rock, some arrangement should be made to establish . . . civil power [there]." Made aware of Curtis' statements, Hindman realized he had to aggressively act to confuse and defeat Curtis' far-flung detachments until more forces could be brought to bear to drive the enemy completely out of the state. Should that be accomplished, Hindman hoped to then throw his mounted forces onto the tenuous supply line in Curtis' rear, with the hope that Curtis might well abandon the entire campaign.[332]

Already, Capt. Alf Johnson's Spy Co. from Texas had set out earlier in May for Des Arc, ostensibly to verify Curtis' movements in the White River area. After a thorough scouting of the area, Johnson had advised Hindman that Curtis' supply line could be easily

---

[331] *Ibid.,* also, *The Civil War,* vol. I, p. 557.

[332] *O.R.,* I, vol. 13, p. 373, in which Curtis advised that his advance would reach Searcy by nightfall on May 9. He expressed concerns as well for a supply line that stretched all the way back to Rolla, Missouri.

disrupted by hard-riding cavalry detachments who could sever enemy supply lines at virtually any point, and should it not force Curtis' withdrawal, it would at least force him to send additional units out to protect his line of communications. And it was while thus engaged in this reconnaissance that Johnson's Spy Co. on May 21 had engaged the enemy in a rather sharp contest, in which the Texans lost only a single man.[333]

With his reconnaissance concluded, Hindman now sent his disposable cavalry forces into the White River basin; most of these were the new Texas regiments just in from the Lone Star State. Col. William Taylor's 17th Texas Cavalry broke camp May 26; he'd been ordered to scout the area in and around Searcy and report his arrival there to Col. William Parsons of the 12th Texas Cavalry. Through Special Order #7, issued June 4, Parsons had advised: "1st. That all citizens above Des Arc Bayou are hereby required to haul with the aid of their own teams and negroes their supplies [of] corn & bacon South of said Bayou," and 2nd: "Col. [William] Taylor will take prompt steps to enforce the order – by compulsion if necessary." A follow-up directive, Special Order #11 on the same date, announced that "Major [John] McClarty commanding detachment of [Col. William] Taylor's 17th Texas Cavalry at Austin will bring every available man in his command & all commissary stores in his possession" to the vicinity of Searcy valley.[334]

Col. Sweet's 15th Texas Cavalry regiment had soon after followed the 17th Texas Cavalry northward, moving out in the same direction on June 4. The men had to travel through dust "so thick you can't see the men before you," according to one private. Having left their tents and cooking equipage behind, the men had to subsist on green apples as their only fare during much of this march, these being the only in-season edibles at the time, as numerous orchards

---

[333] *O.R.*, I, vol. 13, p. 35; also, see "The Flavius Perry Letters", *Military History of Texas and the Southwest*, vol. 13, # 2, p. 16, relating to Johnson's engagement. Raised in Collin County in 1861, the "Spy" Co. had initially been composed of 160 men. For a brief history of its formation and early service, see the *Houston Telegraph*, May 7, 1862.

[334] Anne J. Bailey, ed. In the Saddle with the Texans; Day-By-Day with Parsons's Cavalry Brigade, 1862-1865. Abiline, Texas. McWhiney Foundation Press. 2004. Hereafter cited as *In the Saddle with the Texans*.

dotted the roadside along which they passed. Advised they'd be serving under the command of an Arkansan, BG Albert Rust, Sweet penned a letter on the 11th to the *San Antonio Weekly Herald* of his first meeting with the new commander: "Brigadier General A. Rust commands us at this time, a clever gentleman and good officer; but the boys are quite clamorous for a Texas Brigadier and Maj. Gen to command them – a very natural feeling of state pride, but I have no doubt they will do as good fighting under any other man."[335]

After several days spent scouting the enemy in the vicinity of Searcy, Rust began to rendezvous his forces near that place; at least six regiments of Texas cavalry reached there by June 8. This included not only Parsons' own 12th Texas Cavalry and Col. George Sweet's 15th Texas Cavalry, but Col. William Fitzhugh's 16th Texas Cavalry, Col. William Taylor's 17th Texas Cavalry, and Col. Nicholas Darnell's 18th Texas Cavalry. The 17th Texas had previously found itself engaged in a sharp skirmish on the Little Red River June 6, upon encountering a picket post of Co. L, 3rd Illinois Cavalry; the Texans scattered the Union troops in this affair. Sweet's 15th Texas Cavalry had likewise encountered and fought a small enemy party just beyond the Little Red River, as Union troops tried to draw Sweet's men into an ambush on the east bank.[336]

For its part, whether by luck or sheer ignorance, Sweet's 15th Texas Cavalry had found scant opposition when the regiment cautiously probed fords stretching down the Little Red beyond Searcy on the main road leading to Batesville. Not quite as fortunate,

---

[335] William Young letter of June 12, 1862, CRC, Hill College; *In the Saddle With the Texans*, p. 32, published July 5, 1862.

[336] *O.R.*, I, 13, p. 103, report of Capt. David R. D. Sparks to Col. McCrillis, from Fairview; also, see Norman Delaney, ed., "Diary and Memoirs of Marshall Samuel Pierson, Company C, 17th Regt. Texas Cavalry, 1862-1865," in *Military History of Texas and the Southwest*, 13 (1975), p. 26. Hereafter cited as *Military History of Texas*. Separate accounts of these events are also found in John Q. Anderson, ed., Campaigning with Parsons's Texas Cavalry Brigade, C.S.A.: The War Journal and Letters of the Four Orr Brothers, 12th Texas Cavalry Regiment. Hillsboro, Texas: Hill Jr. College Press. 1967, pp. 47-53. The writer, from the 12th Texas Cavalry, had two brothers who had recently enlisted in Darnell's 18th Texas Cavalry, specifically mentioning the 15th, 17th and 18th Texas, in addition to his own, the 12th Texas Cavalry, as being in that area. Hereafter cited as *Campaigning with Parsons's*, along with the page #.

Taylor's 17th Texas Cavalry had gotten itself engaged in a wild, freewheeling engagement that had shifted first one way, then another as Union reinforcements sent to the scene of their skirmish taught the Texans an important lesson about proper reconnaissance not far from the 17th's contest. Their first taste of combat proved pivotal in one respect, however, as the soldiers on both sides seemed as astounded by the sudden appearance of each other as they were over the outcome. Wrote a captain in the 17th Texas to his wife on June 10:

> I have just had the pleasure of seeing a yankee [sic] and smelling [gun]powder. Just as I sat down for dinner, our pickets came in with news that they had been fired upon at the river, four miles from town. (It was amusing to see some of the boys with pale faces running to me complaining of being sick and not able to go.) Crossing the river, we hear that there were two battalions formed . . . . When they began firing on us, we was [were] ordered to fire one barrel of our [shot]guns, and to reserve the other for the charge. . . . [The] Yanks [now took] to running like frightened mustangs through a wheat-field.[337]

Only one wing of the 17th actually got into this action, the other wing not reaching the battlefield until well after the contest had ended. A member of this latter wing, Pvt. Marshall Pierson of Co. C, wrote of the high anxiety everyone felt as they tried to learn the whereabouts of the other wing:

> The night being so dark, we missed the road [over which the advance had traveled] . . . Those in the rear guard galloped first in one direction, then another, halting every now and again to strike a match and observe whether hoof-print[s] indicated that a body of men had recently advanced along the road they were on: We had attained [such] a state of wildness, until one among them suggested they fire

---

[337] Bryan Marsh in *Chronicles*, vol. 14, #2, p. 11.

a gun and await an answering signal. Straining their ears, some thought they heard a faint reply way off in the distance. Now signaled as to the regiment's location, the men rejoined it, thinking themselves indeed lucky not to have stumbled onto the enemy in the darkness.[338]

On the next day, the as-yet-untested wing finally got its opportunity to "smell gun smoke," displaying their abilities in a brief encounter in the same general area. Crossing the Little Red to the north bank, they soon found an enemy detachment posted along both sides of a narrow road down which the Texans rode in a column, their scouts advising the enemy apparently ready for a fight: "Going on them like a whirlwind," as one cavalryman stated it afterward. All simultaneously charged, screaming "that peculiar Texas yell to the utmost of his ability." The enemy did not stand long, unceremoniously withdrawing from the field and "leaving [their] wagons and teams, commissaries, etc., behind," this provoking one Texas participant to exclaim: "Old Abe's [Lincoln] boys had better look out, and [we] thought it was a great pity there were not more of our sort in the Confederate . . . army."[339]

Satiated by their initial success, the men of the 17th Texas soon after rode westward, passing through a beautiful, mountainous country in neighboring Van Buren County. Here they and their horses rested, and an officer thought this an appropriate time to rid his company of men he felt wanting in the recent skirmishes. Capt. Bryan Marsh of Co. C wrote that he sought discharges for many men, "not for [their] inability to perform military duty," he declared, "but because they are too cowardly to belong to so good a company [as this]."[340]

All too soon, this respite came to an end and the now-rested troops moved back eastward to resume active operations, unaware apparently that their presence in Van Buren County had been made

---

[338] *Military History of Texas*, vol. 13, p. 26.

[339] *Ibid.* See also, *One of Cleburne's Command:* p. xxxiii.

[340] *Chronicles*, vol. 14, #2, p. 12.

known to a small Union force also operating there. Lt. Ferdinand Hansen of the 5th Missouri Cavalry reported to his superiors that: "Texas Rangers had been in this neighborhood, and . . . they were expected to return soon." That this proved not to be the case came through a relieved message from him that the "feared Texas Rangers moved off to the east."[341]

On June 20, the 15th Texas Cavalry was gathered together at the direction of Col. Sweet, who gave them a dramatic speech, bringing it to an end by stating "we are going to punish the enemy this very day, even if we have to go right into Batesville and pull old Curtis' beard till he gets mad enough to entertain us in a war-like manner." Lt. Robert M. Collins of Co. B led the fifteen-man detachment sent out as advance guards, and they came up to a mountaineer's cabin, the old man living there greeting them with a query: "Whose critter company is this and who commands it?" After pausing only briefly enough to enjoy a short companionship with several of his red-haired daughters and partake of a sparse fare, the regiment proceeded on toward Batesville. Nearing there, they encountered a mounted enemy vidette, who fled into the neighboring town to sound the alarm. Collins' men intently listened to the beating of the long roll by Union drummers and the blaring of bugle calls that indicated they just might be up against a formidable force. This disparity in numbers quickly convinced these "Texicans," as the old mountain man had called them, that they might better beat a hasty retreat, Collins dryly noting this to have been done "in what is called in military parlance double quick time."[342]

BG Roane had recalled Taylor's 17th Texas Cavalry to the Batesville area as well; this resulted in a grueling thirty-six-hour march for the regiment to arrive there. Roane had need for every man to implement a plan to capture this strategic hamlet. It was speculated that Curtis had opted to cross over and move down the east bank of the White River, apparently with the hope of linking up with a U.S. gunboat flotilla that had supposedly entered the White and was steaming upstream to link up with Curtis. Toward the end of June, Rust matured plans to first encircle, and then to destroy, any force

---

[341] *O.R.*, I, vol. 13, pp. 128-9.

[342] *Chapters*, pp. 35-7.

still remaining in the White-Cache rivers area. By this time, Sweet's 15th Texas Cavalry had actually preceded Taylor's 17th Texas into Batesville, and Col. Sweet extolled this occasion in a rambling report published July 15: "I entered the town of Batesville in the afternoon of Wednesday, July 2, the town having been evacuated on June 30. Having entertained hopes of intercepting Brig. General Cadwallader Washburn's Illinois Cavalry Brigade, supposedly moving south to augment Curtis' forces." Sweet had quickly lost his nerve and "withdrew my command to Puddell's Mill." Upon returning to Batesville the following day, his regiment "destroyed twenty ambulances and wagons left by the Federals, [for] I had not time to get teams and take them away." Though having missed Washburn's column completely, nevertheless, a fifty-man detachment on July 5 seized another small train of wagons near Sulphur Rock, burning "ten wagons loaded with United States Sutler goods on their way to Jacksonport."[343]

Meanwhile, Rust had decided to make a concentrated attack upon Curtis, utilizing at least five of these Texas Cavalry regiments. Gen. Hindman had ordered Rust "to resist the enemy to the last extremity, blockading roads, burning bridges, [and] destroying all supplies." When heavy rains prevented fording the White opposite Jacksonport, Rust's brigade moved downstream west of the river until reaching Des Arc. From that point, they would cross the Cache River and assault what was thought to be the head of Curtis' column at or beyond Cotton Plant. The units to be included by Rust would be Parsons' 12th Texas Cavalry, Sweet's 15th Texas Cavalry, Fitzhugh's 16th Texas Cavalry, Taylor's 17th Texas Cavalry, and Darnell's 18th Texas Cavalry. After getting across the Cache in the late evening hours of July 6, the Texans encamped only a few miles away from where Curtis' advance rested.[344]

The strategy was to entrap the enemy between two wings, pinch off retreat, and then destroy the enemy force. Unfortunately,

---

[343] *O.R Supplement*, vol. 13, pp. 33-4.

[344] Anne J. Bailey. *Between the Enemy and Texas: Parsons's Texas Cavalry Brigade in the Civil War*. Ft. Worth. T.C.U. Press. 1989. P. 67. The 18th Texas Cavalry had departed Washington, Arkansas on May 30th, "with various banners and fine looking horses [that] presented quite an imposing appearance."

the Battle of Cotton Plant, as Col. Parsons called it, or Cache River, as it came to be called by those in the 17th Texas Cavalry, went horribly awry. Parsons' force first encountered Col. Charles Hovey's 33rd Illinois Infantry, 1st Brigade, 1st Division, Army of the Southwest. Rust instructed Parsons to attack straight ahead upon the enemy column, which had just been augmented on the Federal side by several companies of the 11th Wisconsin Infantry, reinforced by a small-bore steel gun manned by the 1st Indiana Cavalry. But through a lack of coordination, the battle soon took on the makings of a disaster.[345]

Coming up immediately in the rear of the 12th Texas Cavalry was Taylor's 17th Texas Cavalry, whom Rust had instructed to make a grand circuit in order to get into the enemy rear, thereby cutting off a retreat. As Parsons' regiment confronted the head of Hovey's column, and the 17th Texas madly rose off to get into Hovey's rear, the 16th Texas Cavalry made it onto the field just in time to be thrown into line to join the fight. Taylor's 17th Texas had scarcely reached its intended position when gunfire off in the distance signaled that Roane had begun his frontal attack. Unfortunately, additional Union troops from the 1st and 2nd brigades arrived to augment Hovey's force, including a battalion of the 1st Indianan Cavalry bringing up two more of the steel guns, with Rust finally beginning to comprehend its predicament. Poor reconnaissance and insufficient coordination, combined with a rather obstinate defense by a well-concealed enemy in the midst of a cypress swamp, caused Roane to break off the fight, leaving Taylor's regiment perilously exposed at the enemy's rear. Mused one cavalryman in the 17th Texas about this sobering moment: "Then began the races, with our regiment for fifteen or twenty miles [galloping fast] to prevent being cut off, one horse fell from exhaustion, and [its] . . . rider outran every horse in the company . . . ." Neither of the other Texas regiments, the 15th under Sweet or Darnell's 18th, made it into action.[346]

---

[345] *O.R.*, I, 13, p. 37; *Between the Enemy and Texas*:, pp. 67-8.

[346] Capt. Bryan Marsh, Co. C, 17th Texas Cavalry, in *Chronicles*, vol. 14, #2, p. 14.

Remarkably, a 150-man detachment of Sweet's 15th Texas Cavalry had also gained an opportunity to "smell powder" as well; this occurred over a hundred miles away on July 8 near Paroquet Bluff on the Black River, just above Jacksonport. This blocking force had been left in north Arkansas in order to continue intercepting enemy supply trains moving south out of Missouri to reach Curtis' army. As Col. Sweet reported some four days after, having learned of the presence of an enemy force in the area, he had moved in the direction of Orient's Ferry on the 8th, "as rapidly as the excessive heat . . . and the jaded condition of the horses would permit, . . ." After sending a reconnoitering party ahead, he learned that the enemy "had no pickets out, and that we were right on the[ir] main body." This enemy force, also becoming aware of the Texans' approach, consisting of companies A, D, and K of the 5th Kansas Cavalry (already known derisively as "The Redlegs,"), and led by Capt. William Creitz of Co. A, all armed with Sharp's rifles, had deployed to either side of a narrow road that led down to a ferry crossing; the enemy also lay in wait in heavy brush all the way to the opposite side of the crossing.[347]

His men primarily armed with just percussion shotguns (Capt. Alsdorf Faulkner's only armed with sporting rifles), Sweet ordered his men to charge in a column of four abreast right down the road in an effort to drive the enemy away from the train. In the resulting melee, Sweet's horse was shot from under him, and he was forced to swing up behind Capt. Thomas Sherwood in a hail of bullets from enemy carbines just to escape. Just as quickly, the Texans bolted back up the road they had so brashly rushed down. Among the Texans killed during this contest was Capt. Tom Johnson of Tarrant County, shot through the head while leading his company in the charge. Sweet's total loss amounted to seven killed, another seven wounded, and the regiment losing twenty-two horses. Sweet appears to have been attempting to dampen an apparent defeat by stressing in his report the barbarity of the Kansans after the skirmish, though at the end of his report he at last admitted to losing the fight.

---

[347] *O.R. Supplement*, vol. 13, pp. 37-8, Col. Sweet reporting; also, see also *Chapters*, p. 37. Also, see http://www.encyclopediaofkansas.net for another account of this fight.

Of considerable import is a remark recorded later by a participant, Pvt. William Young of Co. A, who noted that although Sweet was on the field, "my opinion is that he was so confounded drunk he could not give a command."[348]

Gen. Hindman had afterward written about another skirmish by this regiment, apparently just prior to the Orient's Ferry fight, in what was the Texan's first true campaign:

> On June 24, certain information reached me that Curtis . . . was in motion . . . and [very near] destitute of supplies. To delay the enemy . . . , Sweet's Texan regiment was thrown across the [White] river above Batesville and fell upon his rear, killing, wounding and capturing over 200 Federals, and taking a number of wagons containing army stores and Sutler goods.[349]

With respect to the capture of this particular train, one of those involved reported afterward that the men enjoyed the "good life" for some days. This officer, Lt. Robert M. Collins of Co. B, reported the wagons had been headed for Jacksonport, and were loaded "to the guards with fancy wet groceries, ginger cakes, sardines, oysters, tobacco, boots, shoes, calico, spool thread, [and such things as] ladies hoop skirts." Obviously, this seemed a treasure

---

[348] William Young letter, July 20, 1862, CRC, Hill College; also *O.R. Supplement*, vol. 13, p. 40. See also Gregory Harmon, "5th Kansas Cavalry: A Photo Album," *Military Images*, vol. 4, (1984), p. 22-4; Sweet's report in *O.R. Supp*, I, vol. 10, pp. 38-9. The federal loss is reported as 1 drowned, 3 wounded, and another 3 missing, in http://www.encyclopediaofarkansas.net. Johnson's father traveled all the way from present-day Arlington, Texas, to retrieve his son's body, bringing him home for burial in a family plot just east of Cooper St. (Hwy. 157) and Spur 303.

[349] *O.R.*, I, 13, p. 36; contrast this to Sweet's report on both the recapture of Batesville, in *O.R. Supplement*, vol. 13, pp. 33-41.

to men who had recently been exposed to a Spartan existence while living in the saddle.[350]

After retaining the goods they could put to use, the cavalrymen elected to dole out the surplus items to civilians living in the vicinity of their camp. As a token of their appreciation, the locals hosted a lavish party for the cavalrymen, which proved a welcome event after weeks of hard service they had experienced. Word began to spread, however, that some of the younger soldiers used these goods as a means to entice some of the local farmgirls into supplying more affection than most deemed appropriate, which almost caused a scandal.[351]

Not surprisingly, during the time the 15th Texas occupied Batesville, several men who'd formerly been printers seized the presses of the pro-Union *Batesville Eagle*, publishing a decidedly pro-Southern edition directed toward the less-supportive readers in that vicinity. This brought about a howl of protests that provoked many a staunch Unionist to come in and cancel their subscriptions. In all likelihood, the only permanent injury done to the community came in the impact of this event upon the newspaper's business.[352]

Sweet's account of the Orient's Ferry fight, composed while at Batesville on July 15, substantially differed from the accounts of others who had been in that late fight. Lt. Collins of Co. B supplied a unique perspective, advising that the enemy cavalrymen had opened upon them with "both carbines and six-shooters," and, suddenly fearing for their own safety, the Texans "took to the woods." So disorganized had been their departure out of the river bottom, he said, that their horses made the "brush pop like a [stampeding] herd of longhorns . . . ."[353]

And Pvt. William Young of Co. A, who had earlier made rather unflattering remarks over his commander's role in this

---

[350] *Chapters*, p. 34; also, see William Young letter of July 20, 1862, William Young papers, CRC. Hill College; and note in *Chapters*, p. 38, Collins advises that eight wagons held Sutler stores, the remainder bearing military supplies.

[351] *Chapters*, p. 38.

[352] *Ibid.*, p. 40.

[353] *Ibid.*, p. 43.

skirmish, told in a letter how enemy "jayhawkers" had followed them off the field, killing several comrades who'd been seriously wounded and had to be left behind. Stories circulated that the "red-legs" had given no quarter, deliberately executing in cold blood every wounded soldier they came across. Some wounded who did survive ultimately rejoined the regiment, though the severity of wounds made further service improbable. Among these was Lt. R. W. Bannister of Co. B, who suffered wounds to both arms, one bullet splintering his right, disqualifying him from further service.[354]

And, according to William Dennis of Co. D, during the panicky retreat, Col. Sweet had tried to leap his horse across a huge bog, only to have the animal land right in the middle. His mount hopelessly bogged down, Dennis dismounted and let Sweet take his animal, with Dennis "jump[ing] up behind a comrade" in order to make good his own escape.[355]

Despite the many hardships incurred, Hindman's hit-and-run strategy had worked to disrupt Curtis' tenuous supply line, and in tandem with a failed naval expedition at St. Charles, where Union gunboats commanded by Lt. James W. Shirk were turned back on the lower White River, this ultimately led Curtis to abandon his present line and shift his base of operations toward Helena, Arkansas. If he safely reached there, he could rely on the Mississippi for both supplies and reinforcements, in the hope that he might use that place as a base from which to renew his advance on Little Rock; though this time he'd approach the city from almost due east. But the principal reason he advanced seemed to have been Shirk's inability to succor his army.[356]

---

[354] William Young letter, July 20, 1862, CRC, Hill College; see also *Chapters*, pp. 52-8.

[355] *Reminiscences:*, p. 184.

[356] It's interesting that the Cache River fight is listed as an action, as opposed to a skirmish in *Chronological Tracking*, p. 75; apparently denoting it as larger than the mere skirmishes preceding it in the weeks previous. This likely occurred because it involved brigade against brigade, rather than smaller parties. See *O.R.*, I, vol. 13, pp. 423-4, Report of Operations between MG Curtis and MG Grant. Also, see *O.R.*, I, vol. 13, pp. 35, 103, 114-5, 423.

Even as Hindman had sent the bulk of his Texas Cavalry regiments pounding northeast toward Batesville in his attempt to forestall Curtis' advance, he had similarly had to direct his attention eastward toward the Memphis-Helena area. For it was between these two communities (in staunchly Union hands) and Little Rock that a second campaign would be conducted. Between Memphis and Little Rock ran the only major rail system that had only come into existence just before the war, and at this time included two existing sections of rail lines existing within Arkansas. One segment ran eastward from Little Rock to DeVall's Bluff on the White River, approximately fifty miles in length. Another segment ran southwest from Memphis to the St. Francis River, about the same distance, and for about another fifty miles lay a third, unfinished section, that bridged many of the major streams and bayous running through that region. Realizing the need for a military force to be situated at the eastern terminus of the western line running from Little Rock to the White River, where the rail line terminated atop DeVall's Bluff, it was essential to have a blocking force in place at that point.[357]

Hindman had, upon becoming aware of the enemy's capabilities of moving up the White with a naval force to link up with Curtis, on June 11 ordered Col. Allison Nelson to move his own regiment, the 10th Texas Infantry, to Brownsville, midway between the capital and the bluff terminus. Just two days before, Nelson's regiment, numbering 40 officers and 767 enlisted men, had been issued 354 muskets and a similar number of equipages in the guise of leather accoutrements. This had been followed on the 11th by a second issue that included 413 muskets, bayonets, etc. Interestingly, this second issue included cartridge boxes, belts and plates, bayonets and scabbards, with gun slings, "for the men that have not [yet] received arms." Of special interest, the two issues included also 300 flints, 200 pistol caps, a hundred pistol cartridges, and one holster case. The requisitions had been approved by the regiment's ordnance officer, Lt. George Jewell; the only items now lacking were cartridges for the arms. The last transpired due to a lack of black powder locally, and neither lead shot not cartridge wrappers were available with which to fabricate ammunition. This led to an

---

[357] *Ibid.*

unnecessary delay in initiating the march Hindman ordered until he could acquire these items in Little Rock.[358]

At last, having finally supplied the later, Nelson had his regiment ferried across the Arkansas on the morning of June 12, the men making an initial march the next day to reach Post Oak Flat. After an especially grueling, dusty eight-mile march on the 13th, the regiment reached Bayou Metoe on the 14th. There the regiment rested on Sunday, the 15th, before continuing on to reach Brownsville, where the men underwent a thorough weapons inspection, including their boxes and knapsacks. The regiment next continued on to DeVall's Bluff; this required a forced march of just over thirty-five miles in about twenty-four hours.[359]

It was as they were marching toward Devall's Bluff that Nelson's regiment encountered several Texas Cavalry regiments belonging to Gen. Rust's brigade, who may well have been moving toward that same point. On June 22, Capt. W. H. Getzendaner of the 12th Texas Cavalry sent a letter to a friend in Texas that he had watched as the 10th Texas Infantry passed them by: "Nelson's Regiment is the pride of Texas, few are sick and the men are stout, strong and hearty[,] and begin to look like and have the step of veterans. Texas may back her honor on them. Colonel Nelson is the Lion wherever he goes in Ark."[360]

Hardly had the 10th reached the Bluffs than Nelson received orders to split his command in order to place them aboard several steamers standing to at the levee, to make a hurried trip downstream toward St. Charles. He was to bolster the small garrison of sailors that manned a small earthen fort situated in a bend of the lower

---

[358] List of Ordnance Returns supplied this writer by Scott McKay from Ordnance Returns, RG 109, NA.

[359] *O.R.*, I, vol. 13, p. 836; also, see James Hurst diary entries, June 13-15, CRC, Hill College; also, *The Bugle:*, p. 11; and Isaiah Harlan letter of June 23, 1862, CRC, Hill College; as well as Roger Q. Mills' letter of June 15, 1862, from Bayou Metoe, State Archives, Austin.

[360] Letter copy acquired through Anne Bailey, and copied from a previous volume written on Parsons's 12th Texas Cavalry (source unknown), but is shown as p. 99. The date was wrongly ascribed to being written January 22, rather than its actual date of June 22, 1862.

White River. Because of snafus, one gunboat and a transport had already gone downstream; this caused Nelson to split his regiment into its wings. Five of the companies were to remain at the bluffs, while the remaining five would have to depart on several smaller steamers making ready to go downstream. Nelson would personally lead the advance of two companies, on one steamer, leaving three others to follow aboard a second transport expected in shortly from downriver to carry them down to St. Charles. The second party would be commanded by Lt. Col. R. Q. Mills, who would trail Nelson aboard a second boat that could handle the other three. It being late in the evening before the first vessel got underway, it would have to make a tortuous 120-mile trip, the Texans aboard thinking they might quickly witness their first taste of combat since arriving in Arkansas earlier that month. Lt. Col. Mills thought the men's morale about his boat appeared appropriate, even if they seemed rather anxious.[361]

    The steamers had barely gotten underway, however, when heavy rains and gale-force winds forced the vessels to heave to and drop anchor for the night; the sailors had to lash their steamers to trees along the levee in an effort to keep from being thrown against the banks or swept uncontrollably downstream in the dark. Long before daylight, the lead steamer, bearing Nelson's companies, sped on downstream, leaving Mills' transport trailing behind at a much slower pace. Aboard Mills' steamer, the captain constantly pleaded with the Texan to authorize his turning back, declaring frankly that Nelson's boat had likely been either taken captive, or worse, sunk. His dogged determinedness, coupled with Mills' suggestion of the use of force if need be, forced the captain to hesitatingly continue down, though not without heightening the tension already growing amongst the soldiers.[362]

    Unbeknownst to those aboard Mills' boat, on approaching St. Charles and learning the post there had likely surrendered already,

---

[361] Lt. Col. R. Q. Mills letter, June 23, 1862, State Archives, Austin. Also, see a letter dated June 22, and signed only as "T.J.S.," published in the *Tri-Weekly Telegraph*, Houston, July 21, 1862, State Archives, p. 1, columns 4 & 5.

[362] *Ibid.*; Isaiah Harlan letter of June 23, 1862, CRC, Hill College; *The Bugle:*, p. 12.

Nelson decided to turn around and go back upstream to join up with Mills' boat. Unaware of this, aboard Mills' vessel, there was suddenly the plaintive cry of: "Smoke!" It was readily apparent that another steamer was fast closing on them from the direction of St. Charles, with only a river bend separating the two vessels.[363]

By now, with his own men having reached a state of near-panic, Mills had the presence of mind to order his companies to load their muskets and take whatever shelter could be found aboard the steamer. Without awaiting an order to do so, the vessel's captain had the engines quickly reversed, putting on all possible steam in his quest to save his threatened ship. Proceeding upstream only a few miles, virtually consuming his remaining firewood in the process and with boiler pressure beginning to rapidly fall, the captain hove to on the east bank, demanding Mills unload his companies, the best guess of everyone being that they were somewhere in the vicinity of Clarendon.[364]

The men hurried ashore to conceal themselves amidst trees and underbrush lining the steep banks, the almost unnerved soldiers now apparently awaiting their fate, for surely the enemy could not be far behind. Much to their chagrin, and embarrassment, when the trailing steamer came chugging around the bend, they could see that it was the one bearing Nelson and his two companies. Obviously, they had not been captured, or sunk, but being short on firewood, Nelson decided to land both companies and immediately send a dispatch to DeVall's Bluff ordering the remaining five companies, along with their train, to march down and meet him on the road leading from Reagan's Bluff to DeVall's.[365]

Exhausted and dispirited, Nelson and Mills' companies spent a miserable night under the stars in a rather muddy bottomland. With fires not allowed and most of the men with few rations in their haversacks, they nervously awaited the arrival of their enemy. They had hastily dropped knapsacks and bedrolls upon offloading, and

---

[363] *Ibid.; ibid.*

[364] *The Bugle:*, p. 13. "T.J.S," in *The Tri-Weekly Telegraph*, July 21, 1862.

[365] *O.R.*, I, vol. 10, pt. 1., p. 836. A map of this area can be seen in *Military Atlas*, as Plate CLIV.

these had been carried atop the levee and placed in shacks, after which they lay down in the muck to try and get some rest. They were roused well before dawn, and details were sent up to retrieve their baggage, after which the companies fell in for the tortuous trek that would see them return to DeVall's Bluff. Soldiers wrote that the mud ran from ankle- to over knee-deep, besides being slippery, making this a trying march, especially the first six miles needed to reach the Clarendon road intersection.[366]

The five companies of the regiment that had departed DeVall's Bluff, meanwhile, also had a hard march to make in the mud, the men moving downstream at the quick-step. Accompanying this column was the regimental train, bearing a mix of rations and ordnance stores, one among them decrying that: "we distance anything in the shape of horseflesh, out travel a cavalry regiment from Texas, and come one hundred miles out of our way" to at last overtake the remaining wing. The wagons were not able to keep up, and as a consequence, the entire regiment spent that first night out sleeping on their arms and having "no supper, no blankets, and the nights here in these damp thick woods are really chilly." The following day saw the reunited regiment ford the river at a point known as Pyburn's Bluff, where they awaited the enemy gunboats' arrival. When the boats didn't appear, the regiment retraced its steps to reach the bluff.[367]

By the time the regiment reached DeVall's Bluff, the men were in a foul mood, miffed at what they thought to have been a monumental miscue, attributing this recent fiasco as the result of bad management on someone's behalf. After their return, Nelson assumed overall command of the troops there, as several additional regiments had come in, with Lt. Col. Mills taking command of the 10th Texas Infantry. Over sixty feet above the water, the bluffs provided a commanding downstream view, from whence they anxiously awaited the enemy's gunboats at any moment. Further

---

[366] Roger Q. Mills' letter, June 23, 1862, State Archives, Austin; also, *The Bugle:*, p. 13.

[367] "T.J.S." in *The Tri-Weekly Telegraph*, July 21, 1862. This writer notes they by this time had designated themselves as the "walkers, for we can outwalk any other regiment in the service!"

exacerbation occurred when, immediately after their return, the men found themselves having to throw up a series of rifle pits atop the bluff in expectation of the enemy's arrival. Worn out physically strength, as well as spiritually, they took to what they felt to be demeaning work, especially as this occurred on what one of the infantrymen declared to be a "very warm day." After working hard all day to finish this work, now "hungry and tired [from] lying in the sun" all day, they waited throughout the evening for an enemy that never showed. A meager meal prompted further grumbling, after which they returned to the works "and slept on our arms . . . for the first time since . . . [entering the] service."[368]

Just how tenuous Hindman's efforts to gather an armed force at this point is readily seen in considering Capt. William Hart's Dallas Artillery; that battery was dispatched, along with other troops, to DeVall's Bluff for service. On June 17, Hindman had ordered Col. Francis Shoup to proceed from Little Rock to the bluff, taking with him the 1st Trans-Mississippi Infantry regiment, along with Daniel's Lamar Artillery and Hart's Co. of Artillery. Shoup was to accompany them there, and "if Col. (Allison) Nelson is not [there], should assume overall command." Upon reporting himself, he otherwise would act as Nelson's second in command. On the 30th, Nelson had written Hindman's assistant adjutant general, William Nelson, that the three heavy guns Shoup had brought with him had been put in place a half-mile south of the depot and that he had sent one of Capt. Daniel's field guns five miles downriver to Pyburn's Bluff as a signal gun in case the enemy came up. This single gun was apt to be the first to face the enemy, but in any case, it could provide some forewarning to those further up. Nelson's report noted that he had completed some 400 yards of entrenchments; these ran in a semicircular arc atop the highest elevation.[369]

---

[368] The *Tri-Weekly Telegraph*, July 21, 1862; also *The Bugle:*, p. 13.

[369] See https://wikepedia.org/wiki.2nd_Ark_Field_Battery.Harts Battery. Also, see Danny Odom's posting "Re: Arms Brought Out by Capt. Hart," in Arkansas in the Civil War Message Board, posted 12/8/2013. # 28884 and Missouri Heritage Hosted Collections, Copybook of Telegraphic Instructions from [General] T. [C.] Hindman, Little Rock. Hart's battery had three sections, two of them 10-pound Parrotts, and one being six-pounder guns.

That the Federals had indeed come very close to engaging the Confederates posted at the bluff can be seen in a series of reports provided by a Union colonel, Graham N. Fitch of the 46th Indiana, when aboard the steamer *White Cloud* as part of the Indiana Brigade that steamed toward the bluff in early July. According to the regimental history, the 46th, along with the 24th Indiana, had occupied Clarendon before moving on to Aberdeen, less than a dozen miles below DeVall's. In fact, this same detachment would actually reach the Bluffs on July 9, only to find that the Confederate forces there had been withdrawn.[370]

Much as they had previously experienced, early July saw continuing hot and humid weather, this discomforting the men, even though they were not being taxed by arduous labor. It was apparent that the enemy had not followed them to this point, and late in the afternoon of the 6th, the 10th Texas moved its camp three miles back of the bluff to a place called Arkapolo. The men here established a most hospitable camp amidst some fine shade trees. Lean-tos and brush arbors predominated their accommodations in camp, with only here and there a tent seeming to sprout like a mushroom off the forest floor.[371]

By now, low morale had begun to make such inroads amongst the Texans that a general sullenness permeated their demeanor; this effectively demonstrated their great displeasure at all things military at this point. It's likely that this may, in part, have stemmed from their not having been paid yet, but it also seems to have sprung from the very rigid discipline on their officers' part, which had seemingly changed demonstrably since they reached Arkansas. Corp. Aaron Estes of Co. B, 10th Texas railed on this subject: "They [his mess-mates] are [completely] out of tobacco and

---

[370] Thomas H. Bringhurst, comp. *History of the 46th Indiana Volunteer Infantry, Sept. 1861 to September, 1865.* Logansport, Indiana. 1888. See pp. 37-8 as regards the "White River Expedition."

[371] Roger Q. Mills letter of June 23, 1862, State Archives, Austin. Also, that Rust's cavalry brigade had arrived at the bluff by then is seen *O.R*, I, 13, p. 453, was a Federal report sent to St. Louis advising that five regiments of Texas Cavalry, an Arkansas Infantry regiment, one Texas Infantry regiment (Nelson's), along with six brass guns and two forty-two-pounder cannons had been emplaced atop the Bluffs.

wee [sic] haven[']t had eny [sic] Whiskey since wee (sic) left Texas." To further frustrate the men, since returning to the bluff after their downriver excursion, the 10th had been thrown into an all-Arkansas brigade that, according to Estes, had as little interest in them seemingly as they had for the "rackensackers."[372]

It was during this trying period that Lt. Col. Roger Q. Mills found himself shocked, then greatly saddened while perusing a dated copy of the *Houston Telegraph,* where he first learned that his brother had been killed at Glorietta Pass, New Mexico Territory, that previous March. In a June 22 letter to his spouse, Mills encouraged her to go and visit the slain brother's wife and invite her to come and stay at their home, and that they would financially care for her should that prove necessary. In this same letter, Mills expressed with great pride how his personal servant, Benjamin, had during the St. Charles expedition grabbed a musket from the wagons and joined the ranks in order to defend against a possible enemy attack. Penned Mills at the time, Ben afterward proudly lay down that night in the rank and file and "slept on his arms" as well.[373]

By July 3, the works the men had labored so hard to improve, now designated as Ft. Hindman, had been completed, and the force atop the bluff augmented such that a Texas noncommissioned officer crowed: "Ower [sic] army [here] amounts to seven or eight thousand. Fort Hindmand [sic] and Devaller [sic] Bluff is all the same." The writer, Aaron Estes of Co. B, 10th Texas Infantry, advised his wife that "wee [sic] have 6 redgements [sic] of Texas troops here and the Arkansaw [sic] husers (?) [and] think wee [sic] can whip the devil out of his den." The only major complaint in this letter arose from the fact that they hadn't been paid up to this point, but "wee [sic] have just bin [sic] muster fore pay and the pay roles has just been made out and will be mailed today." Of particular interest to the learned reader is what he reported last with respect to their defenses: "Wee [sic] have a submarine batry [sic] that is a cask of powder that ways

---

[372] 4th Cpl. Aaron Estes letter, likely drafted around June 18, a transcribed copy found in the Estes Family Special Collections, Baylor University.

[373] Roger Q. Mills letter, June 23, 1862, Roger Q. Mills letters, State Archives, Austin, Texas.

[sic] 200 lbs[.] [and] is sunk in the river where the [enemy] boats have to run over and it will bee [sic] let of[f] buy lecttrisity [sic] conducted under the water buy a wier [sic]." He advised her also that the finished rifle pits appeared to be nearly as tall as the soldiers themselves when standing behind them.[374] Matters would remain in a static state until July 9, when the 10th Texas Infantry (and apparently, all the other troops assembled there) received orders to return to Little Rock. The extensive works completed, it appeared that the possibility of an enemy attack had fallen by the wayside, according to Col. G. N. Fitch of the 46th Indiana Infantry on the Federal side (commanding the Indiana Brigade aboard the steamer *White Cloud*). His force, after occupying Clarendon on June 30, and sending an advance guard to within ten miles of DeVall's Bluff, had not made any other movements. As for why he didn't go any further, he reports that it was speculated the enemy there numbered close to 6,000 men, and in follow-up dispatches of July 6 and 8, he advised that his riverine brigade had approached to within seven miles of the bluff, but by the 14th his force had been withdrawn, as "DeVall's Bluff . . . was [by that time] evacuated, the enemy taking his guns and munitions to Little Rock, [and] tearing up the railroad track behind him."[375]

By this time also, the riverine force had learned that MG Curtis' army had left the White River area and moved on east toward Helena, and thus the amphibious force returned to the Mississippi and made upstream for that point themselves, temporarily leaving a static situation in eastern Arkansas. For their part, the Confederates had spent much of their efforts in early July "engaged in foraging" expeditions to the many small hamlets near the bluffs in an attempt to augment their sparse rations, while many amongst them saw this as an opportune time to send letters to those

---

[374] 4th Cpl. Aaron Estes letter of July 3, 1862, in the Estes Collection, Special Collections, Baylor University. It's believed that the Texas regiments alluded to were the Texas Cavalry regiments that had lately been at Des Arc, the 12th, 15th, 16th, 17th, and 18th Texas Cavalry.

[375] Report of Col. Fitch, White River, in *O.R.*, I, 13, S # 19, pp. 171-3; he reported his brigade as consisting of the 24th, 34th, 43rd, and 46th Indiana Infantry Regiments.

at home. Quite a few had little valuable news, though often the men mention "rumors" of what had been transpiring in the state. One soldier announced that peace would apparently soon come to hand, wishfully thinking, perhaps, that it might have already been consummated. Others repeated the gossip that England had finally come in on the side of the South, or that the U.S. at least stood on the brink of war with the mother country. Of note, however, is that Isaiah Harlan of Co. G, 10th Texas reported the good news to his family from far-off Virginia: "McClellan's army [there] has been routed," and rumor had it that "Washington City has also been destroyed." Spain, too, he wrote, had conveyed it would soon enter a coalition to oppose the North, and that both England and France were working feverishly to bring an end to the war.[376]

That rumors could prove to be of ludicrous proportions can be seen in another letter by this same soldier. Isaiah Harlan penned in a letter how a soldier had reportedly been scheduled to be shot for desertion and that how afterward the soldier had been executed (including that he'd been shot through the head). Only a few hours later, he learned that all of this had been just another rumor, without a germ of truth to it.[377]

So often had this been the case of late around camp that many men downplayed virtually every rumor unless they received confirmation from outside sources. One that had almost come true, however, was when toward the end of June, a paymaster had arrived, with Cpl. Estes of Co. B, 10th Texas, reporting he had come to distribute both wages and cash bonuses due them. Having not received a cent to this point, they earnestly hoped they'd soon receive at least a portion of the monies owed them. Finally, the call came to fall in before the paymaster's tent, though subsequently the men thought themselves to have been taken in again, for even as they discussed what they expected to do with their pay, the sound of gunfire off in the distance, immediately followed by the long roll, forced the men to seize their gear and rush back to the trenches, with ammunition being distributed. As no enemy made an appearance by dark, the men began to believe this to have been a ruse to get them

---

[376] Isaiah Harlan letter, June 23, 1862, CRC, Hill College.

[377] *Ibid.*, Isaiah Harlan to his mother, June 29, 1862., CRC, Hill College.

out of camp while the paymaster departed, again depriving them of their just due.[378]

It was while stationed there at the bluffs that the men of the 10th Texas at least got the opportunity to fire their muskets when, on June 22, thinking the high humidity might have rendered their charges useless, Nelson had the men march down to the river for target practice. A large target had been placed on the opposite bank at a distance estimated to be at least 250 yards. Apparently, everyone had the opportunity to fire his piece; unfortunately, only the hits scored by Co. G seem to have been recorded. If indicative of the regiment as a whole, however, it showed a fair accuracy from their smooth-bore guns, as about fifteen of the fifty rounds fired by this company struck the human-size target. Not bad for soldiers who had only recently been supplied with their arms.[379]

Ever since reaching Arkansas, generally speaking, all of these Texas units had been exposed to privations that caused much suffering, ranging from paltry rations to the incessant heat from an interminably hot summer that made life outdoors anything but enjoyable. Increasingly, as a consequence of such conditions, men began to take sick and then die in ever-increasing numbers. For example, in the 10th Texas, from early June to mid-July, nearly two-thirds of the men suffered some type of disability or illness, in recent weeks caused by an epidemic of measles. Those thought to be but moderate cases found themselves farmed out to residents in the area, put up in private quarters until recovering, with more severe cases shipped to hospitals at either Brownsville or in Little Rock. What was obviously needed to bring the men back to a state of readiness was a long rest, but under current circumstances, this was not apt to happen.[380]

Another contentious matter that made for low morale came from the low opinion most held for the Arkansas troops with whom they had to serve, the perception being that most appeared to be

---

[378] *The Bugle:*, p. 16.

[379] *Ibid.*, p. 14; also, see the *Tri-Weekly Telegraph*, Houston, Texas, July 21, 1862.

[380] Isaiah Harlan letter, June 29, 1862 CRC, Hill College; also, *The Bugle:*, p. 16.

either apathetic to, or ignorant of, their cause. They had seen that sutlers serving the troops and area merchants had no qualms about charging exorbitant prices for the paltry goods possessed, despite authorities' attempts to set prices. As often as not, they thought the women to be every equal companion to their male counterparts, some believing they'd do anything to get a soldier to the altar. These women often went around wearing shabby clothes and kicked about without shoes on, even in mixed company. And recently, even the fighting qualities of Arkansas soldiers had been called into question when, upon learning that Wheat's (Infantry) Battalion had succeeded in dogging a fight in late June, had prompted a soldier of the 10th Texas to complain: "If we had [had] the right sort of men [there,] they would have taken in the whole passel [of them];" instead, "the damned Arkansans run [from the field]."[381]

During this same time, following their mostly unsuccessful forays into Northeast Arkansas that included such skirmishes as that near Batesville with the Kansas "red-legs," or the larger Cache River fight, the Texas Cavalry regiments that had formed part of BG Rust's brigade had begun a retrograde that had them headed back toward Little Rock. By mid-July, the smaller contingent of the 15th Texas Cavalry under Col. Sweet that had been stationed near Batesville had returned to Brownsville, where it awaited those other regiments returning from the Des Arc-DeVall's Bluff area. Here they would remain several days, with rumors once again swirling around that they would likely be dismounted before many more days. If that occurred, it was understood they'd be sent to a camp of instruction to convert these men into infantry soldiers. For the moment, however, all they could do was await their fate. William Young of Co. A, 15th Texas Cavalry noted that "it is certain we will be set afoot." And Z. H. Crow of Co. C of that same regiment wrote on July 16 that his regiment had already been dismounted, and their horses sent back to Texas, leaving him and his comrades "in a very bad fix."[382]

---

[381] *Ibid.*, p. 17.

[382] *Chapters:*, p. 61; an undated William Young letter, CRC, Hill College, and an undated letter of Z. H. Crow in "A Smith County Confederate," *Chronicles*, Vol 4, # 2, p. 13.

Also reaching Brownsville during this time was Fitzhugh's 16th, Moore's 17th, and Darnell's 18th Texas Cavalry regiments; each had spent most of June and the first weeks in July around either Batesville, or near Des Arc, though one writer in the 17th Texas Cavalry noted that at the end of June his regiment had been posted near Augusta, east of Searcy on the Cache River. In fact, one of its wings had been engaged in a minor scrape there with an unknown enemy that had cost several men in Co. F, who had been killed or wounded. A private in Co. A of that regiment, Malcom Scurlock from near Alvarado, in Johnson County, wrote his folks that his captain's brother had been among those severely wounded in this spirited contest. Also joining these commands at this point was the 10th Texas Infantry, which had marched in from DeVall's Bluff about the 10th.[383]

Gen. Hindman's two-month campaign had seemed almost surreal, more than a real campaign, its shotgun-like approach confusing Curtis, but all in all it had confounded him that the Union commander had temporarily given up on his quest to advance upon Little Rock. He had shifted his army to Helena, reaching there July 13. The river town could accommodate his troops and provide him a substantial base in the near future as he planned a new expedition against the Arkansas capital. And Hindman posting of a substantial force in strong works at DeVall's Bluff had frustrated the enemy navy's efforts to join Curtis on the White, while positioning the three Texas regiments under Col. Robert Garland at Pine Bluff had prevented any attempt to advance for the time being via the Arkansas. Having a little breathing room, Hindman could turn his attention to systematically organizing his widely dispersed forces and plan on a new strategy for new regiments, expected to be coming in from Texas, as well as those raised among the conscripted Arkansas soldiers, all of whom desperately needed more drill and discipline.[384]

One expedient had been met already through the forced dismounting of surplus cavalry regiments encamped at Brownsville. The government offered only to either purchase their mounts or let

---

[383] See the Scurlock family letters, *Grandview Tribune*, Dec. 23, 1977; also see Isaiah Harlan letter of July 18, 1862, CRC, Hill College.

[384] *O.R.*, I, 13, pp. 35-6.

the men appoint details for escorting their mounts home to Texas. Issued July 15, his order had stipulated also that a new all-Texas infantry brigade was to be created by combining the dismounted regiments into a single command. Among the reasons given were that there already existed in the department a disproportionate number of cavalry, versus infantry commands, and that the state had been adversely damaged due to a drought that left a severe shortage of forage crops in the Arkansas valley.[385]

For its part, Lt. Col. Mills' 10th Texas Infantry had departed their camp near DeVall's Bluff on July 8; the sick were sent by rail cars, while those men capable of marching would move via Brownsville to Little Rock. Upon reaching the capital, the sick found themselves assigned surgeons in Little Rock who were either unwilling or incapable of treating them in a professional manner. The marching troops didn't reach the city until July 15, by which time many a man had dropped by the wayside due to sickness, or from the stifling heat. All were reunited at Camp Texas some days later, some four or five miles south of town. According to George Allen of Co. A, just 384 of the men had made the entire march, though that number had dwindled to under "200 men [present] and half of them is not able to go ten miles on a forced march."[386]

As one might imagine, the morale of both the cavalrymen and this infantry regiment had plummeted upon learning of the orders issued now from Little Rock. Surprisingly, however, it appeared that the morale of those in the 10th Texas could not have gotten much worse. For the former cavalrymen, however, it could scarcely have been any better, for in addition to the conscription act increasing their term of service from twelve months to three years, it

---

[385] *Chapters*, p. 61. See also, Marshall Pierson, Co. C, 17th Texas Cavalry, in *Military History of Texas*, vol. 13, p. 28. William Young of Co. A, 15th Texas, had likewise sent an undated letter in mid-July advising that the "old men" in his regiment would escort the horses, CRC, Hill College. And Malcolm Scurlock's sister confirms in a letter to a brother the next month that Malcolm had confirmed they had been set afoot the previous month, though the date and place are not given, *Grandview Tribune*, Grandview, Texas, January 27, 1988.

[386] *The Bugle*:, pp. 14-15; also, George Allen letter of July 24, 1862, in "Civil War Letters of George W. Allen," Charleen P. Pollard, ed., in *S.W.H.Q.*, vol. LXXXIII, # 1, pp. 48-9.

had discharged many comrades who were either under eighteen or over thirty-five years in age. Along with this came a reduction in salary of a dollar a month, along with the perception they had that every Texan would scarcely walk across the street back home if he could swing up into a saddle to accomplish such a move. While some former cavalrymen clung to the belief that their dismounting might prove only a temporary measure, the more astute understood they'd likely never be remounted.

Perhaps the most shocking reaction to the morale problems surfaced not with the dismounted cavalrymen, but rather the veterans of the 10th Texas Infantry. When their original commander, Allison Nelson, had been bumped up to brigade command at Little Rock, permanent command of the 10th Texas fell to Lt. Col. Roger Q. Mills on July 16. Mills could never have guessed his command authority would be put to the test so soon, but on the 18th several of his companies refused to turn out for morning roll call. When this was related to him, Mills had personally gone down and ordered the men out, and upon their refusal to do so a second time, he immediately had arrested fifty or more of the ringleaders, before wiring Nelson at Little Rock as to what ought to be done with those men.[387]

Word immediately came back to continue to arrest those unwilling to turn out, and further, to send the leaders to Little Rock for a meeting with the district commander, Hindman. Mills carefully listened to their complaints on never being paid and the taxing service they had recently undergone, persuading them that while he understood their displeasure, he wouldn't brook further insubordination within his army, and he would deal harshly with any person who continued to be engaged in what he bluntly referred to as a mutiny. Some of the men attempted to assuage their guilt by explaining their families desperately needed their support and that they had already made more than enough sacrifices for the cause. They had come to believe that now was the time for the government to make good on its promises to them. Pledging to immediately act on their expressed concerns, Mills sternly lectured the leaders before

---

[387] Isaiah Harlan letter, July 18, 1862, CRC, Hill College; also, *The Bugle:*, p. 18.

sending them off to camp with a threat of the consequences that could be expected by those who bucked his authority in the future. This seemed to produce the desired effects, though Hindman went on to assure the malcontents that they wouldn't want to witness firsthand his brand of military justice should this conduct ever be repeated, going on to state that "he wo[u]ld have ever[y] tenth man shot" if that become necessary to restore order.[388]

Many of those who hadn't participated in this episode worried those at home might not think well of this action, that they were shirkers at best, or worse, out-and-out deserters. Isaiah Harlan of Co. G, who advised that a total of seven companies had initially refused to turn out on parade, acknowledged that most acquiesced soon after, and at the last, forty to fifty malcontents continued their protest: "They complain of no pay, rigid discipline and too much drill." Emotionally wrought over this episode, he recalled that: "I was afraid yesterday the regiment would disgrace Texas and for the first time I regretted very much that I was a member of it."[389]

George Allen of Co. A, who had recently suffered from a relapse of the measles, noted on July 24 that a close comrade from his company, James H. Hurst of Grimes County, had just died of disease (which proved to be typhoid); he'd been taken ill on June 29, and passed away on July 17. Hurst had maintained a diary of the regiment's earliest activities, but especially the marches up from Texas. Depressed by Hurst's death, along with several others in his company, Allen wrote his parents: "I am very tired of Arkansas and want to get out of it very much for it is no place for Texians[,] I assure you." He continued with an explanation of the recent "embarrassment," ending with the statement that: "It is true we volunteered but we are treated like Regulars[,] if not worse. We are the only troops that have not received their pay, or at least the larger portion of it at least."[390]

---

[388] *The Bugle:*, p. 18.

[389] Isaiah Harlan letter to his brother, July 18, 1862, CRC, Hill College.

[390] George Allen letter of July 24, 1862, SWHQ, vol. LXXXIII # 1, pp. 49-50.; also a typed transcript of James Hurst's diary entry of June 29, where he notes he had taken ill; another soldier penning on the last page of the diary that "James H.

Several other issues had been raised besides no pay, one being a recent requirement that the regiment call roll three times daily, which suggested to the men that this had been done to imply their desertion unless under the strict control of their officers. Coupled with a dramatic rise in the number of hours spent in daily drills under a scorching summer sun, this had provoked much displeasure. The increased drills worked to sap men's energy, without providing much benefit, and, like the roll calls, had been implemented from above with no input from the rank and file. Even at this late date, the men's morale seemed to spring from their perception of the duties owed their country, and their demand that fair play ought to be employed, rather than forcing them into compliance.

What made this situation all the more dangerous came from the knowledge that each man had retained the ten rounds issued at DeVall's Bluff and that some of the malcontents had gone so far as to suggest that force would be resorted to should they not receive fair consideration from above. They saw their complaints as legitimate and were unwilling to subordinate themselves to the whims, some complained, of commanders arbitrarily appointed over them. In a letter sent out just days afterward by one of those in the 10th, the writer summed up the prevailing attitude that their more senior officers were "not worth shooting." Though this was likely aimed more at those holding higher posts in the army, he nevertheless chose not to praise his own regimental officers either.[391]

The monetary issue had been quickly addressed through paymasters being dispatched to address what had become a most perplexing problem. Had that not transpired, however, a clear notion of how willing the district commander was to enforce his authority came not long thereafter. Acting under special orders issued August 1 by Hindman, Col. Mills was instructed to select a firing detail for the execution of several Arkansas deserters. Mills appointed Lt. L. M. Barton of Co. G to draft a detail from his company to compose a

---

Hurst, a private in Col. Nelson's Texas Regiment, Co. A, died at the General Hospital, July 17, 1862, of typhoid fever," CRC, Hill College.

[391] William Young letter to Davenport, July 21, 1862, William Young letters, CRC, Hill College.

firing squad, as these men would be charged with executing Arkansans who had in recent months gone over to the enemy, only to be subsequently taken in by their former comrades. A Texan who witnessed the spectacle was moved to write:

> This morning . . . a scene which probably might be interesting to you, [and] to which I believe I have become hardened [occurred here]. I saw five men blindfolded and brought up before the gaze of 10,000 men, . . . compelled to fall on their knees and be shot. There was one in particular that deserved sympathy. He was sixty years old. His hair was white as the driven snow. He tottered up like he was satisfied. One of the others was a Capt.[392]

A similar response came from another private of the 10th who had observed the execution scene: "They fell to the ground and not even a groan was heard, nor did they draw a breath [thereafter]." That this episode brought about the desired effect came from the fact that none of those observing this event spoke a word on their way back to camp. Hindman had obviously proven his point, and the men of the 10th now realized just how far he'd go to enforce military discipline; if it were required, lethal force would be relied upon to produce the desired effects.[393]

During these weeks, the more hectic movements of Rust's former cavalry regiments made it impossible to keep abreast of what oftentimes was happening to them. Pvt. Z. H. Crow of Co. C, 17th Texas had acknowledged in a letter to his sister of July 29, "[we] have gotten no money yet [letter torn] . . . and' don't know when we will." Capt. Bryan Marsh of that same company had written on the same day that their regiment had been dismounted on July 13 and already been placed in "a camp of instruction for

---

[392] Ibid., letter to Nan Davenport, August 12, 1862, CRC, Hill College.

[393] *The Bugle:* p. 19. See as well,

HTTP://cdm.sos.mo.gov/cdm/page_textphp?.cisoroot+/mack&cisoptr+10995cisoptr+11175 & item+290.

infantry service." And it's probable that the 15th, 16th, and 18th Texas Cavalry regiments underwent their dismounting about the same time, for in a letter sent by Malcolm Scurlock of Co. A, 18th Texas Cavalry, to his family in mid-August, he suggested his regiment had been dismounted prior to August 9. In any case, all four of the regiments from Rust's brigade had been recalled to Little Rock, where they found themselves instantly converted into service afoot.[394]

As early as July 20, William Young of Co. A, 15th Texas Cavalry had written his sisters in Texas that his regiment had just "received orders to go up the [Arkansas] river for instructions. It is getting like we are all to be set afoot." He complained intensely about the officers who had been appointed over them in Arkansas, the very next day (the 21st) writing: "We have some of the triflingest (sic) officers. Old Hineman (sic) and Rust. They are not worth shooting."[395]

On Sunday, August 3, Woodson Park of that same company of the 15th Texas Cavalry (since dismounted) had written a sister on how lonely he had become "since Daniel was killed" in the skirmish that had occurred the month before at Orient's Ferry on the Black River in combat with the 5th Kansas Cavalry. The weather had become increasingly hotter, he advised, and the *ARMY REGULATIONS* had recently been read at evening dress parade as a precaution to the soldiers concerning their duties. A final sentence advised that they had at last gotten their "bounty money the other day," this relieving him greatly over his distressed financial situation.[396]

---

[394] Z. H. Crow letter from Little Rock, posted July 16, 1862, *Chronicles* vol. vol. 4, # 2 (fall 1965), p. 13; also, Bryan Marsh to "Mittie" on July 29, 1862, in *Chronicles*, vol. 14, # 2 (winter 1975), pp. 14-15. For the Scurlock letter, see Mollie Scurlock to brother J.W., published in the *Grandview Tribune*, Grandview, Texas, January 13, 1978.

[395] William Young transcript letters of July 20 & 21, 1862, CRC, Hill College. By this time, interestingly enough, Maj. Hindman had relinquished command of the Trans-Mississippi on the 16th, being unliked equally by the Texans, the residents of Arkansas, and even many of his own subordinates.

[396] The Park family letters of Daniel and Woodson were graciously furnished this writer by Betty Troutman, a descendant of the two.

And, on the following day, the 4th, Bryan Marsh of Co. C, 17th Texas Cavalry (also now dismounted) had written his spouse, "Mit," that they were now receiving only half rations at their new camp near Crystal Hill, northwest of Little Rock, and that they had four hour-long drill sessions a day; officers such as himself had to engage in two more a day than enlisted personnel. Of special interest is a note made, apparently in an effort to get a rise out of his wife, that "am pretty, [or] so say the Arkansas women [hereabouts]." And he related that Curtis was believed to have reached Helena, this giving them more time to better prepare for further campaigns down the road.[397]

Also on July 4, Hindman had wired BG John Roane at Pine Bluff that he had just issued orders for Capt. William Hart's Arkansas Battery to move to that point for service under that officer. By this time, a camp of instruction had been established at White Sulphur Springs, some miles out from that borough, where many Arkansas conscripts had arrived in reaction to the recent draft law so they could receive basic training. It's rather interesting to note that Hart's battery had been an early-war unit, which had essentially been disbanded for cowardice at the Battle on Pea Ridge the previous March, but had appealed this suspension and been allowed to reorganize under the same officer. Only a month before, Hindman had ordered BG Albert Pike in the Indian territory to send along ten Parrott rifles to Little Rock to be issued to newly forming artillery units, with six going to Woodruff's battery at Des Arc, and Hart's receiving the remaining four.[398]

On August 5, 1862, the 10th Texas Infantry had passed through Little Rock to reach Crystal Hill, where they would be united with several dismounted Texas Cavalry regiments being sent there. Even though a goodly number of the infantrymen were quite ill, they remained for some time afterward at their former camp south of the capital. Benjamin Seaton of Co. G, in this regiment, noted that on the 4th they had each been paid their bounty money, and his $30 "came in [at] a good time." The regiment had been detached by this time from their former

---

[397] "Bryan Marsh," in *Chronicles*, vol. 14, # 2, p. 15.

[398] *O.R.*, I, 13, p. 187; http://en.wikepedia.org/wiki/2nd_Arkansas_Field_Battery.

association within an Arkansas brigade. On the 11th, according to Benjamin Seaton, "there[e] are five more men to be shot today and it was executed by the Arkansas troops and it was a barbarus [sic] affair. They knelt down to receive the contents of the load-they shot them 2 times before they left them[,] and then left them not dead." On the 12th he advised that all of the convalescents of the regiment had reached the new camp.[399]

William Young of Co. A, 15th Texas Cavalry (also dismounted by now) had sent a letter out on August 10 that his regiment had moved almost "twelve miles above Little Rock [and are now] in the darndest place you ever seed [sic] of." All the sick men seemed to getting well, "though [the] devlisc [sic] water [there]" was apt to cause every one of them to become sick anew. He speculated that there were a great number of men at this new camp, known as Crystal Hill, which had grown with the addition of several new regiments just arrived from Texas and now numbered "about 15,000 men." And recently, a furlough system had been instituted that allowed some comrades to go home to Texas for a well-earned rest.[400]

Another correspondent at Crystal Hill, Lt. Flavius Perry of Co. B, 17th Texas Cavalry (Dismounted), had written on August 11 about the deserters who'd recently been shot to death and the impact this had had on him, as well as the excitement that occurred during the previous evening, when they'd been ordered back to DeVall's Bluff. For some undisclosed reason, this latter order had been rescinded, and the regiments that had just gotten off returned to their former camps. He'd been sick for some time and was staying with a lady in the country who attended him well; he enjoyed the meals she prepared, even "if she . . . is a

---

[399] *The Bugle:*, pp. 19-20. With regards to the executions, they must be the same ones noted in a letter from William Young, Co. A, 15th Texas Cavalry (now dismounted), dated August 8, 1862, CRC, Hill College.

[400] William Young letter of August 10, 1862, transcribed by author from original, CRC, Hill College.

Rackemsacker." As a sad note, of late just fifteen men of his company had been able to turn out for duty.[401]

By now, Col. Allison Nelson had been called upon to serve as brigade commander for this new conglomeration that included his old regiment, the 10th Texas Infantry, now to be used as a role model for the 15th, 16th, 17th, and 18th Texas Cavalry (Dismounted). He had, however, found himself called to Little Rock often to help organize the new regiments just in from Texas, which left little time to oversee the day-to-day operations of his new brigade, with Col. George Sweet of the 15th Texas Cavalry (Dismounted) the next most senior officer in rank having to substitute for Nelson. It was obvious early on that few of the men in Sweet's own regiment, much less the others, cared a whit for him, and this would become a very sensitive issue down the road. In reaction to this, shortly thereafter, in an obvious effort to show their displeasure over their interim commander, several soldiers of the 18th Texas Cavalry (Dismounted) took his horse one night, shaved its mane and tail, then picketed it in front of Sweet's tent. For some days after, whenever Sweet rode out in front of the brigade, some wag in the ranks would loudly holler out: "Whoa, Bob!" And don't think Sweet didn't quickly get the message.[402]

As mentioned previously, Nelson's brigade, as it was fast becoming known, suffered not just from a paucity of rations but from bad water that they found there. Their fare often consisted of just "blue" beef and cornbread, with an occasional issue of molasses sweetener, and less often, small amounts of sugar or syrup coming their way. While a furlough system had been initiated, stringent new rules forbade a soldier leaving camp except when going to or from the hospital, or being sent out under a written pass on military business. This caused the men to seek novel ways to entertain themselves while in camp: card games (or card-sharking), marbles, and a unique form of baseball known as "one-eyed jack," or town-

---

[401] Flavius Perry to family, August 11, 1862, *Military History of Texas*, vol. 13, # 2, p. 17.

[402] *Chapters:*, p. 62. That this was fairly common between enlisted men who thought some officers to be overly haughty, see Col. Harold B. Simpson's *Lee's Grenadier Guard: Hood's Texas Brigade*. Waco. Texian Press. 1970, p. 63.

ball, often provided an enjoyable form of physical exercise as well as giving some relief from boredom.[403]

Meanwhile, back down in Texas, many males who deemed it objectionable to await conscription into the service decided to go up to Arkansas in order to enlist with already-established units, where they'd at least be amongst men they knew. Even some of those hailing from Arkansas itself chose to enlist in Texas commands, perhaps also wanting to escape the onus of being compelled to serve and indiscriminately being assigned to any unit where recruits were needed. This was especially the case with James and Lafayette Orr, from Ellis County, who early that summer made their way to Arkansas in hoped of joining a brother then serving in the 12th Texas Cavalry. But just after reaching southern Arkansas, they were made to understand they would not likely be able to reach their brother's regiment (in the far eastern part of the state). They instead opted to enlist in the 18th Texas Cavalry (Dismounted), as they had several friends there.[404]

While such additions might alleviate, to some extent, the losses to commands from death, disability from incapacitating wounds, or discharge by virtue of the conscription act, this second year of the war wouldn't bring about dramatic increases in numbers, at least to near the level they had had the year before. For their part, many of the older hands welcomed these new recruits, as they often brought information as to what was happening on the home front; though obviously, some took advantage of new recruits by beating them out of extra clothes they had or bargaining for items that had long since disappeared in the service. One Texan thought that the

---

[403] *O.R.*, I, vol. 10, pt. 1, p. 555, Union Gen. A. P. Hovey noting the location of the enemy's camps as being at Crystal Hill. As to ball games, these were antecedents to modern baseball; town-ball usually had eighteen players on a side, the term "town" in this case meaning that the team came from a given community, hence the title. The game of "one-eyed jack" seems to have utilized a single base, along with a home-plate, the players running back and forth between the two in order to rack up "runs".

[404] John Q. Anderson, ed., *Campaigning With Parsons's Texas Cavalry Brigade, CSA: The Journals and Letters of the four Orr Brothers, 12th Texas Cavalry Regiment.* Hill Jt. College Press. Hillsboro, 1967, p. 60. Hereafter cited as *Campaigning:*.

new recruits often took to active service even more capably than his old friends, apparently suffering little stigma from their delayed entry into the army. Also arriving at the camps around Crystal Hill at this time were drill instructors who would whip both old and new soldiers alike into the miseries of *Hardee's Tactics*.[405]

An avid interest of the soldiers at Crystal Hill appeared to be in learning the whereabouts of other Texans in the army, whether that be in Arkansas or on far-distant fields. So they eagerly read newspapers on the exploits of other commands, whether that be in way-off Virginia, or far out in New Mexico, as well as those serving much closer to them. A private in one of Nelson's dismounted regiments passed the news to those back home that he had learned that "Garland's [6th Texas Infantry Regiment] is on the . . . river [some] twenty-five miles south of Little Rock," while "Carter's Brigade [that had included the 24th and 25th Texas Cavalry (Dismounted)] is somewhere east of here." Especially notable were the exploits of Johnson's Texas Spy Co. and Parsons' Cavalry Brigade, who had recently captured "three wagon-loads of ammunition, one of arms, one of commissary stores, and two ambulances . . . " almost within the city limits of Helena.[406]

Hindman having resigned as district commander July 16, MG Theophilus Holmes arrived on the 30th to take overall command of the vast Trans-Mississippi Department that had just come into creation. Immediately after arriving at Little Rock, Holmes began talking about prospects for taking the initiative against the Federals by fall. He early on had advised Nelson that the several brigades undergoing organization, and training, in and around Little Rock would likely be sent to Missouri; he urged that the Texans should work to get his entire brigade prepared for cold-weather operations. What with the government's apparent inability to supply the men's clothing needs, Nelson was instructed to look to Texas for somehow meeting his men's need for winter clothes. Soon after getting this information, he communicated that to his men, who began to write to those at home requesting that "good, thick clothing such as the

---

[405] "Bryan Marsh," in *Chronicles*, vol. 14, # 2, p. 16 (winter 1975).

[406] William Young, Co. A, 15th Texas Cavalry (Dismounted) in a letter to his mother, August 8, 1862, CRC, Hill College.

government may not be able to" furnish be forwarded to Little Rock.[407]

Soldiers generally wanted to receive homespun clothes suitable for everyday use, as these were generally more comfortable and often served as a direct connection reminding them of loved ones at home truly caring about their welfare. Soldiers requested that all such clothing be finished and forwarded as quickly as practicable, as the great distances and cumbersome trains required meant that it needed to be sent immediately if it was to reach them before cold weather set in. If home-made goods couldn't be supplied, they would try to acquire penitentiary cloth, and through active sewing circles, fashion the cloth into the requisite clothing. Isiah Harlan of Co. G, 10th Texas, wrote to his brother, Eliphalet, that he needed a pair of britches, an over-shirt, two pair of drawers, three to four pair of socks, suspenders, and a heavy overcoat. In a separate letter addressed to his mother on the same day, he told her that "my military coat is as yet unworn." Hats and shoes were also in short supply, he noted.[408]

As previously noted, only once during their sojourn at Crystal Hill did it appear that the brigade might get an opportunity to "see the elephant" sooner rather than later. This had occurred on August 13, as Nelson ordered the 10th Texas Infantry to move in the direction of DeVall's Bluff, with the remaining regiments of the brigade following. Thus, the men of the 10th began a forced march that had carried the regiment the distance of eighteen miles in just over six hours, when an order arrived rescinding the march and advising them to return to camp. This appears to have been the first time they had marched at the "double-quick." They spent that first night under the stars, on empty stomachs, as the rations in their haversacks had quickly run out, with the wagons having quickly fallen far behind.

---

[407] Isaiah Harlan, Co. G, 10th Texas, to Eliphalet, August 13, 1862, CRC, Hill College.

[408] Isaiah Harlan letters of August 13, 1862, CRC, Hill College. It should be pointed out that "military coats," or "fighting jackets," as some referred to them, were generally reserved for wearing when going out to battle an enemy; this holdover from the Victorian era stated that a man needed to be properly attired when going out onto the battlefield.

Weary over what they saw as a wasted effort and confronted with grumbling stomachs, many of the men thought this but another example of gross neglect on some officer's part. One of those who had been left behind to trail the 10th Texas Infantry had been William Young of Co. A, 15th Texas Cavalry (Dismounted). He wrote to his wife, "Nan," that the order instructing them to put their arms into order created quite a stir in camp, and only when the 10th Texas returned from their march did this take the edge off for the remaining regiments of the brigade.[409]

The early weeks of August had seen the Texans around Crystal Hill subsisting on half rations, and the days were extraordinarily hot. At least for now they didn't have to be constantly on the move, this allowing the soldiers to continue sending out their letters. Lt. Henry Curl of Co. B, 17th Texas Cavalry (Dismounted) wrote his wife on August 14 that his father was still in their camp on a visit and that he was still sick with a fever, but that Henry had finally reached a decision not to resign his commission. And just days before (August 8), William Young of Co. A, 15th Texas Cavalry (Dismounted) had advised his "ma" that they had finally been separated from the Arkansas regiments and there were now a total of six Texas regiments who had been thrown together; he seemed quite pleased that his regiment now belonged to Nelson's brigade.[410]

Even as the dispirited soldiers encamped around Crystal Hill struggled to adjust to their Spartan circumstances in their new camp of instruction, significant changes were ongoing in the Trans-Mississippi Department. While a district headquarters remained in effect at Little Rock that included Arkansas and the Indian Nations, the neighboring states of Missouri, Louisiana, and Texas had become separate entities within the department, each virtually independent of the other. For now, MG Holmes remained in command of the

---

[409] *The Bugle:*, p. 20. Interestingly, the rancor shown still seemed to have been directed toward their higher-ranked officers and not those at regimental or brigade level. See also, William Young letter of August 15, 1862, transcript from the CRC, Hill College.

[410] Bryan Marsh letter of August 4, 1862, in *Chronicles*, vol. 14 # 2, p. 15; and transcript letter of William Young, August 8, 1862, CRC, Hill College.

department from his headquarters at the Arkansas capital, having assumed command on August 12, and MG Hindman saw himself transferred out to Ft. Smith to take command of an infantry corps there.[411]

Holmes, whose age earned him the sobriquet "Granny," worked assiduously to organize and arrange the forces within the department. At present, he retained Nelson's brigade near Little Rock, while leaving Garland's temporarily at Pine Bluff. While obviously not as energetic as Hindman, he nevertheless proved to be a lesser nuisance in comparison to the latter, whose actions while commander had made him a pariah within the state. As early as August 2nd, Lt. Flavius Perry of the 17th Texas Cavalry (Dismounted) had advised in a letter that there stood a good chance for the Texas regiments near Little Rock to be sent to Austin, some thirty-five miles northeast of the capital. A Federal officer, however, noted on August 10 that the force that had of late been posted at Clarendon, which included these regiments, was ensconced at Little Rock.[412]

In the meantime, Nelson's brigade had been ordered to proceed to Austin, and on August 18, the five regiments composing the brigade (each burdened by its own supply train) began a four-day march that took them to that point. All of the regiments made something like fifteen miles a day in this move, having to backtrack through Little Rock in the process and fording the Arkansas River just east of the city. Most of the sick had to be left at their former camp for some time; they were simply too ill to accompany their regiments as they moved toward their new duty station: "It is sed [sic] to be a butiful [sic] place for a camp to orginnize [sic]."[413]

When arriving there, the men had to first clear a large enough space to encamp an entire division, rumors swirling that several more brigades would follow them to Austin. Holmes advised that as the brigades arrived, Nelson was to oversee their organization, with the

---

[411] Thomas Snead, "The Conquest of Arkansas," in *Battles & Leaders*, vol. III, p. 445.

[412] Lt. Perry letter in *Military History of Texas*, vol. 12, p. 16; also, see *O.R.*, I, 13, p. 555, from HQ, 4th Div., Army of the Southwest.

[413] The Bugle:, p. 20.

understanding that he would ultimately assume command of the new division created. This greatly increased his responsibilities. And it appears that this was likely the reason Col. Sweet had been elevated as temporary brigade commander. Some weeks would be needed to organize a completely new command structure (even on paper) for the division. Nelson quickly ordered separate brigade reviews be immediately held, and on August 27, Sweet held a review of Nelson's old brigade. The next day witnessed a division review that included several new brigades that had arrived. Nelson's elevation to brigadier general would not come until September 12, but the new division commander had begun already to impart to his brigadiers and staffs what was expected of them.[414]

The most recent addition to Nelson's, led by Col. George Flournoy (as senior colonel), included his own 16th Texas Infantry, along with Col. R. T. Allen's 17th Texas Infantry, Col. Richard Waterhouse's 19th Texas Infantry, and Col. William Fitzhugh's 16th Texas Cavalry (Dismounted). This last regiment appears to have been reassigned from Nelson's old brigade prior to its being attached to Flournoy's brigade. An initial return of the brigade at the time reflects a strength of about 4,000 men, but with no artillery assigned at the time. Subsequently, two additional brigades would be assigned to what would become the only Texas division to serve from that state; Nelson was in temporary command of the whole until coming down with typhoid fever later that month. (Upon Nelson's death in October, BG Henry McCulloch would arrive from Texas to act as temporary commander, pending the assignment of MG John G. Walker's taking command of the Greyhound Division, which, less Nelson's old brigade, would continue to serve as the only all-Texan division to serve throughout the war.)[415]

---

[414] *Ibid.*,; for Nelson's prewar and early Confederate service, see *The Handbook of Texas*, Vol. II, p. 289; *Texas in the War*, p. 14; and also, the *Atlanta Historical Society Bulletin*, (fall, 1985), pp. 19-25. In a letter to his wife on August 24, Lt. Col. Mills stated that he'd been in temporary command of Nelson's "old" brigade of five regiments but as of that date, "now only [have] mine." He had been sick for some time and the use of laudanum and mercury-morphine had nearly killed him. R. Q. Mills letters, furnished this writer by Scott McKay of Georgia.

[415] See *Texas in the War*, p. 13.

Their relocation to Austin brought with it a host of new medical problems, not the least of which were intestinally related diseases, probably from the bad water at Crystal Hill, with diarrhea and dysentery the most common complaint. Not easily cured in camp (nor in hospitals, for that matter), the men were treated with everything from laudanum (opium suspended in oil) to home remedies or patent medicines; quite often, these completely failed to alleviate their suffering. Sadly, the use of such dangerous compounds led to many deaths in the regiments. George Allen of Co. A, 10th Texas Infantry advised that though they had reached Austin safely, nine men had died since July, and he was still on the sick list. Many a soldier wouldn't recover from illness, as witnessed by the large number of Texan graves that can still be seen today in cemeteries there. The digging of deeper wells, however, got below the contaminated surface water, and, in association with an early fall, caused many of the sick to gradually improve. But cooler weather also had a favorable impact on their efficacy as well, because it brought about a return to the incessant drills, dress parades, and guard duty.[416] Their relocation to Austin, soon named Camp Hope, brought about many other changes as well, especially with respect to both the quantity of and variety of rations now coming the men's way. One private in the 18th Texas Cavalry (Dismounted) advised that the rations had been increased recently to 3/4 lbs. beef daily, with a quart of meal and bacon issued every eight days. When it arrived, the last was distributed at the rate of a pound per soldier, with the men quickly realizing these could be augmented by the purchase of peaches and watermelons from farmers in the area. The only government-issue treat that continued to come their way proved to be the occasional barrel of molasses or casks of cane sugar, all of which seemingly disappeared as quickly as they reached camps.[417]

For those who served in the dismounted regiments, many still clung to a glimmer of hope that one day they'd be returned to

---

[416] On the death rates at Austin, see the "Civil War letters of George W. Allen," in *S.W.H.Q*, vol. 83, #1, pp. 48-53, and Capt. Bryan Marsh to "Mit," in *Chronicles*, vol. 14, # 2 (Winter 1975), p. 17.

[417] Letter from A. L. Orr to his parents on September 12, 1862, in *Campaigning:*, p. 67-8.

mounted service, but that wouldn't be an easy matter, given that most had either sold their mounts to the government or sent them back to Texas. A former cavalryman claimed to his relatives at the time that the government had made a solemn vow to remount the regiment by the following spring. One note of particular interest is that the dismounted troops chose to hang on to their claim as dismounted cavalry, apparently rejecting the idea of only being viewed as ordinary infantrymen. This arose more from a determination, based more on perception than reality, that they were only temporarily serving in that capacity, and thus theirs was not a permanent condition.[418]

Their conversion to infantry had prompted William Young of the 15th Texas Calvary (Dismounted) to write his wife, "Nan," animatedly on September 6: "We are under the damnedest, strictest rules that a human could study out. It is [now] drill, drill, drill from morning to night." Obviously displeased with their acting brigade commander, Col. Sweet, he pronounced that "as to our colonel, let me tell you we come as near having none as a regiment well could." And as to their morale caused by their dismounting, "our boys all look down-spirited." Feeling much akin to what Malcolm Scurlock had indicated in the last paragraph, "the cry [heard] is when shall I be mounted on a horse again?" In advising a brother not to join the army at this time, he ended by stating: "For a man is as low down as he can get when he has to go as infantry."[419]

The first full division review that included Nelson's old brigade had occurred on August 28, and Pvt. Benjamin Seaton of Co. G, 10th Texas Infantry noted that there were over 6,000 soldiers included. And on September 4, there had been a separate review of Nelson's old brigade at 9:00 a.m., which may have been the event that provoked William Young of the 15th Texas Cavalry (Dismounted) to declare "that a man is as low as he can go" when serving as an infantryman. Lt. Flavius Perry of the 17th Texas Cavalry (Dismounted) wrote at this time that more Texas regiments

---

[418] Malcom Scurlock of the 18th Texas Cavalry (Dismounted) to a brother, in the *Grandview Tribune*, January 28, 1978.

[419] William Young letter, September 5, 1862, transcript copy from CRC, Hill College.

had been coming in at the rate of one or two a day at Austin, "though because of their newness to army life, they will require more drill and discipline." He included for his wife's perusal a copy he had of the "Army Bulletin" that had just begun printing in their camp, this providing some sense to those back home what was transpiring in their camps. Though a recent convert to the infantry arm, he satirically suggested to his spouse that she ought to "see me drill the company."[420]

A rather momentous event for the division had occurred in either late September or early October, described by 5th Sgt. Aaron Estes of Co. B, 10th Texas Infantry. Some thirty wagons loaded with the latest military arms had reportedly reached Little Rock, and the contents were to be distributed by those who either carried obsolete arms or had none. Though most of these would go to men in the new regiments, it's possible this is when the 10th Texas actually received the Enfield rifles they would later be noted as armed with. The new arms would go a long way to arming the troops, though oddly enough, apparently none of them were issued to the dismounted cavalry regiments in Nelson's old brigade, as they continued to utilize shotguns and sporting rifles for several months to come.[421] But Estes specifically states that by the time he wrote another letter on September 16, his regiment had indeed had had them issued to them.[422]

Perhaps the most notable incident to dramatize the men's distaste for Col. Sweet transpired in early October, when he was still in nominal charge of Nelson's old brigade. On the 9th, he decided to bolster his own ego by hosting an open-air dance that evening. Selecting an area about five miles from camp, he had a large section cleared, having sent out invitations to virtually everyone living in the vicinity to attend: "Everybody went," one Texan afterward

---

[420] *The Bugle:*, p. 22; Lt. Flavius Perry to his wife, September 6, 1862, in *Military History of Texas*, vol. 13, # 2 (1975), p. 18.

[421] Aaron Estes' letter of September 6, 1862, in the Estes Special Collection, Baylor University, Waco and a copy furnished this writer by Scott McKay of Georgia.

[422] *The Bugle:*, p. 22; Lt. Flavius Perry to his wife, September 6, 1862, in *Military History of Texas*, vol. 13, # 2 (1975), pp. 18.

complained. "Arkansan, Ingun [sic]; in all about 10,000 men." The great crowd of humanity made it next to impossible for anyone to dance, and Sweet finally had to order an armed guard to try and keep the spectators back. This did no good, and angering everyone concerned, as soldiers and civilians alike simply swept back onto the dance floor as the guard moved away.[423]

Sweet had personally pleaded with the crowd to disperse, exhorting the soldiers to clear the dance floor, but "the more he said the worse it got," said a Texan who was present. As the situation grew worse by the minute, most of the women departed in a huff, leaving the soldiers clamoring for Sweet's hide; it seemed that everyone had witnessed "a general dissatisfaction." The gulf between the commander, and those he commanded, if accounts are to be relied upon, seemed to grow ever worse in the aftermath of this debacle. The episode caused Lt. H. B. Curl of the 17th Texas Cavalry (Dismounted) to refer to Sweet a "brass mounted Colonel . . . and I believe he is detested by every man in camp."[424]

This could not have come at a more critical moment, for although he'd been promoted to the rank of brigadier general on October 12, by that date he had already begun to show signs of being out of sorts. Within a short time, he had come down with a full-blown case of typhoid fever. With the weather becoming progressively cooler (although he may have wanted to see Sweet's deficiencies, or look into Nelson's condition) MG Holmes had come up to inspect the troops at Austin. Obviously, a firm hand was required at this juncture, for the divisions being readied for service required strong leadership. Upon hearing of the state of Nelson's illness, Holmes expressed grave concerns over that officer's recovery: "I am distressed beyond measure," he wired, "and for the sake of the cause, I beseech you to take care of yourself." Holmes further suggested that Nelson come to Little Rock so that he might receive better treatment, offering his own personal surgeon to treat Nelson. But all those efforts would prove to be of no avail, and the

---

[423] *The Bugle:*, p. 22.

[424] H. B. Curl to his wife, October 18, 1862, H. B. Curl papers, CRC, Hill College; see also A. L. Orr's letter of September 12, 1862, about this incident in *Campaigning:*, p. 68.

loss of this subordinate couldn't have come at a worse time, for Curtis appeared to be getting ready to initiate another thrust at Little Rock.[425]

It seemed readily apparent that Sweet's days in command were fast nearing an end, and in less than a month, he would be headed back to Texas, ostensibly to run for political office. With Nelson still unavailable, he needed a very experienced, as well as likeable, officer. He very well may have had one in mind already: the recently arrived Alabaman Col. James Deshler. Deshler had formerly served back east with the 17th Virginia Infantry, before coming west to serve as Gen. Hindman's commissary chief. However, Deshler had remained at Little Rock when Hindman moved out to Ft. Smith, and more recently had served as the liaison officer who oversaw the movement of almost 15,000 muskets sent to the Trans-Mississippi Department. This brought him into Gen. Holmes' purview, and by all accounts, Deshler had the requisite skills for leading soldiers in the field, assuming the Texans accepted him.[426]

Meanwhile, at Helena, the situation was also in a flux, with BG Samuel Curtis having been promoted to major general on August 29, in charge of all field operations in eastern Arkansas. BG Frederick Steele had supplanted him as the field commander of the troops there or reported to be on their way to that point. In September, Steele had begun to wrestle with how best to initiate a new offensive, given that the new troop levies would raise his effective strength to about 40,000 men, more than enough for him to develop a new strategy, against which Holmes could field scarcely 24,000 men. Interestingly, both Steele's and Holmes' troops had recently been designated the same, each the "Army of the Southwest." While Holmes wrangled with how best to utilize his

---

[425] *Houston Telegraph*, November 3, 1862, State Archives, Austin. A. L. Orr of the 18th Texas Cavalry Dismounted in a letter home on September 12, notes that at that time there were eleven Texas and seven Arkansas Regiments at Camp Hope, in *Campaigning:*, pp. 67-8.

[426] *O.R.*, I, vol. 10, pt. 1, pp. 882, 884; also, see "Report from the Proceedings of Granbury's Brigade Association," (Dallas, 1888), p. 290. Some 5,000 stands of arms never reached the Trans-Mississippi, though Deshler was not held responsible for their loss in crossing the Mississippi.

troops in order to hold his present positions, Steele schemed on how best to utilize his own in bringing the state back into the Union.[427]

A department return for Holmes' army from September 17 noted that Sweet's Texas and McRae's Arkansas brigades were each at Austin, while mention was made that Garland's brigade at Pine Bluff possessed an aggregate strength of 1,317 men for duty on the same day. Over the course of the summer, troops that afterward composed Nelson's brigade had moved from near DeVall's Bluff to Little Rock, and thence to Crystal Hill, and ultimately to Austin. Meanwhile, the Texans in Garland's brigade at Pine Bluff had essentially remained in place at Camp Holmes. Though not engaged in active operations, Garland's brigade had made good use of its time in drilling his three Texas regiments, the 6th Infantry and 24th and 25th Cavalry (Dismounted), expecting to take the field as fall came on. As the hot summer months passed, the rank and file had seen few glimpses of combat, the latter's brigade at Pine Bluff watching now and again as enemy soldiers taken captive passed through on their way to Little Rock. But hardly a day had passed from this brigade's inspection when a courier arrived announcing that the enemy was making a demonstration downriver in the vicinity of the Arkansas Post.[428]

With the arrival of a second year of conflict at hand, those encamped at Austin and Pine Bluff awaited an opportunity to prove themselves on the battlefield, though the former cavalrymen now in Deshler's brigade had at least gotten the opportunity to "smell gunsmoke" either at Batesville or over on the White River near Cotton Plant. But the best chance for all would not be far beyond the horizon, and the coming winter would find both brigades down in Southeast Arkansas, where they would get the chance to show their mettle. Barely 150 miles below Little Rock, a major confrontation was brewing at a great bend of the Arkansas River, nor far from its mouth. Destiny was to bring Nelson's old brigade at Austin (now

---

[427] *O.R.*, I, vol. 10, pt. 1, p. 605; & *O.R.*, I, vol. 13, p. 605.

[428] *O.R.*, I, vol. 13, pp. 883-4; also, for a reference to the word arriving on Arkansas Post, see *One of Cleburne's Command:* p. 1. Some 2,000 Union soldiers had supposedly come within eight miles of the post on September 18, and word came the following morning for Garland to move in that direction.

under Deshler) and Garland's stationed at Pine Bluff into close contact, in the process giving everyone more fighting than likely desired.

Chapter 4

"As Pretty a Reveille as I Ever Listened To"
William T. Sherman in his Memoirs

At Austin or Pine Bluff, a stifling summer sun had shown little intent of diminishing as September wore on, the soldiers at both places languishing beneath a broiling orb that gave scant promise of relief. The soldiers found their energy sapped by the scorching temperatures and extraordinarily high humidity. But, if anything, the previous months had been a time of seasoning for those in Nelson's old and Garland's brigades. The summer had brought forth a series of events that had embroiled the men often in controversy, and had on at least on one occasion brought many a man to the brink of mutiny. But as fall approached and the military situation seemed static, and with conditions for the soldiers generally improving, including more varied and better portions of rations, along with improved drinking water and better sanitary and medical treatments, it seemed as if the government had finally gotten a handle on military matters in Central Arkansas. Indeed, it was perhaps just such a perception that caused William Young of the 15th Texas Cavalry (Dismounted) to pen on August 11, 1862: "We will be ready for the fall campaign [provided] we can get the right kind of officers."[429]

Much of the additional paperwork required of officers stemmed from a need to remedy the absence of bimonthly reports, which hadn't been filed for most regiments since they had originally been mustered in. Now, as Bryan Marsh of Co. C, 17th Texas Cavalry (Dismounted) grumbled, Little Rock was now demanding completion and submission of not only the bimonthly returns, but quarterly and others, almost all of which had to be completed in triplicate. The bimonthly forms alone required a tremendous

---

[429] William Young letter, Co. A, 15th Texas Cavalry (Dismounted), CRC, Hill College; along with "Bryan Marsh," in *Chronicles*, vol. 14, #2 (1975), p. 17.

expenditure of effort because they assessed not only the overall capability of the regiments themselves, but that of every soldier, present or absent. These were supplemented by army inspectors who came up to grade each regiment's capacity in six overall areas: instruction, military appearance, arms, accoutrements, instruction, and clothing.[430]

As stated earlier, some had been completed in late August, with these rolls providing some sense of the many variations existing within even smaller organizations, such as companies. A slightly later roll, one dated October 31, shows that Co. A of the 15th Texas Cavalry (Dismounted) were issued U.S. model 1841 rifles, and scored well in all other categories. On the other hand, Co. C of this same regiment had been shown under its "recapitulation" as scoring "good" in accoutrements, discipline, and inspection categories, but just "fair" in military appearance and "deficient" in terms of clothing; its arms were shown as "double-barrel shotguns and sporting rifles." The Co. C roll bears the notation that: "In consequence of having no blank muster rolls, the muster of August 31 has not been completed." Two men from this company had been killed at the Battle of Orient's Ferry on Black River, July 8, 1862. The wounded had by now recovered and returned to duty: "Enemy engaged[,] 5th Kansas[,] c[o]mm[ande]d by Maj. ----. Dismounted and [our] horses sent to Texas on 24 July, 1862. Present for duty: 1 capt., 1 lt., 3 sgt., 3 corp., 1 musician, 34 privates, total: 43. Died from disease: 5 KIA: 2."[431]

Such inspections had to be conducted by officers outside their commands; they then certified whether the men were in or not in compliance. Further, all deficiencies noted required a written explanation. For those who had equipment issued, but not having same at the time of the inspection, had a note appended to the roll as to why this was the case and whether a "stoppage" of wages owed the soldier was in order, i.e., if the loss was attributable to neglect. Though the process caused a mountain of bureaucratic headaches, it

---

[430] See *C.S. Regulations*, Goetzel edition, (Mobile, 1862).

[431] Bimonthly returns, Companies A & C, 15th Texas Cavalry (Dismounted), RG 109, N.A., Washington.

was only through such reports that higher authorities could gauge a unit's combat effectiveness.[432]

Of note, the returns demonstrated well the dichotomy existing between infantry regiments and their recently dismounted counterparts. Not surprisingly, the records reveal that the infantry regiments showed both a better outward physical appearance and a higher drill proficiency than did the dismounted cavalry. In fact, the dismounted men ordinarily scored substantially lower in nearly every category when compared to their infantry counterparts. For example, the 10th Texas Infantry scored "good" in every category at the October muster; the 15th Texas Cavalry (Dismounted), however, was judged only as "fair" with respect to either arms or appearance, and "tolerably deficient" in clothing and accoutrements.[433]

But considering the limited resources within the department overall, it's rather surprising that as much progress had been made as quickly as it had, given the myriad difficulties they had been greeted with just two months earlier. Though months would pass before their clothing shortages had been addressed (and that relating to proper military arms wouldn't so long as they remained in the Trans-Mississippi Department) by fall, their basic needs had been met, and in areas like the drill, most felt they were getting much more proficient than even they would have believed.

Col. Roger Q. Mills of the 10th Texas Infantry had worked diligently in the wake of the mutiny to resolve any outstanding issues; he confided to his wife his dismay that something like 200 men of his regiment had died since reaching Arkansas, and not from battlefield wounds, but from various illnesses. Despite these problems, Little Rock had not sent out qualified physicians, and those that did come seemed to have as little compassion as their higher authorities. Sadly, the department suffered from a dearth of proper medicines, though despite this, the authorities seemed to have no qualms in requiring even the sick to perform their duties. Mills ascribed this to poor leadership at the department headquarters: "Nine-tenths of our army favor Maj. Gen Sterling Price . . . [over]

---

[432] *Ibid.*

[433] Bi-monthly rolls, 15th Texas Cavalry and 10th Texas Infantry, October 31, 1862, in RG 109, N.A., Washington.

Granny Holmes," he noted, as the former officer from Missouri seemed to be genuinely concerned with his soldiers' welfare.[434]

The arrival of more Texas units in the late summer and early fall appeared to have converted portions of Arkansas into proverbial colonies of the Lone Star State. A September 17 departmental return noted that over 8,000 Texans were now serving in the vicinity of Little Rock, while other Texas units besides Garland's were scattered across the eastern part of the state. Nelson's old brigade aggregated 136 officers and 1,614 enlisted men at the time, while Garland's return put his command at 99 officers and 970 privates "for duty."[435]

By September, two more Texas brigades had arrived at Austin, Col. Overton Young's and Col. Horace Randal's, and they were assigned to Nelson's division. Each was composed of five regiments, numbering about 3,000 men, and were assigned to the division effective September 17. It was during this time that Nelson had come down with typhoid fever, and Sweet requested to be relieved shortly afterward, which made it essential to send Deshler over to assume command of Nelson's brigade.[436]

Those who had been in Arkansas for some period studied the recently arrived soldiers through jaundiced eyes. Lt. Robert Collins of the 15th Texas Cavalry (Dismounted) hoped these reinforcements would help bolster the morale of those within his own brigade. That said, "most of them are destitute of drill and discipline, [they] . . . will have to stay in camp [drilling for] some time" in order to be relied upon. The arrival of reinforcements did not bring with it an interruption in their drills, however, as attested to by another 15th Texas Cavalry soldier, who bemoaned: "It is drill, drill, [drill] from morning to night." He concluded own letter by evincing his frustrations over their current predicament, hoping things would eventually change for the better.[437]

---

[434] Roger Q. Mills to his wife, September 5, 1862, State Archives, Austin..

[435] *O.R.*, I, 13, p. 881, Return of Troops, District of Arkansas.

[436] *Ibid.*; also, see Joe R. Wise, ed. "Lt. Flavius Perry, Co. A, 17th Texas Cavalry, 1862-1865," in *Military History of Texas*, vol. 13, #2, p. 18; also, William Young letter of September 5, 1862, CRC, Hill College..

[437] *Chapters:*, p. 105; also, William Young to Nan Davenport, September 5, 1862, CRC, Hill College.

Once settled in, the new regiments found their daily life at Camp Holmes to be one of endless repetitions. Up at 5:30 a.m. for roll call, followed by sick report, and the rest of the morning was spent in squad and company drill, after which the camps were policed and sundry other chores performed. Their officers, in the meantime, were schooled in the tactic's manuals until lunch. The soldiers then spent two to three hours in the afternoon learning the more complicated battalion and brigade drills. Almost without exception, everyone then had to turn out for evening dress parade at 6:00 p.m., followed by the reading of general orders, and to receive assignment to various fatigue parties and guard duty. Officers employed their evening hours to either study or complete reports, after which lights-out came for everyone, except camp guards, at 9:00 p.m.[438]

Sometimes rumors seemed directed to somehow influence morale or deceive the enemy of Confederate intentions in their vicinity. A persistent rumor at this time suggested the troops at Austin might soon go over to the offensive; this prompted Lt. Col. Mills of the 10th Texas Infantry to chortle to his spouse that they might indeed be soon making an advance on St. Louis: "We will soon have a magnificent army here and . . . invite the vandals to [a fight, and] . . . listen to the music of our muskets." While morale did indeed seem to be improving, the rumors of going to Missouri would ultimately turn out to be a complete ruse.[439]

On the other hand, upon Garland receiving word in mid-September to move his brigade to Arkansas Post, he ordered his men to pack their wagons, prepare several days' rations, and be ready to move on the morning of September 19. Garland requested volunteers to precede the column by a series of forced marches, and Capt. Foster of Co. H afterward noted that his entire company had volunteered to move out with enough others to compose a party of some 400 men in the advance. The 6th Texas Infantry and 24th

---

[438] "Lt. Flavius Perry, Co. A, 17th Texas Cavalry, 1862-1865," in *Military History of Texas*, pp. 18-9.

[439] Roger Q. Mills, September 7, 1862, State Archives. The recent visit by General Holmes for a division review had helped fuel the rumor that they might soon be embarking on a new campaign.

Texas Cavalry (Dismounted) would be the first to go, with the 25th Texas Cavalry (Dismounted) apparently detached to serve as train guards at the rear of the column.[440]

At the Post, engineers had begun to survey a point where they felt that erecting a fort might work to Confederate advantage against an enemy expedition coming up the Arkansas River. It was to be called Ft. Hindman, and supervision of the actual labor to be performed fell to Col. John W. Dunnington, a former U.S. naval officer. He was assisted by captains Robert Fitzhugh and A. M. Williams of the Engineers Department, augmented by Capt. S. Clarkson's company of sappers and miners, and a gang of some 200 slaves. The purpose of the fort was obvious, for it must deny access to the Arkansas valley in the wake of the fall of Memphis and Helena's capture, which would enable the enemy to enter the interior of the state by way of that stream.[441]

Arriving almost as a sudden summer shower, this movement assured the men temporary relief from a banal existence outside Pine Bluff, though their marching orders foreshadowed momentous events that would occur in the not-too-distant future. The 6th Texas Infantry and 24th Texas Cavalry (Dismounted) had marched through Pine Bluff and some nineteen miles downstream before camping that first night. Two additional days of marching brought the column to Jourdan Plantation, opposite to and only ten miles from the Post. Here Garland was intercepted by an excited courier who had just ridden in with an urgent dispatch from the Post. This hastily scribbled note advised a heavy enemy force, estimated at 2,000 men, had landed below the Post and was fast moving upriver, expecting to

---

[440] "Jim Turner", in Texana, vol. XII, # 2 (1974), pp. 153-4. also, *One of Cleburne's Command:*, p. 1. In his diary, Capt. Foster had the brigade as reaching the post on the 19th, but they didn't arrive until the 20th. The Arkansas Post had at one time served as the government seat for Arkansas Territory, in 1819, until the capital was relocated to Little Rock some years later.

[441] For a full discussion of events leading up to the Battle of Arkansas Post, see Edwin Bearss, "The Battle of the Post of Arkansas," in the *Arkansas Historical Quarterly*, vol. 18, # 3, (Autumn, 1959), pp. 237-40. Hereafter cited as "Battle of Arkansas Post," *A.H.Q.*, with page #s.

seize the fort prior to Garland reaching reached there.[442] Garland called for volunteers to take part in a relief expedition, proceeding to the Post at the rapidest gait possible, wanting obviously to beat the enemy there. Leaving all extra gear behind, over 400 anxious soldiers departed for the Post not long after dusk arrived. At dawn the following morning, this column of mud-spattered, disheveled Texans suddenly appeared through the mists back of the Post; Garland shortly afterward reported his men's arrival in Little Rock.[443]

Only when they returned to the fort did the Texans learn that no enemy force had been seen anywhere near the Post. The suspected invasion force turned out to be only a small foraging party, trumped up by the locals into a full-scale offensive column. Following a short consultation between Garland and Col. Dunnington, it was agreed to send a reconnaissance party eastward, across the White River, at least until the rest of Garland's brigade reached there. Sent out the next day, however, this party returned with information that only a small party of the enemy had even been in that area and had already retired. Garland's men now settled in for the long haul, though persistent rumors had it that enemy gunboats could soon be expected to arrive in conjunction with an overland force coming from Helena. Union Gen. Steele would later acknowledge that he had sent several scouting parties into the White River area to reconnoiter the Confederate forces there.[444]

It became apparent immediately to those just reaching the Post that the site might prove a poor defensive location, subject to overflow and surrounded by low, swampy ground on three sides, with an unfordable river constituting the fourth. And back to the north lay a smattering of flat woods and choked sloughs, cut by slow-flowing creeks and bayous filled with stagnant water, their sides

---

[442] *Texana*, vol. XII, # 2 (1974), p. 153; *One of Cleburne's Command:*, p. 3; also, *Charles Leuschner*, p. 9.

[443] *A.H.Q.*, vol. 18, #3, p. 237; *One of Cleburne's Command:*, p. 1-2, where Capt. Foster advised that upon arriving they discovered the Post occupied by Capt. L. M. Nutt's Louisiana Cavalry company, these horsemen being immediately sent forth to scout the enemy, and try to draw them into an ambush.

[444] *One of Cleburne's Command:*, p. 6; as to Steele's report, see *O.R.*, I, 13, p. 653, to Henry Halleck.

choked with vegetation. All the land subject to overflow by the Arkansas River during the rainy months, which had just begun, prompted misgivings on the men's parts. Several days later, the remainder of Garland's brigade arrived at the Post, the 25th Texas Cavalry (Dismounted), with the train, the last to arrive. For some days afterward, the men relaxed in the wake of the trying march, giving them a firsthand look at this lackluster position. They would soon find themselves up to their elbows, literally as well as figuratively, laboring alongside the engineers and slave gangs in the construction of the fort.[445]

Also coming in shortly thereafter was Col. Charles Dawson's 19th Arkansas Infantry, apparently with Lt. Col. William Crawford's Arkansas Infantry battalion in tow (the latter had only two companies at this point), but the Post was to be augmented by other commands, including Capt. William Hart's Arkansas Battery and Capt. Matthew Denson's Louisiana Cavalry company. The two former units were assigned to Col. Dunnington, while both Hart's battery and Denson's company found themselves attached to Garland's command; it was understood they would compose a land defense of the fort, giving flexibility, as they could operate far beyond the fort to warn of an enemy's approach. In military parlance, a combination of infantry, artillery, and cavalry was referred to as a mixed-force command.[446] Apparently expecting to remain here for a considerable amount of time, Garland got details to start cleaning off an area behind the fort for winter quarters, in addition supplying labor details for the fort itself, the permanent structures being a plus in this rainy, miasmatic region. About this same time, Garland had instructed his men to send home for winter clothing, provided that could be arranged, given the distance to home. With most of his command originating in far South Texas, it would take a major logistical effort to get any clothing the

---

[445] *Ibid.*; and according to *O.R.*, I, 13, p. 884, initially Col. E. E. Portlock's 24th Arkansas Infantry is shown as being assigned to Garland's brigade per S. O. # 39.

[446] *O.R.*, I, vol. 13, pp. 884-5. Another example of a mixed-force is a legion in that era, which likewise included all three army branches in a single command. Capt. L. M. Nutt's Louisiana Cavalry company had earlier reached the post before Garland's command, and was later assigned to Garland.

home-folks could furnish through their relative's industry. Upon learning of the plight of this group of Texans serving in Arkansas, the *Dallas* Herald of September 13 called upon readers in that area to gather up and forward all heavy clothing that they could in order to help their brethren in the ranks make it through another winter.[447]

As the same conditions would confront both brigades, Garland's and Deshler's, the fall, which had ushered in milder weather, allowed the soldiers in both commands a better opportunity to get ready for the colder, wetter weather expected in Arkansas. It was just such an awareness of their inadequacies that motivated a private in the 18th Texas Cavalry (Dismounted) to advise loved ones: "There is about 1/3 of our regiment bare footed," lamented A. L. Orr in requesting help from those at home, "and [we] can't get shoes [here] at any price."[448]

But even issues that came their way from army headquarters generally amounted to just a fraction of what was needed, and the cooperation of those at home would be needed to supply what military authorities couldn't. In one significant area, however, just prior to departing for the Post, Garland's men found themselves much better off, when just before departing, all three regiments received an issue of arms. This resulted in the 6th Texas Infantry acquiring the latest (1853) pattern British Enfield rifles, in .577 cal.; the 24th Texas Cavalry (Dismounted) received U.S. model 1841 Rifles in .54 cal., replacing shotguns and rifles; whilst the 25th Texas Cavalry (Dismounted) settled for old, if serviceable, U.S. model 1816 muskets, converted to percussion, in .69 cal.[449] Meanwhile, up at Austin, a review of Nelson's division late that same month had

---

[447] Dallas Herald, September 13, 1862, Dallas Public Library Archives, Dallas.

[448] *Campaigning:*, September 12, 1862, p. 69. That not everyone in Deshler's suffered from a want in clothing, on October 10, Capt. Thomas Alexander had requisitioned from the quartermaster on October 10, 1862, and received for the 10th Texas Infantry 98 coats, 131 pair of pants, 160 pair of drawers, 31 pair of socks, 53 pair of shoes, 18 knapsacks and 4 axes. Miscellaneous records of stores issued, RG 109, National Archives, Washington.

[449] *Ibid.*; also, see *One of Cleburne's Command:*, p. 13. This writer has not learned to date whether the latter regiment's .69 cal. muskets had been rifled or not, for the ammunition returns (ordnance) were not found at the National Archives.

drawn a large crowd to observe the Texans, the best estimate of those present being near 20,000. Reviews such as this were perhaps intended to really appeal to higher authority, as Gen. Homes did attend, but those civilians present often stirred up the soldiers who participated as well. The men naturally found themselves demonstrating their tactical capabilities, but a recently formed division brass band certainly added a martial air. That such displays could often serve to boost soldiers' morale was attested to by a 10th Texas soldier, who afterward recalled the exhilaration he felt in the wake of this review:

> When the review was over and [we] started back, we passed where the ladies were, and they commenced waving their handkerchiefs and such a waving of hats [by us] and yelling you never heard before. It made everyone [in the ranks] "feel their weapon," [as the] saying is.[450]

The fall of '62 had turned out most auspiciously for the men of the 7th Texas Infantry also, as the soldiers at Camp Douglas in Chicago learned in August of their pending exchange and return south. Already, their regimental commanders, Col. John Gregg and Maj. Hiram Granbury, had been paroled at Ft. Warren, Boston, for shipment via Baltimore, Maryland, and on to Richmond, Virginia, where they were exchanged. And it was in Boston that Maj. Granbury sat for one of the only images of him in Confederate service, his wife accompanying him there to be treated for a female medical issue. By early September, both had taken the "cars" to

---

[450] Benjamin Seaton in *The Bugle:*, p. 23.

Vicksburg, where they had been advised to expect to soon be reunited with their former charges, expected to be released shortly.[451]

And that appears to have been the case not long after for those in the enlisted ranks, who shortly thereafter boarded rail cars for the first leg of a trip down to Cairo, Illinois. Here they boarded river packets on September 5, bound downriver for Vicksburg, and the freedoms this trip symbolized. In the meantime, Gregg had been confirmed as a brigadier general on August 29. Received in the same wire were instructions to turn over command of his regiment, the 7th Texas Infantry, to Maj. Hiram B. Granbury, who had been elevated in rank to colonel. Gregg was instructed further to report himself to MG John C. Pemberton at Jackson, Mississippi, while Granbury continued on to Vicksburg, where he would take command of the exchanged prisoners.[452] Interestingly, at Vicksburg, Granbury received orders to continue back to Texas, where he was ordered to "recruit his regiment with conscripts and such . . . unattached companies of Texas volunteers now serving in the Trans-Mississippi Dept., as may be necessary to fill said regiment." In the meantime, by virtue of Special Order #235, issued by the War Department, all surviving members of his regiment, once arrived, were to be consolidated into a single company that had been assigned to Col. J. E. Bailey's 49th Tennessee (consolidated) Infantry regiment, which became Co. A. It was understood they would remain organized as such until Granbury and other officers sent back with him on recruiting duty returned with a sufficient number of recruits to

---

[451] See *O.R.*, II, vol. 5, p. 256, reports of the Dix-Hill cartel (G. O. #142), September 25, 1862, provided for exchange points at Aiken's Landing, Virginia, and Vicksburg, Mississippi. See Granbury's record in Register # 1, p. 76, Fort Warren, Boston. It notes he was discharged on July 29, 1862, to report to General Wool in Baltimore, after which he had been shipped by boat to Fortress Monroe, Virginia, on July 31. See also, RG 109, N.A., Washington. In a letter of June 23, Granbury mentions that among the prisoner's pursuits in prison had been "playing football and pitching quoits;" though he and his Texans comrades enjoyed "chess, cards and whiskey occasionally [to] vary the monotony of our indoor life;" artifact # 1998.2.1688 from the William Moody collection, Mary Moody Northern, Inc., Galveston, Texas.

[452] *O.R.*, I, vol. 52, pt. 2, p. 382, S. O. #249, Richmond, October 24, 1862; also, see *Ibid.*, series II, vol. 3, pp. 575 & 640.

warrant the Texans being detached from and reestablished as its own separate organization.[453]

Also continuing with Granbury to Texas on recruit duty (and also charged with bringing back absentees already there in the aftermath on Ft. Donelson) were captains K. M. Van Zandt and William L. Moody. Upon arriving in Texas, they soon encountered Capt. Jack Davis, who, along with several other personnel, had escaped the surrender and made his way back to the Lone Star State. After establishing a recruiting office in Tyler, these four officers utilized both direct appeals and newspaper ads in their quest to gain recruits, the advertisements instructing willing volunteers to Tyler no later than October 22.[454]

To be of help, the *Dallas Herald* deemed it appropriate to publish a short history of the 7th Texas Infantry to that time in an effort to encourage recruits. However, a thorough reading of their travails within the past year might have turned off as many recruits as it attracted. The paper advised that twenty men had been killed at Ft. Donelson and forty wounded. Twenty-eight other men had been discharged during their service on disability certificates, but perhaps most astounding was that some 210 men had died from diseases, and only three had deserted. Perhaps no better endorsement of the severity of military service could have been provided to those wondering what to expect if joining the 7th Texas. Some twelve months before, 300 of the 750 men who had reached Hopkinsville died prior to exchange. Though such statistics might make for a good story, they didn't result in a large enlistment in the regiment.[455]

Meanwhile, back in Arkansas, "Granny" Holmes had struggled for months to provide for the logistical needs of his department, but especially those relating to rations. His former chief of commissary, James Deshler, had had to limit the supply of pork

---

[453] *Ibid.*, I, vol. 4, p. 265.

[454] *Ibid.*, I, vol. 52, pt. 1, pp. 926-7, H.Q., Exchanged prisoners, Jackson, Miss., October 24, 1862; a commutation of $230.06 was paid Granbury from Oct. 14, 1862 to January 15, 1863, for travel to Marshall, Texas, and back on recruiting duty. Found in RG 109, N.A., Washington.

[455] *Dallas Herald*, September 20 and October 11, 1862, Dallas Library Archives, Dallas.

except for hospital usage, General Order #18 being a clear indication of just how lean the supply of this item had become by September. The rapidly increasing number of soldiers there would inevitably face long-term supply problems.[456]

Oddly enough, while Garland's brigade and even many of the newer regiments just arriving in Arkansas gained appropriate arms for their men, such wouldn't be the case with what became Deshler's brigade. Though the 10th Texas Infantry had been issued the "latest model Enfields" to supplant the antiquated U.S. model 1816s they had received the previous year, the four remaining regiments of the brigade would receive few of the latest-model arms. For the present, at least, all of the dismounted cavalry regiments in the brigade would be forced to make do with double-barrel shotguns, firing buck-and-ball cartridges, or carrying the hunting rifles that had been brought from Texas.[457] Deshler had been relieved of staff responsibilities on September 28, apparently preferring an active field command, with Holmes promising quick assignment. And when Sweet's letter of resignation reached Holmes' desk later that month, Holmes obviously tapped Deshler for his replacement. By this time, Nelson's health had deteriorated such that Holmes needed someone at Austin with considerable expertise. Almost concurrent with Deshler's departure from Little Rock came the soon-infamous Special Order #42, Holmes' directive that led to what the Texans at Austin would impolitely refer to as the "Clarendon mud-races."[458]

Over at Clarendon, a very excited BG John S. Roane, thinking himself about to come under massive attack by Steele's army, rumored to be marching from Helena, sent an exaggerated

---

[456] See Col. James Deshler's order, in *O.R.*, I, vol. 13, p. 882. Likewise, see War Depart. memos of Sept. 25 & Oct. 20, 1862, in *O.R.*, I, vol. 13, p. 882 & 889, as it relates to Deshler's attempt to get some 20,000 stands of muskets to the Trans-Mississippi Department.

[457] For the Enfield rifles issued to the 10th Texas, in addition to Sgt. Aaron Estes' letter of September 16th, 1862, Estes Special collection, Baylor University; see *Houston Telegraph*, October 22, 1862, State Archives, Austin.

[458] *O.R.*, I, vol. 13, p. 882 (S.O.# 39) & 978; for the September 28 order to BG Nelson to immediately move his division to Clarendon; see S. O. #42, *O.R.*, I, vol. 13, p. 978.

report of the enemy flooding into his area, followed up by an urgent request for reinforcements to be sent. With virtually no warning beforehand, near 2:00 a.m. on October 1, just hours after bedding down, word arrived from Little Rock that directed Deshler's brigade on the road before daybreak for Clarendon. His lead regiment, the 10th Texas Infantry, moved out well before dawn at a rapid pace eastwardly, the other regiments of the brigade following. Moving off at the double-quick, the 10th Texas quickly went to a route step, the brigade moving fifteen miles along the Des Arc road to reach Hickory Plains. After a short respite there, the regiment covered another twelve miles before camping that first night at Camp Lake, having covered a little over than thirty miles.[459]

    The brigade had hardly reached the camp before a cold front barreled through, preceded by gusting northerly winds that brought with it a heavy downpour. Up before daybreak the following morning, the rain still coming down in torrents, the brigade moved just three miles to get out of the flooded bottomlands, where they halted, stacked arms, and broke ranks to permit everyone to dry themselves and equipages out. Within a matter of minutes, nearly every nearby fence and many tree limbs were covered with their wet togs, the men having to let their body heat dry out their drawers.[460]

    October 3 saw the brigade once again on the march; this resulted in another forced march that carried the command down some 35 miles of boggy roads, the roads becoming soupier the further east they went. Nearly paralleling the White River now, the column entered a flatland area called the Grand Prairie, not far from the previous haunt of the 10th Texas and the three dismounted cavalry regiments of DeVall's Bluff. On Saturday, the 4th, the brigade completed an exhausting sixteen-mile march that brought the men to Clarendon. For much of the way, the infantrymen had to prolong the artillery of Capt. James Daniel's battery through seemingly bottomless mud. The men were already worn to a frazzle by the previous day's marches; this last one proved especially trying,

---

[459] *The Bugle:*, p. 24.

[460] *The Bugle:*, p. 24.

as they had to wrestle the big guns again, the rain adding to their misery.[461]

Deshler's brigade reached Clarendon about the same time as Garland's, which had received similar orders to proceed as rapidly as possible to that point. Lt. J. D. Lum of Co. B, 25th Texas Cavalry (Dismounted) wrote a hurried letter to his wife, Lucinda, on the 1st that they were getting ready to start their march, after reaching the Post just days earlier. He told her that Curtis' army had apparently moved from Helena in their direction and that a collision could be expected shortly. Trying to assuage her fears, he continued: "I do not feel like I will get hurt, still I might be the 1st victim [i.e., casualty to fall]." On the following day, the 2nd, Jim Turner of the 6th Texas Infantry, Garland's brigade, advised that they had started for Clarendon that day. They too encountered extremely wet weather, moving via the Crockett's Bluff road in what turned out to also be a series of forced marches through bottomless mud. Along with Deshler's brigade and several other commands, Garland's command brought the troop strength there to over 8,000 men, rumors abounding that they must expect to encounter Curtis' advance any moment. The next few days instead found everyone sitting around in the rain while gangs of slaves threw a line of fieldworks. If nothing else, the men were seemingly pleased at not having to perform physical labor. The men lounged around camp, some sunning themselves on the ground like so many turtles whenever the sun did break through, their scouting parties scouring every possible approach in a vain effort to locate Curtis' column (actually Steele's), which never made an appearance.[462]

After another three monotonous days at Clarendon, with no sign of the enemy, several detachments started back for their former encampments. Garland's command reached the Post on October 12,

---

[461] Known as the "Lamar Artillery," Daniel's Battery had not long before been assigned to Nelson's Division. See *Texas in the War*, p. 37, and in 131. Also, see *The Bugle:*, p. 24.

[462] See the J. D. Lum letter in the Texas Confederate Museum, Collection # 94.30.5, Midland, Texas; and *One of Cleburne's Command:*, p. 6; also, *Texana*, vol. 12, p. 154, reports Garland's brigade would return to the post October 15, but it may actually have been the 12th, as Capt. Foster of the 24th recalled.

and the men returned to work on their unfinished winter quarters. Even as the men of Deshler's brigade broke camp, word came their beloved division commander, Allison Nelson, who had remained hospitalized at Austin, had passed away, the news casting a pall over everyone: "Col. Nelson was about the best man Texas ever sent out and was about the best and most efficient officer in Arkansas," a division officer remembered afterward. Disheartened by this event, and smarting still from what many perceived as another senseless campaign they had just endured, the men understandably appeared in a foul mood even before they began the return march. Rumor had it that BG Henry McCulloch would soon arrive from Texas to become Nelson's replacement at division headquarters.[463]

Hardly had the men been formed and gotten underway on the 9th than rain began to fall again, first as a light mist, but with every passing hour, it seemed to grow heavier and heavier, until at last it came down in buckets. There would be no frolicking or lighthearted banter on the way back, just as there had been none on the way down. But now, the pouring rain on the return march could not even stifle the grunts and groans of the soldiers, intermixed with constant swearing, the sounds often spliced by an unearthly sucking noise coming from thousands of feet kneading the roadways into an unbelievably deep quagmire. That first day saw a rough march of only twenty miles, given the conditions, the column encamping finally at Prairie's crossroads, where they spent a most miserable night in the continuing downpour. By this time, any chatter had long since disappeared, and the water-logged, filthy uniforms hung loose on their frames, each man lying down in the driving rain in a stone-cold silence.[464]

---

[463] Norman Brown, ed., *Journey to Pleasant Hill: The Civil War Letters of Capt. Elijah Perry*, (San Antonio) 1983, p. 87. The *Houston Telegraph*, November 3, 1862, in publishing Holmes' G. O. #15 advising that Nelson's death had come at 9:15 a.m. on the 7th, State Archives, Austin. His burial took place October 9, with Col. J. W. Speight's 15th Texas Infantry regiment, Morgan's Squadron of Texas Cavalry, and Edgar's Texas Battery serving as funeral escort.

[464] Interestingly, Lt. Henry Curl of Co. B, 17th Texas Cavalry (Dismounted) advised his wife in a letter on October 8 that the march might have been merely a ruse to draw out Curtis' army. He could not advise her how many troops were involved, being prohibited from doing so. Only 200 of the men in his regiment

On the 10th, a Friday, Deshler's brigade saw the front approaching them through the deluge. They reached Brownsville that evening, where they "enjoyed" a short respite following a twenty-two-mile jaunt. This whole day, with the rain seemingly increasing by the hour, they continued their march, the mud "from shoe-mouth to knee-deep, and it very cold." The next day proved to be even more onerous than the previous ones. They slogged some sixteen tortuous miles on the bottomless roads to reach their former camps at Austin. Thinking themselves deserving of time off to recuperate, instead they found themselves once again engaged in the normal "routine of drilling, guard-mount . . . parade and inspection."[465]

The morale of those men in both brigades who'd spent a week of "sloshing" and "counter-sloshing" through the White River region before returning to Arkansas Post and Austin was very poor. Few expressed surprise that they had not encountered an enemy soldier; fewer still saw any amusement in what most felt had been a "wild goose chase." Within days, however, the weather began to gradually improve, and as they got back on their feet (literally), they fervently hoped to spend a quiet winter in quarters, hoping not to be disturbed again before spring arrived.[466]

In one area alone would there be progress during this first week in October. In Austin, Governor Thomas Lubbock had informed acting quartermaster Giddings of the 24th Texas Cavalry that the state would turn over to that officer an order of penitentiary cloth that had originally been assigned to a Capt. Young, who represented BG Albert Pike's Indian Brigade, the following bulk material: 2,501 yards of kersey, 2,491 yards of woolen "plains;" 20,360 yards of osnaburg; and, 9,647 yards of cotton "jeans." This would be escorted by the Reverend Hugh Glass to Holmes's headquarters for distribution to Texans in Arkansas, and this cloth eventually went into making uniforms for the regiments in Garland's

---

were present, and that guard details kept civilians out of their camp. He admonished her to "guard well" their children, "for a good name is worth everything. Teach them . . . modesty, industry, and honesty" CRC, Hill College.

[465] *The Bugle:*, p. 25; *Chapters:*, p. 63.

[466] *One of Cleburne's Command:* p. 7.

brigade. In total, Glass took the entire 35,000 yards of material proffered.[467]

Not long after the "Clarendon mud-races" had occurred, Samuel Cooper, the adjutant and inspector's general officer at Richmond, Virginia, had been in communication with MG Holmes, when on October 15, he ordered Holmes to "send seven Texas regiments from your department to Virginia," as General Robert E. Lee sorely needed replacements for the famed Hood's Texas Brigade in his army, which had almost been destroyed in the wake of the recent Maryland campaign. Unnerved by the request, Holmes temporarily delayed responding to the order, in the meantime telegraphing MG Thomas C. Hindman that: " . . . to complete my depression, I have just received a telegraphic order to send seven regiments of Texas troops to Richmond." He went on: "I will probably send Garland's three regiments . . . ."[468]

Seeming to comply, Holmes had wired Cooper the following day, the 19th, that "I will order Garland's Brigade of three regiments, now at the Post of Arkansas," to move, and further that "Col. Garland will move his brigade as soon as the guns are mounted in the fort now being constructed at the Post, . . . say, in ten days." But apparently, however, in the intervening weeks, with nary a query from Richmond as to this response, Holmes awaited the receipt of peremptory orders before sending off the troops enumerated. And, to the good fortune of the department, if not the troops involved, those orders never arrived.[469]

While in all probability ignorant of the ongoing communications, at Arkansas Post, Garland noted the arrival of Col. C. L. Dawson's 19th Arkansas Infantry, along with Lt. Col. William Crawford's Arkansas Infantry battalion, and heard that Col. E. E. Portlock's 24th Arkansas Infantry, then stationed at St. Charles,

---

[467] See Huntsville Penitentiary Papers, Box 4-8-407, State Archives, Austin.

[468] *O.R.*, I, vol. 13, pp. 888-9.

[469] *Ibid.*, I, 13, p. 889. Though replying within two days to Cooper's demand, his return message was not received at Richmond until November 22! In a letter to his mother on October 20, 1862, Isaiah Harlan of Co. G, 10th Texas Infantry had advised that: "The Texas Brigade there (in Virginia) is said to have been annihilated in the[ir] last battle," CRC, Hill College.

would soon join them there. These troops were to be consolidated into another infantry brigade that would serve as the fort's permanent troop garrison. With the heavy battery positions there nearing completion, lacking only the mounting of the heavy tubes that had recently come off the gunboat *Pontchartrain*, the fort had become quite formidable. To man the fort's heavy guns, a detachment of thirty-five sailors and marines had come ashore to man the heavy battery.[470]

In order to test the garrison's capabilities, Garland ordered a review and inspection in a large clearing back of the Post for October 18. A junior officer in the 24th Texas Cavalry (Dismounted), Sam Foster, left a remarkable account of this, his first experience at such a stirring ceremony:

> It was a grand sight to see about 4,000 soldiers all out at once . . . , with one cavalry company and one [of] artillery. The artillery company had four brass cannons and two wagons with each gun, and to see them unhitch the wagon that has the gun on it and go through the motions of loading and shooting was something new. It was [as they say,] as good as a show.

It's not known if Foster's reference to the cavalry company was Capt. L. M. Nutt's Shreveport Rangers or Capt. Matt Denson's Red River Rangers, for both Louisiana companies had already reached the Post by this date. Denson's company may have been downstream at Napoleon, however.[471]

---

[470] *O.R.*, I, vol. 22, p. 904; also, see Edwin Bearss, "The Battle of the Post of Arkansas," in *A.H.Q.*, 18, #3 (1959), p. 240. Dawson's 19th Arkansas Infantry should not be mistaken for Col. H. P. Smead's 19th Arkansas Infantry, the former originating in western Arkansas and having seen earlier service in the Indian nations. For a brief history of Dawson's regiment, see *A.H.Q.*, vol. 32, #4 (1973), p. 306.

[471] *One of Cleburne's Command:* p. 7. The review encompassed other troops besides Garland's brigade, apparently including the Arkansas regiments as well as the marine detachment that manned the fort's guns.

Back at Austin, the men in Deshler's brigade could scarcely do more than try to ward off the rapidly deteriorating weather. BG Henry McCulloch arrived to take command of the division that Deshler's now belonged to, although most understood his selection to be but a temporary appointment. One advantage came with the cooler weather, which brought with it an improvement in the men's vigor, which translated into their spending less time at hospitals and more with their commands. October had brought with it the first frost of the fall, which had been followed by snowfall, the continuing shortage of tents and blankets forcing men to spoon together often, just to keep themselves warm at night. They criticized staff officers at departmental headquarters, who they blamed for the actual shortages, especially their own quartermasters charged with ensuring that badly needed supplies reached the men.[472]

A major remaining issue for the men of Deshler's brigade was their prospects of having to go into battle with inferior arms: "It is said," an optimistic Texan reported at Camp Nelson (renamed from Camp Hope for their deceased division commander), "[understand] that Holmes is receiving arms from beyond the Mississippi . . . and that 10,000 have [recently] reached Little Rock." While not just idle rumor, instead of the latest arms going to Deshler's men, they went west to Ft. Smith in order to supply BG Hindman's army. Another rumor, which did not come true, had it that Deshler's brigade might be sent to Fayetteville, out in the far northwest part of the state.[473]

On the Federal side of the coin, on October 29, Col. Robert A. Cameron of the U.S. Army had written Col. Charles E Hovey that because of a lack of forage in the Arkansas River valley due to drought, both the 24th and 25th Texas Cavalry had recently been dismounted. While both had indeed been converted to infantry, fortuitously, those two, and their companion regiment, the 6th Texas Infantry, would be recipients of an early Christmas present when, at

---

[472] Z. H. Crow in a letter of Martha, October 17, 1862, in "A Smith County Confederate," in *Chronicles*, vol. 4, #2 (1975), p. 13.

[473] Isaiah Harlan, Co. G, 10th Texas Infantry, October 17, 1862, CRC, Hill College.

the end October, uniforms made from the Huntsville Penitentiary cloth came into camp. When issued to the men on November 1, the distribution provided every man a complete suit of clothes that included short (or "shell") jackets, with matching pairs of pants and caps, each of the same cut and color. For men who had grown accustomed to identifying comrades by their variegated dress, these new uniforms stood in stark contrast to their former clothing. Capt. Sam Foster of the 24th Texas declared: "The men [now] all look so different [from one another, as] you can't tell one from another unless you see his face."[474]

But new clothes alone wouldn't deter the diseases so prevalent in this swampy area, such as that which encircled the Post: "Stout, healthy men [still] take sick one day and die the next," lamented one of Garland's company officers, a rumor circulating that "on the 13th there were 9 buried," and that "a Mexican in [Capt.] Fly's Co. died [whilst] standing on his feet," penned Capt. Foster of the 24th Texas Cavalry (Dismounted).[475]

Especially disconcerting, at least according to Pvt. Robert Hodges of the 24th Texas Cavalry (Dismounted): "I assure you, we can hear the dead march nearly at all times of the day and sometimes in the night." And Capt. Bryan Marsh of the 17th Texas Cavalry (Dismounted) complained that cold weather at night, especially as the season progressed, made it where the men "can't all spoon at the same time."[476]

Another soldier serving in Deshler's brigade at Camp Nelson (Austin) perhaps reflected the belief of many Texans in Arkansas this winter when exclaiming that this "country was never made for white people to live in, nothing but frogs and crawfish can live here long." Though cooler weather had initially eliminated many of the debilitating illnesses soldiers had suffered from, the arrival of severe

---

[474] *O.R.*, I, 13, p. 770, for the Cameron and Hovey account. See *One of Cleburne's Command:*, p. 8, for Capt. Foster's comments.

[475] *One of Cleburne's Command:*, p. 8.

[476] *Ibid.*, 8; and for a reference to the appearance of "black tongue" among those at the Post, see Maury Darst, ed., "Robert Hodges, Jr.:" in *E. T. H.J.*, vol. 9, #1 (1971), p. 33, who had made the previous statement; "Bryan Marsh" letter of October 29, in *Chronicles*, vol. 14, # 2, p. 18-9.

winter conditions began to reverse the trend, with soldiers now struck by colds, the flu, or worse, pneumonia. Lt. Flavius Perry of the 17th Texas Cavalry (Dismounted) wrote to his wife, Eva, on October 28 that it had snowed there even prior to the first frost of the season. A final appendage to this letter attested to the displeasure he felt over their dismounting and that their pay had been reduced to that of infantrymen; they had lost a dollar a month in the process.[477]

If the adverse weather did not flag men's spirits, recent events inside the Lone Star State must have done so. In early November, word began to filter in that Galveston had fallen recently from an enemy naval assault, and that Houston and San Antonio could be expected to follow. Should these prove true, and the latter two weren't, these rumors caused men to ponder why they would want to stay in Arkansas, with their own state about to be overrun. Not surprisingly, some men felt the need to go home, turning up missing at morning roll calls, apparently believing themselves duty-bound to protect those at home rather than continuing to serve in far-off Arkansas.[478]

When heavy snows began falling on October 25, this provided a temporary escape from the rigid drill regimen, but word arrived that the second conscription act had recently passed, which would require all males between the ages of seventeen and forty-five, including most of those men discharged under the first act, to return to military service. Refusal to do so could brand individuals as deserters if they failed to comply with the act. In light of their recent dismounting and the pay reductions ordered for the now-dismounted cavalrymen, this act caused spirits to sag anew. In an effort to assist the existing regiments, papers like the *Dallas Herald* on December 6, 1862, would publish General Order #29, that those formerly discharged from the 15th Texas Cavalry (Dismounted) were ordered to report to Tyler for a return to duty with that command.[479]

---

[477] "The Letters of Lt. Flavius Perry," in *Military History of Texas*, vol. 13, #2, p.24.

[478] "Robert Hodges, Jr.", where the writer tried getting a transfer to a regiment in Texas, rather than remaining in Arkansas, *E.T.H.J.*, vol. 9, #1, (1971), p. 33.

[479] "The Letters of Lt. Flavius Perry," in *Military History of Texas*, vol. 13, #2, p. 24, concerning their pay reduction.

If the regiments affected by such orders could take solace in anything, it may well have been at the expense of the new units that had lately filtered in from Texas. A captain in Deshler's brigade, Bryan Marsh of the 17th Texas Cavalry (Dismounted), observed a new regiment's adjustment to their long-suffering existence:

> It would amuse you to hear the men in the new regiments complaining of [the] strict discipline and hard living. Reducing their [number] of wagons [per regiment] . . . will [shortly] cause them to lay aside camp stools, cots and other creature comforts.

Though perhaps just as miserable as the new men, the old hands had become so used to their treatment that they "look down their noses" at the neophytes trying to make the adjustments.[480]

Though for the most part inactive, the Texans in Arkansas followed the actions of those involved in active theaters. Gen. Holmes had, in issuing General Order #33, praised Capt. Alf Johnson's Texas Spy Co. once again for the recent havoc they had wreaked with enemy foraging parties in the neighborhood of Helena. This independent company had taken, as a result, sixteen wagons, eighty mules, and thirty horses, and in the process had killed twenty and taken twenty-seven others captive. And at Newtonia, Missouri, in late October, a mounted Texas Cavalry brigade had engaged in a memorable fight, instilling still more pride for those from Texas awaiting their own opportunity.[481]

Through the recent issuance of clothing and arms, combined with the items sent from loved ones back home, in one area only had they suffered from the adverse weather of recent weeks. Heading into November, they still faced one tremendous shortage: the lack of shoe leather. This was certainly not good for men who had to hoof it everywhere they went, especially with the weather seemingly growing worse with every passing day. Despite the shortage of

---

[480] "Bryam Marsh" letter of October 29, 1862, to "Mit," in *Chronicles*, vol. 14, # 2, p. 19.

[481] *O.R.*, I, vol. 13, p. 907; see also Robert S. Weddle, *Plow Horse Cavalry: The Caney Creek Boys of the 34th Texas Cavalry*, (Austin, 1981), pp. 54-65.

brogans, a 10th Texas private noted that he otherwise could survive an entire year on what he had just received, provided he "had no bad luck." Obviously unaware of the prophetic nature of this statement, in a touching letter to those at home, he praised a young son, advising that he had included a small token of esteem: somehow, he had found some marbles, and had mailed fourteen as a gift to a son he knew would "continue to support his mother."[482]

Sweet's resignation having become effective October 25, Deshler received assignment as the permanent commander of what had been Nelson's "old" brigade. A more unusual happenstance that occurred during this week saw Capt. James McKnight's Angelina County company reach Austin; it quickly became Co. I of the 17th Texas Cavalry (Dismounted). A lesser event came when Deshler's brigade lost the services of Daniel's Texas Battery, though Capt. Horace Haldeman's Texas Battery would supplant Daniel's.[483]

In early November, Deshler's brigade had been moved to near Little Rock, along with at least a portion of McCulloch's division, to a point midway between Hindman's army at Ft. Smith and Garland's command at Arkansas Post. Holmes ordered that Deshler's brigade be immediately sent to him, with Deshler to hold the regiments in readiness to move, as the situation warranted, to the support of either. Holmes needed the flexibility of reinforcing either of his widely scattered wings in the event of an emergency, the only question being who would need help first. And, to their misfortune, it was this reliance upon Deshler's command that events in Southeast Arkansas would require the brigade to ultimately be sent to the Post.[484]

The origins of this movement came about on November 3, after a reconnaissance force from Helena sent out by BG Alvin P. Hovey prompted that officer to seek permission to take a sizeable

---

[482] As to the clothing issues, see Isaiah Harlan of Co. G, 10th Texas, to his mother, November 9, 1862, CRC, Hill College; and on the marbles gift, see Noah Snider's letter, November 2, 1862, CRC, Hill College.

[483] For the Angelina company, see "Lt. Flavius Perry" in *Military History of Texas*, vol. 13, #2, p. 25; for a history of Haldeman's Battery, see *Texas in the War*, pp. 39-40.

[484] Isaiah Harlan to his mother, November 2, 1862, CRC, Hill College.

force and attempt to seize the Post. Pro-Unionists in the area convinced Holmes that he must expect trouble there sooner or later. With McCulloch's division posted as a rapid-strike force in Little Rock, it meant that he could move quickly to the southeast at a moment's notice, and Holmes now waited to see what the enemy might be doing down south. And it had been a meeting with McCulloch at Austin in early November that Holmes had first briefed McCulloch on just such a prospect.[485]

After a conference with McCulloch, "Old Grannie" had elected to directly speak to the men of that division; he first commended them as the best one in his department, after which he ordered Deshler's brigade to immediately come to the capital. The brigade had just reached there when it saw itself ordered back to Austin. It seemed to the men that they might just spend the entire winter moving back and forth between the two points. Though, with a little luck, they might not be called upon to assist either army wing; alas, if anyone maintained such hopes, they would be in for a major disappointment![486]

Some twenty-five miles above the mouth of the Arkansas River stood a quaint cluster of shacks bearing the imposing name Napoleon, and on November 17 the pickets there stood guard for enemy gunboats and transports. On this day, an observant cavalryman watched as several vessels arrived, and soon after began sounding the depth of the river, one of the videttes dashing upstream to convey the news of the enemy's arrival in the vicinity. That message went out over the wires to Little Rock; Holmes was advised the vessels were conducting preparatory sounding before entering

---

[485] "The Battle of Arkansas Post," *A.H.Q.*, vol. XVIII, # 3, (autumn, 1959), p.240. While Curtis had not approved Hovey's requests, that officer had decided to go ahead and proceed, *O.R.*, I, 13, p. 788.

[486] *The Bugle:*, p. 28, Seaton refers to Holmes' visit and the subsequent orders. Interestingly, Lt. Flavius Perry of the 17th Texas Cavalry (Dismounted) and William Young of the 15th Texas Cavalry (Dismounted) mention a dearth of shoes in their respective commands, with Isaiah Harlan of the 10th Texas Infantry doing so as well, going further to state that the men could not do duty given the weather. See Perry's letter of November 5, 1862, in *Military History of Texas*, vol. 13, # 2, p. 17; William Young letter, Nov. 10, 1862, CRC, Hill College; Isaiah Harlan letter of November 9, 1862, also CRC, Hill College.

either the Arkansas or the White. After dispatching the information to Little Rock, including a request for reinforcements, Garland turned the entire garrison out under arms. He then ordered his own brigade to move downstream to discover the enemy's intent, as their actions clearly presaged a fight in the near future.[487]

Due to low water in the Mississippi, Hovey had taken three days to get his expedition of 6,000 infantrymen and 2,000 cavalrymen downriver to this point. Though not yet receiving approval for this reconnaissance of the Arkansas River valley, he expected to move up the White River, and via a cut-off there, he could then steam on up the Arkansas to reach the Post. Capt. Henry Walke, commander of the Union navy, had charge of the gunboats as well as the transports bearing Hovey's troops; he reported the White accessible even though the water was quite low. Should he succeed in getting over the bar, he could steam up that river to the Arkansas itself, where his gunboats could advance to engage the fort. Provided everything went as planned, Hovey would then be left only with the enviable duty of accepting the Post garrison's surrender.[488]

Upon learning there was 5.5 feet of depth at the bar, Hovey put Col. Cyrus Bussey's 1st Iowa Cavalry regiment ashore on the left bank of the river so that officer could move up with his regiment to seize the ferry across Wild Goose Bayou. Already, Col. George McGinnis' 11th Indiana Infantry had been offloaded at the mouth of the Arkansas, his job being to prevent any enemy troops from being ferried across the river from Prentiss, Mississippi, in order to attack Hovey in his rear. Above the cut-off, the navy found another shallow bar that prevented Hovey's gunboats from going any further, the shallow water not able to accommodate deep-draft gunboats, leaving Hovey with little choice but to reconsider his plan of attack. Knowing that it most likely would require several days to march to the Post from this point, and even more to reduce it, Hovey decided

---

[487] Post of Arkansas:", in *A.H.Q.*, vol. 18, #3 (1971), p. 241; *One of Cleburne's Command:*, p. 9.]

[488] *Ibid.*, p. 242; "The Conquest of Arkansas," in *Battles &Leaders*, vol. III, p. 450, reports on unsuccessful efforts to take the post at that time.

to withdraw after receiving orders from Helena to suspend the operation and return to that point.[489]

By the time Hovey had reached this decision, Bussey's troops had made it to within eight miles of the Post, alarming the sentries, some of whom thought themselves about to be cut off. But even as Hovey recalled Bussey and other detachments on shore to withdraw to the boats, Holmes had finally reacted to the news. Once back aboard, Hovey had the fleet steam away, his only success the destruction of an artillery redoubt and the ferry at Wild Goose Bayou. Though the operation appeared fruitless, nevertheless, it planted the seeds for a later, and larger, operation directed against the Post. Meanwhile, Hovey steamed back up the Mississippi to reach Helena on November 21.[490]

Prior to sending men downstream to confront the approaching force, at midnight Garland had called his junior officers together for a briefing, occurring in the midst of a torrential rainstorm that continued unabated throughout the night. At the meeting, he enumerated what he wanted to see happen should a fight break out. Not long after, the men were jostled out of their beds and ordered to prepare two days' rations of cornbread, after which they sleepily fell into line for the march.[491]

In the pitch-black darkness, Garland's brigade headed downriver in the direction of Col. Notribe's landing, the nearest point it was thought that a sizeable enemy force might be landed on the same bank as the fort. These men had barely covered two miles when word came for the brigade to immediately halt and to start entrenching, as rumors circulated that the enemy had already begun to offload at Notribe's, only two miles away. Garland's troops occupied a low rise on the left bank, their line running almost at right angles from the river itself, from which the men expected to dispute the enemy's approach up the river road at that point. Through assiduous efforts, the men completed rifle pits that averaged six feet

---

[489] "The Battle of Ark. Post," in *A. H. Q.*, vol. XIII, # 3, p. 241.

[490] *Ibid.*, p. 242-3

[491] Newton Allen letter, December 7, 1862, 24th Texas Cavalry (Dismounted), courtesy Joe Browder, Cleburne, Texas.

in width but only a foot in depth, throwing the dirt over to the outside such "that by standing in the ditch [one] . . . can just see over the works."[492]

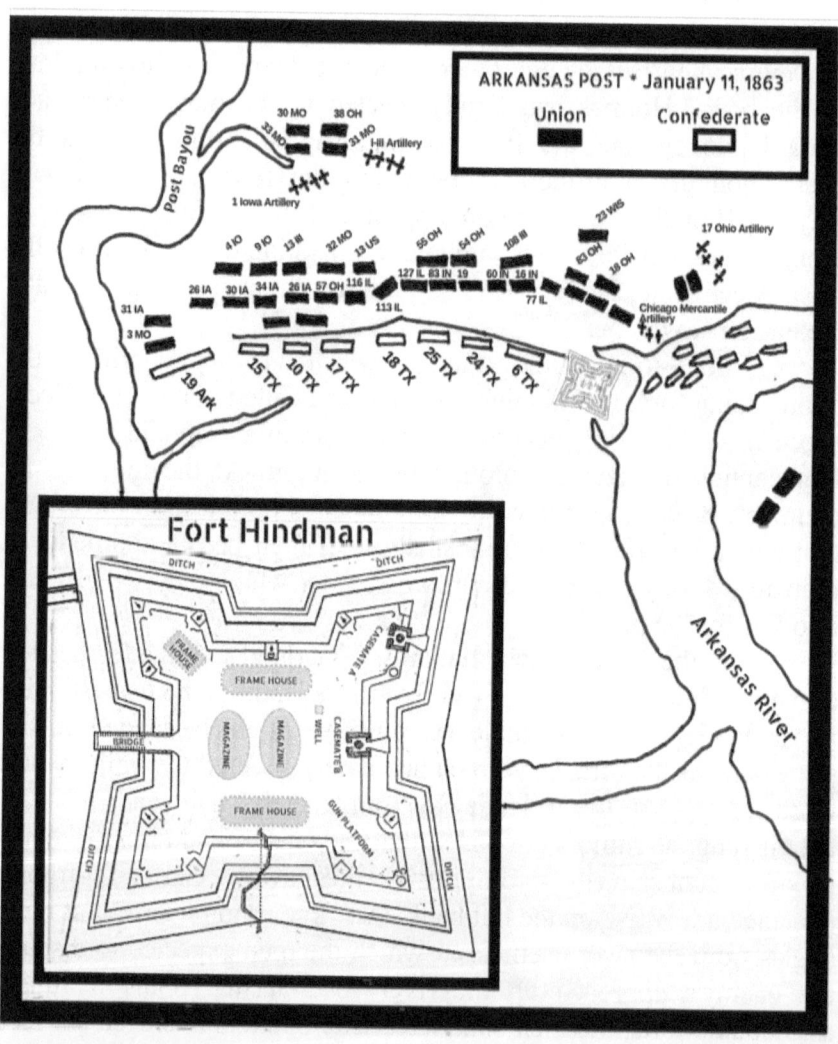

---

[492] *One of Cleburne's Command:*, p. 9. Also, "Post of Arkansas," in *A.H.Q.*, vol. 18, #3, p. 248. The spelling of Notribe's won't use Bearss' spelling, but rather Union Army contemporary accounts.

These works lay atop a natural levee of the river, with the right anchoring on the riverbank itself and his left extending eastward until terminating upon Coyne's Hill, a modest rise a half-mile back from the river. Beyond lay an impassable swamp, thick with underbrush, making any enemy attempt to move in that direction a virtual impossibility. Before midnight, the men had occupied the works, most anxiously scanning the downstream area for signs of enemy smoke. This would signal the close approach of the enemy gunboats, suggesting that the enemy force was being landed further down than Notribe's. With darkness coming on and no obvious signs of the enemy, Garland sent scouts down to observe for signs of the enemy in the distance; they reported back as seeing not one enemy soldier[493].

Capt. Sam Foster of the 24th Texas Cavalry (Dismounted) briefly described these events: how they marched downriver in a column, and how that when they got to the works, there wasn't sufficient room to hold all of the troops. Before heading down to occupy this advance line, " [we] . . . go to the Ordnance wagon and draw 40 rounds . . . for each man; it raining like the blazes." Proud of their accomplishment, "by 2 O'Clock [sic] p.m. we had a very nice breastwork," but having not seen a single enemy soldier, his brigade was withdrawn before dark, the men returning to their camps, "and [with] no one hurt."[494] In Little Rock, Holmes reacted to the reports from the Post by again ordering Deshler's brigade to the capital in order to dispatch that brigade to the Post. About 1:00 a.m. on the 21st, the sergeants began to kick the men awake, everyone hustling into line for roll call as their drums sounded the long roll. After ensuring every man was at his post, ammunition was distributed, each issued the standard forty rounds. They then stacked arms, loaded surplus baggage aboard their wagons, and promptly went back to bed to await the coming of dawn. By 8:00 the next morning, the regiments were ordered into a closed column, and the men were

---

[493] Capt. Samuel Foster, 24th Texas Cavalry (Dismounted), advises that both colonels Wilkes and Gillespie had ridden down to verify reports of the enemy being ashore, but saw no evidence of the enemy "nearer than twelve miles." *One of Cleburne's Command:*, p. 9

[494] *Ibid.*, p. 9.

given a pep talk by McCulloch. According to Benjamin Seaton of Co. G, 10th Texas Infantry, McCulloch "flattered us" in this speech, and the men responded with three cheers, after which they got underway. According to George Allen of Co. A, of the same regiment, the division commander had complimented them by stating "our regiment [is] the best drilled and disciplined regiment in the western army."[495] Up again and breakfasted before 8:00 a.m., their tents struck and wagons ready to move, they anxiously awaited the march to begin. McCulloch came over and "flattered" the men with a rousing talk before they began, and the men "all gave three cheers to the General and off we marched." Pvt. G. W. Allen of Co. A, 10th Texas Infantry seemed genuinely struck by McCulloch's appeal: "He praised our Regt[.] very much and said we was the best drilled and best disciplined Regt[.] in the Western Army, which was saying a heap for us; he also said that if there was a fight [that] we should be in it first!"[496]

The brigade moved in a closed column of regiments toward the capital, arriving there on November 22 after a thirty-five-mile march. It was made known that they would there be loaded aboard river packets for the trip down the Arkansas. On the 23rd, a Saturday, they patiently waited all day for the steamboats to arrive, though they didn't come up until almost dark. According to Benjamin Seaton of the 10th Texas, Holmes himself reviewed them early on Monday morning, after which Mills' regiment boarded the side-wheel steamer, *Arkansas*; this vessel immediately cast off and turned its bow downstream. Next came Col. James Taylor's 17th Texas Cavalry (Dismounted), which went aboard the *Julian Roane*; that vessel departed as soon as everyone got aboard. Other steamers would arrive later that day to load Col. Nicholas Darnell's 18th Texas Cavalry (Dismounted) and Maj. V. P. Sanders' 15th Texas Cavalry (Dismounted), the latter regiment trailing at the rear of the brigade.[497]

---

[495] *The Bugle:*, p. 27.; also, see Isaiah Harlan letter of November 20, 1862, CRC, Hill College.

[496] "The Civil War Letters of George W. Allen" in *S.W.H.Q.*, vol. 83, (July, 1979), p. 52.

[497] *The Bugle:*, p. 28; Isaiah Harlan letter of December 3, 1862, CRC, Hill College; also, see Henry B. Curl letter of November 21, 1862, Henry B. Curl

Obstructions in the river and shallow water slowed their progress, this causing several of the vessels to go aground, temporarily forcing the convoy to a halt. Hardly had they gotten underway when a "blue norther" struck, drenching those in the open with a cold, pelting rain, accompanied by bitterly cold winds that continued throughout the remainder of the trip. Some joked that the weather couldn't have gotten any worse that first day, but each successive one convinced most otherwise, as it was seemingly growing worse on the hour. The inclement weather made this a most grueling trip.[498]

When the vessel carrying Taylor's 17th Texas Cavalry (Dismounted) hove to at the dock at Pine Bluff, the men finally had the opportunity to spend some of their hard-earned cash, many imbibing in the "wet goods" found in riverfront grogshops. A real cavalryman, whose Critter company had only recently arrived in the state but was now on its way to Arkansas Post, watched from the bank as boatload after boatload of reinforcements passed by their camp. W. W. Heartsill, of Capt. Samuel Richardson's W. P. Lane Rangers, advised that while encamped on the river below that city, the cavalrymen watched curiously in the early afternoon hours of November 26 as Col. Mills' 10th Texas Infantry passed by aboard the *Arkansas,* its decks packed with infantrymen. The following morning, the steamer *Julian Roane* passed, its decks loaded down with Taylor's by now spirited men (if we accept Capt. Bryan Marsh's account of the 17th Texas' brief layover at Pine Bluff), huddling together aboard the vessels to ward off the bitter winter wind.[499]

---

papers, wherein he advises that the 10th Texas Infantry actually boarding at 9:00 a.m., CRC, Hill College.

[498] *The Bugle:*, p. 28.

[499] Bryan Marsh," in *Chronicles*, vol. 14, #2, (1975), pp. 19-20; see also Bell I. Wiley, ed., *Fourteen Hundred and 91 Days in the Confederate Army: A Journal Kept by W. W. Heartsill for four years, one month and one Day*, (Jackson, 1953), pp. 81-3. Cited hereafter as *Fourteen Hundred*. That the winds were blustering horrifically is evidenced by a notation from Benjamin Seaton of Co. G, 10th Texas Infantry, who recorded on November 27 that the winds forced the boats to pull ashore until they subsided. See *The Bugle:*, p. 28, wherein he notes this in a diary entry of that date.

Richardson's Lane Rangers had only been in Arkansas briefly before being ordered to proceed to the Post; the men followed the winding river road along the south bank to reach there. The boats had hardly passed when Richardson's company received orders to push forward in all haste to the Post. After a strenuous ride, the cavalrymen reached the riverbank opposite Ft. Hindman, a place known locally as Stilwell's Point, on the 30th. It was discovered that BG Thomas J. Churchill had in the meantime also arrived to assume overall command of the Post forces, and that officer advised Richardson to put his men into camp before reporting to headquarters for instructions. As Heartsill remembered, the men pitched their tents in a beautiful grove of trees that framed the huge fortress in the distance. The cavalrymen designated this site as Camp Gil McKay, in honor of a captain serving in Taylor's 17th Texas Cavalry (Dismounted), which had only just arrived at the Post before Capt. Richardson's company.[500]

As with the remaining regiments in Deshler's brigade that arrived via steamer during this time, the 17th Texas Cavalry (Dismounted) had encountered several problems in getting there. To compound matters, only days after arriving, Capt. Gill McKay of Co. I, with several other officers of the 17th Texas Cavalry (Dismounted), came to pay their respects to their comrades in Richardson's Lane Rangers. What appeared to capture everyone's attention had begun with a candid reflection by McKay that conditions at the Post seemed remarkably like what he had learned about Ft. Donelson the previous February. Virtually anyone with cursory military knowledge who viewed the environs of Ft. Hindman thought it not a well-situated fort. As confirmation of that fact, on December 3, Isaiah Harlan of Co. G, 10th Texas wrote home that the fort itself was a strong work, "[though] it seems to me that if the enemy should bring a force large enough to take the place, that they would [easily] take us too."[501]

---

[500] *Ibid.*, p. 85. W. W. Heartsill kept a very detailed account of his war-time experiences, and these often help fill gaps that otherwise would not have been made known of the Texans at the Post, or afterward in the Army of Tennessee.

[501] *Ibid.*; also, Isaiah Harlan letter of December 3, 1862, CRC, Hill College.

With Deshler's arrival, there were now close to three full infantry brigades either on hand or on their way. This being a sufficient number, a decision was reached to combine all three into a single division structure, Churchill bearing overall responsibility for integrating Garland's, Deshler's, and Col. John Dunnington's Arkansas regiments into the new division. Though Garland's and Deshler's were nominally all-Texan, Dunnington's was to incorporate the 19th and 24th Arkansas Infantry, along with the two companies of William Crawford's Arkansas Infantry battalion, including the sailors and marines from the gunboat *Pontchartrain*, with the last assigned to the big guns of the fort. Capt. Bryan Marsh of the 17th Texas Cavalry (Dismounted) appears to have been unimpressed with the new command: "We have but two Brigades at this place, only Garland's & Deshler's, with one or two company's [i.e., regiments] of Ark. Conscripts, but they are not worth a curse." In addition to the infantry and the heavy artillery contingent of sailors and marines, some four companies of cavalry (including Capt. Richardson's just-arrived Lane Rangers) were to act as the eyes of the garrison, and were sent downriver on scouting duty to guard the various approaches to the Post, as well as to connect the Post with army headquarters at Little Rock. Initially, Hart's Arkansas Battery would continue to remain attached to Garland's brigade.[502]

The most central position of importance at Arkansas Post consisted of the four-bastioned earthwork known as Ft. Hindman, which had been constructed atop a twenty-five-foot levee on the left (north) bank of the Arkansas. It overlooked a great bend of the river. Its four bastions, or wings, radiated from a core, each ninety degrees on a side and all a hundred yards in length, looking like one of the four points of a compass. Along the outer sides, a ditch of some eight foot in depth and twenty across enclosed a parapet wall; the earth from the ditch was used to make the berm for the parapet. While from a distance, the fort might appear to be just slightly above the plain upon which it sat, the parapet actually stood eight feet higher

---

[502] "Bryan Marsh," in *Chronicles*, vol. 14, # 2 (1975), p. 20; also, *O.R.*, I, vol. 22, p. 904. Of interest is that somehow the 17th Texas Cavalry (Dismounted) was omitted from Deshler's organization, and obviously Haldeman's battery had not traveled to the post with that brigade.

and measured fifteen feet thicker at the base than the levee itself. Its exterior walls sloped inward from this outer ditch, its purpose to deflect even heavy artillery projectiles. Inside the walls, there were two fifteen-by-eighteen-foot casemated structures called "bombproofs" by the men, which had been constructed in the bastions facing downstream. Both these rooms had walls of eight feet in height, constructed of oak timbers of fourteen inches square, each laid in alternating directions, with the roof being covered in the same material and topped by a 7/8-inch thickness of railroad iron for additional protection, giving them a very sturdy look.[503]

Capt. Samuel Foster of the 24th Texas Cavalry (Dismounted) compared the two bombproofs to the only things he knew them to be similar to: They "are [like]. . . a house made of Oak logs hewn 12" square and laid flat on one another, . . . put on like the half of the roof of a house--with the eves next to the river--and so low that the muzzle of the cannon shoots just under the end of the top logs--Then on top of the logs is a layer of railroad iron, and it **looks like it is impossible to damage it** [author's emphasis])."[504]

Each of the casemates held a huge, smooth-bore Columbiad, one of eight inches in diameter, the other a nine-inch gun, while a third Columbiad, also of nine-inch bore, sat atop an in-barbette (or open) on a center-pintle gun carriage atop the westernmost bastion looking upstream. The lower gun in the first casemate was built into the flank of the eastward, or downriver facing bastion, while the second sat in the curtain (or angle) that separated the two bastions. On a landward-facing arm that looked north, the guns there consisted of four 10-pound Parrott rifles (of iron) and a similar number of six-pounder smooth-bore guns. And, like the 9-inch Columbiad in the westward-facing bastion, all eight guns on the landward side stood in the open, on field-gun carriages, which would make them easy targets for well-posted enemy guns.[505]

---

[503] "Post of Arkansas," in *A.H.Q.*, vol. 18, #3 (1959), pp. 83-5; and, *One of Cleburne's Command:*, p. 7.

[504] *One of Cleburne's Command:*, p. 7.

[505] "Post of Arkansas," in *A.H.Q.*, vol. 18, #3 (1959), p. 239.

From the terminal, or distal, end of the north-facing bastion, a line had been marked off by the engineers, upon which to construct fieldworks in the event that an enemy approached the fort from the landward side. This line ran a little over 700 yards in length and terminated 200 yards short of Post Bayou, a sluggish stream that curved around the northern part of the Post to empty into the river back behind Ft. Hindman. Apparently, no one had considered the length of the staked-out portion of this line with respect to how many troops would be needed to occupy it. Should an enemy attack this point between the bayou and the staked-out line, or get beyond the bayou itself, the line would be flanked, and the fort taken from reverse.[506]

Gen. Thomas J. Churchill had, until just recently, served east of the Mississippi River, but had at Holmes' request been transferred to his native state to take command of the Post. By early December, Churchill had completed the organization of what would be known as the 2nd Division of Holmes' department, McCulloch's reserve division at Austin being the 1st. While the majority of Churchill's division consisted of Texas regiments, some came from Arkansas and Louisiana, mostly in Dunnington's brigade. Though most of those assigned had arrived at the Post by mid-December, some of the Arkansans remained in the vicinity of St. Charles.[507]

Churchill's 1st Brigade consisted of Col. Robert R. Garland's three regiments, including his former 6th Texas Infantry (now under Lt. Col. Phillip Swearingen), along with Col. Franklin Wilkes' 24th Texas Cavalry (Dismounted) and Col. Clayton Gillespie's 25th Texas Cavalry (Dismounted); it also included Capt. Matthew Denson's (Louisiana) Cavalry Co. and Capt. William Hart's Arkansas Battery. The 2nd Brigade, led by Col. James Deshler, contained Col. R. Q. Mills' 10th Texas Infantry, Maj. V. P. Sanders' 15th Texas Cavalry (Dismounted), and Col. Robert Taylor's 17th Texas Cavalry (Dismounted), along with Lt. Col. John T. Coit's 18th Texas Cavalry (Dismounted), there being no artillery provided for it.[508]

---

[506] As will be seen, this early on proved to be the enemy's main effort, as will be seen in Brig. George W. Morgan's (U.S.) reports in *O.R.*, I, vol. 17, pt. 1, p. 721.

[507] *O.R.*, I, vol. 22, p. 904.

[508] *O.R.*, I, 17, pt. 1, p. 783, and 791.

Churchill's 3rd Brigade, led by Col. John Dunnington, held Lt. Col. William Crawford's Arkansas Battalion, Col. C. L. Dawson's 19th and Col. E. E. Portlock's 24th Arkansas Infantry regiments, along with the Marine Battery and Capt. L. M. Nutt's (Louisiana) Cavalry Co. It's interesting to note that Capt. Richardson's W. P. Lane Rangers went unreported; it appears that this Texans Cavalry company served as Churchill's personal escort. Also not reflected on the organizational chart, but would be present during the battle, was Capt. Alf Johnson's Texas Spy Co. All told, the Confederate force at the Post amounted to almost 6,000 rank and file.[509]

November had ended without bringing the engagement many had felt imminent, leaving the men at the Post with just two objectives: first was to finish their winter quarters (or, in the case of Deshler's, to build them), the heavy rains and sleet making this a miserable proposition; secondly, most of the men had an innate interest in letting loved ones at home know where they were and what they had been up to of late, especially with the holiday season near. Continuing bad weather forced a suspension of drills, "as it rains here all the time," one perplexed Texan pointed out, and "if we go into our tents we freeze, and if we go to a fire to get warm, we get nearly drowned." He advised his spouse that they would be attacked as soon as the river got up, perhaps presaging things to come.[510]

Still a much-debated topic for discussion among the Texans centered on the fighting capability of the Arkansas troops at the Post, Capt. Bryan Marsh of the 17th Texas Cavalry (Dismounted) noting that they left a lot to be desired. Should a battle happen soon, they'd likely "skedaddle," leaving his fellow Texans to bear the brunt of the fighting. In the letter wherein he voices his discontent, he apologizes for the poor penmanship, his excuse being that wind-driven rain entering his tent had completely numbed his hands.[511]

---

[509] *Ibid.*, p. 904, shows a fourth brigade, BG J. M. Hawes', but like Haldeman's battery, didn't reach the post. For the composition of Hart's battery, see *A. H.Q.*, vol. 22, #3, p. 260.

[510] Newton Allen to his wife, December 7, 1862, courtesy of Tom Browder of Cleburne. Allan had just been selected as the third sergeant of his company, this entailing him to serve as commissary sergeant for the company. He advised that this date marked his thirty-second birthday, coming while he wrote this letter.

[511] Bryan Marsh," in *Chronicles*, vol. 14 #2, p. 20.

Others recounted their travels of late to loved ones back home. A 10th Texas private wrote about their trip down to the Post, and his concern that exposure to the harsh conditions might well make everyone sick. And after observing the low, swampy ground at the back of the fort, he believed the place not conducive to maintaining good health, for it subjected them to lung disorders, like pneumonia. And recent heavy rains had made finding firewood a difficult task, and hard to light when one did find it; keeping it going once aflame proving to be virtually impossible. Plus, if deeper wells were not dug soon, he grumbled, the loved ones at home should expect to find all their names in the obituary columns.[512]

And relations' replies often did little to help morale. One anxious sister's letter as to her brother's whereabouts and his health continued by expounding on the extent of suffering borne by those at home. What few supplies she found in Johnson County, she confessed, now brought unbelievably high prices, with flour selling for $5.00 a bushel, cotton cards at $25.00 a pair, and plain jeans beginning at $7.00 a yard! But what had really provoked her into writing her brother, Malcolm Scurlock of the 18th Texas Cavalry (Dismounted), was making him aware that those at home faced as much danger in their daily lives, from hostile Indians, as the soldiers at the front.[513]

As if high prices and a scarcity of materials were not enough, the hostiles had recently made an appearance in the western part of the county, the Comanches in western Johnson County killing and burning settlers out. Heightening her fears, the few men capable of defending them, an uncle and a cousin of Malcolm's, had recently departed for Vicksburg with a cattle herd, leaving the families with virtually no one for protection should the hostiles appear again. To top matters off, they had heard nothing from the frontier troops that were charged with defending their western border.[514]

---

[512] Isaiah Harlan to Eliphalet, December 3, 1862, CRC, Hill College

[513] Mollie Scurlock to Malcolm, in the *Grandview Tribune*, January 8, 1977. Her brother, Malcolm, is afterward listed in *Confederate Soldiers and Sailors who died at Camp Butler, Illinois*, as having died while incarcerated on March 15, 1863, after his capture at the post.

[514] *Ibid.*

Even to those inexperienced in military matters, the situation at the Post, with swamp on three sides and a rising river on the fourth, suggested they might all be easily boxed in if hit by a combined land and naval assault. Some expressed concerns that their new chief seemed to have little experience in such situations: "General Churchill . . . thinks that we can hold the place against the world," one Texan noted, while others "think that a large force could easily bag the whole of us." As if able to anticipate this last, he confided that "it seems to me that we would be in a critical position should we be overpowered."[515]

On December 17, the steamer *Key West* hove to at the landing at the Post, returning some 300 convalescent soldiers to their commands from Little Rock hospitals. The river, on the rise as a consequence of the recent heavy rains, had become somewhat easier to communicate by boat with Holmes' headquarters by boat. It was during this time that scouts downriver at Napoleon began to report that a large number of enemy ships were moving down the Mississippi toward Vicksburg; this provoked a cavalry officer there to suggest placing a field piece or two at the mouth of the Arkansas in order to disrupt Union shipping.[516]

December 7 through 18 saw letters and reports by those in the most recently arrived brigade, Deshler's, to provide readers a glimpse of their new circumstances. Col. Mills of the 10th Texas Infantry wrote his wife on Sunday, the 7th, that his regiment had witnessed a substantial reduction in numbers since reaching Arkansas, with 748 men present from their high of 967. On that same date, Pvt. Newton Allen of the 24th Texas Cavalry (Dismounted) stated that "if we go in our tents we freeze, and if we go to the fire to get warm, we get nearly drowned." But, according to Allen, Arkansas Post was "the key to the state and [therefore] a post of honor." On the 10th, several writers brought their families up to date on recent activities. Capt. Bryan Marsh of the 17th Texas Cavalry

---

[515] Isaiah Harlan to brother, Alpheus, December 18, 1862, CRC, Hill College; also, see "Marshall Pierson," in *Military History of Texas*, vol. 13, p. 28, wherein Pierson imparts his impression that the Post wouldn't hold out long if heavily attacked.

[516] *Fourteen Hundred*, p. 87.

(Dismounted) told his wife of his despondency over the fact that the rest of the troops had winter quarters but not his brigade; it appeared, he said, that "we are small fish in Arkansas." Bryan promised to celebrate her birthday on this date in camp by eating hominy and pork, cautioning her to "wash Hen's (their son) face and kissing him for me . . .;" in any event do "not whip the little fellow for being ill before breakfast. It is hereditary with him." And Isaiah Harlan of Co. G, 10th Texas Infantry told family members that he had had diarrhea, but that the regiment would soon commence winter quarters despite his illness. And on the 11th, according to Benjamin Seaton of Co. G, 10th Texas, they had moved their camp two miles, ostensibly to acquire the space required on which to build their huts.[517]

With the exception of the 18th Texas Cavalry (Dismounted), the more recently arrived regiments of Deshler's had their huts finished before Christmas, so they could now settle in for the winter, or so they thought. Colder weather, in the form of sleet and freezing rain, had led to the suspension of everything except the completion of menial chores associated with organizing their quarters. With more idle time, the men often gathered around their roaring campfires at night, singing songs or recounting the latest camp gossip. With the Christmas holiday approaching, men's thoughts naturally turned to those at home who, like they did, were suffering through another winter.[518]

The music ranged from the frivolous to that of a more religious significance, often interspersed by melancholic tunes that helped wile away the time, as well as in some way linking them with those back home. On many a night, Deshler's brass band supplied musical entertainment. On one emotionally stirring evening, Sgt. W. W. Heartsill of Richardson's Lane Rangers penned in his diary: "The distant brigade bands occasionally cheer up the long, lazy hours," and then, as if dramatizing the melancholia he felt in that instant, he

---

[517] R. Q. Mills letter of December 7, copy furnished by Scott McKay of Georgia; "Bryan Marsh" letters in *Chronicles*, vol. 14, #2, p. 20-1; Newton Allen letter of December 7, 1862, courtesy of Joe Browder of Cleburne, Texas; and lastly, Seaton diary of December 11, 1862 in *The Bugle:*, p. 29.

[518] *Campaigning*, p. 89; *The Bugle;*, p. 30.

recorded that "the sentinel at his post cries out: 'Alls well at Post #1'."[519]

A most interesting account of how higher-ranked officers often abused their lesser-grade ones became the subject of a letter penned by Lt. Sebron Sneed of Co. G, 6th Texas Infantry on December 18. He had been out visiting a Catholic family in the neighborhood of the Post, learning that the wife had recently expired. He believed them to be quite decent folks, for Creoles, afterward learning that Churchill had forced the family out of their home so he could have it as his headquarters. It's obvious Sneed felt that the cause they were fighting for was betrayed when important individuals used their offices to perform such an act: "My Heart grew bitter, not against our enemy, but against the military despotism that would turn that desolate family, heart-broken[,] from their home . . . "[520] On the same day Lt. Sneed had drafted his letter, Isaiah Harlan of Co. G, 10th Texas Infantry wrote his brother, Alpheus, that Deshler's brigade consisted of "Sweet's [15th Texas Cavalry Dismounted]," "Taylor's [17th Texas Cavalry Dismounted]," and "Darnell's [18th Texas Cavalry Dismounted]," along with his own 10th Texas Infantry. Of great interest, he complains of their overall commander in his letter, but from a rather different perspective. Said Harlan: "Churchill who commands the post (sic) thinks we can hold the place against the world[,] whilst others think that **a large force could easily bag the whole of us.**" [author's emphasis added] Expressing his own thoughts, he stated that "it seems to me that we would be in a critical position should we be overpowered."[521]

Of note, interestingly, Sgt. W. W. Heartsill of Richardson's Lane Rangers recorded in his dairy that the 18th Texas Cavalry (Dismounted), which had seemingly been long delayed in getting to the Post, arrived on the 19th to consolidate the entire brigade in one place. An interesting sidebar to his note was made, that with the river

---

[519] *Fourteen Hundred*, p. 87. The nighttime sing-alongs helped turn men's thoughts away from their troubles and helped to somehow bind them together in ways those not in service could fathom.

[520] Lt. Sebron Sneed letter to wife, Fannie, copy courtesy of family member from Austin, Texas.

[521] Isaiah Harlan letter, December 18, 1862, CRC, Hill College.

on the rise, soon the enemy's gunboats would be enabled to steam upriver to confront the garrison of the Post.[522]

The only remarkable event occurring before Christmas came on December 20, when for the first time, Churchill reviewed his assembled division, after which the marine detachment in Ft. Hindman test-fired the massive guns there. The deafening peal of the guns, followed afterward by stark silence as massive smoke clouds rolled downriver with the current, then gave way to reverberations that echoed from far across the intervening swamps. Almost as if a consequence of this event, several letter writers wrote the day afterward, Sunday the 21st, that it looked much like spring outdoors, and this facilitated the continued work on their quarters, one soldier finding them to be like "negro quarters," being about 16 feet square on average and with mud daubed into the cracks between the rough planks for sealing out the weather.[523]

Otherwise, the soldiers at the Post began observing the approaching yuletide season, though few opportunities to properly celebrate came about. Christmas Day found Deshler's men still felling trees and hewing logs for their winter huts, while the mumps had suddenly made an appearance in Richardson's Lane Rangers; their sick were ferried across the river to the division hospital. Lt. Sebron Sneed of the 6th Texas Infantry told his wife how he had "an elegant breakfast – corn bread, beef, corn coffee and molasses," with the expectation that "dinner the same and supper will be the same again." He had, however, been able to commandeer some eggnog from a fellow officer, and for a late night treat they were to brew "a large pot of coffee (real coffee)" in his mess. Cal Horton of Co. I, 25th Texas Cavalry (Dismounted) announced to his wife that he'd been so sick he seemed to be living solely of late on "blue mass and calomel." And Capt. Sam Foster of the 24th Texas Cavalry (Dismounted) noted only that the good weather would keep them drilling and that he hadn't been able to procure eggnog anywhere.

---

[522] *Fourteen Hundred*, p. 87.

[523] Aaron Estes letter of December 21, 1862, Estes Special Collection, Baylor University, Waco; Flavius Perry letter to "Eva," in *Military History of Texas*, vol. 13, #2, p. 15; and "Bryan Marsh" letter of same date to "Mit," in *Chronicles*, vol. pp. 21-2.

Perhaps the poorest postscript on Christmas came from the pen of Lt. R. M. Collins, 15th Texas Cavalry (Dismounted), who noted that his hut sat only yards from the cemetery and that details were passing back and forth to bury the dead every day and night.[524]

Unfortunately for the soldiers and sailors of both sides, that final week in December would see a seemingly innocuous event transpire near Napoleon, an episode that would forever transform the lives of everyone involved. For most of the Texans at the Post, it would prove to be a seminal moment in their collective lives. (Known today as the Battle of Arkansas Post, it signaled the most vivid experience, ranging from the horrific to the sublime as to a major battle the likes of which they had not a clue as to what to expect.) As the old year gradually turned into the new, most men sought solace in the fact that, at least at this moment, they hadn't had to witness the full panoply of war. It all began when Capt. Nutt's Louisiana cavalrymen swarmed aboard a Union supply boat they had captured. With sufficient water in the river, they brought it upstream to the Post.[525]

For those having been long separated from luxury gods, the ship's hold quickly yielded a treasure trove of goods. For men used to "blue" beef and cornbread, the flour, coffee, apples, whiskey, and salt excited salivary glands. Ordnance officers came away with a great haul as well; there was a large amount of artillery stores and small-arms cartridges, plus a small supply of muskets and pistols. Almost as interesting to the rank and file, however, had to be the capture of a

---

[524] *Fourteen Hundred*, p. 88.; *One of Cleburne's Command:* p. 12; *Chapters*, p. 64; and for the Horton letter, see www.civilwarbull.org.forum/messages.4343.html. Lt. Sebron Sneed letter of December 25, 1862, courtesy of a family member, wherein he states to his wife: "Fan[,] there is a vast amount of humbegery in the army, . . . "There is one thing that I do take a malicious pleasure in . . . , [that] Col. Garland has not received the appointment of Brig. ., and what is more he will not receive it . . . The hopes and expectations among mighty hosts of little puppies who have licked Garland's boots, and lapped the drippings from the sanctuary where he sits enthroned . . . , will all fail." Garland's subsequent conduct at the post battle would settle the promotion matter forever.

[525] "Post of Arkansas," *A.H.Q.*, vol. 18, #3 (1959), p. 244; also, *Campaigning*, p. 88; *Fourteen Hundred*, p. 88; also, see the Andrew S. Murphey biography in *Reminiscences*, pp. 551-2.

goodly quantity of mail sacks, one source reporting eighteen bags, each stuffed with letters, packages for Union soldiers, and a host of the latest Northern papers. Originally thought to be a godsend, the *Blue Wing's* seizure would ultimately prove the Post's undoing. Gratified in sharing the contents of the mail bags, few gave thought as to how dynamic the enemy's reaction might be over what the Confederates took to be but a trifling loss.[526]

That the *Blue Wing's* capture was not a trivial issue came quickly in the guise of one MG John A. McClernand, who not long before had arrived at Helena at the head of a large army that had recently been sent down to link up with MG William T. Sherman in a campaign aimed at taking Vicksburg. Together, the two forces, each a full infantry corps, augmented by artillery and cavalry components, were to be united in a composite force whose objective was to take the vital citadel on the Mississippi. Sherman had actually preceded McClernand to the vicinity and, without hesitating, had attempted to carry the bastion through a combined Army-Navy attack on December 27that had seen disastrous consequences. Thinking himself senior to Sherman in rank, upon learning of the latter's debacle on the Yazoo bluffs, McClernand beckoned Sherman to come up to Helena to consult with himself and the U.S. fleet commander, Adm. David D. Porter, on a new strategy. As fleet commander of the gunboats and transports on the lower Mississippi, Porter had agreed to supply both gunboats and transports for the army, wherever and whenever the two officers agreed to go, coordinating a naval assault of his forces in concert with any land engagement they might agree upon.[527]

Among the many items discussed, the three senior officers eventually seemed to dwell on how best to react to the seizure of the

---

[526] "Lt. Flavius Perry," *Military History of Texas*, vol. 13, #2, pp. 29-30; "Post of Arkansas," *A.H.Q.*,vol. 18, #3 (1959), p. 244; and *One of Cleburne's Command:*, p. 11. Sgt. Heartsill, in *Fourteen Hundred*, p. 30, notes there were sixteen mail sacks, enough to let everyone have the latest info on the enemy.

[527] "Post of Arkansas," in *A.H.Q.*, vol. 18, #3 (1959), pp. 245-6; William T. Sherman, *Memoirs of General William T. Sherman: By Himself*, (Bloomington, 1957), pp. 296-7. Hereafter cited as *Memoirs*, readers ought to be aware that this latter work is replete with errors relating to Arkansas Post and confirm his assertions in that volume.

Blue Wing and the potential threat the presence of a large rebel force on the lower Arkansas was for downriver operations should the Post remain intact. McClernand proposed, and Sherman agreed, to reduce the fort in an effort to prevent the potential for it to wreak further havoc upon the Union communications line. At McClernand's recommendation, it was mutually agreed to reduce the Post before initiating new operations around Vicksburg. The ultimate decision emerging from the conference was a decision to utilize both McClernand's 13th and Sherman's 15th Corps (the latter still at Chickasaw Bluffs), along with a grand naval assault through combined operations.[528]

Porter was not overly fond of McClernand. Nevertheless, for his part, Porter promised sufficient transport to carry both Sherman's and McClernand's corps up to the Post, along with a sufficient number of gunboats to reduce the fort. Designating his force the "Army of the Mississippi," McClernand ordered Sherman to rendezvous his corps near his at the mouth of the White River, from whence each would continue up that stream until reaching the cut-off that led from the White over to the Arkansas and thence up that river to the Post. Assuming overall command, McClernand assigned BG George Morgan command of the 13th Corps. Together, the two corps had nine infantry brigades, organized into two separate divisions in each corps. Along with artillery support and cavalry detachments, the whole force numbered close to 35,000 men, certainly more than enough to defeat, if not totally destroy, Churchill's force of near 5,000.[529]

Porter had available for duty the heavy ironclads *Dekalb*, *Cincinnati*, and *Louisville*, along with several lighter, shallow-draft "tinclad" vessels, including the lightly armored *Rattler*, more than enough firepower to dominate the shallow waters often encountered in the Arkansas. In contrast to McClernand's nine infantry brigades, Churchill had just three, and not all of their components had arrived at the Post. His nearest reinforcements, in fact, consisted of a single

---

[528] *Ibid.*

[529] "Post of Arkansas," in *A.H.Q.*, vol. 18, #3 (1959), p. 247; also, see Thomas L. Snead, "The Conquest of Arkansas," in *Battles and Leaders*, vol. III, pp. 452-3.

infantry regiment and only one cavalry company, each near St. Charles and over forty miles away.[530]

The New Year had seen continued good weather, although heavy rains continued falling, what the men called a "false spring." Lt. Flavius Perry had written his spouse, Eva, that this was the day Lincoln had decreed the end of slavery in the seceded states. He went on to recount the recent *Blue Wing* episode, which had provided them a load of "real" flour, "genuine" coffee, some whiskey, salt, apples, and a host of cotton cards, and if the Federals hadn't made this gift possible, they'd have been out of salt within a matter of days. Also on that day, Lt. Sebron Sneed had written his wife that in reading the letters and newspapers, he learned that the morale of the Union soldiers seemed to be at a rather low point: "All their letters were longing for peace, some of them were for peace on any terms." All of this confirmed to those in the Southern ranks that the enemy seemed to be of the same low feeling, "so it seems that we poor rebels are not all who are sighing for our homes and the olive branch." Only a day later, a scout brought word up that a gunboat had been seen down at Napoleon and that he had learned somehow that the enemy had been decisively defeated in their recent attempt to take Vicksburg by way of the Yazoo Pass above that city.[531]

During the early morning hours of January 4, 1863, a hundred-plus vessels began firing up their boilers and, with steam up, began moving upstream from Vicksburg, bearing the whole of Sherman's corps. McClernand's corps left Helena going south, each expecting to affect a junction near the mouth of the White River, where, like Hovey's expedition the previous November, they hoped to steam up the White until reaching the cut-off, then crossing over into the Arkansas not far below the Post. Plans were to put the army

---

[530] "Post of Arkansas," in *A.H.Q.*, vol. 18, #3 (1950), p. 247. While Churchill in recent weeks had gotten wooden piles driven to the waterline across much of the river, he mentions that uprooted trees drifting downstream in the recent freshets had severely damaged them, leaving him with little more than the three heavy guns, some field artillery pieces, and a meager infantry force with which to oppose the enemy.

[531] Flavius Perry letter, January 1, 1863, in *Military History of Texas,* vol. 13, #2, p. 17. As to the Yazoo expedition outcome, see Sgt. Heartsill's confirmation of same in *Fourteen Hundred*, p. 89.

ashore on the left (or north) bank, which in that area ran almost south to north, where they would march up toward the Post, deploying for a grand assault. After its human cargo disembarked, the gunboat portion of the fleet would then steam up to employ its heavy metal to batter Ft. Hindman into submission. To ensure the best chance for success, the plan required quick execution, plus the application of superior force before the garrison could either be withdrawn or reinforced.[532]

Interestingly enough, at this time Pvt. Malcolm Scurlock of Co. A, 18th Texas Cavalry (Dismounted) wrote to a brother serving east of the Mississippi with the 10th Texas Cavalry (Dismounted) that reports had it a great number of vessels had of late been observed going both up and downriver, the latter apparently headed for Vicksburg. He also mentioned the recent boat capture that had seen them take in twenty-four Union sailors, along with six Negroes, and a cargo valued at over $300,000. And on that same day, A. L. Orr of Co. I, 18th Texas Cavalry (Dismounted) advised his mother of that same capture, stating that the regiment was now in winter quarters and that they were well fortified, and he was in good health. He asked his mom to advise a family friend: "[Tell] Sammy, . . . when he gets to the fort not to get sceared [sic] at the big guns and run back, that they are only hear [sic] to wake up the babyes [sic] in Arkansas."[533]

Thus, it was that during the late evening hours of January 8, 1863 that Capt. Sam Richardson's W. P. Lane Rangers, accompanied by a section of Capt. William Hart's Arkansas Battery, which had been down at Napoleon, arrived back at the Post. As Sgt. W. W. Heartsill noted in his diary that night, after visiting his captain, "the atmosphere begins to smell a little gunpowderish [sic] around here." On the morning of the 9th, a courier dashed up, bringing word that the "entire fleet is now in the Arkansas river steaming their way with

---

[532] *Ibid.*, p. 246; also, see "The Conquest of Arkansas," in *B. & L.*, vol. III, pp. 452-3.

[533] Malcolm Scurlock letter, January 4, 1863, Grandview Tribune, January 13, 1977; for Orr's letter, see *Parsons's Texas Cavalry Brigade*, pp. 87-9. This would be Malcolm Scurlock's final letter, for he'd die in a Union prison camp in March, before being exchanged.

all possible dispatch for this place." Hurriedly, the cavalrymen of that company on the opposite side of the river loaded their wagons and sent them and their ambulance up the south (or right) bank. The men, meanwhile, began preparing to cross the river to the fort side. In the act of so doing, several long-range shots were fired in their direction from near Fletcher's plantation; the men also observed wisps of smoke on the horizon that marked the approach of the fleet. With this activity, it was readily apparent to everyone ashore that their time "for watching the elephant" lay at hand. Something extraordinarily fearsome seemed to be in the offing, and that something now seemed to be coming directly toward the Post.[534]

On the 8th, Lt. Sebron Sneed of the 6th Texas Infantry had written his wife that the men in his Co. G were as ready to fight as was he. Stating that he'd "volunteered in the army to sustain a cause by every means in my power, even to giving my life," instead "I feel and know that Col. G has no desire for active service . . . and has managed to keep all the troops under his command out of service . . . in the present stirring times when every man should be face to face with the enemy." Though there was little that could be done by this time, needless to say, "I get mad whenever I begin to think . . . about the manner in which our regiment is connected and the cowardly imbecility of our Colonel who wants nothing but his ease."[535]

The Indian summer had continued well into the month all across Southeastern Arkansas after New Year's Day, the unseasonable weather continuing without exception even as the Federals plied the river on their way to the Post. For the Confederates, as a consequence, the men were out and about without having to wear their heavy winter clothing; that attire was safely stored away in their huts. This anomaly, unfortunately, would set the stage for a great disaster that would befall the men after the close of the upcoming fight, due to a failure on their part to retrieve that

---

[534] *Fourteen Hundred:*, p. 90. Churchill would afterward dispute knowing to have been aware of the enemy's arrival until their fleet entered the Arkansas, though it's apparent that virtually everyone had some forewarning of the enemy's coming due to the warnings spread by Richardson's Cavalry Co.

[535] Sebron Sneed letter of January 8, 1863, typescript copy from family member shared with this writer.

clothing from their cabins. However, like the proverbial turtle, many a man soaked up the sun's warming rays along the river's edge, most of the garrison basking atop the parapet or arraying themselves in many small clusters in the vicinity of their camps. Most of the men would never forget their error in not recovering their clothing while they still might have.[536]

Just after learning of McClernand's arrival at the cut-off on the 9th, Churchill fired off a telegram to Little Rock, advising Holmes, and once again requesting reinforcements be sent to him. He followed that up with a dispatch to Col. E. E. Portlock's 24th Arkansas Infantry and Capt. Alf Johnson's Spy Co., both at St. Charles, to march posthaste for the Post. That done, he turned his attention to readying his forces on hand for what he suspected would be a major endeavor by his enemy. He sent word to all three subordinates, colonels Garland (1st Brigade), Deshler (2nd Brigade), and Dunnington (3rd Brigade) to have the men immediately cook three days' rations and see to the distribution of ammunition, and in less than thirty minutes, each had his brigade formed and under arms. Knowing that many of his men had deficient cartridge boxes, rather than issuing ammunition directly, Deshler kept his issues in their thousand-round wooden crates; these would accompany the regiments when they started from camp.[537]

Already arrived on the same side of the river before dark on the 9th, Capt. Samuel Richardson's Lane Rangers had initially been posted at the rear of Ft. Hindman, but about midnight had been moved forward to Churchill's headquarters so as to be available for

---

[536] *Fourteen Hundred*, pp. 89-90. For an idea of the arrangements of their possessions within their huts, see Lt. Sebron Sneed, 6th Texas Infantry, letter of January 8, 1863, wherein he discloses to his wife that he had a log cabin with a shed kitchen at one end and a fireplace at the other, a small window, plank bed with a red coverlet on it, a small table, and several stools to sit on. One wall sported he and his comrade's knapsacks, canteens, haversacks, swords and pistols, sashes, and the like, whilst another had a mantel on it, on which he "piled books and you will see a box of tobacco, and some long-stemmed pipes, etc." Typescript copy obtained courtesy of a family member, Austin, Texas.

[537] *O.R.*, I, vol. 17, pt. 1, p. 790, Report of Col. James Deshler (#41), C.S. Army, commanding Brigade, March 25, 1863. Also, see Brig. Churchill's report # 39, in the same *O.R.*, pp. 780-82.

assignment as required. Sgt. Heartsill advised that the men had only been issued three hard-bread crackers that evening, were already famished, and had few prospects of obtaining anything else to eat. Previous to this, the brigades of Garland, Deshler, and Dunnington had been ordered to advance downstream several miles to occupy the lower line of works, these being the ones thrown up the previous November upon Hovey's near approach. Screened out front by A. M. Nutt and Matthew Denson's Louisiana cavalry companies, Deshler reported his brigade in motion before 3:00 p.m. It's mystifying as to why Churchill would send all his infantry to the lower works, for they exceeded the capacity required to occupy them and the surplus might have been better employed, as shall be seen, in preparing the landward-side works which had heretofore been marked out but had remained untouched to this point. Perhaps he considered throwing his entire disposable force onto the enemy, as it was unloaded at the landing just below the downstream works, but he never stated such.[538]

Hardly had Deshler gotten underway than an orderly overtook him bearing orders to halt his command at an upper work situated only a mile and a quarter below the Post, and there await further developments. In the meantime, Churchill had been advised that the enemy had supposedly reached the landing known as Notribe's Plantation, two miles further downstream, which made occupying the lower works further downstream, perhaps, improbable. Garland advises his command didn't reach this upper area until right at dark, but that for some reason, he continued on down to occupy the lowest works. He immediately shook out five companies from the 6th Texas Infantry, led by Maj. Phillips, and 24th Texas Cavalry (Dismounted), led by Lt. Col. Swearingen, as advance skirmishers. The latter pressed on further down, with Garland advising that his remaining regiments had been "posted some distance in the rear of the first line, [then] occupying the rifle-pits." His right flank rested adjacent the riverbank itself, his left running at a right angle eastward until anchored on a sluggish bayou. To his right, nearest the river, he put Hart's Arkansas Battery in place so as to command the river channel. The men began throwing up

---

[538] *Ibid.*

works, utilizing both brush and timber wherever practicable to protect the men. According to him, the gunboats came up just at dark to shell his works, as well as toward the fort back upriver.[539]

That Deshler's brigade remained instead at the middle works that first night out is attested in his report, "the general line being convex to the front [as the Union map on p. 711 shows]," though little had been done beforehand to make this an entrenched line; and though "the engineer officer had traced the ditch, . . . it was quite far from being completed." Extending that line further to the left during the night, he linked his left to Dunnington's brigade, which had apparently arrived not long after his. Felling timber out in front to construct an abatis, "we worked the entire night," though "the want of tools, axes, spades etc., was a very serious drawback." Oddly enough, however, he infers that Hart's battery was situated in the intervals between the companies of his rightmost regiment, the 10th Texas, which contrasts with Garland's report that states Hart's battery was with his brigade at the time.[540]

Dunnington's troops must have trailed Deshler's, as traditionally, being formed on his left suggests that his regiments were deployed from right to left, a rule during that era. As the men of both Garland's and Deshler's brigades busied themselves with improving their separate points, Sgt. W. W. Heartsill of Capt. Richardson's Cavalry Co. advises that the Lane Rangers passed on beyond the advanced infantry skirmishers at the lower works, where they soon met up with captains Matthew Denson and L. M. Nutt's Louisiana Cavalry companies. And, according to Heartsill, the first gunboat targets proved to be these cavalrymen; he counted nine of their gunboats as they steamed up late that night. Hardly anyone on either side got much sleep that night, reflecting on what the morrow must inevitably bring their way.[541]

Thus, fully deployed before midnight of the 9th, the Confederates could only watch and await the arrival of the enemy's

---

[539] Garland's Official Report, # 40, is found in *O.R.*, I, 17, pt. 1, p. 783.

[540] Deshler in *O.R.*, I, 17, pt. 1, p. 790. Hart's having six guns, they may have been split up at the time.

[541] Deshler's report verifies that Dunnington's troops had formed on his left, *O.R.* I, 17, pt. 1, p. 790; also, see *Fourteen Hundred*, p. 91.

land forces in their front. They were expected to follow the gunboats up early the next morning. On his behalf, McClernand's advance, consisting of Sherman's entire XIV Corps, had reached Notribe's landing, where it was expected to disembark, hopefully doing so without opposition. But with darkness now at hand, it would be a close match to get ashore, whether they encountered the enemy or not. Also arriving about dusk was Morgan's XIII Corps, which had made it to Fletcher's Landing, some nine miles back downstream from Notribe's plantation. It was understood the XIII Corps would await Sherman's offloading before steaming on up to Notribe's to disembark. Though somewhat late in gaining these points, nevertheless, McClernand now had his entire force a scant five or so miles below the Post. With that accomplished, he set in motion his plan for reducing Arkansas Post.[542]

But with darkness having fully set in, this and other considerations made it such that neither Sherman's nor Morgan's troops got ashore that evening, though this had not prevented Porter's sending several gunboats upriver to toss a few rounds into the area of the lower works to let the Southerners know of their arrival. After gaining the distance, they sent forth a combination of solid shot and shells, the Confederates within the rifle pits referring to these projectiles by the not-so-affectionate term of "wash-kettles." Some Texans had been imprudent enough to steal over to the riverbank to observe the monstrous vessels, dispersing quickly, however, when the huge naval rounds began to fly in their direction. By 10:00 p.m. this firing had stopped, the vessels dropping back downstream some distance, with the anxious rebels pondering on what was to come their way. After which, as one put it, we "laid our blankets down on the ground and stretched out with our guns in our arms." And, as Surgeon C. M. Smith would later report, the men "remained all night in a pelting rain storm."[543]

---

[542] *O.R.*, I, vol. 17, pt. 1, p. 721, Report # 4, BG George W. Morgan, commanding 13th Army Corps.

[543] *O.R.*, I, vol. 17, pt. 1, p. 790; p. 723; also, *One of Cleburne's Command:*, p. 14.; "Coller," *Military History of Texas*, vol. 9, #2 (1972), p. 133. And for C. M. Smith's report, see the *Galveston Tri-Weekly News*, typescript copy provided by Scott McKay from microfilm original found at the Dallas Public Library.

His plan now pushed back until the following morning, McClernand retired for the night, but only after ordering Sherman to land his XV Corps at daybreak and advance up the river road to deploy his forces by extending intervals to the far right, expecting that his subordinate officer might actually succeed in getting troops out beyond Post Bayou and thereby flank the enemy works. Morgan's XIII Corps was to trail Sherman's move, disembarking at Notribe's as soon as Sherman's columns had cleared the landing, Morgan expecting to follow Sherman's troops. But a heavy fog the following morning prevented Sherman's getting ashore at an early hour; in fact, so much time was consumed in getting off the boats that his lead division didn't get on the roadway until near 11:00 a.m., when it steadily advanced upriver on the road directly leading to the Post.[544]

About the time Sherman began debouching his corps from their transports, Morgan's XIII Corps left Fletcher's Landing for Notribe's. But before departing, Morgan ordered that Col. Daniel Lindsay's Infantry Brigade from Peter Osterhaus' 2nd Division, reinforced by a Parrott-gun detachment from the Chicago Mercantile Battery, land on the opposite shore and proceed up the south bank in order to occupy Stilwell Point, placing him directly opposite Ft. Hindman. Should this detachment obtain its objective, its guns could actually be posted slightly above the Post, preventing the garrisons either being evacuated or receiving reinforcements via Pine Bluff. For his part, Sherman had put BG Frederick Steele's division of three infantry brigades in the vanguard, its skirmishers barely getting underway before Steele's men reported coming under scattered small-arms fire.[545]

Even earlier, the lightly armored gunboats *Rattler* and *Blackhawk* steamed upriver to test the Post's heavy guns, and, when bypassing the Confederates entrenched below, tossed several rounds in the infantrymen's direction. The shells did little damage, though they brought to a halt the felling of trees out in front of the rebel works. After delivering this initial "salute," the gunboats steamed on

---

[544] See "Post of Arkansas," in *A.H.Q.*, vol. 18, #3 (1959), pp. 249-251; also, Sherman's *Memoirs*, p. 297.

[545] *Ibid.*, pp. 250-1.

up, Hart's gunners having learned that they couldn't inflict observable damage on even these thinly armored tinclads with their smaller field guns, so things quickly fell silent.[546]

At the head of Steele's division marched BG Charles Hovey's brigade, his five regiments advancing up the river road in a closed, compact column. To Hovey's rear marched BG John M. Thayer's Iowa Brigade, also five regiments strong, also well closed, followed by BG Frank Blair, Jr.'s brigade of six regiments. After easily brushing back the few cavalrymen encountered in the early part of their advance, the Union soldiers soon began to encounter heavier cavalry resistance, then enemy infantry skirmishers concealed by a dense forest, this prompting Steele to send for Battery F, 2nd Missouri Artillery so as to shell the enemy from these concealed positions. Apparently, these skirmishers were the five companies of the 10th Texas Infantry, led by Lt. Col. Robert Young of that regiment, his men "coming under a heavy skirmishing fire."[547]

On reaching the intersection of the Crockett's Bluff road with the river road some miles below the Post, Sherman directed Steele to swing his brigade to the right, these men unknowingly marching away from the river in the direction of several impenetrable swamps. Sherman had entertained hopes of using this connecting road to get well out beyond the enemy's left flank, in which case his corps could quickly sweep around to the north of Post Bayou to cut off the rebel garrison's only viable means of escape. Once over Post Bayou, he could quickly march parallel up that fetid stream, before turning back to drive the rebels south of the bayou back into the Arkansas River. He had not gotten very far on the Crockett's Bluff road before encountering a dammed-up creek that had completely flooded the roadbed, preventing his continuing the movement in that direction. With no other route available, Sherman had little recourse but to

---

[546] *O.R.*, I, vol. 17, pt. 1, p. 791, wherein Deshler reports the enemy fired at Hart's battery until near noon.

[547] "Post of Arkansas," in *A.H.Q.*, vol. 18, #3 (1959), p. 251; Sherman's *Memoirs*, p. 297; also, Deshler's report from *O.R.*, I, 17 pt. 1, 791.

double back on the same road to reach the river road, thence resuming his advance directly toward the Post.[548]

Back at Notribe's, Morgan's XIII Corps had been offloaded, and an advance begun. It made good headway, since there was no resistance, and he made it to the intersection of the river road with that of Crockett's Bluff, his lead division actually reaching that point about the time of the return of Steele's division, forcing a delay as both corps had come to a halt, resulting in further delays. In the meantime, Gen. McClernand had sent some of his cavalry up the river road toward the Post pending the separation of the XIII and XIV corps, with Sherman's 2nd Division, led by BG David Stuart, moving north first along the winding river road. He immediately came into contact with the enemy again, only to witness them hastily vacating the lower works that they obviously had manned since the previous evening. Upon learning this, McClernand demanded that Stuart be pushed forward in order to facilitate his cavalry's driving the rebels back upon their main line. McClernand entertained hopes that should Stuart push forward with vigor, he might just follow the enemy into his works, rendering an all-out assault all but unnecessary.[549]

As for the Confederates, when Churchill had earlier been made aware of Sherman's effort to pursue a flanking route down the Crockett's Bluff road, rather that advancing to attack, he hurriedly chose to abandon his downstream positions. He first sent out three cavalry companies to demonstrate and thus hold the enemy in check in order to cover the withdrawal. He next ordered Deshler to post a strong rearguard to further retard the enemy's advance, while at the same time ordering Garland to employ his brigade as the train guard in order to get the artillery and wagons back safely to the Post. Remaining on scene just long enough to see Garland get off, Churchill then instructed Col. Dunnington to fall in behind Garland, Deshler to bring up the rear. Meanwhile, Deshler had shaken out five

---

[548] *Ibid.*; O.R., I, vol. 17, pt. 1, p. 722; *Memoirs*, p. 297. This postwar work by Sherman is a decidedly biased account and suspect in any number of ways, warranting confirmation if used as a source.

[549] "Post of Arkansas," in *A.H.Q.*, vol. 18, #3 (1959), p. 252; *O.R.*, I, 17, pt. 1, p. 726; *Memoirs*, p. 298.

companies from the 10th Texas Infantry to act as skirmishers to cover the withdrawal.[550]

Charged with the safety of the artillery and supply train, upon reaching the fort, Garland ordered his men to begin construction of a line of works previously staked out that ran almost due north from the point where it intersected the sally port of the northernmost bastion wall of the fort. Lt. Col. A. S. Hutchinson's 19th Arkansas regiment of Dunnington's brigade had accompanied Garland's command, and upon arriving, had taken post with the fort itself, apparently augmented by Crawford's Arkansas Infantry battalion. Deshler was to buy time by slowing the enemy's advance such that, upon arrival, he could assume a position on Garland's left, extending Garland's line northward toward the sluggish Post Bayou. Known as a tactical withdrawal, when executed in the immediate presence of an overwhelming enemy, it often required as much luck as skill to properly execute. Withdrawal, given such circumstances by untried (if well-trained) infantry, as Deshler's brigade had become, was nevertheless fraught with great danger, and even if successfully accomplished, could work to adversely affect the morale of all involved.[551]

What's most surprising, given later circumstances, is that the troops most unnerved by this enterprise appeared to have been several regiments in Garland's brigade. Perhaps this came from their initially being the furthest downriver when ordered to evacuate their posts, which they might presume would make them the most likely to be the first attacked. Or it may have been that they had the greater distance to travel to reach the comparative safety of the main works. In any case, Garland had barely gotten his three regiments out of their downstream position and headed back upriver when word arrived, supposedly from Churchill, that Garland must refrain from attempting to withdraw using the river road, and instead to move cross-country to reach the Post. This may have arisen from the fact that the cavalry companies covering their withdrawal had been sent off to the east to see if the enemy had already gotten around them. In

---

[550] *O.R.*, I, vol. 17, pt. 1, p. 780; p. 783; p. 791; and p. 730, report of BG Stephen G. Burbridge, U.S. Army, commanding 1st Brigade, 1st Division, 13th Corps.

[551] *Ibid.*, p. 791.

any event, not long after, as Garland's column hurriedly passed through a large, cleared field, men were heard to start shouting that "ten thousand cavalry" had gotten beyond them, threatening to cut them off from the fort. What ensued was wholesale panic, which quickly spread the length of Garland's column. Of particular interest, in light of afterward events, for reasons apparently only known to the men in the 24th Texas Cavalry (Dismounted), as soon as they heard this, they bolted in a panic-stricken mass into the rear of the lead regiment, the 6th Texas Infantry, with each seemingly disintegrating and running for the Post as fast as the men's legs could carry them. This prompted the rear regiment, the 25th Texas Cavalry (Dismounted), to break apart and flee. As Capt. Sam Foster of the 24th Texas Cavalry noted of this affair: "So here we go--all get mixed up, and all get in front, and if it were not for the Colonel we would have run over those ahead of us."[552]

For several panic-stricken minutes, only slightly subsiding as the men became winded by their dash, terror reigned in Garland's brigade; in fact, many of the men didn't regain composure until reaching the environs of Ft. Hindman itself, when, apparently due to embarrassment, the men began to slow down and regain a sense of order. Interestingly, in his after-action report of the campaign, Garland conveniently fails to mention this event, instead declaring that the brigade "had to move slowly" because it was encumbered by both the artillery and ordnance train. This writer believes that the implications that knowledge of such an occurrence would have provoked fellow officers, and he deliberately chose to make no mention of it in his official report.[553]

On the other hand, Deshler, ably assisted by the three cavalry companies cooperating with his skirmish companies, not only succeeded in extricating his own troops safely after Dunnington's commands got away, but harassed the enemy so effectively as to slow considerably its approach to the Post. Several times during the withdrawal, Deshler had had to halt his command to face his regiments about to confront, albeit temporarily, the enemy's progress. Following each display of resistance, Deshler would then resume the

---

[552] *One of Cleburne's Command:*, p. 15.

[553] *O.R.*, I, vol. 17, pt. 1, p. 783.

retreat toward the Post, and upon reaching there, learned that his brigade had been assigned to that portion of the staked-out line that extended from Garland's left all the way over to Post Bayou. As he afterward observed, "my right touching the left of Garland's Brigade and my left prolonged toward a bayou, which ran into the Arkansas in my rear . . ."[554] Deshler quickly discovered that the portion of the line assigned him appeared greatly overextended, and as with Garland's on his right, at a right angle from the river, his men having to somehow occupy all the intervening ground over the bayou. He discerned that he couldn't maintain contact with Garland's brigade, however, and still occupy the entire distance to his left. To his credit, Churchill had ordered the cavalry to go back out front to further delay the enemy approach, this giving Deshler some time in which to set his men to work on throwing up fortifications. And, just as Garland's men before him, the men in Deshler's brigade had to make do with the few entrenching tools they had, axes and spades, forcing the men to resort to using bayonets, cups, plates, and even wooden planks as a means for throwing up works. With only a few hours of daylight remaining, and the enemy fast closing upon them, they had precious little time to complete their entrenchments.[555]

That the two infantry brigades outside the fort walls had made good progress in throwing up these works is attested to by Sgt. W. W. Heartsill of Capt. Richardson's Cavalry Co., who returned from out front about dark: "We find [the infantry] have not been idle while we were in front, but now at dark have tolerable breastworks thrown up; where four hours since there was not a clod of earth dug up . . . ." And Franz Coller of Co. H, 6th Texas Infantry told how those working outside the fort walls had food carried to them by those inside so they could continue to work without interruption. He, like many other soldiers, had had little to no sleep for the past several nights and, unfortunately, it "fell to my lot to be picket for our camp tonight." Coller found himself able to stand his post this third night, "as I was tired but not sleepy, for such affairs don't let one sleep!"[556]

---

[554] *O.R.*, I, vol. 17, pt.1, p. 791; p. 780.

[555] *Ibid.*, pp. 780-1, 784, 791.

[556] *Fourteen Hundred*, p. 94; and "Coller," in *Military History of Texas*, vol. 9, #2 (1972), p. 134.

Upon learning of the predicament of those outside the fort, Churchill had assigned six companies of Lt. Col. A. S. Hutchinson's 19th Arkansas Infantry and Capt. William Hart's battery to Garland. This permitted Garland to shift his three regiments further to their left, yet remain in contact with the fort. Garland had deployed his brigade in the following order, from right to left: on the left of the 19th Arkansas came Hart's battery; followed by Lt. Col. T. S. Anderson's 6th Texas Infantry of 542 men, posted to the left of Hart's three sections; next came Col. Franklin Wilkes' 24th Texas Cavalry (Dismounted), 587 strong; and lastly, Col. Clayton C. Gillespie's 25th Texas Cavalry (dismounted), of 552 men, which was connected to Deshler's right regiment. All told, Garland had 1,681 men of his brigade present for duty at the start of the contest.[557]

Deshler had posted his brigade from right to left, with Lt. Col. John T. Coit's 18th Texas Cavalry (Dismounted) just touching Gillespie's 25th Texas Cavalry (Dismounted), next came Col. James Taylor's 17th Texas Cavalry (Dismounted), followed by Col. R. Q. Mills' 10th Texas Infantry, and lastly Maj. V. P. Sanders' 15th Texas Cavalry (Dismounted). Deshler would later estimate his strength at the commencement of the battle as being close to 1600 men, rank and file. The weakest part of Deshler's line, obviously, remained his far left, where Sanders' 15th Texas Cavalry (Dismounted) found over 200 yards separating its left flank from the sluggish bayou. In military parlance, this placed Deshler's left flank for the time being "in the air;" in other words, not anchored upon a natural feature that would prevent its being flanked from that direction.[558]

For the present, Churchill maintained his headquarters inside the fort proper, and Deshler searched him out there to report about his vulnerable left. After some discussion, an agreement was reached that Deshler would cause Sanders' 15th Texas Cavalry (Dismounted) to construct wooden traverses at the width of a company front to his left rear, on each of his five left companies, at 90-degree angles. This

---

[557] *O.R.*, I, vol. 17, pt. 1, p. 784.

[558] *Ibid.*, in his report Deshler estimates his strength, as he lost his papers in the aftermath of the battle. "In the air" is meant that a line regiment has no strong-point upon which to anchor its exposed flank, such as a hill, bayou, river, marsh, etc.

would permit a rapid change of front to the northwest should that regiment be flanked via the bayou, or else by an enemy force that moved west beyond the bayou to reaching their rear. A temporary expedient, these companies must hold the enemy in check until reinforcements could reach the threatened point. Churchill had promised support, but in truth that officer had no disposable troops with which to reinforce Deshler's left in any event, at least without drawing them from some other point on the existing line! This must have caused the men at the far left to ponder on just how tenuous this flank would be in case of an attack from that quarter. Obviously, Churchill didn't have a sufficient number of men to cover the fort on the far right, as well as the improvised works off to his west; therefore, the dispatching of any force to that point must necessarily leave a gap somewhere along the line. To provide at least some means of resistance on his left, soon after Deshler ordered that Capt. Duncan Preston's Co. F, 17th Texas Cavalry (Dismounted) be deployed as skirmishers to his left rear, creating a very thin line that linked Sanders' left to the aforementioned stream.[559]

About dusk, sporadic gunfire erupted out in front of Deshler's left-center, where he had sent work parties to level the huts belonging to the 19th Arkansas. They would have harbored sharpshooters, and he needed a clear field of fire out front in any case, plus the lumber thus secured could be utilized in bolstering their rifle pits. Even as this work progressed, at the opposite end of the line, artillery fire commenced about dark as Union gunboats came up to commence a heavy fire upon Ft. Hindman, which continued until late in the night.[560]

Adm. David Porter well knew the importance of silencing the fort's heavy battery prior to the land forces making any attempt to storm the works, and had therefore at about 6:00 p.m. sent three heavy ironclads, *Baron DeKalb, Louisville,* and the *Cincinnati,* to within a quarter mile of the fort, each having been assigned a heavy

---

[559] *Ibid.*, p. 791; "Marshall S. Pierson" in *Military History of Texas*, vol. 13, p. 29.

[560] *Ibid.*, I, vol. 17, pt. 1, p. 780. A major concern of the Confederates would be if enemy gunboats got beyond the fort and took them in reverse; or that forces on the opposite shore along Stillwell's Point might accomplish a similar object.

gun to be taken out. Additionally, they were accompanied by the shallow-draft gunboats, *Lexington* and *Blackhawk*, which approached to throw shrapnel and shell into the interior of the fort. This heavy gunfire caused the fort's gunners to slacken return fire, especially when the tinclad *Rattler* drew up almost to the fort's embrasures to fire point-blank into its two casemated positions nearest their guns. In doing so, the latter vessel ran upon sunken piles and was solidly raked in the process by the fort's heavy guns, forcing the ship to helplessly drift back downstream.[561]

During this exchange, one of the gunboats scored a direct hit on the muzzle of the forward casemate gun, splintering its tube and sending forth fragments that either killed or maimed nearly all of the gun crew serving the piece. Others struck the iron rail sheathing covering the roofs of the casemated guns, not only splintering or twisting the rails, but also similarly doing the same to the massive 14-by-14-inch oak timbers beneath the rails, the splinters careening along the walls like so many barbed arrows. An officer of the 24th Texas Cavalry (Dismounted), watching this spectacle from a distance (he had found himself almost in a direct line behind the fort), chronicled the bombardment, much impressed by the destruction caused by the enemy's huge naval guns as they belched massive flames and emitted noises that sounded to him much like nearby thunder.[562]

Whilst purely coincidental, almost simultaneous with the last salvo fired by the gunboats, the only reinforcements to reach the Post prior to its surrender came in the arrival of Capt. Alf Johnson's Texas Spy Co., which had miraculously made its way from St. Charles to reach the Confederate lines about 10:00 p.m. The cavalrymen advised that additional troops were on their way, provided the Post garrison could hold out long enough, in the guise of Col. E. E. Portlock's 24th Arkansas Infantry, which was marching from the same place as they but coming at a much slower pace than their mounted counterparts. By now, whether inside or outside the fortifications, virtually everyone realized instinctively that before the end of another day, they must all witness an overwhelming assault by

---

[561] "Post of Arkansas," in *A.H.Q.*, vol. 18, #3 (1959), p. 256.

[562] *Fourteen Hundred*, p. 95; also, *One of Cleburne's Command:*, p. 16.

the Federals. Due to the proximity of the enemy out in front, fires were again prohibited within the infantry works, and with the night turning chilly, some of those inside their ditches must have reflected that they should have attempted to retrieve their winter clothes from their quarters.[563]

McClernand's hopes of taking the Post in one fell swoop on January 10 had failed, but as that second day passed into darkness, he realized that neither Sherman nor Morgan could reach their assigned positions from which to launch their attacks. Indeed, both corps struggled late into the night in mostly vain efforts to get into position, the XIII Corps having barely arrived on the field and Sherman's still engaged in sloshing along at the right in order to stave off escape in that direction. Delays resulting from Sherman being inable to reach the point where he'd been ordered, compounded by the many difficulties experienced in deploying into line during the late evening hours, slowed the Union advance to a crawl."[564]

To recap, the XIII Corps hadn't disembarked until the early afternoon hours, having laid over the preceding night at Mudlins, some seven miles further downstream from Notribe's. Having just two days' rations in their haversacks, and feeling the extra weight due to carrying sixty rounds of ammunition, along with lugging knapsacks and blankets, the march to the Post had proven quite trying. BG A. J. Smith's 1st division of Morgan's corps led off the advance, with BG Stephen Burbridge's brigade of six regiments in the van, followed by Col. William Landrum's brigade, which numbered six regiments as well. To the rear of Smith's Division came BG Peter Osterhaus' 2nd Division, composed of Col. Lionel Sheldon's 1st and John De Courcy's 3rd brigades; Col. Daniel Lindsay's 2nd brigade had been earlier sent across to Stilwell Point on the south side of the river.[565]

---

[563] *Fourteen Hundred*, p. 93; *One of Cleburne's Command:*, p. 16. See also a letter drafted that same night, attributed to Capt. E. B. Pickett of Co. I, 25th Texas Cavalry (Dismounted), of several making just such an effort in civilwarbull.org/forum/messages/4485.html.

[564] Post of Arkansas," in *A.H.Q.*, vol. 18, #3 (1959), pp. 255, 258-9.

[565] *O.R.*, I, vol. 17, pt. 1, pp. 716, 723; *A.H.Q.* vol. XVIII, # 3, pp.254-5.

As these members of the XIII Corps passed through the hastily abandoned lower works of the rebels, unfortunately, intermingling had taken place between Morgan's and Sherman's corps. After separation, BG Andrew J. Smith's 1st Division trailed Sherman's corps up the river road, the latter still hoping to find maneuvering room out to his right, Burbridge's 1st brigade still at the front of Smith's division. By the time this division reached the field immediately in front of the fort, evening shadows had begun to pass into complete darkness. Landrum's 2nd brigade arrived later, reaching its position in complete darkness and encamping in a column of regiments that stretched far back down the river road. Even further than that came BG Peter Osterhaus 2nd Division, which went into camp astraddle the Crockett's Bluff road intersection, well in the rear of Landrum's brigade. Now, nearly all of McClernand's disposable force had come to within striking distance of the Confederates and, ere the coming of dawn, would be quickly deployed and prepared to strike.[566]

Even as Morgan's several divisions settled in for the night, Sherman continued his extension toward the right, causing his corps to march northward and away from the river in the direction of Post Bayou, though he seemed not yet to be fully aware that possession of that stream would place him directly opposite Deshler's unanchored left. For his part, McClernand had previous to this dispatched Capt. James Spark's Co. L, 3rd Illinois Cavalry, to reconnoiter the bayou itself; this officer returned to report the torpid stream could be easily forded, and he further advised that "one brigade and a battery" be thrown across "for the purpose of cutting off retreat and enfilading their rifle pits." Either Sherman didn't receive this information, or he failed to act on it. And, just before turning in for the night, McClernand had ordered Capt. Jacob Foster's 1st Wisconsin Battery of 30-pounder Parrotts to join Lindsay's brigade on Stilwell Point, to augment the section of 10-pound Parrott guns of the Chicago Mercantile Battery, which had accompanied Lindsay there.[567]

---

[566] *Ibid.*, pp. 723, 726, 730-31; *Ibid,* p. 255.

[567] See especially *O.R.*, I, vol. 17, pt. 1, pp. 720-1 for the cavalry reconnaissance; also, *Memoirs*, p. 298, for Sherman's effort to explain away his not taking advantage of this missed opportunity.

In his memoirs, Sherman would lead readers to believe he indeed had conducted a personal reconnaissance of the enemy positions out in his front under a "bright moonlight . . . close up," and found the rebels all withdrawn "in and about the fort." Waxing poetically in his narrative as to his supposed personal observations, Sherman advised readers that he "could hear the enemy hard at work, pulling down houses, cutting with axes, and building entrenchments." This continued until dawn came, "and I was thus listening when, about 4:00 a.m., the bugler in the rebel camp sounded as pretty a reveille as I ever listened to."[568]

Obviously, all was not calm in the Confederate lines, as the nighttime hours pressed in upon the rebels huddled in their works. It had turned rather cold, and this made the men quite uncomfortable, the few with blankets sharing with those that had none. Some, in fact, went looking for ways to ward off the coldness. However, notably, two soldiers of Co. I, 25th Texas Cavalry (Dismounted) ventured forth in a search for their own winter gear. A surviving account of this quest, apparently penned early the next morning, dramatically captures those moments, thus revealing the mindset of the Texans in the fieldworks. Most likely the note, or handwritten letter if it was intended to be that, originated from Capt. E. B. Pickett, who commanded that company during the night and the following day:

> Lt. [J. J.] Pickett and [John] Manly went into quarters last night [the 10th] after dark & brought out their baggage - A rather daring act & one attended with much risk, as the enemy were all around them. Our breastworks are completed & must be impenetrable. Large logs were laid on the ground, covered well with dirt on [top]. Two layers of house logs were placed on the inside, one end resting on the ground & the other on top of the works - The [w]ho[l]e well braced with abutment logs on the inside. The enemy's skirmishers[,] or sharpshooters, have come up in our front behind logs and stumps, and already a brisk fire is going on between them and our skirmishers, while

---

[568] *Memoirs*, p. 298.

balls are whistling over our heads. The desperate struggle must soon begin. It is surprising to see how unconcerned the men are while some few faces express a deal of agitation, most of them seem totally indifferent.

To me it is a solemn, anxious and impressive occasion and one calculated to fill the mind with a thousand contending emotions. Here we are a little band not exceeding 4,000, opposed by a force numbering probably ten to one with perhaps twenty times as much artillery, probably surrounded and all chances of retreat all cut off. Our commander has said he will not surrender, & we have agreed to make good his declaration. Consequently, it is victory or death, and who can feel a reasonable hope that we can survive the struggle. To my mind the chances are a hundred to one against us, I would speak falsely to say that I feel indifferent or unconcerned, but I am resolved to take the chances, & fight them to the end for **I had rather die than be whipped.**[569] [author's emphasis added]

A decidedly frosty morning greeted friend and foe alike in the early hours of Sunday, January 11, though the sun gave promise of quickly driving away both the darkness and the vapors that developed in the lowland swamp back of the Post. As soon as the ground out in front of Deshler's line became visible, he observed several enemy columns well out beyond the range of his Texans' small arms; these columns all seemed to be moving further out beyond his left, massing in-depth, especially in the vicinity of the bayou. The previous night had found Gen. Churchill wiring Lt. General Holmes at Little Rock of the likelihood of a dawn assault and requesting reinforcements; he'd received a telegraphic response that stated that Churchill must hold out at all costs; or to use Holmes'

---

[569] Emphasis added by writer. Posted by Ron Blake on January 11, 2000, it can be seen on the website, www.civilwarbull.org/forum/messages.

words, " . . . to hold out till help arrived are until all [are] dead!" And it's apparent, based upon the preceding paragraph, that Churchill had certainly conveyed that message to each of his subordinate commanders.[570]

By the time that Holmes' reply had come back, Churchill had turned his attention to last-minute troop movements. For he had become aware that opposite Deshler's far left, BG Charles Hovey's 2nd brigade of Sherman's corps had already begun to deploy, his right attached to the bayou itself, and this officer would be the first to send forth his six regiments; they charged to aim for the river behind Deshler's left. Aware by now of Hovey's objective of soon attempting to turn his left, Deshler had taken two companies from each of his other three regiments, excepting only Maj. Sanders' 15th Texas Cavalry (Dismounted), already posted there, then sending them along to bolster the skirmish companies that had been previously sent out under Lt. Col. Sebron Noble of the 17th Texas Cavalry (Dismounted). The firing in this area erupted soon after daybreak, Hovey having delayed only long enough to organize his front line, consisting of the 3rd and 17th Missouri Infantry, and a savage firefight developed.[571]

Overly concerned about his exposed left, not long after sunrise, with "not a company in reserve," Deshler had requested that additional reinforcements be sent him from Garland's brigade on his right, this having previously been agreed upon by all the parties in a meeting the night before. For his part, Deshler could see the enemy as they passed through the huts of Garland's old camp. Garland, in the meantime, reacted by sending over six companies of 19th Arkansas Infantry, which had been posted outside the fort on Garland's right, along with two sections of Hart's Arkansas Battery, to report to directly to Deshler. Even as these units made ready to move, well out in Deshler's front, these Texans watched nervously as

---

[570] *O.R.*, 1, 17, p. 781. Holmes would order MG Henry McCulloch's former division (all Texans), then under the command of MG John G. Walker (soon to be known as Walker's "Greyhound" Division), to move toward the Post from near Little Rock, but it would not likely arrive in time to be play a role in relieving the besieged garrison.

[571] *A.H.Q.*, vol. XVIII, # 3, p. 260.

what seemed to be long strands of "blue yarn," still moving at great distance toward their own right, their rifles tipped by what appeared to be shiny, straight pins (actually burnished bayonets). The enemy regiments moved in the same general direction as Deshler's oncoming reinforcements. Just afterward, Churchill personally sent over Capt. Alf Johnson's Texas Rangers, in tandem with Capt. Matthew Denson's and L. M. Nutt's Louisiana Cavalry companies. These were deployed immediately in open order back to the west along the bayou's south bank, starting at Deshler's left and extending all the way westward until reaching the river near the mouth of the creek to prevent the enemy's getting that far into his rear. These three cavalry companies gave Deshler an additional 120 men only, however. Now began a race between the moving Union and Confederate columns, the outcome of which would inevitably prove to be a matter of life and death for those involved.[572]

Hovey's men had been up and in place well before sunrise; he, soon after daybreak, had received orders to move directly at Deshler's perilously exposed left. This presented a danger of the greatest possible magnitude. Now properly aligned and well-dressed, Hovey's men advanced in a column of regiments as they passed through the intervening woods and across several cultivated fields to arrive directly opposite Deshler's left. As before stated, Hovey had, upon reaching an agreed point previously selected, formed the 3rd and 17th Missouri Infantry regiments in a front line, followed by a second composed of the 25th and 31st Iowa and 76th Ohio, the latter line following the former at a full wheeling distance. Having fully established Deshler's location with his skirmishers, Hovey halted only temporarily to await the arrival of troops on his left.[573]

Hardly had this transpired than the Arkansas Infantry companies scurrying westward now reported in to Deshler. All of a sudden, a tremendous crashing noise exploded in front of Deshler's line as Hovey's men opened upon the Texans; the men there immediately returned fire. It was during this momentous time frame, with sheets of flame and columns of smoke gushing forth, the staccato rattle reverberating across the fields in the early morning

---

[572] *O.R.*, I, vol. 17, pt. 1, pp. 781, 784, & 792; *A.H.Q.*, vol. XVIII, # 3, p. 261.

[573] *Ibid.*, p. 792.

stillness, that Hart's sections of 6-pounders and 10-pound Parrott rifles reached the threatened point, then immediately were put into line. Deshler quickly dispatched the Arkansas infantrymen to the left of Maj. Sanders' 15th Texas Cavalry (Dismounted), the battalion placed in line in an echelon formation at the left-rear of Sanders' works. This enabled the nearby Texans to obliquely sweep the ground to their left, in front of the Arkansas soldiers, for the latter had scant protection other than a slight rise, and the men went prone immediately. In the interval, the two sections of Hart's guns, under Lt. E. A. Du Bose and W. T. Tiller, had been put into position near the center of Deshler's brigade; the guns were situated beginning on the right-most company of the 10th Texas Infantry. In other words, they were situated between the intervals of each successive company to the left of the first gun.[574]

Even with the insertion of Hutchinson's six Arkansas companies on Sanders' left and with the two gun sections situated, Deshler still found after extending his intervals to the left that a gap yet existed encompassing over a hundred yards from Hutchinson's right to Sanders' left, and with an equal distance between the Arkansans' left and the bayou. The "rackensackers" had scant opportunity to throw up works, having come under heavy fire as soon as they arrived, the men taking a prone position alone behind the slight rise they had discovered there. Tough Hart's guns hadn't occupied much space; nevertheless, they tremendously increased Deshler's overall firepower, thus providing comfort to infantrymen supporting these guns.[575]

Though with not a single reserve on hand, Deshler thought he could hang on for the time being. Hardly had these last reinforcements arrived than Deshler withdrew his previously deployed infantry skirmishers at the bayou, supplanting them with the three dismounted cavalry companies that had recently reported, deploying them at right angles to his line so as to form an extension toward the left rear, while simultaneously throwing some of these men across the bayou in order to watch for the enemy. As with the

---

[574] *Ibid.*; also, *One of Cleburne's Command:*, p. 95.

[575] *Ibid.*

Arkansans before them, these cavalrymen sought what little protection the brush and timber growing along the bayou afforded.[576]

To fill the void left by the detachment of the 19th Arkansas battalion and the two sections of Hart's battery on his front, Garland caused his remaining troops to extend to their right in order to remain in contact with the fort. As the enemy assaults had thus far been directed only against Deshler's front, this could be readily accomplished due to a lack of incoming fire. He accomplished this by extending intervals to the right, deploying the remaining men in a single line of battle, and did so without losing a man. However, with noon now approaching, the gunboats came up once again to complete the wreck of the main fort, and soon a strange cacophony of sounds began drifting over Garland's line, heavier perhaps on the right as the Union's large navy guns opened up amidst the noise of steamboat whistles. These sounds punctuated slightly less in reverberation on the far left, where a groundswell of field guns, intermixed with volleys of small-arms musketry, the agonizing wails of wounded livestock, amidst lusty cheering, all apparently ensconced within a pall of acrid smoke that drifted across the fields to mask what was actually transpiring. The noise made everyone on both sides, if anything, even more jittery.[577]

The continuous rattle of musketry at the far left had gradually commingled with the even louder reverberations from the thunderous explosions in and adjacent to the fort, which by now had diminished in response to the fire of gunboats attempting to silence the Confederates therein. The concussions reverberated up and downstream and across the intervening woods, further enhancing the anxiety of those involved. Not surprisingly, the smoke and noise combined to further heighten an already increased state of nervousness that enveloped even those in Garland's brigade, who seemed to be witnesses to the spectacle of endless firing that by now had enveloped both flanks. The billowing smoke on the right, however, couldn't conceal the damage being inflicted upon the fort's

---

[576] *Ibid.*; also, see *Fourteen Hundred:*, p. 96

[577] *One of Cleburne's Command:*, pp. 17 & 19; "Jim Turner," in *Texana*, vol. 13, pp. 156-7; *Charles Leuschner*, p. 12; and "Franz Coller," in *Military History Of Texas*, vol. IX, # 2, pp. 135-6.

walls: "See the railroad iron fly 30' high doubled in all sorts of shape," wrote Capt. Sam Foster, a company officer with the 24th Texas (Dismounted) as a nearby casemated position was instantly shattered: "Then [this] . . . same shell," he recorded, "pass[ed] behind us crashing and breaking everything in [its] . . . track."[578]

The fighting that had begun initially on Deshler's left had gradually expanded to his right prior to noon as additional enemy units had begun their own "in-echelon" advances. By this time, Hovey had lost a substantial number of killed and wounded, his men slackening their fire, albeit briefly, thus giving the 15th Texas Cavalry (Dismounted) and the left wing of the 10th Texas Infantry an opportunity to regain some composure. Those moments had quickly been exploded by an artillery barrage that commenced from where Garland's winter camp had been situated, and immediately thereafter BG John Thayer's all-Iowa 3rd Brigade advanced to the attack on Hovey's left. Aimed directly upon Deshler's center, and again advancing in an echelon formation, with right in front, his five Iowa regiments now sprinted forward. The brigade's right had overlapped with Hovey's left, thus becoming intermixed somewhat with Hovey's as the Iowans approached the works, resulting in some amount of hesitation. Again allowing the enemy to come within a hundred yards after emitting a hefty "Texas" cheer, the two regiments posted in their front opened upon the Iowans, with results similar to those Hovey had experienced from behind their protective walls.[579]

Deshler recorded the effects of his men's fire as the enemy arrived within point-blank range. They had reserved their fire until they knew they could score hits amongst the enemy:

> We did not open fire upon this column with small-arms until its head was within 80 to 100 yards from our line; then we gave them a very deadly [volley]

---

[578] *One of Cleburne's Command:*, p. 17; also, "Coller," in *Military History Of Texas*, vol. IX, # 2, p. 135.

[579] *O.R.*, I, vol. 17, pt. 1, p. 793. Deshler admits having just 315 Enfield Rifles (in the 10th Texas Infantry) the three other regiments being mostly armed with percussion shotguns and sporting arms.

fire, . . . [then] firing by file, and with marked effect, as after our first volley those not killed or wounded fell back in great confusion to the shelter of the timber, from whence they kept up a very heavy skirmishing fire.[580]

Those not hit withdrew as rapidly as they had come on, regrouping in a nearby wood-line to be reformed again and return to their work, but the Enfield rifles, smooth-bore muskets, and shotguns utilizing buck-and-ball loads, combined with other regiments that directed an oblique fire upon the enemy again as they reached Deshler's center, caused great havoc. Even more punishing fire came from Hart's four guns, each of which spat both shell and canister rounds into the enemy infantrymen, which, combined with the rifle balls and buckshot fired by the infantry, forced Thayer's men to go to ground out front. However, these men fired back from their concealed positions as best they could through the blinding smoke, gradually working their way forward in the following minutes in the direction of the Texans' works.[581]

Across the debris-strewn fields, still new lines of Union infantrymen could be seen deploying forward, most carefully threading their way through stunted undergrowth to get into position for assaults upon Garland's thinly stretched line. It seemed obvious that, sooner or later, such efforts must inevitably breach the line, as the sheer numbers of those approaching, coupled with the many batteries of guns being sighted, gave a startling image to these men as their foes began moving again. Men were surely thinking as they witnessed this spectacle, blue waves appearing like so many ocean breakers, that they must inevitably sweep away those still attempting to resist their enemy.

Over on Deshler's front, not long after noon, Hovey's men had clawed their way through dense shrubbery to take up positions as close as possible to the enemy works, directing a menacing fire at anyone that dared lift his head above the parapet, even for a second. Opposite Deshler's center, sharpshooters from the 76th Ohio Infantry

---

[580] *Ibid.*, pp. 793-4.

[581] *Ibid.*, p. 793.

had discovered an especially good vantage point from which to drive Hart's artillerymen from their four guns, in the process killing or wounding eighty of the eighty-two horses that had been picketed at the rear of the guns. In between these detachments, Thayer's Iowans had also continued to fire following their second assault, his men effecting a lodgment not over a hundred paces in front of Deshler's line. In their initial advance, this brigade had precisely executed a "forward into line" movement from a column of regiments, the 26th and 30th Iowa regiments suffering many casualties while executing that maneuver. In fact, these two regiments alone from this brigade would suffer the highest casualty rate of any unit on the Federal side.[582]

Not long after Thayer's attack had stalled out, to his left, BG Stuart's division had been next in line to launch an attack. His two brigades also deployed in-echelon, right in front, their assault aimed directly at Deshler's extreme right. Led respectively by senior colonels Giles and T. K. Smith, the two brigades made little headway against the shotguns and antiquated guns wielded by the 17th and 18th Texas Cavalry (Dismounted), facilitated somewhat by the 10th Texas Infantry, whose men swept Stuart's line at a right oblique with their Enfields. Recoiling from this concentrated fire, the men of both brigades sought whatever cover they could out in front of Deshler's works. The tide of battle having shifted gradually from Deshler's left to his center, and now to his right, signaled to the two left regiments of Garland's brigade they too must soon be exposed to an increasing rattle of musketry. To their chagrin, to their left and front they witnessed an ever-growing number of Union field guns that arrived to mingle with their shells to the infantry fire that raised great concern amongst those in 25th and 24th Texas Cavalry (Dismounted) regiments, who lay in that order in their works.[583]

Persistent enemy attacks along the whole of Deshler's front ultimately forced him to once again call on help from Garland. Still having no reserves in hand, Churchill had little choice but to once again approve Deshler's request, even though Garland's left

---

[582] "Post of Arkansas," in *A.H.Q.*, vol. 18, #3 (1959), p. 266.

[583] *O.R.*, I, vol. 17, pt. 1, p. 784; "Post of Arkansas," *A.H.Q*, vol. XVIII, # 3, p. 267-8.

regiments had apparently help beat off the attack against Deshler's right, and Garland once again agreed to send additional reinforcements over to the left. Having been made aware that this might be the case, Garland reacted quickly, sending off two companies of the 6th Texas Infantry under Maj. A. H. Phillips, along with the alternate (five in all from each) companies of the 24th and 25th Texas Cavalry (Dismounted), under Lt. Col. P. H. Swearingen and Lt. Col. William Neyland respectively, over to Deshler's front. Though this would obviously weaken Garland's own position, he again extended the intervals of the remaining companies of the 6th Texas in order to man his entire line; they deployed in a single rank. The extraordinary fire on Deshler's front had grown to such an extent that those moving there from the right had to traverse the entire distance by scurrying on all fours in an attempt to avoid being struck down by either enemy shells or bullets that whistled just overhead.[584]

Just after noon, BG A. J. Smith had drawn his division up to the left of David Stuart's, receiving instructions to attack in-echelon as well, right in front, the point of his attack being the works on Garland's front. BG Stephen Burbridge's 1st Brigade of Smith's division found itself directly opposite Garland's left regiment, the 25th Texas Cavalry (Dismounted), the Union soldiers quickly running afoul of the percussion muskets wielded by the men of the 25th, aided by oblique fire from the Mississippi Rifles carried by those in the 24th Texas Cavalry (Dismounted). That the resulting firepower directed upon this single attack proved especially destructive is the fact that in this one advance, Burbridge's loss amounted to a fourth of the XIII Corps casualties sustained, that officer noting a loss of 37 killed, 305 wounded, and 7 missing.[585]

Up until this moment, the Texans in the works occupied by Garland's remaining soldiers had, for the most part, contented themselves as spectators, hunkering down in their works to listen to

---

[584] *Ibid.*, I, vol. 17, pt. 1, p. 782. Lt. Col. Anderson of the 6th Texas Infantry advised that to man the portion of the line assigned him, he had deployed his remaining men in "open order" in a single rank just to maintain contact with Dunnington's troops within the fort.

[585] *Ibid.*, I, vol. 17, pt. 1, p. 716; "Post of Arkansas," *A.H.Q.*, vol. XVIII, # 3, pp. 268-9.

the music of the iron and lead balls that whistled overhead. A thick pall of smoke had by now drifted over their position, obscuring vision and further exacerbating the anxiety felt. One junior officer of the 124th Texas Cavalry (Dismounted), posted toward the left-center of his brigade, tried to explain the fear being felt: "Oh, what is the matter?--Is this the end of the world?--Is this war?-- Is this fighting?--If it is, Lord, [please] deliver us!"[586]

To seemingly add insult to injury, on the left of Burbridge's brigade, Col. William Landrum's 2nd Brigade of Smith's 1st Division now began an advance; it had to pass through intervening woods midway across a flat plain from their starting point and the rebel works, and while this vegetation offered scant protection, it created alignment difficulties that somewhat slowed the infantry's advance. These men got no nearer to Garland's right than those to their right, with Landrum's regiments having to seek cover when only a hundred steps from the Texans' works. Though directing considerable fire upon Garland's right, Landrum's regiments would sustain a loss of just eighty-five men in this firefight.[587]

Lastly, nearest the river, BG Peter Osterhaus sent forward a single brigade from his own 2nd Division, Col. Lionel Sheldon's 1st Brigade, consisting of three regiments, all of which aimed directly at Ft. Hindman. Delivered in a handsome manner, the attack saw the 120th Ohio Infantry effecting a lodgment upon the outer parapet wall, though it didn't quite achieve its object of getting within the fort walls. However, this led to an excited call by Dunnington for Garland to come to his assistance as well. Realizing this to be an especially critical situation, Garland reacted a final time by dispatching the two right companies of the 6th Texas Infantry, under Lt. Col. Anderson, to bolster the fort's defense.[588]

The reinforcements sent by him apparently helped stave off Sheldon's effort to breach Hindman's walls, the 108th Illinois Infantry subsequently bogging down near the drawbridge that

---

[586] *One of Cleburne's Command:*, p. 19.

[587] *Ibid.*; and "Post of Arkansas," *A.H.Q.*, vol. 13, # 3, p.269.

[588] *O.R.*, I, vol. 17, pt. 1, p. 784. And according to Garland, it was during this time that the gunboats had forced their way past the fort and into the Confederate rear.

entered the fort's easternmost bastion, where it connected with Garland's remaining troops. The Illinois and Ohio soldiers clung tenaciously to the outer earthen walls, and additional reinforcements would be not long in coming, as Osterhaus had other regiments that could be brought to bear if needed, allowing them to carry the fort and conceivably swing around to their right so as to easily roll up Garland's line.[589]

By this time, Garland's efforts of sustaining Dunnington's position had stretched his remaining forces to their breaking point. Undoubtedly, the critical moment was at hand, with artillery rounds and small-arms projectiles shrieking along the works, akin to a violent summer rain; in this case, the drops first came from the north, then increasingly eastward, and lastly from every direction simultaneously. Men were seen to respond by pulling hat brims down over their eyes, others simply hunkering down, if that were possible, further into their tranches, while seemingly awaiting the final assault they knew must be in the making. And virtually everyone in the area of Garland's part of the line realized that when it did, it must sweep them all away.[590]

On the far right of the fort, the shelling had grown in tempo once the gunboats *DeKalb, Lexington,* and *Louisville* began to unleash their guns at point-blank range. Upon coming opposite the fort, a solid shot struck and dismounted the single remaining heavy gun situated in the rear casemate, both the forward casemate and in-barbette (traversing) gun situated atop the parapet to their rear having previously been knocked out so that before 4:00 p.m. not a single gun in Ft. Hindman could be brought to bear upon the river. Indeed, only a single field gun on the landward side yet remained active. Since none of the Confederate guns could be put back into order, this permitted the gunboats *Glide* and *Rattler,* along with the steam-ram *Monarch,* to move upstream to shell both the fort and the landward-side trenches to a point beyond where Garland's left lay. In reality, already rounds had begun to take effect in those fieldworks

---

[589] *Ibid.*

[590] *O.R.,* I, vol. 17, pt. 1, p. 784.

immediately to the rear of the fort, where Garland's men huddled within their trenches.[591]

With all the artillery, large and small, having been silenced, Churchill now had only the manpower he possessed in the infantry and dismounted cavalry in order to hang on. Then, suddenly, shells from Parrott rifles stationed on the opposite bank of the river on Stillwell Point began to enfilade the fort, some passing beyond to explode within the infantrymen's lines; these seemingly came to be an endless stream. The gunboats had passed on up some distance to maximize their fire; they began to turn their guns upon the rear of the Confederate line, this rendering impossible the arrival of reinforcements from Pine Bluff or Little Rock. The end was obviously in sight. Adding to the discomfort of those in Garland's brigade, sharpshooters from the 23rd Wisconsin Infantry worked their way through the abatis out front to secure advantageous positions up on the left flank of the 24th Texas Cavalry (Dismounted), and were able to cut down anyone who attempted to stand and return fire. The only question remaining centered on what, and when, that single event would occur to bring an end to the conflagration.[592]

As might have been seen relative to the previous day's reaction during the retreat of Garland's brigade from their downstream positions, the 24th Texas Cavalry (Dismounted) once again stood on the precipice of disaster, albeit this time a more realistic one. One officer of that regiment described the catastrophic effects caused by shells fired from the steam-ram *Monarch*, which had by now also gotten completely into the rear, and coupled with the fire of those guns from across the river, seemed to impact every point occupied by these men:

> The first shot from [the guns posted at Stillwell Point] passed directly over the regimental flag [of the 24th].

---

[591] *Memoirs*, p. 299; also, see "Post of Arkansas," in *A.H.Q.*, vol. 18, #3, pp. 260-1; for the attack on Ft. Hindman, see p. 264. One of these vessels took the 7th Kentucky Infantry aboard at Stillwell Point to proceed upstream some ten miles to destroy a ferry to prevent any final chance for escape.

[592] "Post of Arkansas," in *A.H.Q.*, vol. 18, #3 (1959), p. 271.

> The next . . . goes nearly in at the same place, . . . killing one man and cutting both legs off his brother. The one that has the legs . . . off turned . . . halfway [around] to his brother, not knowing he was dead. As soon as he saw [that] he takes his pistol . . . , puts it to his head and kills himself.[593]

Shells had begun to explode directly overhead as the range was found, hurtling hot iron fragments and lead balls into their works, the explosions often tossing huge clods up upon bursting. All of a sudden, from somewhere in the midst of the left-wing companies of the 24th Texas Cavalry (Dismounted), white handkerchiefs began to go up on rammers and bayonets, and from his post at the left flank of his old regiment, the 6th Texas Infantry, Garland observed the display, hearing immediately thereafter the plaintive cry of men hollering: "Raise the flag; by order of General Churchill." As if lending credence to the statement, other voices immediately called out to: "Pass the order up the line."[594]

Soon after the firing began to subside, at least other than on Deshler's front, additional white flags could now be seen going up in the nearby fort, everyone on both sides clearly interpreting the meaning of them, and apparently, no one appeared to be overly concerned as to whether that was an official ceasefire that had been ordered. In observing the enemy on his front beginning to do likewise, Deshler looked out over his front to see "four distinct and parallel lines of battle . . . extending along my entire front and as far to the right and left as I could see," these men appearing to be move directly upon his own portion of the line. From about 400 yards behind, in the vicinity of Ft. Hindman, BG Churchill appeared mystified by what he took to be "several white flags . . . [being] displayed in the Twenty-fourth Regiment Texas Dismounted Cavalry." Afterward, it would be Garland's contention that he'd not sanctioned surrender, though Churchill would vehemently swear he hadn't approved of such a move either.[595]

---

[593] *One of Cleburne's Command:*, p. 19.

[594] *O.R.*, I, vol. 17, pt. 1, p. 785; 781; *One of Cleburne's Command:*, p. 20.

[595] *O.R.*, I, vol. 17, pt. 1, pp. 794, 781, 785.

Confusion reigned for some time along all parts of the line, except, that is, on Deshler's front, where his men continued fire unabated for some time after it had clearly come to an end off to his right. Garland later contended that, before he could suppress the flags displayed within his brigade, Union soldiers crowded upon his works, with Col. Burbridge riding up to pointedly demanded that Garland have his men "ground arms," which seems to have been done without further incident. Chagrined by what he perceived to be an inexcusable act, Churchill soon found himself having to be escorted over to Deshler's front in order to stop the fighting still going on at the far left, Deshler having patently refused to surrender without a specific order from the division commander. Sherman would later report that when he rode into Deshler's line, he explicitly stated to the Alabaman on his refusal to surrender: "You are a regular officer, and ought to know better." When Churchill finally did make it over to order Deshler's surrender, that officer promptly ordered his men to stack arms, his overall commander trying to mollify the situation by advising: "We are in their power, and you may surrender." After which, Deshler turned to his staff to pass to the regiments that they "stack arms." And with this final act, the Battle of Arkansas Post came to an embarrassing end.[596]

Ironically, just as Deshler decided to approve the enemy's demand for surrender, a jaded column of 190 men from Col. E. E. Portlock's 24th Arkansas Infantry arrived from St. Charles to enter the rebel line. They had completed a remarkable forty-mile forced march in a little over twenty-four hours to find themselves also made captives of the enemy. Remarkably, in the attendant chaos relative to the final surrender, some Texans and Arkansans, including a whole company from the 17th Texas Cavalry (Dismounted), simply walked off into the surrounding woods to prevent their being taken prisoners of war.[597]

Gen. McClernand's after-action report of the battle acknowledged the taking of 4,791 prisoners, seventeen pieces of artillery, 3,000 stands of arms, and seven rebel flags. Perhaps of

---

[596] *Ibid.*, pp. 724, 726, 731, 781, 785, 795; "Post of Arkansas," in *A.H.Q.*, vol. 18, #3 (1959), p. 271; *Memoirs*, p. 299.

[597] *Ibid.*, I, vol. 17, pt. 1, p. 781.

more than a little interest, among the stores he acquired was the lot of ammunition that had been taken in the earlier seizure of the transport *Blue Wing* by the Confederates the month previous, that property once again coming into the Union Navy's hands. In the capture of the Post, however, McClernand had paid a significant cost, noting 134 Unionists killed, 898 others wounded, and twenty-nine men missing, making the total rise to 1050 casualties. And this didn't reflect the Navy's losses, which would be separately reported later.[598]

For his part, Churchill's much-later report listed sixty rebels killed, seventy-five to eighty seriously wounded, with 3500 men captured. Garland reported his brigade's loss as twenty-five dead, sixty-four wounded, and sixty-eight missing; he attributed most of those to be from artillery fire. He had carried 1,797 men into the fight on the 9th, the 24th Texas Cavalry (Dismounted) sustaining the greatest loss, with twelve killed, seventeen wounded, and twenty-five missing. This regiment sustained nearly half of the casualties suffered by the brigade, which also included the 6th Texas Infantry and 25th Texas Cavalry (Dismounted), Hart's Arkansas Battery and Matthew Denson's Louisiana Cavalry Co., which, altogether, had not suffered more than the 24th Texas had. Comparatively, Deshler, who advised he had fended off eight separate assaults on his line, compared to only two by Garland's, stated his total loss as just three dead and seventeen wounded; he had entered the battle with close to 1600 men present.[599] Churchill didn't list Dunnington's loss in his official report, as either that officer didn't submit one, or else did so after the division commander submitted his. The greatest single complaint came from the rebel side came in Deshler's report: he stated that U.S. artillery pieces had clearly fired upon a marked hospital, and in so doing killed a surgeon and killed or wounded several litter bearers when shells exploded over that structure. In reporting the death of Surgeon Nathan Wynkoop of the 15th Texas Cavalry (Dismounted), Deshler railed against his enemy: "Painful as the reflection is, I am forced to believe that the enemy's gunboats fired upon our division hospital, though our flag was displayed from it. . . . the position of the hospital building was such that it does not

---

[598] *Ibid.*, I, vol. 17, pt. 1, pp. 708, 716-19.

[599] *Ibid.*, pp. 785, 795.

seem possible to me that it could have been in range of the gunboats if firing at the fort." Of special interest is Deshler's praise of both Lt. Col. A. S. Hutchinson's 19th Arkansas Infantry and Hart's Arkansas Battery, for each had been under his direct observation, as were several Texas and Louisiana Cavalry companies.[600]

For his part, MG Sherman afterward dramatized the massive damage inflicted upon the rebel works when compiling an account of the battle. The fort's parapet had been "knocked down in many places, and dead men lay around very thick." He also reported on a rather heated conversation he overheard between Gen. Churchill and Col. Garland, which supposedly transpired just upon the former's entering the rebel line. During this conversation, Sherman recalled that Garland stated he allowed the white flag to continue being waved, but only after "I received orders to do so from one of your staff." Remarkably, in what had to be a unique situation, the night after the battle, Sherman invited Garland to share accommodations at a nearby house that he had commandeered because, as he related it: "There seemed to be a good deal of feeling among the rebel officers against Garland, who asked leave to stay with me . . ."[601]

Night came not long after the close of battle, and its settling in prevented Union troops from doing anything other than herding the Post prisoners together in a ravine near the river's edge and posting a strong guard to watch over them. The prisoners had been driven at bayonet point into a nearby depression just at the back of the fort, in essence a square being formed between parallel gullies that emptied into the river, with the guards taking position along the creek banks and high ground at back of them, the river constituting a fourth side. Unfortunately for the battle-weary prisoners, the night of January 12-13 proved to be one of great misery, as temperatures plunged not long after sunset. Just about dawn, cattle boats and other auxiliary vessels began to arrive to take on the now-shivering survivors of the Post battle. Clambering aboard the filthy decks of boats that had heretofore been used for transporting cattle, the men

---

[600] *Ibid.* I, vol. 17, pt. 1, p. 79.

[601] *Memoirs.*, p. 301-2.

could overhear engineering officers discussing how best to completely destroy the Confederate works.[602]

Earlier, when MG U. S. Grant learned of Gen. McClernand's strategy of capturing the Post, that officer quickly sent word to McClernand to cease operations and return forthwith to Vicksburg. Unfortunately for the rebels, his message hadn't reached McClernand until the day after the battle; Grant had ordered McClernand to report at once to Milliken's Bend, whether the Post had fallen or not. This action did forestall a grandiose scheme of McClernand to continue up the Arkansas to seize Little Rock, however. Even as engineers oversaw the destruction of the rebel works, McClernand had turned his attention to transporting both his and Sherman's corps, as well as the Post prisoners, downstream to Vicksburg. Much of the 15th was spent in working out the final details with the Navy for moving the two groups of men.[603]

Observing the destruction of their former works, on which they had so recently labored, little remained otherwise except to be loaded up with McClernand's own army and see to the escort of the Post prisoners to the Mississippi. A great concern confronted the captives, centering on whether they were to be repatriated as soon as they reached the environs of Vicksburg, or be sent on to Northern internment camps. Rumors began spreading that the former was apt to happen, as the two adversaries had not long before mutually agreed that Vicksburg would be one of two only major exchange points for paroling prisoners. Many a man afterward felt that, given their ultimate fate, the rumors may well have a ruse all along by a nefarious enemy who desired keeping them docile during their

---

[602] Post of Arkansas," in *A.H.Q.*, vol. 18, #3 (1959), p. 276. Sgt. W. W. heartsill of the "Lane Rangers," recalled the men of Capt. Richardson's cavalry company used the intervening hours in disposing of their arms: "we have thrown them into deep muddy Bayou," *Fourteen Hundred*, p. 97.

[603] *Ibid.*, p. 277; also, see Richard Rush, et al, eds., *O.R.*, I, vol. 24, p. 106, wherein Grant had earlier reported to Halleck in Washington that: "McClernand has fallen back to White River and gone on a wild-goose chase to the Post of Arkansas."

downstream trip. For now, the prisoners could only watch and wait, many pondering what their immediate future would bring.[604]

No doubt many reflected upon their service to this point, having spent the better part of a year or more in adjusting to military life, then seeing their first major combat role come to such an ignominious conclusion. Though they had, at last, "seen the elephant," certainly the majority of them couldn't have been less pleased with the outcome. Though only a small handful of men had paid the ultimate price in the actual battle, a plethora of others had died in the many months that had passed before they arrived at Arkansas Post. Some may well have reflected upon a recent theory evinced by the famed naturalist, Charles Darwin, that in life, "only the fittest survive." In essence, it appeared as if the military had worked in a similar fashion to remove those unable or unwilling to make the great physical or mental adjustments needed for personal survival.

To those who'd survived to this point, however, life in the army had been unlike anything they might have imagined it to be. Death or impairment by disease, desertion, or discharge from being over- or under-age had forced many a comrade from their ranks. Along with the rude dismounting of the cavalrymen and the political infighting they had witnessed, not surprisingly, all had acted to wreck that sense of fairness and honor they had taken to be a part of war in civilized society.

As to what negative effects imprisonment would have upon them, should they survive, time alone would tell. Yet, even as they clung to the false prospects of being quickly repatriated, many pondered just what had really led to this embarrassing surrender. No easy answer appeared evident, and as would be the case in many another fight they'd engage in, the entire process wasn't ever to be easily understood. Dallas Herndon, in his *Centennial History of Arkansas*, concluded that the surrender at the Post came about as "the white flag was displayed through a mistake of one of the Texas

---

[604] For speculation on their probable exchange, see *One of Cleburne's Command:*, p. 22; and *Fourteen Hundred*, p. 100.

regiments[,] but this is not well authenticated." And in reality, perhaps it was as easy as that to dismiss the entire episode.[605]

There can be little doubt that while their exact motivations are not likely ever to be fully known, it's not surprising, given the signs that had appeared early on, specifically in the 24th Texas Cavalry (Dismounted), but in Garland's brigade as a whole, had actually been demonstrated well before the actual battle began; even before the fighting commenced, the brigade had almost totally dissolved upon hearing that they might have been cut off in their retreat to the Post. Yet it's readily apparent that during the fight, as Garland's report concludes, the 24th Texas Cavalry (Dismounted) suffered the highest casualty rate of any in the division (certainly far more than those of Deshler's Texans). And later on, such losses as experienced at Arkansas Post pale in comparison to what they encountered in this extraordinary affair.[606]

In the final analysis, the 24th Texas Cavalry (Dismounted) had found itself strained beyond both its physical and emotional limit, with half their men being detached and sent off to another part of the battlefield, after which the remaining men had been required to extend to the right in order to simply remain in contact with both Deshler's and Dunnington's brigades. And it should be pointed out as well that increasing and effective artillery fire by the enemy toward the end of the battle, coming from in front and from both Stillwell Point and the gunboats that had gotten behind them, appeared to have singularly converged on the works help by the 24th Texas.[607]

But it also appears that neither of the other two regiments in the brigade had any more confidence in Garland, their brigade commander, than Lt. Sebron Sneed of Co. G, 6th Texas Infantry had so cogently expressed the previous month, when declaring near Christmas:

---

[605] Dallas T. Herndon, ed., *Centennial History of Arkansas*, Chicago, 1922, p. 675.

[606] *O.R.*, I, vol. 17, pt. 1, p. 785.

[607] Garland's report in the *O.R.*, I, vol. 17, pt. 1, p. 785

There is one thing that I do take a malicious pleasure in, which is that Col. Garland has not received the appointment of Brigadier General, and what is more, he will not receive it if rumor is correct that our Delegates in Congress refuse to name his claims, as he is not a Texan. The hopes and expectations among mighty hosts of little puppies who have licked Garland's boots and lapped the drippings from the sanctuary where he sits enthroned in state, will all fail.

In another, similar post made at the time, that officer had complained that: "I feel and know that Col. G[arland] has no desire for active service . . . and he [will] keep out of danger, will and has managed to keep all the troops under his command out of service . . . , and in a state of such masterly inactivity in the present stirring times when every man should be face to face with the enemy."[608]

In the final analysis, it's likely that a combination of things actually made surrender at Arkansas Post inevitable. Confronted by overwhelming numbers, possessing an inadequate reserve close at hand, with no way to get away, and ordered to "hold out at until all dead," by a commander ensconced some 150 miles away at Little Rock, it was only a question of time. Add Churchill's obvious errors in not having entrenched either the middle works downstream nor that portion of the line running from the fort to Post Bayou, though having been in command since December 10, with no easy escape available, surrender or death seem to have been the only possible results. Of great import, however, their surrender on January 11 at least ensured that many would live to fight another day. Hard-pressed afterward to explain the debacle which had occurred, "Granny" Holmes would write on June 8 from Little Rock that: "It never occurred to me when the order was issued ['to hold out till help arrived or until all dead'], that such an overpowering command would be devoted to an end so trivial." This writer doesn't think that

---

[608] Sebron Sneed letters to Fannie, December 25, 1862 & January 8, 1863, typescript copy of Sebron Sneed letters, courtesy of family member, Austin, Texas.

either the Texans or the Arkansans would have considered Arkansas Post such a trivial matter.[609]

End of Part One

---

[609] *O.R.*, I, vol. 17, pt.1, p. 782.

A Force to Be Reckoned With Volume II coming soon;

Some miles outside of Atlanta, Georgia, on May 27, 1864, Granbury's brigade would confront one of its greatest tests in trying to thwart Gen. William T. Sherman's infamous campaign to wrest that city out of Confederate hands. Closing in on New Hope Church and Pickett's Mill, Sherman dispatched a column of several divisions back northward toward the railroad to Atlanta in a plan to get beyond the Confederate right flank and roll up Gen. Joseph E. Johnston's line. Almost at the same time, MG Pat Cleburne's famed division struck out for its own army's far right, hoping to stave off disaster by preventing U.S. troops getting around their far right. Arriving at a long ridge after a rapid march, Granbury's Texas Brigade of Cleburne's Division arrived just in time to be deployed, though not soon enough to throw up even temporary fieldworks. Advancing to the western brim of the rise, the men could observe what appeared to be at least three massed Federal divisions moving directly onto their position. As the Unionists approached the swales below the Texans, the men could plainly hear enemy soldiers proclaiming: "By damn you, we've caught you without your works now," obviously bent upon overwhelming the Texans in an irresistible blue tide.

It was during the subsequent hand-to-hand imbroglio that occurred one of those unique events that participants would remember for as long as they lived. This came when Maj. John Kennard of the 10th Texas Infantry stood impassively delivering several religious verses in a tongue-lashing invective aimed in the direction of the enemy, hoping to encourage his stalwarts to stand firm to this ongoing test of arms. After loudly proclaiming to those within earshot, "Put your faith in God, men, for he is with us," Kennard turned toward the seething masses of the enemy, proclaiming, "We are demoralized! Come on [and take us]." Shortly after making the statement, a spent ball struck Kennard right between the eyes. As the men loaded their commander onto a stretcher for the trip to a field hospital, Kennard cautioned them about lying even to the enemy, for his injury was but a clear sign from God that men should not bear false witness, even to their adversaries! [Excerpted from Mary A. H. Gay's, Life in Dixie, pp. 40-1.]

**To stay up to date on appearances, events, and new releases, please consider subscribing to my newsletter via this link:
http://tiny.cc/SessumsNewsletter**

ABOUT THE AUTHOR

Danny Sessums has been a historian, educator, and museum professional for most of his career. After completing his undergraduate work at Texas Tech University in anthropology, he later received his master's degree at the University of Texas at Arlington. *A Force to be Reckoned With* is a culmination of the research that he began for his doctoral dissertation at Louisiana State University and continued for over thirty years. Sessums has also been an avid living Civil War historian, studying the lifestyle and experience of the "common soldier" during the War Between the States. In 2009, he retired from Houston Baptist University, and today, he and his wife reside in East Texas.

Facebook: https://www.facebook.com/DannySessumsPhD/
Website: http://www.dannysessums.com/
Email: dannysessums@gmail.com

Bibliography

Primary Works

Drake, Rebecca Blackwell, & Holder, Thomas D. *Lone Star General: Hiram B. Granbury*. Hood County Historical Society. 2004. [Life narrative]

Purdue, Howell & Elizabeth. *Pat Cleburne: Confederate General*. Portals Press: Tuscaloosa, Ala. 1977. [Authoritative work on the general.]

Symonds, Craig L. *Stonewall of the West: Patrick Cleburne and the Civil War*. University of Kansas Press: Lawrence. 1997. [need to read and highlight]

McDonough, James Lee & Connelly, Thomas L. *Five Tragic Hours: The Battle of Franklin*. University of Tenn. Press. Knoxville. 1983. [Very fine account.]

Groom, Winston. *Shrouds of Glory, From Atlanta to Nashville: The Last Great Campaign of the Civil War*. Simon & Schuster: NY. 1995. [Broughton Maps]

Wallace, Lee A., Jr. *17th Virginia Infantry*. H. E. Howard, Inc.: Lynchburg, Va. 1990.
[James Deshler, Irving Buck info]

Bearss, Edwin & Grabau. *The Battle of Jackson: The Siege of Jackson: Three Other Post-Vicksburg Actions*. Gateway Press, Inc. Baltimore. 1981.

Grear, Charles, ed. *The Fate of Texas: The Civil War and the Lone Star State*. Fayetteville: University of Arkansas. 2008. [Need to study thoroughly, good essays]

-----. *Confederate Military History*. Unknown: The Blue & Grey Press [See Vol. # 11, "Texas By Col. O. M. Roberts"] Reprint edition.

Wright, Marcus J., BG, C.S.A., comp. & Simpson, Harold B. Col. U.S.A.F (Ret.), ed. *Texas In The War: 1861-1865*. Hillsboro, Texas: The Hill Junior College Press. 1965.

McCaffrey, James M. *This Band of Heroes: Granbury's Texas Brigade, C.S.A.* Austin: Eakin Press. 1985.

Spurlin, Charles D., ed. *The Civil War Diary of Charles A. Leuschner*. Austin: Eakin Press. 1st Ed. 1992. [6th Texas Infantry, Co. B..]

McCaffrey, James M. *Only a Private: A Texan Remembers the Civil War*. Houston: Halcyon Press, Ltd. 2004. (William Oliphant memoirs of the ar.]

Myres, Sandra L. ed. *Force Without Fanfare: The Autobiography of K. M. Van Zandt*. Fort Worth: T.C.U. Press. 1968. [From enlistment till returning to Texas.]

Simpson, Col. Harold B., ed. *The Bugle Softly Blows: The Confederate Diary of Benjamin M. Seaton*. Waco; Texian Press. 1965. [Co. G, 10th Texas Infantry.]

Wynn, W. O. *The Biographical Sketch of the Life of an Old Confederate Soldier; as a Cowboy on the Frontier of Texas*. Greenville, Texas. Greenville Printing Co. 1916. A Xerox copy of this volume is in this writer's possession. [Serving in Co. C of the 10th, nevertheless, while some good source material is there, all his statements ought to be corroborated with other sources prior to being used.]

Gay, Mary A. H. *Life in Dixie During the War*. Atlanta: Forte & Davis Co. 1894. [See pp. 47-79, & 175-239, for communications with Lt. Thomas Stokes, Co. G, 10th Texas Infantry, from 1863 through 1864.]

Collins, R. M. *Chapters from An Unwritten History of the War Between The States, or the Incidents in the life of a Confederate Soldier in Camp, on the March, in the Great Battles, and in Prison.* St. Louis: Nixon-Jones Printing Co. 1893. re-print copy from Southern Heritage Press, Widener, Arkansas. [Co. B, 15th Texas Cavalry.]

Anderson, John Q. *Campaigning with Parsons's Texas Cavalry Brigade, CSA.* Hillsboro: Hill Junior College Press. 1967. [Letters of A. L. & James, Co. I, 18th Texas Cavalry.]

Brown, Norman D., ed. *One of Cleburne's Command: The Civil War Reminiscences and Diary of Capt. Samuel T. Foster, Granbury's Texas Brigade, CSA.* Austin: University of Texas Press. 1980. [Co. H, 24th Texas Cavalry.]

Douglas, Lucia Rutherford, comp. *Douglas' Texas Battery, CSA.* Tyler: Smith County Historical Society. 1966. [Letters from James P. to family members.]

Sumrall, Alan K. *Battle Flags of Texans in the Confederacy.* Austin: Eakin Press. 1995. [45, 57, 65, 67 for regimental flags]

Davis, Major George B., U.S. Army. *The Official Military Atlas of the Civil War.* NY: Fairfax Press. 1983.

Heartsill, W. W. *Fourteen Hundred and 91 Days in the Confederate Army: A Journal Kept by W. W. Heartsill for four years, one month and one Day, or Camp Life; Day By Day, of the 'W. P. Lane Rangers' from April 19, 1861 to May 20, 1865.* Wiley, Bell Irvin, ed. Jackson, Tenn.: McCowat-Mercer Press (reprint). 1953. [While serving with the 10th Texas Infantry.]

Scott, Robert N., et. al. *The War of the Rebellion: A Compilation of the Official Records of the Union and Confederate Armies.* Wash, D.C.: Government Printing Office. 1880.

Anne J. Bailey, ed. *In the Saddle with the Texans: Day-by-Day with Parsons's Cavalry Brigade, 1862-1865.* Abilene, Texas: McWhiney Foundation Press. 2004.

Anne J. Bailey. *Between the Enemy and Texas: Parsons's Texas Cavalry in the Civil War.* Ft. Worth: T.C.U. Press. 1989.

Also note a *Supplement to the O.R.s* was published in more recent years and will be noted using the same designation of *O.R.*s as is the above referenced 128 vol. set shown here.

Lundberg, John R. *The Finishing Stroke: Texans in the 1864 Tennessee Campaign.* Military History of Texas Series. Abilene: McWhiney Foundation Press. 2002.

McKay, Scott. *A Time Line History of the 10th Texas Infantry.* A voluminous, unpublished manuscript of regimental returns and interspaced with reports, copies of letters, and sundry other materials relating to both the regiment & Granbury's Brigade.

Jerry Thompson, ed. Tejanos in Gray: Civil War letters of Capt. Raphael de la Garza and Manuel Yturri. College Station. Texas A & M Press.2011.

Secondary Works:

State of Texas, Census manuscript copies, by county, 1860: "Population by Age and Sex," pp. 472-90; & "Miscellaneous Statistics of the Churches in the State of Texas, By Counties," pp. 471-474. Austin: State Archives.

State of Texas, Johnson County, June, 1860: 726 registrants (Occupations), courtesy Layland Museum, Cleburne, Texas.

——————, *The Confederate Soldier in the Civil War: The Campaigns, Battles, Sieges, Charges and Skirmishes.* Fairfax Press. 1977. [For references to Texas regimental losses, see pp. 376-382; note 7th Texas 47th highest % loss in any battle; also, 6th and 24th Texas at Arkansas Post.]

Wheat, James E & Josiah, Ed, "The Civil War and Tyler County History," in *Sketches of Tyler County History.* Bevil Oaks, Texas: Whitmeyer Printing. 1986.. [Companies raised for the 24th Texas Cavalry, Co. D, E, G, H.]

Sowell, A. J. *History of Fort Bend County: Containing Biographical Sketches of Many Noted Characters.* Houston: W. H. Coyle & Co. 1904. [See list of dead men from Co. F, 24th Texas Cavalry.]

Cox, Jacob D., L. L. D. *Atlanta.* NY: Blue and Gray Press. 1980. [pp. 169-70 tell of McPherson's death and Cleburne's skirmishers encountering the 64th Illinois, armed with Henry rifles.]

Partlow, Miriam. *Liberty, Liberty County, and the Atascosito District.* Austin: Pemberton Press, Jenkins Publishing Co., 1974. [Raising of Capt. W. D. Davis' Co. G, and Capt. E. B. Picket's Co. I, 25th Texas Cavalry, along with muster rolls for both.]

Henderson, H. M. *Texas in the Confederacy.* San Antonio: Naylor & Co. 1955. [Mortality rate in prison over 30%.]

Jewell, Carey C. *Harvest of Death: A Detailed Account of the Army of Tennessee at the Battle of Franklin.* Hicksville, NY: Exposition Press. 1976.

——————————————— *Confederate Military History.* The Blue & Grey Press. Vol. XI. Texas & Florida. Unknown date (reprint). See pp. 58-249.

Henderson, H. M. *Texas in the Confederacy*. San Antonio: Naylor Co. 1955. pp, 97-100.

Periodicals:

"Allison Nelson: Atlanta Mayor, Texas Hero, Confederate General," *Atlanta Historical Quarterly Bulletin*, fall, 1985, pp. 19 – 25.

"Wounded Texan's Trip Home on Crutches," Joseph McClure, Ft. Worth, Texas, in the *Confederate Veteran*, vol. XVII, # 4, (April 1909), pp. 162-3. [Co. A, 18th Texas soldier wounded at the Battle of Atlanta, July 21, 1864; his trip home at war's end.]

Turner, Jim, "Jim Turner, Co. G, 6th Texas Infantry, C.S.A., from 1861 to 1865," in "*Texana*, Vol. XII, # 2 (1974), pp. 149-78. [Very good narrative.]

"Long Delayed Letter," from F. E. Blossman, Co. A, 6th Texas Infantry, *Confederate Veteran*, Vol. VII, # 5, pp. 212.[Chattahoochie line, July 8, 1864. Delivered thirty-three years after being mailed!]

"Lt. Flavius Perry letters," Co. B, 17th Texas Cavalry, as edited by Joe R. Wise and published in *Military History of Texas and the Southwest*, vol. 13, # 2, (1975), pp. 12 through 37. [Very good source letters on early days of the 17th, until his death in 1864]

Notes and Documents, "Civil War letters of George W. Allen," Co. A, 10th Texas Infantry, Pollard, Charleen Plumly, ed., *Southwestern Historical Quarterly*, unk. vol. #, pp. 47-52. [Arkansas service to the Post.]

"The Confederate Letters of Bryan Marsh," *Chronicles of Smith County*, vol. 14, # 2 (Winter 1975), pp. 9-55, as published by the Smith County Historical Society, Tyler Texas.[Co. C, 17th Texas Cavalry.]

"Journal of Marshall Samuel Pierson," Co. C, 17th Texas Cavalry, as published in *Military History of Texas and the Southwest*, Norman C. Delaney, ed., vol. 13, # 2, (1975), pp. 25-29. [The Smith County company's activities from muster-in until surrender of Arkansas Post.]

"A Smith County Confederate Writes Home," Letters from J. H. Crow, Co. C, 17th Texas Cavalry, *Chronicles of Smith County*, F. Lee Lawrence and Robert W. Glover, eds., vol. 4, # 2 (fall, 1965), pp. 11-14., by the Smith County Historical Society, Tyler, Texas.

"Memoirs of Samuel Alonzo Cook," Co. E, 17th Texas Cavalry, *Southwestern Historical Quarterly*, vol. 74, # 4 (April, 1971), pp. 536-548. [Not as accurate as could be.]

"One Man's War: Capt. Joseph H. Bruton, 1861-1865," Co. H, 17th Texas Cavalry, by Douglas Hale, *East Texas Historical Journal*, vol. XX # 2 (1982), pp. 28-45. [Details from enlistment in 1861 until 1864].

Darst, Maury, ed.: "Robert Hodges, Jr.: Confederate Soldier," *East Texas Historical Journal*, Vol. IX, # 1 (March, 1971), pp. 21-47. [Letters begin Feb. 22, 1861 and go to March 25, 1865.]

"We Are Prisoners of War, A Texans Account of the Capture of Fort Hindman," *Civil War Times Illustrated*, unknown date, Xerox copies of pp. 24-33 in writer's possession. [See One of Cleburne's Command: by Norman Brown]

"The 25th Texas Cavalry Regiment, Co. B & H," Liberty County, in *Liberty County History* from the following wwebsite: http://libertycountyhistory.blogspot.com/2006/07/25th-texas0cavalry-regiment-company-b.html & same for Co. H, except –H before HTML designation.

25th Texas Cavalry Regiment notes posted on "The Civil War Message Board," Dec. 24, and 26, 1999, at http://www.civilwarbull.org/forum/messages/4339.html. [Also, see #s 4340, 4343, & 4366. Letters from Silvier P. Baillio, Co. I, dated July 17, 1862, Keatchie, La.; July 27, 1862, unknown location, but possibly Shreveport; Sept. 2, 1862, from Shreveport; and Calvin B. M. Horton, Shreveport (a substitute for Abner McMurtry.

"Over the River and Through the Trees," *Confederate Philatelist*, Vol. 7, # 7, (July, 1962) . pp. 6-7, 70-3. A very long letter from Major John Formwalt's wife to him from Acton (then Johnson County, Texas), dated March 31, 1864; copy in author's possession.

"Family History: Hiram B. Granbury," in http://www.battleofraymond.org/holder.htm Tom Holder of Ft. Worth, Texas.

Sessums, Danny M.: "Capt. Edward Thomas Broughton, Jr., Letters," 7th Texas Infantry, C.S.A.," *Chronicles of Smith County, Texas*, Vol. 45, (Spring, 2015), pp. 23-36.

Sessums, Danny M.: "Capt. Edward Thomas Broughton, Jr., Letters," 7th Texas Infantry, C.S.A.," *Chronicles of Smith County, Texas*, Vol. 46, (Fall, 2015), pp. 19-36.

Sessums, Danny M.: "Co. D, 4th Texas, Arizona Brigade, the 'Ellis County Bengal Tigers'," *Military Images*, vol. 3, p. 4

Newspapers:

"Darnell's Regiment to Rendezvous (here) January 15, 1862," in the *Dallas Herald*, January 8, 1862, edition, p.2.

"Johnson County Co. of Darnell's Rgt. marched to Quarters at Reunion . . . ," *Dallas Herald*, January 22, 1862, p. 3 [Lists Company Officers from Capt. To Corporals.]

"Capt. John T. Coit's Co., numbering 90 odd men . . . ," *Dallas Herald*, January 22, 1862, p. 3, [Notes the Dallas Co. has just mustered into service.]

"Another Company for Darnell's Rgt. has reached the River yesterday . . . ," *Dallas Herald*, January 22, 1862, p. 3 [Co. raised at Belton.]

"Denton County Rebels, 3 miles southeast of town . . . ," *Dallas Herald*, January 22, 1862, p. 3. [They and Montague Pioneers in line drilling.]

"The 'Morgan Rangers' arrived here Friday for Col. Darnell's Rgt," *Dallas Herald*, January 22, 1862, p. 3. [Wearing penitentiary uniforms, Officers enumerated.]

"Capt. Ed. Browder's Co. mustered in to Darnell's Rgt. last Saturday," *Dallas Herald*, January 29, 1863, p. 3.

Col. Darnell's has 8 companies already and mustered," *Dallas Herald*, January 29, 1862, p. 3

"Muster roll of John T. Coit's Co. of Dallas County for Darnell's Rgt:," *Dallas Herald*, p. 3. [Lists officers from Capt. down to Corporals, 92 privates.]

"Hays and Williamson (Counties) 'Blues' for Darnell's Rgt." *Dallas Herald*, February 5, 1862, p. 2. [Lists officers and non-coms. Note: Ensign.]

"Capt. Morgan accidentally knocks pistol off hook, wounding self." *Dallas Herald*, February 5, 1862, p. 3. [Hiram Morgan has a company from Bastrop & Travis Counties.]

"Letter of Editor, from Richmond paper: Darnell ordered to Kentucky." *Dallas Herald*, February 12, 1862, p. 2.

"Another Company from Dallas County." *Dallas Herald*, February 12, 1862. [Capt. Middleton Perry's Company. Officers and 83 men sworn into service. [Lists officers and non-coms.]

"*Washington* (Ark.) *Telegraph* reports Col. Darnell's Rgt. arrived, 6 Cos. Today, the rest with the train." Reprinted in the *Dallas Herald* edition of June 7, 1862, p. 2.

"Rgt. (Darnell's) camp near Brownsville, Arkansas, August 4, 1862," *Dallas Herald*, p. 2

"Col. Darnell's Rgt., 18th (Texas) Cavalry for purchasing clothing (and) blankets . . .," *Dallas Herald*, September 13, 1862, p. 2. [Address James C. Foreman at Plano, Collin County.]

"Camp Holmes, Ark. Army of the West: 2 Divisions, 1st Brigade Sweet's (15th Texas Dismounted Cavalry), Taylor's (17th Texas Dismounted Cavalry), . . . , Nelson's (10th Texas Infantry), and Darnell's (18th Texas Dismounted Cavalry), under (command of) Col. (George Sweet." *Dallas Herald*, October 11, 1862, p. 2. [Under the command of Col. Deshler by this time.]

"General Order # 29 H.Q. 15th Texas Cavalry, Camp Nelson, Austin Arkansas." *Dallas Herald*, p. 2. [Men previously released over 35 to report to Tyler "to be marched back to the army."]

"Col. (George) Sweet, 15th Texas Cavalry, passed through this place . . ." *Dallas Herald*, January 7, 1863, p. 2. [On his way home in San Antonio].

"Letter from A. M. Cochran, (Co. C, 18th Texas Cavalry)< 29 December, (1862). *Dallas Herald*, January 21, 1863, p. 2. [List of deaths in command between March and Dec.]

"4,500 troops captured. Darnell's has 2 Cos. From this county. *Dallas Herald*, February 4, 1863, p. 1. [Darnell and Maj. W. A. Ryan not captured: Darnell absent with pneumonia, Ryan wounded 1st day. Marshall, Texas also had 2 Cos. Present there.]

"Recruits for Granbury's (7th Texas Infantry) Rgt. (wanted). $75 bounty, Rgt. now at Port Hudson." *Dallas Herald*, February 11, 1863, contact Adj. W. D. Douglas.[Lt. Will be given to any man raising 25-30 men!]

"Military," dated May 28, 1862, in the *Washington* (Arkansas) *Telegraph*, p. 2, 1st column, bottom of page: "The splendid infantry regiment from Texas under command of A. Nelson, struck their tents and marched . . . ." [Good condition, orderly conduct, excellent drill, etc.]

"Military. The (18th Texas) cavalry regiment from Texas under command of N. H. Darnell is now here." *Washington Telegraph*, May 28, 1862, p. 2. [6 co.s, 4 behind with train, ordered to Little Rock. The men crowd our streets.]

"Soldiers Funeral." *Washington Telegraph*, June 4, 1862, p. 1 lower right column.

"The Splendid Cavalry regiment under command of Col. Darnell 18th Texas) left here last Friday morning." *Washington Telegraph*, June 4, 1862, p. 2, lower left column. [With Various banners and fine looking horses presented quite an imposing appearance.

"Remember Me." A poem by C. E. Crockett, a private in Darnell's (18th Texas) Cavalry. *Washington Telegraph*, June 11, 1862, p. 1 right column.

"Col. Nelson's Infantry Rgt. arrived yesterday (at Little Rock), and are encamped on the southern road," from the *Washington Telegraph*, June 11, 1862, p. 2, middle column, mid-page.

"The Little Rock Gazette Reports." On the 7th instant, Col. Taylor's command (17th Texas Cavalry?) with Capt. Alf Johnson's command, attacked equal number of Federals and defeated them. *Washington Telegraph*, June (July) 11?, 1862, p. 2 middle column. [Likely the Battle of Cache River.]

"Special: Capt. Thomas J. Johnson (Sweet's Texas Rgt.) was killed in a scout against the enemy in Izzard County." *Washington Telegraph*, July 30, 1862, p. 2 1st column. [Shot through heart while leading a dozen men to the attack.]

"Letter from Arkansas," signed only "T.J.S." of Nelson's Regiment (10th Texas Infantry, *The Tri-Weekly Telegraph* (Houston, Texas), Vol. XXVIII- N0. 54, Whole # 3549, Monday, July 21, 1862. [Report on the St. Charles expedition, dated June 22nd.]

"Capt. Montgomery of Gillespie's (25th Texas Dismounted Cavalry) Rgt. states the Federal Officers buried separately." *Galveston News*, February 25, 1863. [Battle aftermath of Ark. Post.]

Article by J. B. Ahrens, Chaplain, 24th Texas Cavalry (dis.), dated May 2, 1863, from Chappell Hill, Texas, in the *Tri-Weekly Telegraph*, Houston, Texas, May 8, 1863 edition, Vol. XXIX-No. 23, p. 1.

"Brutal Treatment of Confederates," from *The Tri-Weekly Telegraph*, Houston, Texas, May 13, 1863. [Report by Gen. Churchill to Col. Hoffman, U.S., of POW treatment]

"Special Orders # 49, June 3d, 1863, H.Q. Trans-Miss. Dept., Shreveport, La.": *The Tri-Weekly Telegraph*, (Houston,

Texas), 2nd column from right, mid-page. [Orders to Col. N. H. Darnell, 18th Texas Cavalry, to proceed to Texas to gather up absent men of the regiment for return to the front.]

"Special Orders # 51, June 5th, 1863, H.Q. Trans-Miss. Dept., Shreveport, La.:" *The Tri-Weekly Telegraph*, (Houston, Texas), 2nd column from right, mid page. [Orders Lt. Col. R. R. Swearingen, 24th Texas Cavalry, to proceed to Texas to gather up absent men of the regiment.]

"Report on the Battle of Arkansas Post," by BG T.J. Churchill, May 6, 1863, under the heading of "Pony Express," *Houston Telegraph*, July 1, 1863.

"Application for Transfer," by BG Thomas J. Churchill, July 9, 1863, endorsed approved by "P. R. Cleburne," compiled service records of Churchill.

"General Orders # 31, July 24, 1863, D. H. Hill, Lt. Gen., published in the *Memphis Daily Appeal*, printed at Atlanta, Georgia.

"List of Men Died out of Col. F. C. Wilkes' Regiment, 24th Texas Cavalry, at Camp Butler, Illinois," *Houston Weekly Telegraph*, Houston, Texas, Sept. 4, 1863. [Also lists desertions by company as well.]

"Casualties from The Battle of Arkansas Post and thereafter prior to exchange at Model Barracks, Va.," by Surgeon D. F. Stewart, and Asst. Surgeon Thomas C. Foster, 10th Texas Infantry, printed in Sept. 7, 1863 *Houston Weekly Telegraph*, Vol. XXX, # 121.

"Letter from Beatus," Co. B, 24th Texas Cavalry (dis.), from the *Houston Daily Telegraph*, June 3, 1864, Vol. XXX, # 61, p. 2. [Upbeat article on brigade reorganization that has seen Granbury put in charge, and his manners.]

"List of Patients at Texas Hospitals, Auburn, Ga., James Richle, Whole # 3933, Aug. 3, 1864, in *Houston Daily Telegraph*, Houston, Texas.

"The Mobile "Army and C?, of July 9, 1864, carries a list of "Hospital Reports" for Texans, as re-published in the Aug. 12, 1864, *Houston Daily Telegraph*.

"We copy the following from a letter from John R. Baylor to the news," regarding Dr. Bryan's Hospital, Auburn Ga., *Houston Daily Telegraph*, Aug. 17, 1864, p. 2, col. 2

"Cleburne's Victory at Ringgold-Intemperance in the Army," copied from the *Savannah Republican* in the *Memphis Daily Appeal*, Atlanta edition, December 19, 1863. [Nice account of Cleburne's defense at Taylor's Ridge, plus accusations of drunkenness.]

"Letter From Atlanta," from P. K. Smith of Liberty, to his wife, published in *The Houston Daily Telegraph*, Unknown issue #, but printed Sept. 14, 1864, p. 1, 2 & 3 columns from left, top of page. [Dated Aug. 1, it details exploits of Granbury's during the critical Atlanta campaign.]

"Published List of Casualties of the 6th and 15th Texas, Army of Tennessee," from May 8 through Nov. 30, 1864, by Sgt. Maj. M. O'Donohue, in *Galveston News*, Houston, Texas, March ?, 1865.

"Casualties in Granbury's Texas Infantry Brigade at the Battle of Atlanta," printed in Sept. 2, 1864 edition of the *Houston Telegraph*.

"List of Casualties in Co. C, 24th Texas Cavalry, from C. M. King, Lieut. Commd'g, Co.," in Oct. 21, 1864, edition of the *Houston Telegraph*.

"Came to Texas When Indians Roamed Prairies," Capt. J. H. Collet of Austin, Texas," in *The Galveston Daily News*, Jan. 31, 1915; also see "Civil War Veteran Regains Gun Given U.S. Officer in 1862," in *Austin American*, Sunday, April 30, 1916.

Aberdeen Examiner (Miss.), 1890, biography of Robert Amos Jordan, Co. K, 27th Mississippi Infantry, found in the Miss. Dept. of Archives and History by Gary Pierce and shared with this writer: AS to New Hope Church, on page 29: "Granbury's Texas Brigade, . . . faced to the front, and in not more than two or three volleys almost annihilated a line of Federal Infantry in some places not over 10 or 20 steps from us . . . , it was said . . . the next day about 700 Feds were buried . . . and some 200 prisoners taken that night."

"Scurlock Family Correspondence, 1862-1863," published in several copies of the *Grandview Tribune*, Grandview, Texas, from Nov. 25, 1977, on. Malcolm Scurlock served in Co. A, 18th Texas Cavalry and the letters commence on Jan. 7, 1862 and continue on until Feb. 21, 1865. [Sister Mollie, writes to brothers Malcolm and James.]

"Saluria, Fort Esperanza, and Military Operations on the Texas Coast, 1861-1864," by Leste N. Fitzhugh, *The Southwestern Historical Quaterly*, vol. LI, # 1, (July 1957), pp. 69-75.

"The Texas Slave Insurrection of 1860," by William W. White, *The Southwestern Historical Quarterly*, vol. LII, # 3 (January 1959), pp. 261-285.

Letters:

John Gregg & Hiram Granbury letters, March, 1862 through July 1, 1862, found in the Mary Moody Northern collection, 1988.2, from the Moody Library, Galveston, Texas.

William E. Stanton letters, Co. A, 6th Texas Infantry, Jan. 17, and March 30, 1865, Box 2J-132, Texas State Archives, Austin, Texas.

William A. Stanton letters, Co. A, 6th Texas Infantry, U-T Archives, Austin, Texas. [Both letters are from early 1865, and most informative.]

Letters from Col. John Gregg and Maj. Hiram Granbury, commanders of the 7th Texas Infantry, drafted between March 8, 1862 through July 1, 1862, Xerox copies from Mary Moody Northern, Inc., Coll. # 1988.z.1688, transcribed by Lori Hartman.]

Lt. Col. J. M. Clough, Jan. 19, 1862, 7th Texas Infantry, from Van Zandt autobiography, Myres, ed., *Force Without Fanfare:*, p.83-5. [Sickness in regiment, Pre-Ft. Donelson.]

John T. Pace letters, Co. C, 7th Texas Infantry, Feb. 13 to Aug. 12, 1863 (died Canton, Mississippi of sickness, June 3rd), transcribed from James Wilkins Collection, Smith County Historical Society, Tyler, Texas.

Edward T. Broughton, Jr., letters, Co. C, 7th Texas Infantry, Sept. 17, 1861 to Nov. 2, 1864, originals in Coll. # 1993.24, Smith County Historical Society, Tyler Texas.

Milton Carter family letters, Co. F, 7th Texas Infantry, Aug. 8, 1863 & Nov. 15, 1863. [Transcribed copies via Smith County Historical Society, Tyler, Texas.]

William H. Henderson letters, Co. G, 7th Texas Infantry, Pearce Civil War Collection, Navarro College, Corsicana, Texas. [9/4/1864, Jonesboro; 11/18/64, Florence. Ala.]

George A. Bacon letter to Capt. J. H. Collett, 7th Texas Infantry, written July 9, 1866, regarding the pistol captured from Collett at Ft. Donelson, Tn., Feb. 1862; another by G. A.

Bacon, July 16, 1895, regarding getting a permit for Granbury from Grant after Ft. Donelson to take his wife to Clarksville, Tn. [J. H. Collett family papers, Collett B. Dilworth, Austin, Texas.]

R. W. Ford letters, Co. B, 7th Texas Infantry, *Civil War Times Illustrated* collection, Dec. 25, 1862 – Feb. 7, 1863, transcribed copies obtained from U.S. Military History Institute, Carlisle Barracks, Pa. Includes diary entries made May 21, to July 14, 1863, Port Hudson, La. [He commanded 7th Texas contingent left at Port Hudson when the regiment moved to Woodville, Miss. About May 1st.]

Roger Q. Mills letters, commencing Jan. 22, 1861, to Nov. 29, 1863, from Box 2F42, Mills Papers, University of Texas Archives, Austin.

Letters of Cpl. Aaron Estes, Co. B, 10th Texas Infantry, Estes Collection, Special Collections, Baylor University, from Nov. 29, 1861, to Dec. 30, 1863. [Very good info on his observations and activities.]

Hosea Garrett letter, Co. G, 10th Texas Infantry, Aug. 1, 1864, conveyed to Scott McKay by Dennis Kelly of Kennesaw Mt., Ga., typescript copy of original in possession of Mrs. S. L. Byrd, Chattanooga, Tennessee. Hosea carried the regimental colors. [Battle of Atlanta and just after.]

Isaiah Harlan letters, Co. G, 10th Texas Infantry, Nov. 1, 1861 to April 9, 1864, typescript copies obtained by the writer from the Confederate Research Center, Hill Jr. College, Hillsboro, Texas. [Very good source on unit.]

Noah Snider letter, Co. K, 10th Texas Infantry, Nov. 2, 1862, typescript copy located by writer at Confederate Research Center, Hill Jr. College, Hillsboro, Texas.

William A. Young transcribed letters, Co. A, 15th Texas Cavalry, March 22, 1862 through Nov. 18, 1864, courtesy Confederate Research Center, Hill Jr. College, Hillsboro, Texas. [Very good material.]

Letters from Daniel and Woods Park, brothers serving in Co. A, 15th Texas Cavalry, from Feb. 20, 1862, to Feb. 14, 1863. Xerox copies provided by Betty Troutman, a familial descendant. [Includes Compiled Service Records for Daniel Park.]

R. M. Cockran letter, written to "Jimmy" of Co. A, 15th Texas Cavalry, April 5/6/1864, Pearce Civil War Museum, Navarro College, Corsicana, Texas. [Not much meat here.]

Letter from Alonzo Steele, Co. F, 15th Texas Cavalry, transcribed copy dated June 8, 1864, provided by Bill Holmes of Houston, Texas, SCV Camp 67. [Brother Hampton Steele also enlisted in the same company but was discharged after being disabled in an accident at Clarksville, Texas, just a month later. A third sibling, Alvarado Steele, had earlier enlisted in Co. B, 10th Texas Infantry.]

Unidentified letters of a private soldier serving in Co. A, 17th Texas Cavalry, beginning May 13, 1862, and running through Dec. 19, 1863. [Several persons named in letters identified.]

Unidentified writer, No. 1, May 13, 1862, drafted at Camden, Arkansas, and obviously a 17th Texas Cavalry soldier, Xerox copy of original from unidentified source. [Measles outbreak, trip to Camden, Ark. And camp rumors.]

Henry Curl letters, Co. B, 17th Texas Cavalry, from June 3, 1862 to April 27, 1864, one from Joe Walker of Waco, Texas, the remainder being obtained from the Confederate Research Center, Hill Jr. College, Hillsboro, Texas.

John T. Coit & family letters, copied "From a calendar of the Coit and Moore papers prepared by Jesse Guy Smith as an M.S. (thesis), Commerce, Texas, 1936. [Details Coit's move to Texas, then his involvement in the civil war with N. H. Darnell's 18th Texas Cavalry, letters commencing July 15, 1861 and going through July, 1864. Note especially the letter of Aug. 18, 1863, from Graysville Depot, Ga.]

F. N. Hamilton letter, Co. I, 18th Texas Cavalry, Xerox copy of original dated April 26, 1863. [By family descendant, Della Mae Nelson, 303 Oak Creek, Jacksboro, TX 76056]

Letter to J. M. Harper, Dr., June 16, 1862 for the purchase of 532 bushels of corn purchased for the benefit of Col. Carter's command by F. Fauntleroy, of 1st regiment, Carter's Command. Found at the following location: http://freepages.genealogy.rootsweb.ancestry.com/-barrettbranches/researchers/karen%2.html [A John Harper is listed in the 1860 census as living in Henderson County, just west of Smith County (Tyler).

Letter of Maj. William A. Taylor to the father of Lt. Col. (Robert) Young, dated Feb. 5, 1865, posted by Granbury's Texas Brigade Camp, S.C.V. Camp 1479, Conroe, Texas, at their website. See http://granburytexasbrigade.org/units/granburysbrigade.html [Sad letter expressing sympathy to the family.

Newton Allen letters, Co. F, 24th Texas Cavalry, Xerox copies transcribed by this writer, Beginning May 18, 1862, to Feb. 24, 1864. [Courtesy of Joe Browder, Cleburne, TX]

Letters of Sgt. & 2nd Lt. J. D. Lum, Co. B, 25th Texas Cavalry, from Aug. 22, 1862 and Oct. 1, 1862, (Ark. Post). [Courtesy T.C.M., Midland, Texas. Coll. #s: TCM 94.30.1; 94.30.2, etc.; TCM 94.30.7; TCM 94.30.5. Shreveport, Aug. 22, Ark. Post in Oct.]

W. S. Boothe letters, Co. G., 25th Texas Cavalry, Pearce Civil War Museum, Corsicana, TX. [Aug. 15, 1862, Shreveport; Oct. 11, 1863, Chattanooga, TN.]

John R. Hardison letters, Co. G, 25th Texas Cavalry, courtesy, Elizabeth Ryan (family). [March 16, 1862, Tarkington's Prairie, TX; Atlanta, GA., Aug. 14, 1864; Sept. 7, 1864, Lovejoy's Church, GA.]

J. P. Jones' letters, Co. D, 10th Texas Infantry, special collections, Baylor University, Dec. 1, 1861 through Oct. 20, 1864.

Diaries:

Private James H. Hurst, Co. A, 10th Texas Infantry, April 18, 1862, to June 29, 1862, typescript copy in writer's possession as obtained from the Confederate Research Center, Hill Jr. College, Hillsboro, Texas. [Movement to Arkansas.]

William A. Young Co. A, 15th Texas Cavalry, transcribed diary entries from May 1, 1864 June 1, 1865. [Accompanied letters listed above.]

Maps:

General Area:

Southern Tennessee, north Alabama, northwest Georgia, Plate CXLIX, *The Official Military Atlas of the Civil War* (previously cited, shown hereafter as *O.R. Atlas*).

Kentucky, northern Tennessee, Plate CL, *O.R. Atlas*.

Southern Illinois, eastern Missouri, Plate CLII, *O.R. Atlas*.

Northeast Arkansas, southern Missouri, western Tennessee & Kentucky, Plate CLIII, *O.R. Atlas*.

Central and southern Arkansas, western Mississippi, Plate CLIV *O.R.Atlas*,

Southern Texas, Plate CLVII, *O.R. Atlas*.

Central Texas, Plate CLVIII, *O.R. Atlas*.

North Texas, southern Indian Territory, western Arkansas, Plate CLIX, *O.R. Atlas*.

Operational Maps:

Central Kentucky, northern Tennessee, Operations of the 7th Texas Infantry, 1861-2, Map # 3, Plate XXIV, *O.R. Atlas*.

Central Tennessee, Operations of Granbury's Brigade, late 1864, Map # 2, Plate # XXX, *O.R. Atlas*.

Western Mississippi, Operations of the 7th Texas Infantry, 1863, Map # 1, Plate XXXVI, *O.R. Atlas*.

Specialized Maps:

Marietta & Dallas, Ga., Operations of Granbury's Brigade, May-June, 1863, Maps # 4, 5,6, & 9, Plate XLIII, *O.R. Atlas*.

Missionary Ridge, Tn., Battle of, U.S. & "rebel" forces shown, Map # 8, Plate XLV, *O.R. Atlas*.

Chickamauga, Ga., Battle of, U.S. & "rebel" positions at various times, Maps # 1, 2 & 4, Plate XLVI, *O.R. Atlas*.

Chickamauga, Ga., Battle of, U.S. & "rebel" positions at various times, Maps # 2, 3, & 7, Plate XLVII, *O.R. Atlas*.

New Hope-Dallas, Ga., Battle of, U.S. & "rebel" positions at various times, Maps # 3 & 4, Plate XLVIII, *O.R. Atlas*.

Missionary Ridge, Tn., Battle of, U.S. & "rebel" positions at various times, Maps # 1 & 2, Plate XLIX, *O.R. Atlas.*

Chattanooga, Tn., & Vicinity, campaign showing various mountain passes (gaps), Map # 5, Plate L, *O.R. Atlas.*

Atlanta, Ga., Battle of July 22, 1864, showing "rebel attack", Map # 6, Plate LVI, *O.R. Atlas.*

Atlanta, Ga., Campaign Map, from Chattanooga to Atlanta, Map # 3, Plate LVII, *O.R. Atlas.*

New Hope Church, Ga., Battle of, Map # 5, Plate LIX, *O.R. Atlas.*

Jonesboro, Ga., Battle of, showing U.S. & "rebel" positions, Map # 6, Plate LIX, *O.R. Atlas.*

Atlanta, Ga., Battle of, July 22, U.S. & "rebel" positions marked, Maps # 2 & #, Plate LXI, *O.R. Atlas.*

Lovejoy's Station, Ga., location of U.S. & "rebel" positions, Map # 1, Plate LXI, *O.R. Atlas.*

Jonesboro, Ga., Battle of, Aug. 31-Sept. 1, U.S. & "rebel" positions, Map # 5 & 7, Plate LXI, *O.R. Atlas*

Atlanta, Ga., Battle of, U.S. & "rebel" positions, Map # 8 & 12, Plate LXII, *O.R. Atlas.*

Johnson's Island, Ohio, POW camp, Map # 10, Plate LXVI, *O.R. Atlas.*

Bentonville, N.C., March 19, 1865, Map # 5, Plate LXVIII, *O.R. Atlas.*

Franklin, Tn., Battle of, Nov. 30, 1864, U. S. & C.S. forces, Map 1, Plate LXXII, *O.R. Atlas.*

Nashville, Tn., Battle of, Dec. 15-16, 1864, U.S. & "rebel" forces, Map # 2, Plate # LXXII, *O.R. Atlas.*

Franklin, Tn., Battle of, Nov. 30, 1864, U.S. positions & Stewart's "rebel" corps assault, Maps # 3 & 4, Plate LXIII, *O.R. Atlas.*

Nashville, Tn., Battle of, Dec. 15-16, 1864, topo. map of overall battlefield and the position of Stewart's Corps on both days, Maps # 1 & 2, Plate LXXIII, *O.R. Atlas.*

Bentonville, N.C., Battle of, March 19, 1865, Map # 4, Plate LXXIX, *O.R. Atlas.*

Averysborough, N.C., Battle of, March 16, 1865, Map # 5, Plate LXXIX, *O.R. Atlas.*

Bentonville, N.C., Battle of, March 19, 1865, Map # 10, Plate LXXX, *O.R. Atlas.*

Averysborough, N.C., Battle of March 16, 1865, Map # 11, Plate LXXX, *O.R. Atlas.*

Goldsborough, N.C., Area of Operations, Maps # 7, 8 & 16, Plate LXXXVI, *O.R. Atlas.*

Atlanta, Ga., Siege of, July, 1864, Map #s 1 & 2, Plate LXXXVIII, *O.R. Atlas.*

Chickamauga, Ga., Battle of, Sept. 20, 1863, showing Deshler's Brigade, Cleburne's Division, Map # 4, Plate XCVI, *O.R. Atlas.*

Chattanooga, Tn., area of Operations, Map # 1, Plate XCVII, *O.R. Atlas.*

Chickamauga, Ga., Battle of, Sept. 19, 1863, Map # 3, Plate XCVII, *O.R. Atlas.*

Chickamauga, Ga., Battle of, Sept. 20, 1863, location of Greggs & Deshler's assaults, Map # 2, Plate XCVIII, *O.R. Atlas.*

West Harpeth River, Tn., Battle of, Dec. 17, 1864, Map # 6, Plate CV, *O.R. Atlas.*

Atlanta, Ga. Battle of, July 22, 1864, U.S. & "rebel" positions, Maps # 3(a & b), Plate CXXXI, *O.R. Atlas.*

Averysborough, N.C., Battle of, March 16, 1865, showing both U.S. and "rebel" positions, Map # 1, Plate CXXXIII, *O.R. Atlas.*

Bentonville, N. C. , Battle of, March 19, 1865, Map # 2, Plate CXXXIII, *O.R. Atlas.*

Franklin, Tn., Battle of, Nov. 30, 1864, showing U.S. lines and attacking force, Map # 1, Plate CXXXV-B, *O.R. Atlas.*

Franklin, Tn., Battle of, Nov. 30, 1864, showing U.S. "field works,", Map # 5, Plate CXXXV-C, *O.R. Atlas.*

Also, see Nashville, Tn., Battle of, maps of Broughton's Texas Inf. Brig., in Groom, *Shrouds of Glory*, as cited in primary works.

Unknown, *Confederate Arkansas – 1862*

Unknown, "Raymond: Pre-Battle Deployment," in the *Clarion Ledger*, Jackson, Mississippi, 1958.

Unknown, "Battle of Jackson, Mississippi, from *Civil War Times Illustrated*, furnished via the Jefferson Davis camp, SCV, Jackson, Miss. (Compiled and drawn by Ed. Bearss)

Sessums, Danny. Map 5, "Carter Hill," using the same titled map sans platting the assault of Granbury's Brigade thereto as initially published in Cox, Jacob D. *The Battle of Franklin.* NY: ?

"County Map of Texas, 1860" as copied from an original in the State Archives, Austin, Texas.

Photographs:

Later war-time image of John S. Pickle, with his wife, he seated in chair, Co. Co. B, 18th Texas Cavalry, Austin History Center, Austin, Texas. [Need copy and permission to publish.]

Capt. William M. Allison, Co. E, 18th Texas Cavalry, circa Arkansas Post? http://texansinthecivilwar.com/biographies/william_allison.html.

Co. G, 18th Texas Cavalry, post-war image of seven identified veterans from "The Portal to Texas History." See http://texashistory.unt.edu/ark:/67531/metapth15477/m1/1.

Print copy of Pat Cleburne's Navy pistol, Layland Museum, Cleburne, Texas.

Print copy of cdv of Hiram B. Granbury, taken at Baltimore, Md., 1862, from Lawrence T. Jones collection, now at S.M.U., Dallas, Texas.

Enlarged print photo of cased image (ambrotype?) of Col. John Gregg, seated, holding sword, undated.

Print copy from a sleeved image of P. Jeptha Wilson, Co. G, 6th Texas Infantry, "Travis Rifles," Lawrence Jones III collection, now at S.M.U., Dallas, Texas.

Poor quality print of P. Henry Elms, Co. F, 6th Texas Infantry, holding a U.S. musket across his chest, unknown contributor.

Copy of 1/6 plate ambrotype of P. Thomas F. Bates, Co. D, 6th Texas Infantry, Library of Congress, Prints and Photographs Division, Wash., D.C.

Copy of ferrotype of William J. Oliphant, Co. G, 6th Texas Infantry, with musket and in uniform. Courtesy Austin History Center, Austin, Texas. [Need copy-print image and permission.]

Print copy from a Daguerreotype of K. M. Van Zandt, circa 1850, as a young man. Later served as a Major in the 7th Texas Infantry.

Sepia-tone post-war image of James A. Hughes, Co. K, 10th Texas Infantry, courtesy of Cheryl Abbott, Mesquite, Texas. [Holding what appears to be a grand-child.]

Post-war print of David R. Myres, Co. G, 10th Texas Infantry, from Layland Museum, Cleburne, TX.

Print copy of what appears to be a pre-war ferrotype of Capt. John Johnson, Co. A, 15th Texas Cavalry, courtesy of Gary Ritchie, Amarillo, TX. [Very sharp image.]

Poor Xerox copy of P. James P. Craver, Co. D, 15th Texas Cavalry, war-time image, with turned up hat, pinned with Texas star. [Need better copy of same.]

War-time, touched-up image of Moses M. Beckner, Co. C, 17th Texas Cavalry, holding a double barrel shotgun, wearing large side-knife. [Unknown how we got this image.]

Xerox copy of oval, war-time image(?) of P. Jess J. Johns, Co. C, 17th Texas Cavalry, in civilian winter clothes, with hand on lapel. [Need better quality image.]

Large print copy of P. Malcolm Hornsby, Co. B, 18th Texas Cavalry, wearing penitentiary uniform, hat in hand. [Malcolm was a direct antecedent of the great baseball player, Rogers Hornsby.]

Large print copy of P. Jonah Pickle, Co. B, 18th Texas Cavalry, wearing penitentiary uniform, with a Whitney-style revolver held across his front. [A descendant, also named Pickle served in public office in Texas some years back.]

Copy-print photo of a cased image of William Michael Westmoreland, 1st Texas Mounted Volunteers. [Note two pistols stuffed in belt.]

Companion print to above, also a print of a csed image of James Alexander Westmoreland, Co. E, 17th Texas Cavalry. [Note two pistols in belt, another in one hand, a sword in the other.]

A copy-print photo of P. John David Brantley, Co. K, 24th Texas Cavalry, seated with P. Thomas Glimp, Shiloh Home Guard? [Need a better image copy]

Post-war print of P. David Myres, Co. G, 10th Texas Infantry, in front yard of home. [Reputed to have helped bring in the bodies of Cleburne and Granbury after Franklin.]

Post-war reunion photo of William A. and Isaac Bates, Co. B, 10th Texas Infantry, made by Blair of Gatesville, TX. [Also a later photo of William., and photos of him in a buggy.]

Pictures of headstone and C.S.A. marked of William A. Bates, as above

Miscellaneous:

Compiled Service Record, Hiram B. Granbury, Record Group 109, Old Army and Navy Records, National Archives, Washington, D. C. [Xerox copies made by writer]

Descriptive list of Prisoners of War of the 7th Texas Infantry that died while held at Camp Douglas, Illinois, in 1862-3, by company, Record Group 109 (hereafter simply R.G.), National Archives (hereafter N.A.), Wash., D. C.

Descriptive list of Prisoners of War of the 6th Texas Infantry that died while held at Camp Butler, Illinois, 1863, by company, R. G 109, N. A., Wash., D. C.

Descriptive list of Prisoners of War of the 10th Texas Infantry that died at Camp Douglas, Illinois, in 1863, by Company, R. G. 109, N.A., Wash., N.A.

Descriptive list of Prisoners of War of the 15th Texas Cavalry that died at Camp Douglas, Illinois, in 1863, by company, R. G. 109, N.A., Wash., D.C.

Descriptive list of Prisoners of War of the 17th Texas Cavalry that died at Camp Douglas, Illinois, in 1863, by company, R. G. 109, Wash. D. C.

Descriptive list of Prisoners of War of the 18th Texas Cavalry that died at Camp Douglas, Illinois, in 1863, by company, R. G. 109, N.A., Wash., D.C.

Descriptive list of Prisoners of War of the 24th Texas Cavalry that died at Camp Butler, Illinois, in 1863, by company, R. G. 109, Wash. D. C.

Descriptive list of Prisoners of War of the 25th Texas Cavalry that died at Camp Butler, Illinois, in 1863, by company, R. G. 109, N.A., Wash., D.C.

Disposition of Texas Prisoners of War held at various Illinois camps, from Record Book # 725, R. G. 109, N.A, Wash, D.C. (Alton, Butler, & Rock Island)

Disposition of the 24th Texas Cavalry prisoners taken at the Battle of Arkansas Post, January, 1863, from Record Book # 657, R. G. 109, N.A., Wash., D. C. [Includes negroes owned by soldiers, shipped to City Point, Va.]

Enrolled prisoners of the 6th Texas Infantry at Camp Butler, Illinois, taken at the Battle of Arkansas Post, January, 1863, Record Book # unknown, fragment), R. G. 109, N.A., Wash., D. C.

Enrolled prisoners of the 24th Texas Cavalry at Camp Butler, Illinois, taken at the Battle of Arkansas Post, January, 1863, Record Book # unknown, fragment).

Enrolled prisoners of the 25th Texas Cavalry at Camp Butler, Illinois, taken at the Battle of Arkansas Post, January, 1863, Record Book # (unknown, fragment), N.A., Wash, D. C.

Disposition of Texas POWs held by various Illinois camps, contained in record book # 725, RG 109, NA, Wash., D.C. [Includes mostly the 6th, 24th & 25th Texas
Miscellaneous prisoners of war that died at Camp Butler, Illinois, taken at Arkansas Post, January, 1863, from Record Book # (unknown, fragment), R. G. 109, N.A., Wash, D. C.

Record Book for Accounting of Louisiana, Arkansas, and Texas soldiers crossing northern Louisiana between October & December, 1862, Monroe Depot, N.A. Birge papers, L.S.U. archives, Baton Rouge, La.

Special Order, "To All Whom It May Concern," missive to 2nd Lt. M. J. Dean, Co. F, 7th Texas Infantry, from Capt. W. H. Smith, approved by John Gregg, Col.?; to escort to return the bodies of two company members who died in service at

Camp Alcorn, Jan. 7, 1862, from *Chronicles of Smith County* Vol. 3, # 2, (Fall, 1964), Smith County Historical Society, Tyler, Texas.

Special Orders # 79, "Extract – Hd. Qtrs. Western Dept, ?, June 12, 1862, Pt. IV, "In consequence of the capture of his command, the resignation of 2nd Lt. M. J. Dean of 7th Texas Vols. Is accepted and he is honorably discharged the service." "By Command Gen. Beauregard, George Wm. Brent, Acting Chief of Staff," *Chronicles of Smith County*, Vol. 3, # 2 (Fall, 1964), Smith County Historical Society.

Clothing Return, Sept. 15, 1863 for the 10th Texas Infantry, compiled service record of Quartermaster, Capt. Allen Banks, 318 pair of shoes. [Issued just prior to Chickamauga]

Clothing Return, Sept. 30, 1863, for the 10th Texas Infantry, compiled service record of Quartermaster, Capt. Allen Banks, 177 shirts, 175 drawers, 54 pair of shoes, 34 hats, 1 cap for NCO. {Shows the loss of men attendant to Chickamauga]

William A. Bates, Co. B, 10th Texas Infantry, biographical file courtesy of Louise Johnson, family descendant, Round Rock, TX. [reminiscences of brothers in 10th.]

Muster-roll of Co. D, 10th Texas Infantry, Fairfield, Freestone County, Oct. 26, 1861, researched by Scott McKay, shared with this writer. [Shows disposition of soldiers during the war.]

Reminiscences of Overton Davenport, Co. K, 10th Texas Infantry, from enlistment in late 1861 until 1865, typescript copy provided this writer by descendant, Joe R. Davenport, of San Antonio, Texas. [very good accounts of marches, battles, etc.]

Descriptive list of Pay, Clothing, Bounty, etc., for William Young, Co. A, 15th Texas Cavalry, March16, 1865. [Very good Xerox copy of original.]

Penitentiary records, "Lone Star Mill," Huntsville, Texas, Box 4-8/707, State Archives, Austin, Texas. [Kerseys, Osnaburgs, etc. issued to Texas regiments, 6th, 18th, & 24th.]

Madden/Westmoreland family history, referencing James Alexander and William Michael (Billy) Westmoreland, both of who served in Co. E, 17th Texas Cavalry, provided by Robert Madden, a descendant of both. [Family involved in the Edens-Madden Massacre, 1830s R.O.T. state marker. See flag story from Harrison County Hist. Mus.]

Capt. Robert A. Poole, Co. A, 24th Texas Cavalry, as recorded by Karen McCann Hett, print copies from the following site: http://freepages.military.rootsweb.ancestry.com/-mccannkin.co_a_24/poole.html [Note a 2nd Co. from Montgomery County, under Capt. Samuel D. Wooldridge, became Co. B in the same regiment.]

Image of returned flag of the 17th & 18th Texas Consolidated, Hardee pattern, Courtesy Texas State Archives, Austin, Texas. [Captured at Atlanta, Ga., July 22, 1864, by the 15th Michigan Infantry Rgt.]

Muster Rolls:

6th Texas Infantry: Cos. H, G, K (Texas Archives, Austin, Texas)

7th Texas Infantry

10th Texas Infantry

15th Texas Cavalry

17th Texas Cavalry

18th Texas Cavalry: Cos. A, B, C, E, F, K (Texas Archives, Austin, Texas)

24th Texas Cavalry: Cos. B (from *The Tri-Weekly Telegraph*, Houston, Texas, May 8, 1863), C, H

25th Texas Cavalry: Cos. B, G, H, I

www.ingramcontent.com/pod-product-compliance
Lightning Source LLC
Chambersburg PA
CBHW021117300426
44113CB00006B/178